T0051591

Immortal Poems

of the

English Language

TO LOVE,
TO SUFFER,
TO THINK...
is to seek poetry.

The last six hundred years in British and American literature have given us some of the most moving and memorable poems in all of literature. The pursuits, longings, and sentiments of these great poets will echo eternally in their immortal poems.

In this unique edition, Oscar Williams has selected the masterpieces of one hundred fifty poets, and arranged them chronologically in a book that reflects the immortality of the poetic soul.

Immortal Poems

of the

English Language

An Anthology
Edited by Oscar Williams

G

GALLERY BOOKS

New York   London   Toronto   Sydney   New Delhi

G

Gallery Books
An Imprint of Simon & Schuster, Inc.
1230 Avenue of the Americas
New York, NY 10020

This Gallery Books trade paperback edition June 2022

GALLERY BOOKS and colophon are registered trademarks of Simon & Schuster, Inc.

For information about special discounts for bulk purchases, please contact Simon & Schuster Special Sales at 1-866-506-1949 or business@simonandschuster.com.

The Simon & Schuster Speakers Bureau can bring authors to your live event. For more information or to book an event, contact the Simon & Schuster Speakers Bureau at 1-866-248-3049 or visit our website at www.simonspeakers.com.

Interior design by Kathryn A. Kenney-Peterson

10 9 8 7 6 5 4 3 2 1

ISBN 978-1-9821-9154-2

COPYRIGHT NOTICES AND ACKNOWLEDGMENTS

Many of the poems in this anthology are protected by copyright, and may not be reproduced in any form without the consent of the poets, their publishers, or their agents. Since this page cannot legibly accommodate all the copyright notices, the two pages following constitute an extension of the copyright page. Thanks are due to the following poets, their representatives, and publishers for permission to include certain poems in this anthology:

BRANDT & BRANDT—for "Recuerdo" from *A Few Figs from Thistles*, published by Harper & Row, copyright, 1922, 1950, by Edna St. Vincent Millay; for "what if a much of a which of a wind" from *1 × 1*, published by Henry Holt & Co., Inc., copyright, 1944, by E. E. Cummings; for "i sing of Olaf glad and big" from *Collected Poems of E. E. Cummings*, published by Harcourt, Brace & World, Inc., copyright, 1931, by E. E. Cummings.

JONATHAN CAPE, Ltd.—for "Naming of Parts" from *A Map of Verona* by Henry Reed;—(and Mrs. W. H. Davies) for "A Great Time" from *The Collected Poems of W. H. Davies*.

CHATTO & WINDUS—for the selections by Wilfred Owen from *The Poems of Wilfred Owen*; for

CONTENTS

INTRODUCTION

> *It is absurd to think that the only way to tell if a poem is lasting is to wait and see if it lasts. The right reader of a good poem can tell the moment it strikes him that he has taken an immortal wound—that he will never get over it. That is to say, permanence in poetry, as in love, is perceived instantly. It hasn't to await the test of time. The proof of a poem is not that we have never forgotten it, but we knew at sight we never could forget it.*
>
> —Robert Frost

A poem is immortal not only because it continues to be read by generation after generation of readers but also because each sensitive reader, having once experienced the poem, absorbs the experience and continues to feel it always, and further, because a true poem expresses an immortal human truth. Anyone who knows how to love, or to suffer, or to think, anyone who wishes to live fully, needs and seeks poetry. But not everyone finds it easy to buy all the books he wants and certainly no one can carry his entire library in his pocket. It is for these reasons that I have compiled this Pocket Anthology of *Immortal Poems of the English Language*.

A poem that excites us is not like a novel or an article, to be read and finished. A poem, if it is a good one, is inexhaustible; we want to read it to refresh the dull moments of the day, over and over, wherever we may be. This collection is designed for that purpose. The selections are as comprehensive and representative of the great poetry of the English language, by both American and British poets, as is possible in a pocket-size book; and the arrangement is chronological. In addition to 400 shorter songs, lyrics and passages from plays, I have used many long poems in all their exciting entirety, including *The Rape of the Lock* by Alexander Pope, *A Song to David* by Christopher Smart, *The Rime of the Ancient Mariner* by S. T. Coleridge, *Tam O'Shanter* by Robert Burns, Lycidas, *Il Penseroso* and *Ode on the Morning of Christ's Nativity* by John Milton, *Adonais* by Percy Bysshe Shelley, *The Deserted Village* by Oliver Goldsmith, *The*

Scholar-Gypsy by Matthew Arnold, *The Eve of St. Agnes* by John Keats, *The Rubáiyát of Omar Khayyám*, *The Wreck of the Deutschland* by Gerard Manley Hopkins, most of which have never, within my knowledge, been included thus in a book of this scope and price. I have represented, with especial amplitude, those poets who are generally considered "major," because of quantity, quality and reputation, such as Shakespeare, Donne, Milton, Blake, Wordsworth, Keats, Tennyson, Whitman. I have also given a fair percentage of the space to poetry of the twentieth century, the most important poetry perhaps, for a twentieth-century reader; the work of such poets as Emily Dickinson, G. M. Hopkins, W. B. Yeats, Robert Frost, T S. Eliot, Wilfred Owen, W. H. Auden, Dylan Thomas, is presented generously. For we of today want to hear the contemporary poet expressing the strange, fearful and wonderful experiences of our own time. These poems are also immortal although they have not yet spent centuries in print, for they are alive, alive with the force of our own living time. I believe that their quality is such that the reader will see for himself that they are worthy to live for future generations as well.

Every selection herein has given this editor that "immortal wound" of which Robert Frost speaks. I hope that the reader, with his own sensibility, will be receptive to the sting and permanence of each poem, so that through his own immortal wounds he extends, for his generation, the influence and immortality of the poems.

—Oscar Williams

Immortal Poems

of the

English Language

GEOFFREY CHAUCER
1340?–1400

Balade

Hyd, Absolon, thy gilte tresses clere;
Ester, ley thou thy meknesse al a-doun;
Hyd, Jonathas, al thy frendly manere;
Penalopee, and Marcia Catoun,
Mak of your wyfhod no comparisoun;
Hyde ye your beautes, Isoude and Eleyne,
Alceste is here, that al that may desteyne.

Thy faire bodye, lat hit nat appere,
Lavyne; and thou, Lucresse of Rome toun,
And Polixene, that boghte love so dere,
Eek Cleopatre, with al thy passioun,
Hyde ye your trouthe in love and your renoun;
And thou, Tisbe, that hast for love swich peyne:
Alceste is here, that al that may desteyne.

Herro, Dido, Laudomia, alle in-fere,
Eek Phyllis, hanging for thy Demophoun,
And Canace, espyed by thy chere,
Ysiphile, betrayed with Jasoun,
Mak of your trouthe in love no bost ne soun;
Nor Ypermistre or Adriane, ne pleyne;
Alceste is here, that al that may desteyne.

The Complaint of Chaucer to His Purse

To you, my purse, and to non other wight
Complayne I, for ye be my lady dere!
I am so sory, now that ye been light;
For certes, but ye make me hevy chere,
Me were as leef be layd upon my bere;
For whiche unto your mercy thus I crye:
Beth hevy ageyn, or elles moote I dye!

Now voucheth sauf this day, or hit be night,
That I of you the blisful soun may here,
Or see your colour lyk the sonne bright,
That of yelownesse haddle never pere.

Ye be my lyf, ye be myn hertes stere,
Quene of comfort and of good companye:
Beth hevy ageyn, or elles moote I dye!

Now purse, that be to me my lyves light,
And saveour, as doun in this world here,
Out of this toune help me through your might,
Sin that ye wole nat been my tresorere;
For I am shave as nye as any frere.
But yet I pray unto your curtesye:
Beth hevy ageyn, or elles moote I dye!

L'ENVOY DE CHAUCER

O conquerour of Brutes Albyon,
Which that by lyne and free eleccion
Ben verray king, this song to you I send;
And ye, that mowen al our harmes amend,
Have mind upon my supplicacioun!

Hyd, hide; *gilte*, golden; *clere*, bright;
desteyne, bedim; *swich*, such; *peyne*,
distress; *in-fere*, together; *eek*, also;
espyed, disclosed; *chere*, appearance; *bost*,
boast; *soun*, sound; *pleyne*, lament.

JOHN SKELTON
1460?–1529

Lullay, Lullay

With, Lullay, lullay, like a childe
Thou slepist to long, thou art begilde.
"My darling dere, my daisy flowre,
    Let me," quod he, "ly in your lap."
"Ly still," quod she, "my paramoure,
    Ly still hardely, and take a nap."
    His hed was hevy, such was his hap,
All drowsy dreming, drownd in slepe,
That of his love he toke no kepe,
                    With, Hey, lullay, etc.

With ba, ba, ba, and bas, bas, bas,
   She cherished him both cheke and chin,
That he wist never where he was;
   He had forgotten all dedely sin,
   He wantid wit her love to win:
He trusted her payment, and lost all his pay:
She left him sleeping, and stale away.

The river routh, the waters wan;
   She sparid not to wete here fete;
She wadid over, she found a man
   That halsid her hartely and kist her swete:
   Thus after her cold she cought a hete.
"My lefe," she said, "routith in his bed;
Ywis he had an hevy hed."

What dremist thou, drunchard, drousy pate!
   Thy lust and liking is from thee gone;
Thou blinkerd blowboll, thou wakist to late,
   Behold, thou lieste, luggard, alone!
   Well may thou sigh, well may thou grone,
To dele with her so cowardly:
Ywis, poule-hachet, she blerid thine i.

Stere, pilot; *nye*, close; *frere*, friar; *lyne*, descent;
mowen, have power to; *harnes*, misfortune.
Hardely, confidently; *kepe*, heed; *ba*, kiss;
wist, knew; *stale*, stole; *routh*, rough; *halsid*, hugged;
lefe, beloved; *routith*, snores; *ywis*, indeed;
blinkerd blowboll, shut-eye blow-bowl; *luggard*, sluggard;
poule-hachet, hatchet-face; *blerid thine i*, deceived you.

ANONYMOUS: SONGS & BALLADS

Sumer Is Icumen In

Sumer is icumen in,
   Lhudè sing cuccu;
Groweth sed and bloweth med
   And springth the wudè nu.
      Sing cuccu!

Awè bleteth after lomb,
   Lhouth after calvè cu;
Bulluc sterteth, buckè verteth;
   Murie sing cuccu.
     Cuccu, cuccu,
   Wel singès thu, cuccu,
   Ne swik thu naver nu.
Sing cuccu nu! Sing cuccu!
Sing cuccu! Sing cuccu nu!

I Sing of a Maiden

I sing of a maiden
   That is makeles;
King of all kings
   To her son she ches.

He came al so still
   There his mother was,
As dew in April
   That falleth on the grass.

He came al so still
   To his mother's bour,
As dew in April
   That falleth on the flour.

He came al so still
   There his mother lay,
As dew in April
   That falleth on the spray.

Mother and maiden
   Was never none but she;
Well may such a lady
   Goddess mother be.

Icumen, come; *lhudè*, loud;
sed, seed; *med*, mead;
nu, now; *awe*, ewe;
lhouth, lows; *cu*, cow; *sterteth*, leaps;
verteth, seeks cover; *murie*, merry;
swik, stop;
makeles, matchless; *ches*, chose.

The Falcon

Lully, lulley! lully, lulley!
The faucon hath borne my make away!

He bare him up, he bare him down,
He bare him into an orchard brown.

In that orchard there was an halle,
That was hangéd with purple and pall.

And in that hall there was a bed,
It was hangéd with gold sa red.

And in that bed there li'th a knight,
His woundés bleeding day and night.

At that bed's foot there li'th a hound,
Licking the blood as it runs down.

By that bed-side kneeleth a may,
And she weepeth both night and day.

And at that bed's head standeth a stone,
Corpus Christi written thereon.
Lully, lulley! lully, lulley!
The faucon hath borne my make away.

Make, mate;
may, maid.

My Love in Her Attire

My love in her attire doth show her wit,
    It doth so well become her:
For every season she hath dressings fit,
    For winter, spring, and summer.
    No beauty she doth miss,
    When all her robes are on:
    But Beauty's self she is,
    When all her robes are gone.

O Western Wind

O western wind, when wilt thou blow,
That the small rain down can rain?
Christ, if my love were in my arms
And I in my bed again!

Love Not Me

Love not me for comely grace,
For my pleasing eye or face,
Nor for any outward part:
No, nor for a constant heart!
For these may fail or turn to ill:
    So thou and I shall sever.
Keep therefore a true woman's eye,
And love me still, but know not why!
So hast thou the same reason still
    To doat upon me ever.

There Is a Lady Sweet and Kind

There is a Lady sweet and kind,
Was never face so pleased my mind;
I did but see her passing by,
And yet I love her till I die.

Her gesture, motion, and her smiles,
Her wit, her voice my heart beguiles,
Beguiles my heart, I know not why,
And yet I love her till I die.

Cupid is wingèd and doth range,
Her country so my love doth change:
But change she earth, or change she sky,
Yet will I love her till I die.

Who Is at My Window?

Who is at my window? Who? Who?
Go from my window! Go! Go!
Who calls there, like a strangèr,
Go from my window! Go!

—Lord, I am here, a wretched mortàl,
That for thy mercy doth cry and call
Unto thee, my lord celestiàl,
See who is at thy window, who?—

Remember thy sin, remember thy smart,
And also for thee what was my part,
Remember the spear that pierced my heart,
And in at my door thou shalt go.

I ask no thing of thee therefore,
But love for love, to lay in store.
Give me thy heart; I ask no more,
And in at my door thou shalt go.

Who is at my window? Who?
Go from my window! Go!
Cry no more there, like a strangèr,
But in at my door thou go!

Quia Amore Langueo

In a valley of this restles mind
I sought in mountain and in mead,
Trusting a true love for to find.
Upon an hill then took I heed;
A voice I heard (and near I yede)
In great dolour complaining tho:
See, dear soul, how my sides bleed
  Quia amore langueo.

Upon this hill I found a tree,
Under a tree a man sitting;
From head to foot wounded was he;
His hearte blood I saw bleeding:
A seemly man to be a king,
A gracious face to look unto.
I askèd why he had paining;
  Quia amore langueo.

I am true love that false was never;
My sister, man's soul, I loved her thus.
Because we would in no wise dissever
I left my kingdom glorious.
I purveyed her a palace full precious;
She fled, I followed, I loved her so
That I suffered this pain piteous
  Quia amore langueo.

My fair love and my spouse bright!
I saved her from beating, and she hath me bet;
I clothed her in grace and heavenly light;
This bloody shirt she hath on me set;
For longing of love yet would I not let;
Sweet strokes are these: lo!
I have loved her ever as I her het
  Quia amore langueo.

I crowned her with bliss and she me with thorn;
I led her to chamber and she me to die;
I brought her to worship and she me to scorn;
I did her reverence and she me villainy.
To love that loveth is no maistry;
Her hate made never my love her foe
Ask me then no question why—
  Quia amore langueo.

Look unto mine handes, man!
These gloves were given me when I her sought;
They be not white, but red and wan;
Embroidered with blood my spouse them brought.
They will not off; I loose hem nought:
I woo her with hem wherever she go.
These hands for her so friendly fought
  Quia amore langueo.

Marvel not, man, though I sit still.
See, love hath shod me wonder strait:
Buckled my feet, as was her will,
With sharp nails (well thou may'st wait!)

In my love was never desait;
All my membres I have opened her to;
My body I made her herte's bait
   Quia amore langueo.

In my side I have made her nest;
Look in, how wet a wound is here!
This is her chamber, here shall she rest,
That she and I may sleep in fere.
Here may she wash, if any filth were;
Here is seat for all her woe;
Come when she will, she shall have cheer
   Quia amore langueo.

I will abide till she be ready,
I will her sue if she say nay;
If she be retchless I will be greedy,
If she be dangerous I will her pray;
If she weep, then bide I ne may:
Mine arms ben spread to clip her me to.
Cry once, I come: now, soul, assay!
   Quia amore langueo.

Fair love, let us go play:
Apples ben ripe in my gardayne.
I shall thee clothe in a new array,
Thy meat shall be milk, honey and wine.
Fair love, let us go dine:
Thy sustenance is in my crippe, lo!
Tarry thou not, my fair spouse mine,
   Quia amore langueo.

If thou be foul, I shall thee make clean;
If thou be sick, I shall thee heal;
If thou mourn ought, I shall thee mene;
Why wilt thou not, fair love, with me deal?
Foundest thou ever love so leal?
What wilt thou, soul, that I shall do?
I may not unkindly thee appeal,
   Quia amore langueo.

What shall I do now with my spouse
But abide her of my gentleness,
Till that she look out of her house
Of fleshly affection? love mine she is;
Her bed is made, her bolster is bliss,
Her chamber is chosen; is there none mo.
Look out on me at the window of kindness,
   Quia amore langueo.

My love is in her chamber: hold your peace!
Make ye no noise, but let her sleep.
My babe I would not were in disease,
I may not hear my dear child weep.
With my pap I shall her keep;
Ne marvel ye not though I tend her to:
This wound in my side had ne'er been so deep
   But Quia amore langueo.

Long thou for love never so high,
My love is more than thine may be.
Thou weepest, thou gladdest, I sit thee by:
Yet wouldst thou once, love, look unto me!
Should I always feede thee
With children meat? Nay, love, not so!
I will prove thy love with adversitè,
   Quia amore langueo.

Wax not weary, mine own wife!
What mede is aye to live in comfort?
In tribulation I reign more rife
Ofter times than in disport.
In weal and in woe I am aye to support:
Mine own wife, go not me fro!
Thy mede is marked, when thou art mort:
   Quia amore langueo.

Yede, went.
Het, promised.
Crippe, scrip;
mene, care for.

Sir Patrick Spens

The king sits in Dumferling toune,
  Drinking the blude-reid wine:
"O whar will I get guid sailor,
  To sail this schip of mine?"

Up and spak an eldern knicht,
  Sat at the kings richt kne:
"Sir Patrick Spens is the best sailor,
  That sails upon the se."

The king has written a braid letter,
  And signd it wi his hand,
And sent it to Sir Patrick Spens,
  Was walking on the sand.

The first line that Sir Patrick red,
  A loud lauch lauchèd he;
The next line that Sir Patrick red,
  The teir blinded his ee.

"O wha is this has don this deid,
  This ill deid don to me,
To send me out this time o' the yeir,
  To sail upon the se!

"Mak haste, mak haste, my mirry men all,
  Our guid schip sails the morne."
"O say na sae, my master deir,
  For I feir a deadlie storme.

"Late, late yestreen I saw the new moone,
  Wi the auld moone in hir arme,
And I feir, I feir my deir master,
  That we will cum to harme."

O our Scots nobles wer richt laith
  To weet their cork-heild schoone;
Bot lang owre a' the play wer playd,
  Thair hats they swam aboone.

O lang, lang may their ladies sit,
   Wi thair fans into their hand,
Or eir they se Sir Patrick Spens
   Cum sailing to the land.

O lang, lang may the ladies stand,
   Wi thair gold kems in their hair,
Waiting for thair ain deir lords,
   For they'll se thame na mair.

Haf owre, haf owre to Aberdour,
   It's fiftie fadom deip,
And thair lies guid Sir Patrick Spens,
   Wi the Scots lords at his feit.

Lauch, laugh.
Laith, loth; *owre*, before;
swam aboone, floated above;
kems, combs.

Lord Randal

"O where hae ye been, Lord Randal, my son?
O where hae ye been, my handsome young man?"
"I hae been to the wild wood; mother, make my bed soon,
For I'm weary wi hunting, and fain wald lie down."

"Where gat ye your dinner, Lord Randal, my son?
Where gat ye your dinner, my handsome young man?"
"I din'd wi my true-love; mother, make my bed soon,
For I'm weary wi hunting, and fain wald lie down."

"What gat ye to your dinner, Lord Randal, my son?
What gat ye to your dinner, my handsome young man?"
"I gat eels boiled in broo; mother, make my bed soon,
For I'm weary wi hunting, and fain wald lie down."

"What became of your bloodhounds, Lord Randal, my son?
What became of your bloodhounds, my handsome young man?"
"O they swelld and they died; mother, make my bed soon,
For I'm weary wi hunting, and fain wald lie down."

"O I fear ye are poisond, Lord Randal, my son!
O I fear ye are poisond, my handsome young man!"
"O yes! I am poisond; mother, make my bed soon,
For I'm sick at the heart, and I fain wald lie down."

Helen of Kirconnell

I wish I were where Helen lies,
Night and day on me she cries;
O that I were where Helen lies,
   On fair Kirconnell lea!

Curst be the heart that thought the thought,
And curst the hand that fired the shot,
When in my arms burd Helen dropt,
   And died to succour me!

O think na ye my heart was sair,
When my Love droop'd and spak nae mair!
There did she swoon wi' meikle care,
   On fair Kirconnell lea.

As I went down the water side,
None but my foe to be my guide,
None but my foe to be my guide,
   On fair Kirconnell lea;

I lighted down my sword to draw,
I hackéd him in pieces sma',
I hackéd him in pieces sma',
   For her sake that died for me.

O Helen fair, beyond compare!
I'll mak a garland o' thy hair,
Shall bind my heart for evermair,
   Until the day I die!

O that I were where Helen lies!
Night and day on me she cries;
Out of my bed she bids me rise,
   Says, "Haste, and come to me!"

O Helen fair! O Helen chaste!
If I were with thee, I'd be blest,
Where thou lies low and taks thy rest,
    On fair Kirconnell lea.

I wish my grave were growing green,
A winding-sheet drawn owre my een,
And I in Helen's arms lying,
    On fair Kirconnell lea.

I wish I were where Helen lies!
Night and day on me she cries;
And I am weary of the skies,
    For her sake that died for me.

The Wife of Usher's Well

There lived a wife at Usher's Well,
    And a wealthy wife was she;
She had three stout and stalwart sons,
    And sent them o'er the sea.

They hadna been a week from her,
    A week but barely ane,
Whan word came to the carline wife
    That her three sons were gane.

They hadna been a week from her,
    A week but barely three,
Whan word came to the carline wife
    That her sons she'd never see.

"I wish the wind may never cease,
    Nor fashes in the flood,
Till my three sons come hame to me,
    In earthly flesh and blood."

It fell about the Martinmas,
    When nights are lang and mirk,
The carline wife's three sons came home,
    And their hats were o the birk.

It neither grew in syke nor ditch,
   Nor yet in ony sheugh;
But at the gates o' Paradise,
   That birk grew fair eneugh.

"Blow up the fire, my maidens,
   Bring water from the well;
For a' my house shall feast this night,
   Since my three sons are well."

And she has made to them a bed,
   She's made it large and wide,
And she's taen her mantle her about,
   Sat down at the bed-side.

Up then crew the red, red cock,
   And up and crew the gray;
The eldest to the youngest said,
   "'T is time we were away."

The cock he hadna crawd but once,
   And clappd his wings at a',
When the youngest to the eldest said,
   "Brother we must awa.

"The cock doth craw, the day doth daw,
   The channerin worm doth chide;
Gin we be mist out o our place,
   A sair pain we maun bide.

"Fare ye weel, my mother dear!
   Fareweel to barn and byre!
And fare ye weel, the bonny lass
   That kindles my mother's fire!"

Carline, peasant;
fashes, troubles;
birk, birch;
syke, trench;
sheugh, furrow.
Channerin, devouring;
byre, cattle-shed.

Tom O' Bedlam's Song

From the hag and hungry goblin
    That into rags would rend ye,
And the spirit that stands by the naked man
    In the book of moons, defend ye,
That of your five sound senses
    You never be forsaken,
Nor wander from yourselves with Tom,
    Abroad to beg your bacon.

    While I do sing: Any food,
        Any feeding, drink, or clothing?
    Come, dame or maid, be not afraid,
        Poor Tom will injure nothing.

Of thirty bare years have I
    Twice twenty been enragèd,
And of forty been three times fifteen
    In durance soundly cagèd
On the lordly lofts of Bedlam,
    With stubble soft and dainty,
Brave bracelets strong, sweet whips, ding-dong,
    With wholesome hunger plenty.

    And now I sing: Any food, etc.

With a thought I took for Maudlin,
    And a cruse of cockle pottage,
With a thing thus tall, sky bless you all,
    I befell into this dotage.
I slept not since the Conquest,
    Till then I never wakèd,
Till the roguish boy of love where I lay
    Me found and stripped me naked.

    And now I sing: Any food, etc.

When I short have shorn my sour-face,
    And swigged my horny barrel,
In an oaken inn I pound my skin,
    As a suit of gilt apparel.

The moon's my constant mistress,
    And the lowly owl my morrow;
The flaming drake and the night-crow make
    Me music to my sorrow.
        While I do sing: Any food, etc.

The palsy plagues my pulses,
    When I prig your pigs or pullen,
Your culvers take, or matchless make
    Your chanticleer or sullen.
When I want provant, with Humphry
    I sup, and when benighted,
I repose in Powles with waking souls,
    Yet never am affrighted.
        But I do sing: Any food, etc.

I know more than Apollo,
    For oft when he lies sleeping,
I see the stars at bloody wars
    In the wounded welkin weeping,
The moon embrace her shepherd,
    And the queen of love her warrior,
While the first doth horn the star of morn,
    And the next the heavenly Farrier.
        While I do sing: Any food, etc.

The gipsy Snap and Pedro
    Are none of Tom's comradoes.
The punk I scorn, and the cutpurse sworn,
    And the roaring boys' bravadoes.
The meek, the white, the gentle,
    Me handle, touch, and spare not;
But those that cross Tom Rhinoceros
    Do what the panther dare not.
        Although I sing: Any food, etc.

With an host of furious fancies
　　Whereof I am commander,
With a burning spear and a horse of air
　　To the wilderness I wander.
By a knight of ghosts and shadows
　　I summoned am to tourney
Ten leagues beyond the wide world's end,
　　Methinks it is no journey.

　　　Yet will I sing: Any food, etc.

SIR THOMAS WYATT
1503–1542

They Flee from Me

They flee from me that sometime did me seek,
With naked foot stalking in my chamber.
I have seen them gentle, tame, and meek,
That now are wild, and do not remember
That some time they put themselves in danger
To take bread at my hand; and now they range,
Busily seeking with a continual change.

Thanked be fortune, it hath been otherwise
Twenty times better; but once, in speciall,
In thin array, after a pleasant guise,
When her loose gown from her shoulders did fall,
And she me caught in her arms long and small,
Therewith all sweetly did me kiss,
And softly said, Dear heart, how like you this?

It was no dream; I lay broad awaking.
But all is turned now through my gentleness
Into a strange fashion of forsaking;
And I have leave to go of her goodness,
And she also to use newfangleness.
But since that I so kindly am served,
I fain would know what *she* hath deserved.

SIR PHILIP SIDNEY
1554–1586

Desire

Thou blind man's mark, thou fool's self-chosen snare,
Fond Fancy's scum and dregs of scattered thought,
Band of all evils, cradle of causeless care,
Thou web of will whose end is never wrought;
Desire! desire, I have too dearly bought
With price of mangled mind thy worthless ware;
Too long, too long asleep thou hast me brought,
Who should my mind to higher things prepare.
But yet in vain thou hast my ruin sought,
In vain thou mad'st me to vain things aspire,
In vain thou kindlest all thy smoky fire.
For virtue hath this better lesson taught,
Within myself to seek my only hire,
Desiring nought but how to kill desire.

Loving in Truth

Loving in truth, and fain in verse my love to show,
That she, dear she, might take some pleasure of my pain,
Pleasure might cause her read, reading might make her know,
Knowledge might pity win, and pity grace obtain,—
I sought fit words to paint the blackest face of woe;
Studying inventions fine, her wits to entertain,
Oft turning others' leaves to see if thence would flow
Some fresh and fruitful showers upon my sun-burned brain.
But words came halting forth, wanting invention's stay;
Invention, nature's child, fled step-dame Study's blows,
And others' feet still seemed but strangers in my way.
Thus, great with child to speak, and helpless in my throes,
Biting my truant pen, beating myself for spite,
Fool, said my muse to me, look in thy heart and write.

Double Sestine

STREPHON

You goat-herd Gods, that love the grassy mountains,
You nymphs that haunt the springs in pleasant valleys,
You Satyrs joyed with free and quiet forests,
Vouchsafe your silent ears to playning music,
Which to my woes gives still an early morning:
And draws the dolour on till weary evening.

KLAIUS

O Mercury, forgoer to the evening,
O heavenly huntress of the savage mountains,
O lovely star, entitled of the morning,
While that my voice doth fill these woeful valleys
Vouchsafe your silent ears to playning music,
Which oft doth *Echo* tired in secret forests.

STREPHON

I that was once free-burgess of the forests
Where shade from sun, and sports I sought at evening,
I that was once esteemed for pleasant music,
Am banished now among the monstrous mountains
Of huge despair, and foul affliction's valleys,
Am grown a screech-owl to myself each morning.

KLAIUS

I that was once delighted every morning,
Hunting the wild inhabiters of forests,
I that was once the music of these valleys,
So darkened am, that all my day is evening,
Heart-broken so, that mole-hills seem high mountains,
And fill the vales with cries instead of music.

STREPHON

Long since, alas, my deadly Swannish music
Hath made itself a crier of the morning,
And hath with wailing strength climbed highest mountains:
Long since my thoughts more desert be than forests:
Long since I see my joys come to their evening,
And state thrown down to over-trodden valleys.

KLAIUS

Long since the happy dwellers of these valleys,
Have prayed me leave my strange exclaiming music,
Which troubles their day's work, and joys of evening:
Long since I hate the night, more hate the morning:
Long since my thoughts chase me like beasts in forests,
And make me wish myself laid under mountains.

STREPHON

Meseems I see the high and stately mountains
Transform themselves to low dejected valleys:
Meseems I hear in these ill-changèd forests
The nightingales do learn of owls their music:
Meseems I feel the comfort of the morning
Turned to the mortal serene of an evening.

KLAIUS

Meseems I see a filthy cloudy evening,
As soon as sun begins to climb the mountains:
Meseems I feel a noisome scent, the morning
When I do smell the flowers of these valleys:
Meseems I hear, when I do hear sweet music,
The dreadful cries of murdered men in forests.

STREPHON

I wish to fire the trees of all these forests:
I give the sun a last farewell each evening;
I curse the fiddling finders out of music:
With envy do I hate the lofty mountains;
And with despite despise the humble valleys:
I do detest night, evening, day, and morning.

KLAIUS

Curse of myself my prayer is, the morning:
My fire is more, than can be made with forests;
My state more base, than are the basest valleys:
I wish no evening more to see, each evening;
Shamed I have myself in sight of mountains,
And stop mine ears, lest I go mad with music.

STREPHON

For she, whose parts maintained a perfect music,
Whose beauty shined more than the blushing morning,
Who much did pass in state the stately mountains,
In straightness passed the cedars of the forests,
Hath cast me wretch into eternal evening,
By taking her two suns from these dark valleys.

KLAIUS

For she, to whom compared, the Alps are valleys,
She, whose least word brings from the spheres their music,
At whose approach the sun rose in the evening,
Who, where she went, bare in her forehead morning,
Is gone, is gone from these our spoiled forests,
Turning to deserts our best pastured mountains.

STREPHON These mountains witness shall, so shall these valleys,
KLAIUS These forests eke, made wretched by our music,
STREPHON Our morning hymn is this,
KLAIUS   and song at evening.

SIR WALTER RALEIGH
1552–1618

The Nymph's Reply to the Shepherd*

If all the world and love were young
And truth in every shepherd's tongue,
These pretty pleasures might me move
To live with thee and be thy love.

Time drives the flocks from field to fold
When rivers rage and rocks grow cold,
And Philomel becometh dumb;
The rest complain of cares to come.

The flowers do fade, and wanton fields
To wayward winter reckoning yields;

A honey tongue, a heart of gall,
Is fancy's spring, but sorrow's fall.

Thy gowns, thy shoes, thy beds or roses,
Thy cap, thy kirtle, and thy posies
Soon break, soon wither, soon forgotten,
In folly ripe, in reason rotten.

Thy belt of straw and ivy buds,
Thy coral clasps and amber studs,
All these in me no means can move
To come to thee and be thy love.

But could youth last and love still breed,
Had joys no date nor age no need,
Then these delights my mind might move
To live with thee and be thy love.

Even Such Is Time

Even such is Time, which takes in trust
    Our youth, and joys, and all we have;
And pays us but with age and dust,
    Which, in the dark and silent grave,
When we have wandered all our ways,
Shuts up the story of our days:
    And from which earth and grave and dust
    The Lord shall raise me up, I trust.

The Lie

Go, Soul, the body's guest,
Upon a thankless arrant:
Fear not to touch the best;
The truth shall be thy warrant:
Go, since I needs must die,
And give the world the lie.

Say to the court, it glows
And shines like rotten wood;
Say to the church, it shows
What's good, and doth no good:
If church and court reply,
Then give them both the lie.

Tell potentates, they live
Acting by others' action;
Not loved unless they give,
Not strong but by a faction:
If potentates reply,
Give potentates the lie.

Tell men of high condition,
That manage the estate,
Their purpose is ambition,
Their practice only hate:
And if they once reply,
Then give them all the lie.

Tell them that brave it most,
They beg for more by spending,
Who, in their greatest cost,
Seek nothing but commending:
And if they make reply,
Then give them all the lie.

Tell zeal it wants devotion;
Tell love it is but lust:
Tell time it is but motion;
Tell flesh it is but dust:
And wish them not reply,
For thou must give the lie.

Tell age it daily wasteth;
Tell honour how it alters;
Tell beauty how she blasteth;
Tell favour how it falters:
And as they shall reply,
Give every one the lie.

Tell wit how much it wrangles
In tickle points of niceness;
Tell wisdom she entangles
Herself in over-wiseness:
And when they do reply,
Straight give them both the lie.

Tell physic of her boldness;
Tell skill it is pretension;
Tell charity of coldness;
Tell law it is contention:
And as they do reply,
So give them still the lie.

Tell fortune of her blindness;
Tell nature of decay;
Tell friendship of unkindness;
Tell justice of delay:
And if they will reply,
Then give them all the lie.

Tell arts they have no soundness,
But vary by esteeming;
Tell schools they want profoundness,
And stand too much on seeming:
If arts and schools reply,
Give arts and schools the lie.

Tell faith it's fled the city;
Tell how the country erreth;
Tell manhood shakes off pity
And virtue least preferreth:
And if they do reply,
Spare not to give the lie.

So when thou hast, as I
Commanded thee, done blabbing
—Although to give the lie
Deserves no less than stabbing—
Stab at thee he that will,
No stab the soul can kill.

SIR EDWARD DYER
1550?–1607

My Mind to Me a Kingdom Is

My mind to me a kingdom is,
   Such present joys therein I find
That it excels all other bliss
   That earth affords or grows by kind:
Though much I want which most would have,
Yet still my mind forbids to crave.

No princely pomp, no wealthy store,
   No force to win the victory,
No wily wit to salve a sore,
   No shape to feed a loving eye;
To none of these I yield as thrall:
For why? My mind doth serve for all.

I see how plenty surfeits oft,
   And hasty climbers soon do fall;
I see that those which are aloft
   Mishap doth threaten most of all;
They get with toil, they keep with fear:
Such cares my mind could never bear.

Content to live, this is my stay;
   I seek no more than may suffice;
I press to bear no haughty sway;
   Look, what I lack my mind supplies:
Lo, thus I triumph like a king,
Content with that my mind doth bring.

Some have too much, yet still do crave;
   I little have, and seek no more.
They are but poor, though much they have,
   And I am rich with little store:
They poor, I rich; they beg, I give;
They lack, I leave; they pine, I live.

I laugh not at another's loss;
   I grudge not at another's pain;

No worldly waves my mind can toss;
  My state at one doth still remain:
I fear no foe, I fawn no friend;
I loathe not life, nor dread my end.

Some weigh their pleasure by their lust,
  Their wisdom by their rage of will;
Their treasure is their only trust;
  A cloaked craft their store of skill:
But all the pleasure that I find
Is to maintain a quiet mind.

My wealth is health and perfect ease;
  My conscience clear my chief defence;
I neither seek by bribes to please,
  Nor by deceit to breed offence:
Thus do I live; thus will I die;
Would all did so as well as I!

EDMUND SPENSER
1552–1599

My Love Is Like to Ice

My love is like to ice, and I to fire:
How comes it then that this her cold so great
Is not dissolved through my so hot desire,
But harder grows the more I her entreat?
Or how comes it that my exceeding heat
Is not allayed by her heart-frozen cold,
But that I burn much more in boiling sweat,
And feel my flames augmented manifold?
What more miraculous thing may be told,
That fire, which all things melts, should harden ice,
And ice, which is congealed with senseless cold,
Should kindle fire by wonderful device?
Such is the power of love in gentle mind,
That it can alter all the course of kind.

One Day I Wrote Her Name

One day I wrote her name upon the strand,
But came the waves and washèd it away:
Again I wrote it with a second hand,
But came the tide and made my pains his prey.
"Vain man," said she, "that dost in vain essay
A mortal thing so to immortalize;
For I myself shall like to this decay,
And eke my name be wipèd out likewise."
"Not so," quoth I; "let baser things devise
To die in dust, but you shall live by fame;
My verse your virtues rare shall eternize,
And in the heavens write your glorious name:
Where, whenas Death shall all the world subdue,
Our love shall live, and later life renew."

Prothalamion

Calm was the day, and through the trembling air
Sweet, breathing Zephyrus did softly play
A gentle spirit, that lightly did delay
Hot Titan's beams, which then did glister fair;
When I (whom sullen care,
Through discontent of my long fruitless stay
In princes' court, and expectation vain
Of idle hopes, which still to fly away,
Like empty shadows, did afflict my brain)
Walked forth to ease my pain
Along the shore of silver streaming Thames;
Whose rutty bank, the which his river hems,
Was painted all with variable flowers,
And all the meads adorned with dainty gems
Fit to deck maidens' bowers,
And crown their paramours
Against the bridal day, which is not long—
    Sweet Thames! run softly, till I end my song.

There, in a meadow, by the river's side,
A flock of nymphs I chancéd to espy,
All lovely daughters of the flood thereby,
With goodly greenish locks, all loose untied,
As each had been a bride.

And each one had a little wicker basket,
Made of fine twigs, entrailéd curiously,
In which they gathered flowers to fill their flasket,
And with fine fingers cropt full feateously
The tender stalks on high.
Of every sort, which in that meadow grew,
They gathered some: the violet, pallid blue,
The little daisy, that at evening closes,
The virgin lily, and the primrose true,
With store of vermeil roses,
To deck their bridegroom's posies
Against the bridal day, which was not long—
  Sweet Thames! run softly, till I end my song.

With that I saw two swans of goodly hue
Come softly swimming down along the Lee;
Two fairer birds I yet did never see.
The snow, which doth the top of Pindus strew,
Did never whiter shew,
Nor Jove himself, when he a swan would be
For love of Leda, whiter did appear;
Yet Leda was, they say, as white as he,
Yet not so white as these, nor nothing near;
So purely white they were,
That even the gentle stream, the which them bare,
Seemed foul to them, and bade his billows spare
To wet their silken feathers, lest they might
Soil their fair plumes with water not so fair,
And mar their beauties bright,
That shone as heaven's light,
Against their bridal day, which was not long—
  Sweet Thames! run softly, till I end my song.

Eftsoons the nymphs, which now had flowers their fill,
Ran all in haste to see that silver brood,
As they came floating on the crystal flood;
Whom when they saw, they stood amazéd still,
Their wondering eyes to fill;
Them seemed they never saw a sight so fair
Of fowls so lovely, that they sure did deem

Them heavenly born, or to be that same pair
Which through the sky draw Venus' silver team;
For sure they did not seem
To be begot of any earthly seed,
But rather angels, or of angels' breed;
Yet were they bred of summer's heat, they say,
In sweetest season, when each flower and weed
The earth did fresh array;
So fresh they seemed as day,
Even as their bridal day, which was not long—
    Sweet Thames! run softly, till I end my song.

Then forth they all out of their baskets drew
Great store of flowers, the honor of the field,
That to the sense did fragrant odors yield,
All which upon those goodly birds they threw
And all the waves did strew,
That like old Peneus' waters they did seem,
When down along by pleasant Tempe's shore,
Scattered with flowers, through Thessaly they stream,
That they appear, through lilies' plenteous store,
Like a bride's chamber floor.
Two of those nymphs meanwhile, two garlands bound
Of freshest flowers which in that mead they found,
The which presenting all in trim array,
Their snowy foreheads there withal they crowned,
Whilst one did sing this lay,
Prepared against that day,
Against their bridal day, which was not long—
    Sweet Thames! run softly, till I end my song.

"Ye gentle birds! the world's fair ornament,
And heaven's glory, whom this happy hour
Doth lead unto your lover's blissful bower,
Joy may you have, and gentle heart's content
Of your love's couplement;
And let fair Venus, that is queen of love,
With her heart-quelling son upon you smile,
Whose smile, they say, hath virtue to remove
All love's dislike, and friendship's faulty guile
Forever to assoil;

Let endless peace your steadfast hearts accord,
And blessed plenty wait upon your board;
And let your bed with pleasures chaste abound,
That fruitful issue may to you afford,
Which may your foes confound,
And make your joys redound
Upon your bridal day, which is not long—"
    Sweet Thames! run softly, till I end my song.

So ended she; and all the rest around
To her redoubled that her undersong,
Which said their bridal day should not be long.
And gentle Echo from the neighbor ground
Their accents did resound.
So forth those joyous birds did pass along,
Adown the Lee, that to them murmured low,
As he would speak, but that he lacked a tongue,
Yet did by signs his glad affection show,
Making his stream run slow.
And all the fowl which in his flood did dwell
'Gan flock about these twain, that did excel
The rest, so far as Cynthia doth shend
The lesser stars. So they, enrangéd well,
Did on those two attend,
And their best service lend
Against their wedding day, which was not long—
    Sweet Thames! run softly, till I end my song.

At length they all to merry London came,
To merry London, my most kindly nurse,
That to me gave this life's first native source,
Though from another place I take my name,
An house of ancient fame.
There when they came, whereas those bricky towers
The which on Thames' broad, aged back do ride,
Where now the studious lawyers have their bowers,
There whilom wont the Templar Knights to bide
Till they decayed through pride.
Next whereunto there stands a stately place,
Where oft I gainéd gifts and goodly grace
Of that great lord, which therein wont to dwell,
Whose want too well now feels my friendless case;

But ah! here fits not well
Old woes, but joys, to tell
Against the bridal day, which is not long—
   Sweet Thames! run softly, till I end my song.

Yet therein now doth lodge a noble peer,
Great England's glory, and the world's wide wonder,
Whose dreadful name late through all Spain did thunder,
And Hercules' two pillars standing near
Did make to quake and fear:
Fair branch of honor, flower of chivalry!
That fillest England with thy triumph's fame,
Joy have thou of thy noble victory,
And endless happiness of thine own name,
That promiseth the same;
That through thy prowess, and victorious arms,
Thy country may be freed from foreign harms;
And great Elisa's glorious name may ring
Through all the world, filled with thy wide alarms,
Which some brave muse may sing
To ages following,
Upon the bridal day, which is not long—
   Sweet Thames! run softly, till I end my song.

From those high towers this noble lord issuing,
Like radiant Hesper, when his golden hair
In th' ocean billows he hath bathéd fair,
Descended to the river's open viewing,
With a great train ensuing.
Above the rest were goodly to be seen
Two gentle knights of lovely face and feature
Beseeming well the bower of any queen,
With gifts of wit, and ornaments of nature,
Fit for so goodly stature,
That like the twins of Jove they seemed in sight,
Which deck the baldrick of the heavens bright;
They two, forth pacing to the river's side,
Received those two fair brides, their love's delight;
Which, at th' appointed tide,
Each one did make his bride
Against their bridal day, which is not long—
   Sweet Thames! run softly, till I end my song.

GEORGE PEELE
1558–1598

Bathsheba's Song

Hot sun, cool fire, tempered with sweet air,
Black shade, fair nurse, shadow my white hair.
Shine, sun; burn, fire; breathe, air, and ease me;
Black shade, fair nurse, shroud me and please me;
Shadow, my sweet nurse, keep me from burning,
Make not my glad cause cause of mourning.
    Let not my beauty's fire
    Inflame unstaid desire,
    Nor pierce any bright eye
    That wand'reth lightly.

SAMUEL DANIEL
1562–1619

Care-charmer Sleep

Care-charmer Sleep, son of the sable Night,
Brother to Death, in silent darkness born,
Relieve my languish, and restore the light,
With dark forgetting of my cares return.
And let the day be time enough to mourn
The shipwreck of my ill-adventur'd youth;
Let waking eyes suffice to wail their scorn,
Without the torment of the night's untruth.
Cease, dreams, the images of day-desires,
To model forth the passions of the morrow;
Never let rising sun approve you liars,
To add more grief to aggravate my sorrow.
Still let me sleep, embracing clouds in vain;
And never wake to feel the day's disdain.

MICHAEL DRAYTON
1563–1631

Farewell to Love

Since there's no help, come let us kiss and part;
Nay I have done, you get no more of me;
And I am glad, yea, glad with all my heart,
That thus so cleanly I myself can free;
Shake hands for ever, cancel all our vows,
And when we meet at any time again,
Be it not seen in either of our brows
That we one jot of former love retain.
Now at the last gasp of love's latest breath,
When his pulse failing, passion speechless lies,
When faith is kneeling by his bed of death,
And innocence is closing up his eyes,
Now if thou would'st, when all have given him over,
From death to life thou might'st him yet recover.

CHRISTOPHER MARLOWE
1564–1593

The Passionate Shepherd to His Love*

Come live with me and be my love,
And we will all the pleasures prove,
That valleys, groves, hills and fields,
Woods or steepy mountains yields.

And we will sit upon the rocks,
Seeing the shepherds feed their flocks
By shallow rivers, to whose falls
Melodious birds sing madrigals.

And I will make thee beds of roses,
And a thousand fragrant posies,
A cap of flowers and a kirtle
Embroidered all with leaves of myrtle;

*See page 22

A gown made of the finest wool,
Which from our pretty lambs we pull;
Fair-linèd slippers for the cold,
With buckles of the purest gold;

A belt of straw and ivy buds,
With coral clasps and amber studs;
And if these pleasures may thee move,
Come live with me and be my love.

The shepherd swains shall dance and sing
For thy delight each May morning;
If these delights thy mind may move,
Then live with me and be my love.

What Is Beauty?

What is beauty, saith my sufferings, then?
If all the pens that ever poets held
Had fed the feeling of their masters' thoughts,
And every sweetness that inspir'd their hearts,
Their minds, and muses on admired themes;
If all the heavenly quintessence they still
From their immortal flowers of poesy,
Wherein as in a mirror we perceive
The highest reaches of a human wit—
If these had made one poem's period,
And all combin'd in beauty's worthiness,
Yet should there hover in their restless heads
One thought, one grace, one wonder, at the least,
Which into words no virtue can digest.

From *Tamburlaine the Great*

Who Ever Loved, That Loved Not at First Sight?

It lies not in our power to love or hate,
For will in us is overruled by fate.
When two are stripped, long ere the course begin,
We wish that one should lose, the other win;
And one especially do we affect
Of two gold ingots, like in each respect:
The reason no man knows; let it suffice
What we behold is censured by our eyes.

Where both deliberate, the love is slight:
Who ever loved, that loved not at first sight?

From *Hero and Leander*

Helen

Was this the face that launched a thousand ships,
And burned the topless towers of Ilium?—
Sweet Helen, make me immortal with a kiss!—
Her lips suck forth my soul: see where it flees!—
Come, Helen, come, give me my soul again.
Here will I dwell, for heaven is in these lips,
And all is dross that is not Helena.
I will be Paris, and for love of thee,
Instead of Troy, shall Wittenberg be sacked,
And I will combat with weak Menelaus,
And wear thy colours on my plumèd crest;
Yes, I will wound Achilles in the heel,
And then return to Helen for a kiss.
Oh, thou art fairer than the evening air
Clad in the beauty of a thousand stars;
Brighter art thou than flaming Jupiter
When he appeared to hapless Semele;
More lovely than the monarch of the sky
In wanton Arethusa's azured arms;
And none but thou shalt be my paramour!

From *The Tragical History of Dr. Faustus*

WILLIAM SHAKESPEARE
1564–1616

Who Is Silvia?

Who is Silvia? what is she,
    That all our swains commend her?
Holy, fair, and wise is she;
    The heaven such grace did lend her,
That she might admirèd be.

Is she kind as she is fair?
    For beauty lives with kindness.
Love doth to her eyes repair,
    To help him of his blindness,
And, being help'd, inhabits there.

Then to Silvia let us sing,
    That Silvia is excelling;
She excels each mortal thing
    Upon the dull earth dwelling:
To her let us garlands bring.

Spring

When daisies pied and violets blue
    And lady-smocks all silver-white
And cuckoo buds of yellow hue
    Do paint the meadows with delight,
The cuckoo then, on every tree,
Mocks married men; for thus sings he,
        Cuckoo;
Cuckoo, cuckoo: O word of fear,
Unpleasing to a married ear.

When shepherds pipe on oaten straws,
    And merry larks are ploughmen's clocks,
When turtles tread, and rooks, and daws,
    And maidens bleach their summer smocks,
The cuckoo then, on every tree,
Mocks married men; for thus sings he,
        Cuckoo;
Cuckoo, cuckoo: O word of fear,
Unpleasing to a married ear.

Under the Greenwood Tree

Under the greenwood tree
Who loves to lie with me,
And turn his merry note
Unto the sweet bird's throat,
Come hither, come hither, come hither:

Here shall he see
No enemy
But winter and rough weather.

Who doth ambition shun,
And loves to live i' the sun,
Seeking the food he eats,
And pleased with what he gets,
Come hither, come hither, come hither:
Here shall he see
No enemy
But winter and rough weather.

Blow, Blow, Thou Winter Wind

Blow, blow, thou winter wind,
Thou art not so unkind
   As man's ingratitude;
Thy tooth is not so keen,
Because thou art not seen,
   Although thy breath be rude.
Heigh-ho! sing, heigh-ho! unto the green holly:
Most friendship is feigning, most loving mere folly:
   Then, heigh-ho, the holly!
   This life is most jolly.

Freeze, freeze, thou bitter sky,
That dost not bite so nigh
   As benefits forgot:
Though thou the waters warp,
Thy sting is not so sharp
   As friends remember'd not.
Heigh-ho! sing, heigh-ho! unto the green holly:
Most friendship is feigning, most loving mere folly:
   Then, heigh-ho, the holly!
   This life is most jolly.

It Was a Lover and His Lass

It was a lover and his lass,
　With a hey, and a ho, and hey nonino,
That o'er the green corn-field did pass
　In the spring time, the only pretty ring time,
When birds do sing, hey ding a ding, ding:
Sweet lovers love the spring.

Between the acres of the rye,
　With a hey, and a ho, and a hey nonino,
These pretty country folk would lie,
　In the spring time, the only pretty ring time,
When birds do sing, hey ding a ding, ding:
Sweet lovers love the spring.

This carol they began that hour,
　With a hey, and a ho, and a hey nonino,
How that a life was but a flower
　In the spring time, the only pretty ring time,
When birds do sing, hey ding a ding, ding:
Sweet lovers love the spring.

And therefore take the present time,
　With a hey, and a ho, and a hey nonino,
For love is crowned with the prime
　In the spring time, the only pretty ring time,
When birds do sing, hey ding a ding, ding:
Sweet lovers love the spring.

When That I Was and a Little Tiny Boy

When that I was and a little tiny boy,
　With hey, ho, the wind and the rain,
A foolish thing was but a toy,
　For the rain it raineth every day.

But when I came to man's estate
　With hey, ho, the wind and the rain,
'Gainst knaves and thieves men shut the gate,
　For the rain it raineth every day.

But when I came, alas! to wive,
   With hey, ho, the wind and the rain,
By swaggering could I never thrive,
   For the rain it raineth every day.

But when I came unto my beds,
   With hey, ho, the wind and the rain,
With toss-pots still had drunken heads,
   For the rain it raineth every day.

A great while ago the world begun,
   With hey, ho, the wind and the rain,
But that's all one, our play is done,
   And we'll strive to please you every day.

O Mistress Mine

O Mistress mine, where are you roaming?
O, stay and hear; your true love's coming,
   That can sing both high and low:
Trip no further, pretty sweeting;
Journeys end in lovers meeting,
   Every wise man's son doth know.

What is love? 'Tis not hereafter;
Present mirth hath present laughter;
   What's to come is still unsure:
In delay there lies no plenty;
Then, come kiss me, sweet and twenty,
   Youth's a stuff will not endure.

Winter

When icicles hang by the wall,
   And Dick the shepherd blows his nail,
And Tom bears logs into the hall,
   And milk comes frozen home in pail,
When blood is nipp'd and ways be foul,
Then nightly sings the staring owl,
    Tu-whit;
Tu-who, a merry note,
While greasy Joan doth keel the pot.

But thy eternal Summer shall not fade
Nor lose possession of that fair thou ow'st;
Nor shall Death brag thou wander'st in his shade,
When in eternal lines to time thou grow'st:
So long as men can breathe, or eyes can see,
So long lives this, and this gives life to thee.

When, in Disgrace with Fortune

When, in disgrace with fortune and men's eyes,
I all alone beweep my outcast state,
And trouble deaf heaven with my bootless cries,
And look upon myself, and curse my fate,
Wishing me like to one more rich in hope,
Featured like him, like him with friends possest,
Desiring this man's art and that man's scope,
With what I most enjoy contented least;

Yet in these thoughts myself almost despising—
Haply I think on thee: and then my state,
Like to the lark at break of day arising
From sullen earth, sings hymns at Heaven's gate;
For thy sweet love rememb'red such wealth brings
That then I scorn to change my state with kings.

When to the Sessions

When to the sessions of sweet silent thought
I summon up remembrance of things past,
I sigh the lack of many a thing I sought,
And with old woes new wail my dear time's waste:
Then can I drown an eye, unused to flow,
For precious friends hid in death's dateless night,
And weep afresh love's long-since-cancell'd woe,
And moan th' expense of many a vanish'd sight:

Then can I grieve at grievances foregone,
And heavily from woe to woe tell o'er
The sad account of fore-bemoanèd moan,
Which I new pay as if not paid before.
But if the while I think on thee, dear friend,
All losses are restored and sorrows end.

Full Many a Glorious Morning

Full many a glorious morning have I seen
Flatter the mountain-tops with sovereign eye,
Kissing with golden face the meadows green,
Gilding pale streams with heavenly alchemy;
Anon permit the basest clouds to ride
With ugly rack on his celestial face,
And from the forlorn world his visage hide,
Stealing unseen to west with this disgrace:

Even so my sun one early morn did shine
With all-triumphant splendour on my brow;
But out, alack! he was but one hour mine;
The region cloud hath mask'd him from me now.
Yet him for this my love no whit disdaineth;
Suns of the world may stain when heaven's sun staineth.

What Is Your Substance

What is your substance, whereof are you made,
That millions of strange shadows on you tend?
Since every one hath, every one, one shade,
And you, but one, can every shadow lend.
Describe Adonis, and the counterfeit
Is poorly imitated after you;
On Helen's cheek all art of beauty set,
And you in Grecian tires are painted new:

Speak of the spring and plenty of the year,
The one doth shadow of your beauty show,
The other as your bounty doth appear;
And you in every blessèd shape we know.
In all external grace you have some part,
But you like none, none you, for constant heart.

Not Marble, nor the Gilded Monuments

Not marble, nor the gilded monuments
Of princes, shall outlive this powerful rhyme;
But you shall shine more bright in these contents
Than unswept stone besmear'd with sluttish time.

When wasteful war shall statues overturn,
And broils root out the work of masonry,
Nor Mars his sword nor war's quick fire shall burn
The living record of your memory.

'Gainst death and all-oblivious enmity
Shall you pace forth; your praise shall still find room
Even in the eyes of all posterity
That wears this world out to the ending doom.
So, till the judgment that yourself arise,
You live in this, and dwell in lovers' eyes.

Like as the Waves

Like as the waves make towards the pebbled shore,
So do our minutes hasten to their end;
Each changing place with that which goes before,
In sequent toil all forwards do contend.
Nativity, once in the main of light,
Crawls to maturity, wherewith being crown'd,
Crooked eclipses 'gainst his glory fight,
And Time that gave doth now his gift confound.

Time doth transfix the flourish set on youth
And delves the parallels in beauty's brow,
Feeds on the rarities of nature's truth,
And nothing stands but for his scythe to mow:
And yet to times in hope my verse shall stand,
Praising thy worth, despite his cruel hand.

When I Have Seen by Time's Fell Hand

When I have seen by Time's fell hand defaced
The rich proud cost of outworn buried age;
When sometime lofty towers I see down-razed
And brass eternal slave to mortal rage;
When I have seen the hungry ocean gain
Advantage on the kingdom of the shore,
And the firm soil win of the watery main,
Increasing store with loss and loss with store;

When I have seen such interchange of state,
Or state itself confounded to decay;
Ruin hath taught me thus to ruminate,
That Time will come and take my love away.
This thought is as a death, which cannot choose
But weep to have that which it fears to lose.

Since Brass, nor Stone, nor Earth

Since brass, nor stone, nor earth, nor boundless sea,
But sad mortality o'er-sways their power,
How with this rage shall beauty hold a plea,
Whose action is no stronger than a flower?
O, how shall summer's honey breath hold out
Against the wrackful siege of battering days,
When rocks impregnable are not so stout,
Nor gates of steel so strong, but Time decays?

O fearful meditation! where, alack,
Shall Time's best jewel from Time's chest lie hid?
Or what strong hand can hold his swift foot back?
Or who his spoil of beauty can forbid?
O, none, unless this miracle have might,
That in black ink my love may still shine bright.

Tired with All These

Tired with all these, for restful death I cry,—
As, to behold desert a beggar born,
And needy nothing trimm'd in jollity,
And purest faith unhappily forsworn,
And gilded honour shamefully misplaced,
And maiden virtue rudely strumpeted,
And right perfection wrongfully disgraced,
And strength by limping sway disablèd,

And art made tongue-tied by authority,
And folly doctor-like controlling skill,
And simple truth miscall'd simplicity,
And captive good attending captain ill:
Tired with all these, from these would I be gone,
Save that, to die, I leave my love alone.

No Longer Mourn for Me

No longer mourn for me when I am dead
Than you shall hear the surly sullen bell
Give warning to the world that I am fled
From this vile world, with vilest worms to dwell:
Nay, if you read this line, remember not
The hand that writ it; for I love you so
That I in your sweet thoughts would be forgot
If thinking on me then should make you woe.

O, if, I say, you look upon this verse
When I perhaps compounded am with clay,
Do not so much as my poor name rehearse,
But let your love even with my life decay,
Lest the wise world should look into your moan
And mock you with me after I am gone.

That Time of Year

That time of year thou mayst in me behold
When yellow leaves, or none, or few, do hang
Upon those boughs which shake against the cold,
Bare ruin'd choirs, where late the sweet birds sang.
In me thou see'st the twilight of such day,
As after sunset fadeth in the west,
Which by and by black night doth take away,
Death's second self, that seals up all in rest.

In me thou see'st the glowing of such fire
That on the ashes of his youth doth lie,
As the death-bed whereon it must expire
Consumed with that which it was nourish'd by.
This thou perceiv'st, which makes thy love more strong,
To love that well which thou must leave ere long.

Farewell! Thou Art too Dear

Farewell! thou art too dear for my possessing,
And like enough thou know'st thy estimate:
The charter of thy worth gives thee releasing;
My bonds in thee are all determinate.

For how do I hold thee but by thy granting?
And for that riches where is my deserving?
The cause of this fair gift in me is wanting,
And so my patent back again is swerving.

Thyself thou gav'st, thy own worth then not knowing,
Or me, to whom thou gav'st it, else mistaking;
So thy great gift, upon misprision growing,
Comes home again, on better judgement making.
Thus have I had thee, as a dream doth flatter
In sleep a king; but waking no such matter.

They That Have Power to Hurt

They that have power to hurt, and will do none,
That do not do the thing they most do show,
Who, moving others, are themselves as stone,
Unmovèd, cold, and to temptation slow,—
They rightly do inherit heaven's graces,
And husband nature's riches from expense;
They are the lords and owners of their faces,
Others, but stewards of their excellence.

The summer's flower is to the summer sweet
Though to itself it only live and die;
But if that flower with base infection meet,
The basest weed outbraves his dignity:
For sweetest things turn sourest by their deeds;
Lilies that fester smell far worse than weeds.

From You Have I Been Absent

From you have I been absent in the spring,
When proud-pied April, dress'd in all his trim,
Hath put a spirit of youth in everything,
That heavy Saturn laugh'd and leap'd with him.
Yet nor the lays of birds, nor the sweet smell
Of different flowers in odour and in hue,
Could make me any summer's story tell,
Or from their proud lap pluck them where they grew;

Nor did I wonder at the lily's white,
Nor praise the deep vermilion in the rose;
They were but sweet, but figures of delight,
Drawn after you, you pattern of all those.
Yet seem'd it winter still, and, you away,
As with your shadow I with these did play.

No More Be Grieved

No more be grieved at that which thou hast done,
Roses have thorns, and silver fountains mud,
Clouds and eclipses stain both moon and sun,
And loathsome canker lives in sweetest bud.
All men make faults, and even I in this,
Authorizing thy trespass with compare,
Myself corrupting, salving thy amiss,
Excusing thy sins more than thy sins are:

For to thy sensual fault I bring in sense,
Thy adverse party is thy advocate,
And 'gainst myself a lawful plea commence,
Such civil war is in my love and hate,
That I an accessory needs must be,
To that sweet thief which sourly robs from me.

When in the Chronicle

When in the chronicle of wasted time
I see descriptions of the fairest wights,
And beauty making beautiful old rhyme
In praise of ladies dead and lovely knights,
Then, in the blazon of sweet beauty's best,
Of hand, of foot, of lip, of eye, of brow,
I see their antique pen would have express'd
Even such a beauty as you master now.

So all their praises are but prophecies
Of this our time, all you prefiguring;
And, for they look'd but with divining eyes,
They had not skill enough your worth to sing:
For we, which now behold these present days,
Have eyes to wonder, but lack tongues to praise.

Not Mine Own Fears

Not mine own fears, nor the prophetic soul
Of the wide world dreaming on things to come,
Can yet the lease of my true love control,
Supposed as forfeit to a confined doom.
The mortal moon hath her eclipse endured,
And the sad augurs mock their own presage;
Incertainties now crown themselves assured,
And peace proclaims olives of endless age.

Now with the drops of this most balmy time
My love looks fresh, and Death to me subscribes,
Since, spite of him, I'll live in this poor rhyme,
While he insults o'er dull and speechless tribes:
And thou in this shalt find thy monument,
When tyrants' crests and tombs of brass are spent.

The Marriage of True Minds

Let me not to the marriage of true minds
Admit impediments. Love is not love
Which alters when it alteration finds,
Or bends with the remover to remove:
O, no! it is an ever-fixèd mark,
That looks on tempests and is never shaken;
It is the star to every wand'ring bark,
Whose worth's unknown, although his height be taken.

Love's not Time's fool, though rosy lips and cheeks
Within his bending sickle's compass come;
Love alters not with his brief hours and weeks,
But bears it out even to the edge of doom:—
If this be error and upon me proved,
I never writ, nor no man ever loved.

The Expense of Spirit

The expense of spirit in a waste of shame
Is lust in action; and till action, lust
Is perjur'd, murd'rous, bloody, full of blame,
Savage, extreme, rude, cruel, not to trust:

Enjoy'd no sooner but despised straight;
Past reason hunted, and no sooner had,
Past reason hated, as a swallow'd bait
On purpose laid to make the taker mad:

Mad in pursuit and in possession so;
Had, having, and in quest to have, extreme;
A bliss in proof, and prov'd, a very woe;
Before, a joy propos'd; behind, a dream.
All this the world well knows; yet none knows well
To shun the heaven that leads men to this hell.

My Mistress' Eyes

My mistress' eyes are nothing like the sun;
Coral is far more red than her lips red;
If snow be white, why then her breasts are dun;
If hairs be wires, black wires grow on her head.
I have seen roses damask'd, red and white,
But no such roses see I in her cheeks;
And in some perfumes is there more delight
Than in the breath that from my mistress reeks.

I love to hear her speak, yet well I know
That music hath a far more pleasing sound;
I grant I never saw a goddess go;
My mistress, when she walks, treads on the ground:
And yet, by heaven, I think my love as rare
As any she belied with false compare.

Poor Soul, the Centre

Poor soul, the centre of my sinful earth,
Thrall to these rebel powers that thee array,
Why dost thou pine within and suffer dearth,
Painting thy outward walls so costly gay?
Why so large cost, having so short a lease,
Dost thou upon thy fading mansion spend?
Shall worms, inheritors of this excess,
Eat up thy charge? Is this thy body's end?

Then, soul, live thou upon thy servant's loss,
And let that pine to aggravate thy store;
Buy terms divine in selling hours of dross;
Within be fed, without be rich no more:
So shalt thou feed on Death, that feeds on men,
And Death once dead, there's no more dying then.

The Heavenly Rhetoric

Did not the heavenly rhetoric of thine eye,
'Gainst whom the world cannot hold argument,
Persuade my heart to this false perjury?
Vows for thee broke deserve not punishment.
A woman I forswore; but I will prove,
Thou being a goddess, I forswore not thee:
My vow was earthly, thou a heavenly love;
Thy grace being gain'd cures all disgrace in me.
Vows are but breath, and breath a vapour is:
Then thou, fair sun, which on my earth doth shine,
Exhalest this vapour-vow; in thee it is:
If broken then, it is no fault of mine:
If by me broke, what fool is not so wise
To lose an oath to win a paradise?

From *Love's Labour's Lost*

Imagination

Lovers and madmen have such seething brains,
Such shaping fantasies, that apprehend
More than cool reason ever comprehends.
The lunatic, the lover, and the poet
Are of imagination all compact:—
One sees more devils than vast hell can hold,—
That is the madman: the lover, all as frantic,
Sees Helen's beauty in a brow of Egypt:
The poet's eye, in a fine frenzy rolling,
Doth glance from heaven to earth, from earth to heaven;
And, as imagination bodies forth
The forms of things unknown, the poet's pen
Turns them to shapes, and gives to airy nothing
A local habitation and a name.

Such tricks hath strong imagination,
That, if it would but apprehend some joy,
It comprehends some bringer of that joy;
Or in the night, imagining some fear,
How easy is a bush supposed a bear!

From *A Midsummer Night's Dream*

He Jests at Scars

He jests at scars, that never felt a wound.
But, soft! what light through yonder window breaks?
It is the east, and Juliet is the sun!
Arise, fair sun, and kill the envious moon,
Who is already sick and pale with grief,
That thou her maid art far more fair than she:
Be not her maid, since she is envious;
Her vestal livery is but sick and green,
And none but fools do wear it; cast it off.
It is my lady; O! it is my love:
O! that she knew she were.
She speaks, yet she says nothing: what of that?
Her eye discourses; I will answer it.
I am too bold, 'tis not to me she speaks:
Two of the fairest stars in all the heaven,
Having some business, do entreat her eyes
To twinkle in their spheres till they return.
What if her eyes were there, they in her head?
The brightness of her cheek would shame those stars
As daylight doth a lamp; her eyes in heaven
Would through the airy region stream so bright
That birds would sing and think it were not night.
See! how she leans her cheek upon her hand:
O! that I were a glove upon that hand,
That I might touch that cheek.

From *Romeo and Juliet*

Age Cannot Wither Her

Age cannot wither her, nor custom stale
Her infinite variety; other women cloy
The appetites they feed, but she makes hungry
Where most she satisfies.

From *Antony and Cleopatra*

Ulysses Advises Achilles

Time hath, my Lord, a wallet at his back,
Wherein he puts alms for oblivion,
A great-siz'd monster of ingratitudes:
Those scraps are good deeds past; which are devour'd
As fast as they are made, forgot as soon
As done: perseverance, dear my Lord,
Keeps honour bright: to have done, is to hang
Quite out of fashion, like a rusty mail
In monumental mockery. Take the instant way;
For honour travels in a strait so narrow
Where one but goes abreast: keep, then, the path;
For emulation hath a thousand sons
That one by one pursue: if you give way,
Or hedge aside from the direct forthright,
Like to an enter'd tide they all rush by
And leave you hindmost;
Or, like a gallant horse fall'n in first rank,
Lie there for pavement to the abject rear,
O'errun and trampled on: then what they do in present,
Though less than your sin past, most o'er top yours;
For time is like a fashionable host,
That slightly shakes his parting guest by the hand,
And with his arms outstretched, as he would fly,
Grasps in the comer: welcome ever smiles,
And farewell goes out sighing. O! let not virtue seek
Remuneration for the thing it was;
For beauty, wit,
High birth, vigour of bone, desert in service,
Love, friendship, charity, are subjects all
To envious and calumniating time.
One touch of nature makes the whole world kin,
That all with one consent praise new-born gawds,
Though they are made and moulded of things past,
And give to dust that is a little gilt
More laud than gilt o'er-dusted.

From *Troilus and Cressida*

To Gild Refinèd Gold

To gild refinèd gold, to paint the lily,
To throw perfume on the violet,
To smooth the ice, or add another hue
Unto the rainbow, or with taper-light
To seek the beauteous eye of heaven to garnish,
Is wasteful and ridiculous excess.

From *King John*

To Thine Own Self Be True

There, my blessing with thee!
And these few precepts in thy memory
Look thou character. Give thy thoughts no tongue,
Nor any unproportioned thought his act.
Be thou familiar, but by no means vulgar;
The friends thou hast, and their adoption tried,
Grapple them to thy soul with hoops of steel;
But do not dull thy palm with entertainment
Of each new-hatched, unfledged comrade. Beware
Of entrance to a quarrel, but, being in,
Bear 't that the opposèd may beware of thee.
Give every man thine ear, but few thy voice;
Take each man's censure, but reserve thy judgement.
Costly thy habit as thy purse can buy,
But not expressed in fancy; rich, not gaudy;
For the apparel oft proclaims the man,
And they in France of the best rank and station
Are most select and generous, chief in that.
Neither a borrower, nor a lender be;
For loan oft loses both itself and friend,
And borrowing dulls the edge of husbandry.
This above all: to thine own self be true,
And it must follow, as the night the day,
Thou canst not then be false to any man.

From *Hamlet*

To Be, or Not to Be

To be, or not to be: that is the question:
Whether 'tis nobler in the mind to suffer
The slings and arrows of outrageous fortune,
Or to take arms against a sea of troubles,
And by opposing end them? To die: to sleep;
No more; and, by a sleep to say we end
The heart-ache and the thousand natural shocks
That flesh is heir to, 'tis a consummation
Devoutly to be wished. To die, to sleep;
To sleep: perchance to dream: aye, there's the rub;
For in that sleep of death what dreams may come
When we have shuffled off this mortal coil,
Must give us pause: there's the respect
That makes calamity of so long life;
For who would bear the whips and scorns of time,
The oppressor's wrong, the proud man's contumely,
The pangs of disprized love, the law's delay,
The insolence of office, and the spurns
That patient merit of the unworthy takes,
When he himself might his quietus make
With a bare bodkin? who would fardels bear,
To grunt and sweat under a weary life,
But that the dread of something after death,
The undiscovered country from whose bourn
No traveller returns, puzzles the will,
And makes us rather bear those ills we have
Than fly to others that we know not of?
Thus conscience does make cowards of us all;
And thus the native hue of resolution
Is sicklied o'er with the pale cast of thought,
And enterprises of great pith and moment
With this regard their currents turn awry,
And lose the name of action.

From Hamlet

The Seven Ages of Man

All the world's a stage,
And all the men and women merely players:
They have their exits and their entrances;
And one man in his time plays many parts,

His acts being seven ages. At first the infant,
Mewling and puking in the nurse's arms.
And then the whining school-boy, with his satchel,
And shining morning face, creeping like snail
Unwillingly to school. And then the lover
Sighing like furnace, with a woeful ballad
Made to his mistress' eyebrow. Then a soldier,
Full of strange oaths, and bearded like the pard,
Jealous in honour, sudden and quick in quarrel,
Seeking the bubble reputation
Even in the cannon's mouth. And then the justice,
In fair round belly with good capon lin'd,
With eyes severe, and beard of formal cut,
Full of wise saws and modern instances;
And so he plays his part. The sixth age shifts
Into the lean and slipper'd pantaloon,
With spectacles on nose and pouch on side,
His youthful hose well sav'd a world too wide
For his shrunk shank; and his big manly voice,
Turning again toward childish treble, pipes
And whistles in his sound. Last scene of all,
That ends this strange eventful history,
Is second childishness and mere oblivion,
Sans teeth, sans eyes, sans taste, sans everything.

From *As You Like It*

Tomorrow, and Tomorrow, and Tomorrow

Tomorrow, and tomorrow, and tomorrow,
Creeps in this petty pace from day to day
To the last syllable of recorded time,
And all our yesterdays have lighted fools
The way to dusty death. Out, out, brief candle!
Life's but a walking shadow, a poor player
That struts and frets his hour upon the stage
And then is heard no more; it is a tale
Told by an idiot, full of sound and fury,
Signifying nothing.

From *Macbeth*

The Quality of Mercy

The quality of mercy is not strained,
It droppeth as the gentle rain from heaven
Upon the place beneath: it is twice blessed;
It blesseth him that gives and him that takes:
'Tis mightiest in the mightiest; it becomes
The thronèd monarch better than his crown;
His sceptre shows the force of temporal power,
The attribute to awe and majesty,
Wherein doth sit the dread and fear of kings;
But mercy is above this sceptred sway,
It is enthronèd in the hearts of kings;
It is an attribute to God himself,
And earthly power doth then show likest God's
When mercy seasons justice. Therefore, Jew,
Though justice be thy plea, consider this,
That in the course of justice none of us
Should see salvation: we do pray for mercy,
And that same prayer doth teach us all to render
The deeds of mercy.

From The Merchant of Venice

Our Revels Now Are Ended

Our revels now are ended. These our actors,
As I foretold you, were all spirits, and
Are melted into air, into thin air;
And, like the baseless fabric of this vision,
The cloud-capped towers, the gorgeous palaces,
The solemn temples, the great globe itself,
Yea, all which it inherit, shall dissolve,
And, like this insubstantial pageant faded,
Leave not a rack behind. We are such stuff
As dreams are made on, and our little life
Is rounded with a sleep.

From The Tempest

The Phœnix and the Turtle

Let the bird of loudest lay
  On the sole Arabian tree,
  Herald sad and trumpet be,
To whose sound chaste wings obey.

But thou shrieking harbinger,
   Foul precurrer of the fiend,
   Augur of the fever's end,
To this troop come thou not near.

From this session interdict
   Every fowl of tyrant wing
   Save the eagle, feathered king.
Keep the obsequy so strict.

Let the priest in surplice white
   That defunctive music can,
   Be the death-divining swan,
Lest the requiem lack his right.

And thou, treble-dated crow,
   That thy sable gender mak'st
   With the breath thou giv'st and tak'st,
'Mongst our mourners shalt thou go.

Here the anthem doth commence:—
   Love and constancy is dead;
   Phœnix and the turtle fled
In a mutual flame from hence.

So they loved, as love in twain
   Had the essence but in one;
   Two distincts, division none;
Number there in love was slain.

Hearts remote, yet not asunder;
   Distance, and no space was seen
   'Twixt the turtle and his queen:
But in them it were a wonder.

So between them love did shine,
   That the turtle saw his right
   Flaming in the phœnix' sight;
Either was the other's mine.

Property was thus appalled,
   That the self was not the same;
   Single nature's double name
Neither two nor one was called.

Reason, in itself confounded,
   Saw division grow together;
   To themselves yet either neither;
Simple were so well compounded,

That it cried, "How true a twain
   Seemeth this concordant one!
   Love hath reason, reason none
If what parts can so remain."

Whereupon it made this threne
   To the phœnix and the dove,
   Co-supremes and stars of love,
As chorus to their tragic scene.

THRENOS

Beauty, truth, and rarity,
Grace in all simplicity,
Here enclosèd in cinders lie.

Death is now the phœnix' nest;
And the turtle's loyal breast
To eternity doth rest,

Leaving no posterity:
'Twas not their infirmity,
It was married chastity.

Truth may seem, but cannot be;
Beauty brag, but 'tis not she;
Truth and beauty buried be.

To this urn let those repair
That are either true or fair;
For these dead birds sigh a prayer.

THOMAS NASHE
1567–1602

Spring, the Sweet Spring

Spring, the sweet Spring, is the year's pleasant king;
Then blooms each thing, then maids dance in a ring,
Cold doth not sting, the pretty birds do sing,
    Cuckoo, jug, jug, pu we, to witta woo.

The palm and may make country houses gay,
Lambs frisk and play, the shepherds pipe all day,
And we hear aye birds tune this merry lay,
    Cuckoo, jug, jug, pu we, to witta woo.

The fields breathe sweet, the daisies kiss our feet,
Young lovers meet, old wives a-sunning sit,
In every street these tunes our ears do greet,
    Cuckoo, jug, jug, pu we, to witta woo.
        Spring, the sweet spring!

THOMAS CAMPION
1567–1620

There Is a Garden in Her Face

There is a garden in her face
Where roses and white lilies grow;
A heavenly paradise is that place
Wherein all pleasant fruits do flow.
    There cherries grow which none may buy,
    Till "Cherry ripe" themselves do cry.

Those cherries fairly do enclose
Of orient pearl a double row,
Which when her lovely laughter shows,
They look like rose-buds filled with snow;
    Yet them nor peer nor prince can buy,
    Till "Cherry ripe" themselves do cry.

Her eyes like angels watch them still,
Her brows like bended bows do stand,
Threatening with piercing frowns to kill
All that attempt, with eye or hand,
    Those sacred cherries to come nigh
    Till "Cherry ripe" themselves do cry.

BEN JONSON
1573–1637

To Celia

Drink to me only with thine eyes,
    And I will pledge with mine;
Or leave a kiss but in the cup
    And I'll not look for wine.
The thirst that from the soul doth rise
    Doth ask a drink divine;
But might I of Jove's nectar sup,
    I would not change for thine.

I sent thee late a rosy wreath,
    Not so much honouring thee
As giving it a hope that there
    It could not withered be;
But thou thereon didst only breathe
    And sent'st it back to me;
Since when it grows, and smells, I swear
    Not of itself but thee!

It Is Not Growing Like a Tree

It is not growing like a tree
In bulk, doth make Man better be;
Or standing long an oak, three hundred year,
To fall a log at last, dry, bald, and sere:
    A lily of a day
    Is fairer far in May,
Although it fall and die that night—
It was the plant and flower of Light.

In small proportions we just beauties see;
And in short measures life may perfect be.

The Hour Glass

Consider this small dust, here in the glass,
 By atoms moved:
Could you believe that this the body was
 Of one that loved;
And in his mistress' flame playing like a fly,
Was turned to cinders by her eye:
Yes, and in death, as life unblessed,
 To have it expressed,
Even ashes of lovers find no rest.

JOHN DONNE
1573–1631

Song

Go and catch a falling star,
 Get with child a mandrake root,
Tell me where all past years are,
 Or who cleft the devil's foot,
Teach me to hear mermaids' singing,
Or to keep off envy's stinging,
  And find
  What wind
Serves to advance an honest mind.

If thou be'st born to strange sights,
 Things invisible go see,
Ride ten thousand days and nights,
 Till Age snow white hairs on thee;
Thou, when thou return'st, wilt tell me
All strange wonders that befell thee,
  And swear
  No where
Lives a woman true and fair.

If thou find'st one, let me know;
   Such a pilgrimage were sweet,
Yet do not; I would not go,
   Though at next door we might meet.
Though she were true when you met her,
And last till you write your letter,
      Yet she
      Will be
False, ere I come, to two or three.

Love's Deity

I long to talk with some old lover's ghost
   Who died before the god of love was born.
I cannot think that he who then loved most,
   Sunk so low as to love one which did scorn.
But since this god produced a destiny
And that vice-nature, custom, lets it be,
   I must love her that loves not me.

Sure, they which made him god, meant not so much,
   Nor he in his young godhead practiced it.
But when an even flame two hearts did touch,
   His office was indulgently to fit
Actives to passives. Correspondency
Only his subject was; it cannot be
   Love, till I love her who loves me.

But every modern god will not extend
   His vast prerogative as far as Jove.
To rage, to lust, to write to, to commend,
   All is the purlieu of the god of love.
O! were we wakened by this tyranny
To ungod this child again, it could not be
   I should love her who loves not me.

Rebel and atheist too, why murmur I,
   As though I felt the worst that love could do?
Love may make me leave loving, or might try
   A deeper plague, to make her love me too;
Which, since she loves before, I'm loth to see.
Falsehood is worse than hate; and that must be,
   If she whom I love, should love me.

The Good Morrow

I wonder, by my troth, what thou and I
Did till we loved? were we not weaned till then,
But sucked on country pleasures, childishly?
Or snorted we in the Seven Sleepers' den?
'Twas so; but this, all pleasures fancies be.
If ever any beauty I did see
Which I desired, and got, 'twas but a dream of thee.

And now good morrow to our waking souls,
Which watch not one another out of fear;
For love all love of other sights controls,
And makes one little room an everywhere.
Let sea-discoverers to new worlds have gone;
Let maps to other, worlds on worlds have shown;
Let us possess one world; each hath one, and is one.

My face in thine eye, thine in mine appears,
And true, plain hearts do in the faces rest;
Where can we find two better hemispheres
Without sharp north, without declining west?
Whatever dies, was not mixed equally;
If our two loves be one, or thou and I
Love so-alike that none do slacken, none can die.

The Funeral

Whoever comes to shroud me, do not harm
    Nor question much
That subtle wreath of hair about mine arm;
The mystery, the sign you must not touch,
    For 'tis my outward soul,
Viceroy to that which, unto heav'n being gone,
    Will leave this to control
And keep these limbs, her provinces, from dissolution.

For if the sinewy thread my brain lets fall
    Through every part
Can tie those parts, and make me one of all;
These hairs, which upward grew, and strength and art
    Have from a better brain,

Can better do 't: except she meant that I
        By this should know my pain,
As prisoners then are manacled, when they're condemned to die.

Whate'er she meant by 't, bury it with me,
        For since I am
Love's martyr, it might breed idolatry
If into other hands these reliques came.
        As 'twas humility
To afford to it all that a soul can do,
        So 'tis some bravery
That, since you would have none of me, I bury some of you.

The Blossom

        Little think'st thou, poor flower,
        Whom I have watched six or seven days,
    And seen thy birth, and seen what every hour
    Gave to thy growth, thee to this height to raise,
    And now dost laugh and triumph on this bough,
            Little think'st thou
    That it will freeze anon, and that I shall
    Tomorrow find thee fallen, or not at all.

        Little think'st thou, poor heart
        That labour'st yet to nestle thee,
    And think'st by hovering here to get a part
    In a forbidden or forbidding tree,
    And hop'st her stiffness by long siege to bow;
            Little think'st thou,
    That thou tomorrow, ere that sun doth wake,
    Must with this sun and me a journey take.

        But thou which lov'st to be
        Subtle to plague thyself, wilt say,
    Alas, if you must go, what's that to me?
    Here lies my business, and here I will stay:
    You go to friends, whose love and means present
            Various content
    To your eyes, ears, and tongue, and every part.
    If then your body go, what need you a heart?

Well then, stay here; but know,
　　When thou hast stayed and done thy most;
A naked thinking heart, that makes no show,
Is to a woman but a kind of ghost;
How shall she know my heart; or having none,
　　　　Know thee for one?
Practice may make her know some other part,
But take my word, she doth not know a heart.

　　Meet me at London, then,
　　Twenty days hence, and thou shalt see
Me fresher, and more fat, by being with men,
Than if I had stayed still with her and thee.
For God's sake, if you can, be you so too:
　　　　I would give you
There to another friend, whom we shall find
As glad to have my body as my mind.

A Lecture Upon the Shadow

Stand still, and I will read to thee
A lecture, love, in Love's philosophy.
　　　　These three hours that we have spent,
　　　　Walking here, two shadows went
Along with us, which we ourselves produced;
　　　　But, now the sun is just above our head,
　　　　We do those shadows tread,
And to brave clearness all things are reduced.
　　　　So whilst our infant loves did grow,
　　　　Disguises did, and shadows, flow
　　　　From us and our cares; but, now 'tis not so.

That love hath not attained the highest degree,
Which is still diligent lest others see.

Except our loves at this noon stay,
We shall new shadows make the other way.
　　　　As the first were made to blind
　　　　Others, these which come behind
Will work upon ourselves, and blind our eyes.
　　　　If our loves faint, and westwardly decline,
　　　　To me thou, falsely, thine,

And I to thee, mine actions shall disguise.
　　The morning shadows wear away,
　　But these grow longer all the day;
　　But oh, love's day is short, if love decay.

Love is a growing, or full constant light,
And his first minute after noon, is night.

The Relic

When my grave is broke up again
Some second guest to entertain,
(For graves have learn'd that womanhead
To be to more than one a bed)
　　And he that digs it, spies
A bracelet of bright hair about the bone,
　　Will he not let'us alone,
And think that there a loving couple lies,
Who thought that this device might be some way
To make their souls, at the last busy day,
Meet at this grave, and make a little stay?

If this fall in a time, or land,
Where mis-devotion doth command,
Then he that digs us up will bring
Us to the Bishop and the King,
　　To make us Relics; then
Thou shalt be a Mary Magdalen, and I
　　A something else thereby;
All women shall adore us, and some men;
And since at such time, miracles are sought,
I would have that age by this paper taught
What miracles we harmless lovers wrought.

First, we lov'd well and faithfully,
Yet knew not what we lov'd, nor why,
Difference of sex no more we knew
Than our Guardian Angels do;
　　Coming and going, we
Perchance might kiss, but not between those meals;
　　Our hands ne'er touch'd the seals

Which nature, injur'd by late law, sets free:
These miracles we did; but now alas,
All measure, and all language, I should pass
Should I tell what a miracle she was.

The Ecstasy

Where, like a pillow on a bed,
　A pregnant bank swell'd up, to rest
The violet's reclining head,
　Sat we two, one another's best.
Our hands were firmly cemented
　By a fast balm, which thence did spring;
Our eye-beams twisted, and did thread
　Our eyes upon one double string;
So t' entergraft our hands, as yet
　Was all the means to make us one;
And pictures in our eyes to get
　Was all our propagation.
As, 'twixt two equal armies, Fate
　Suspends uncertain victory,
Our souls (which to advance their state
　Were gone out) hung 'twixt her, and me.
And whilst our souls negotiate there,
　We like sepulchral statues lay;
All day, the same our postures were,
　And we said nothing, all the day.
If any, so by love refin'd,
　That he soul's language understood,
And by good love were grown all mind,
　Within convenient distance stood,
He (though he knew not which soul spake,
　Because both meant, both spake the same)
Might thence a new concoction take,
　And part far purer than he came.
This ecstasy doth unperplex
　(We said) and tell us what we love;
We see by this, it was not sex;
　We see, we saw not what did move:
But as all several souls contain
　Mixture of things, they know not what,
Love, these mix'd souls, doth mix again,
　And makes both one, each this and that.

A single violet transplant,
   The strength, the colour, and the size
(All which before was poor and scant)
   Redoubles still, and multiplies.
When love with one another so
   Interanimates two souls,
That abler soul, which thence doth flow,
   Defects of loneliness controls.
We then, who are this new soul, know,
   Of what we are compos'd, and made,
For th'atomies of which we grow,
   Are souls, whom no change can invade.
But, O alas! so long, so far
   Our bodies why do we forbear?
They are ours, though not we; we are
   Th'intelligences, they the sphere.
We owe them thanks, because they thus
   Did us, to us, at first convey,
Yielded their senses' force to us,
   Nor are dross to us, but allay.
On man heaven's influence works not so,
   But that it first imprints the air;
For soul into the soul may flow,
   Though it to body first repair.
As our blood labours to beget
   Spirits, as like souls as it can,
Because such fingers need to knit
   That subtle knot, which makes us man;
So must pure lovers' souls descend
   T' affections, and to faculties,
Which sense may reach and apprehend,
   Else a great prince in prison lies.
To'our bodies turn we then, that so
   Weak men on love reveal'd may look;
Love's mysteries in souls do grow,
   But yet the body is his book.
And if some lover, such as we,
   Have heard this dialogue of one,
Let him still mark us, he shall see
   Small change when we're to bodies gone.

Batter My Heart

Batter my heart, three personed God; for you
As yet but knock, breathe, shine, and seek to mend;
That I may rise and stand, o'erthrow me and bend
Your force to break, blow, burn and make me new.
I, like an usurped town, to another due,
Labour to admit you, but Oh, to no end;
Reason, your viceroy in me, me should defend,
But is captived and proves weak or untrue.

Yet dearly I love you and would be loved fain,
But am betrothed unto your enemy:
Divorce me, untie or break that knot again,
Take me to you, imprison me, for I
Except you enthrall me, never shall be free,
Nor ever chaste, except you ravish me.

Death, Be Not Proud

Death, be not proud, though some have callèd thee
Mighty and dreadful, for thou art not so;
For those whom thou think'st thou dost overthrow
Die not, poor Death; nor yet canst thou kill me.
From rest and sleep, which but thy pictures be,
Much pleasure; then from thee much more must flow;
And soonest our best men with thee do go—
Rest of their bones and souls' delivery!
Thou'rt slave to fate, chance, kings, and desperate men,
And dost with poison, war, and sickness dwell;
And poppy or charms can make us sleep as well
And better than thy stroke. Why swell'st thou then?
One short sleep past, we wake eternally,
And Death shall be no more: Death, thou shalt die.

Hymn to God, My God, in My Sickness

Since I am coming to that holy room,
    Where, with thy choir of saints for evermore,
I shall be made thy music; as I come
    I tune the instrument here at the door,
    And what I must do then, think here before.

Whilst my physicians by their love are grown
 Cosmographers, and I their map, who lie
Flat on this bed, that by them may be shown
 That this is my south-west discovery
  Per fretum febris, by these straits to die,

I joy, that in these straits, I see my west;
 For, though their currents yield return to none,
What shall my west hurt me? As west and east
 In all flat maps (and I am one) are one,
  So death doth touch the Resurrection.

Is the Pacific sea my home? Or are
 The eastern riches? Is *Jerusalem?*
Anyan, and *Magellan*, and *Gibraltar*,
 All straits, and none but straits, are ways to them,
  Whether where *Japhet* dwelt, or *Cham*, or *Sem*.

We think that *Paradise* and *Calvary*,
 Christ's cross, and *Adam's* tree, stood in one place;
Look, Lord, and find both *Adams* met in me;
 As the first *Adam's* sweat surrounds my face,
  May the last *Adam's* blood my soul embrace.

So, in his purple wrapped receive me Lord,
 By these his thorns give me his other crown;
And as to others' souls I preached thy word,
 Be this my text, my sermon to mine own,
  Therefore that he may raise, the Lord throws down.

A Valediction Forbidding Mourning

 As virtuous men pass mildly away,
  And whisper to their souls to go,
 Whilst some of their sad friends do say,
  The breath goes now, and some say, No:

 So let us melt, and make no noise,
  No tear-floods, nor sigh-tempests move;
 'Twere profanation of our joys
  To tell the laity our love.

Moving of th' earth brings harms and fears,
    Men reckon what it did, and meant;
But trepidation of the spheres,
    Though greater far, is innocent.

Dull sublunary lovers' love
    —Whose soul is sense—cannot admit
Absence, because it doth remove
    Those things which elemented it.

But we by a love so much refined
    That ourselves know not what it is,
Inter-assurèd of the mind,
    Care less eyes, lips and hands to miss.

Our two souls therefore, which are one,
    Though I must go, endure not yet
A breach, but an expansion,
    Like gold to airy thinness beat.

If they be two, they are two so
    As stiff twin compasses are two;
Thy soul, the fix'd foot, makes no show
    To move, but doth, if th' other do.

And though it in the centre sit,
    Yet, when the other far doth roam,
It leans, and hearkens after it,
    And grows erect, as that comes home.

Such wilt thou be to me, who must,
    Like th' other foot, obliquely run;
Thy firmness makes my circle just,
    And makes me end where I begun.

The Will

Before I sigh my last gasp, let me breathe,
Great Love, some legacies: here I bequeath
Mine eyes to Argus, if mine eyes can see;
If they be blind, then, Love, I give them thee;

My tongue to Fame; to ambassadors mine ears;
    To women or the sea, my tears;
  Thou, Love, hast taught me heretofore
  By making me serve her who had twenty more
That I should give to none, but such as had too much before.

My constancy I to the planets give;
My truth to them who at the court do live;
Mine ingenuity and openness,
To Jesuits; to buffoons my pensiveness;
My silence to any, who abroad have been;
    My money to a Capuchin:
  Thou, Love, taught'st me, by appointing me
  To love there, where no love received can be,
Only to give to such as have an incapacity.

My faith I give to Roman Catholics;
All my good works unto the schismatics
Of Amsterdam; my best civility
And courtship to an University;
My modesty I give to shoulders bare;
    My patience let gamesters share:
  Thou, Love, taught'st me, by making me
  Love her that holds my love disparity,
Only to give to such as have an incapacity.

I give my reputation to those
Which were my friends; mine industry to foes;
To schoolmen I bequeath my doubtfulness;
My sickness to physicians, or excess;
To Nature all that I in rhyme have writ;
    And to my company my wit:
  Thou, Love, by making me adore
  Her, who begot this love in me before,
Taught'st me to make, as though I gave, when I do but restore.

To him, for whom the passing-bell next tolls,
I give my physic-books; my written rolls
Of moral counsels I to Bedlam give;
My brazen medals unto them which live
In want of bread; to them which pass among

All foreigners, mine English tongue:
Thou, Love, by making me love one
Who thinks her friendship a fit portion
For younger lovers, dost my gifts thus disproportion.

Therefore I'll give no more, but I'll undo
The world by dying; because Love dies too.
Then all your beauties will be no more worth
Than gold in mines, where none doth draw it forth;
And all your graces no more use shall have,
       Than a sun-dial in a grave:
Thou, Love, taught'st me, by making me
Love her, who doth neglect both me and thee,
To invent & practice this one way to annihilate all three.

If Poisonous Minerals

If poisonous minerals, and if that tree
Whose fruit threw death on else immortal us,
If lecherous goats, if serpents envious
Cannot be damned, Alas! why should I be?
Why should intent or reason, born in me,
Make sins, else equal, in me more heinous?
And mercy being easy, and glorious
To God, in his stern wrath why threatens he?

But who am I, that dare dispute with thee,
O God? O! of thine only worthy blood,
And my tears, make a heavenly Lethean flood,
And drown in it my sin's black memory;
That thou remember them, some claim as debt,
I think it mercy, if thou wilt forget.

What If This Present

What if this present were the world's last night?
Mark in my heart, O Soul, where thou dost dwell,
The picture of Christ crucified, and tell
Whether that countenance can thee affright:
Tears in his eyes quench the amazing light,
Blood fills his frowns, which from his pierc'd head fell.
And can that tongue adjudge thee unto hell,
Which pray'd forgiveness for his foes' fierce spite?

No, no; but as in my idolatry
I said to all my profane mistresses,
Beauty, of pity, foulness only is
A sign of rigour: so I say to thee,
To wicked spirits are horrid shapes assign'd,
This beauteous form assures a piteous mind.

At the Round Earth's Imagined Corners

At the round earth's imagined corners, blow
Your trumpets, angels, and arise, arise
From death, you numberless infinities
Of souls, and to your scattered bodies go;
All whom the flood did, and fire shall o'erthrow;
All whom war, dearth, age, agues, tyrannies,
Despair, law, chance, hath slain, and you whose eyes
Shall behold God, and never taste death's woe.

But let them sleep, Lord, and me mourn a space,
For, if above all these, my sins abound,
'Tis late to ask abundance of Thy grace,
When we are there; here on this lowly ground,
Teach me how to repent; for that's as good
As if Thou hadst sealed my pardon with Thy blood.

The Flea

Mark but this flea, and mark in this,
How little that which thou deny'st me is;
It sucked me first, and now sucks thee,
And in this flea our two bloods mingled be;
Thou know'st that this cannot be said
A sin, nor shame, nor loss of maidenhead;
    Yet this enjoys before it woo,
    And pampered swells with one blood made of two,
    And this, alas, is more than we would do.

Oh stay, three lives in one flea spare,
Where we almost, yea, more than married are.
This flea is you and I, and this
Our marriage bed, and marriage temple is;
Though parents grudge, and you, w' are met,
And cloistered in these living walls of jet.

Though use make you apt to kill me,
Let not to that, self-murder added be,
And sacrilege, three sins in killing three.

Cruel and sudden, hast thou since
Purpled thy nail in blood of innocence?
Wherein could this flea guilty be,
Except in that drop which it sucked from thee?
Yet thou triumph'st and say'st that thou
Find'st not thyself, nor me the weaker now;
　'Tis true, then learn how false fears be:
　Just so much honor, when thou yield'st to me,
　Will waste, as this flea's death took life from thee.

JOHN WEBSTER
1580?–1630?

All the Flowers of the Spring

All the flowers of the spring
Meet to perfume our burying;
These have but their growing prime,
And man doth flourish but his time:
Survey our progress from our birth;
We are set, we grow, we turn to earth.
Courts adieu, and all delights,
All bewitching appetites.
Sweetest breath and clearest eye,
Like perfumes, go out and die;
And consequently this is done
As shadows wait upon the sun.
Vain the ambition of kings
Who seek by trophies and dead things
To leave a living name behind,
And weave but nets to catch the wind.

ROBERT HERRICK
1591–1674

Upon Julia's Clothes

Whenas in silks my Julia goes,
Then, then, methinks, how sweetly flows
The liquefaction of her clothes.

Next, when I cast mine eyes, and see
That brave vibration, each way free,
O, how that glittering taketh me!

To the Virgins, to Make Much of Time

Gather ye rosebuds while ye may,
    Old Time is still a-flying;
And this same flower that smiles to-day,
    To-morrow will be dying.

The glorious lamp of heaven, the sun,
    The higher he's a-getting,
The sooner will his race be run,
    And nearer he's to setting.

That age is best which is the first,
    When youth and blood are warmer;
But being spent, the worse and worst
    Times still succeed the former.

Then be not coy, but use your time,
    And while ye may, go marry;
For, having lost but once your prime,
    You may forever tarry.

Sweet Disorder

A sweet disorder in the dress
Kindles in clothes a wantonness:
A lawn about the shoulders thrown
Into a fine distraction—
An erring lace, which here and there
Enthrals the crimson stomacher—

A cuff neglectful, and thereby
Ribbands to flow confusedly—
A winning wave, deserving note,
In the tempestuous petticoat—
A careless shoe-string, in whose tie
I see a wild civility—
Do more bewitch me than when art
Is too precise in every part.

The Argument of His Book

I sing of brooks, of blossoms, birds, and bowers,
Of April, May, of June and July flowers.
I sing of Maypoles, hock-carts, wassails, wakes,
Of bridegrooms, brides, and of their bridal-cakes.
I write of youth, of love, and have access
By these to sing of cleanly wantonness.
I sing of dews, of rains, and, piece by piece
Of balm, of oil, of spice, and ambergris.
I sing of times trans-shifting, and I write
How roses first came red and lilies white.
I write of groves, of twilights, and I sing
The court of Mab and of the fairy king.
I write of hell; I sing (and ever shall)
Of heaven, and hope to have it after all.

GEORGE HERBERT
1593–1633

The Collar

I struck the board, and cried, "No more;
    I will abroad!
What, shall I ever sigh and pine?
My lines and life are free; free as the road,
    Loose as the wind, as large as store.
        Shall I be still in suit?
    Have I no harvest but a thorn
    To let me blood, and not restore
What I have lost with cordial fruit?

Sure there was wine
Before my sighs did dry it; there was corn
Before my tears did drown it;
Is the year only lost to me?
Have I no bays to crown it,
No flowers, no garlands gay? all blasted,
All wasted?
Not so, my heart; but there is fruit,
And thou hast hands.
Recover all thy sigh-blown age
On double pleasures; leave thy cold dispute
Of what is fit and not; forsake thy cage,
Thy rope of sands
Which petty thoughts have made; and made to thee
Good cable, to enforce and draw,
And be thy law,
While thou didst wink and wouldst not see.
Away! take heed;
I will abroad.
Call in thy death's head there, tie up thy fears:
He that forbears
To suit and serve his need
Deserves his load."
But as I raved, and grew more fierce and wild
At every word,
Methought I heard one calling, "Child";
And I replied, "My Lord."

The Pulley

When God at first made man,
Having a glass of blessings standing by—
Let us (said he) pour on him all we can;
Let the world's riches, which dispersed lie,
Contract into a span.

So strength first made a way,
Then beauty flow'd, then wisdom, honour, pleasure:
When almost all was out, God made a stay,
Perceiving that, alone of all His treasure,
Rest in the bottom lay.

For if I should (said he)
Bestow this jewel also on My creature,
He would adore My gifts instead of Me,
And rest in Nature, not the God of Nature:
    So both should losers be.

Yet let him keep the rest,
But keep them with repining restlessness;
Let him be rich and weary, that at least,
If goodness lead him not, yet weariness
    May toss him to My breast.

Paradise

I bless thee, Lord, because I grow
Among the trees, which in a row
To thee both fruit and order owe.

What open force, or hidden charm
Can blast my fruit, or bring me harm,
While the inclosure is thine arm?

Inclose me still for fear I start;
Be to me rather sharp and tart,
Than let me want thy hand and art.

When thou dost greater judgments spare,
And with thy knife but prune and pare,
Even fruitful trees more fruitful are:

Such sharpness shows the sweetest friend,
Such cuttings rather heal than rend,
And such beginnings touch their end.

Love

Love bade me welcome; yet my soul drew back,
    Guilty of dust and sin.
But quick-ey'd Love, observing me grow slack
    From my first entrance in,
Drew nearer to me, sweetly questioning
    If I lack'd anything.

"A guest," I answer'd, "worthy to be here";
  Love said, "You shall be he."
"I, the unkind, ungrateful? Ah, my dear,
  I cannot look on Thee."
Love took my hand, and smiling did reply,
  "Who made the eyes but I?"

"Truth, Lord; but I have marr'd them; let my shame
  Go where it doth deserve."
"And know you not," says Love, "who bore the blame?"
  "My dear, then I will serve."
"You must sit down," says Love, "and taste My meat."
  So I did sit and eat.

Man

  My God, I heard this day
That none doth build a stately habitation
  But he that means to dwell therein.
  What house more stately hath there been,
Or can be, than is man, to whose creation
  All things are in decay?

  For man is everything,
And more: he is a tree, yet bears no fruit;
  A beast, yet is, or should be, more;
  Reason and speech we only bring;
Parrots may thank us if they are not mute,
  They go upon the score.

  Man is all symmetry,
Full of proportions, one limb to another,
  And all to all the world besides.
  Each part may call the farthest brother,
For head with foot hath private amity,
  And both with moons and tides.

  Nothing hath got so far
But man hath caught and kept it as his prey:
  His eyes dismount the highest star;
  He is in little all the sphere;

Herbs gladly cure our flesh, because that they
    Find their acquaintance there.

    For us the winds do blow,
The earth doth rest, heav'n move, and fountains flow.
  Nothing we see but means our good,
    As our delight, or as our treasure;
The whole is either our cupboard of food,
    Or cabinet of pleasure.

    The stars have us to bed;
Night draws the curtain, which the sun withdraws;
  Music and light attend our head;
  All things unto our flesh are kind
In their descent and being, to our mind
    In their ascent and cause.

    Each thing is full of duty:
Waters united are our navigation;
  Distinguishéd, our habitation;
  Below, our drink; above, our meat;
Both are our cleanliness. Hath one such beauty?
    Then how are all things neat!

    More servants wait on man
Than he'll take notice of; in every path
  He treads down that which doth befriend him
  When sickness makes him pale and wan.
Oh, mighty love! Man is one world and hath
    Another to attend him.

    Since then, my God, thou hast
So brave a palace built, O dwell in it,
  That it may dwell with thee at last!
  Till then afford us so much wit
That as the world serves us we may serve thee,
    And both thy servants be.

JAMES SHIRLEY
1596–1666

Death the Leveller

The glories of our blood and state
   Are shadows, not substantial things;
There is no armour against Fate;
   Death lays his icy hand on kings:
      Sceptre and crown
      Must tumble down,
And in the dust be equal made
With the poor crookèd scythe and spade.

Some men with swords may reap the field,
   And plant fresh laurels where they kill;
But their strong nerves at last must yield;
   They tame but one another still:
      Early or late
      They stoop to fate,
And must give up their murmuring breath
When they, pale captives, creep to death.

The garlands wither on your brow;
   Then boast no more your mighty deeds!
Upon Death's purple altar now
   See where the victor-victim bleeds.
      Your heads must come
      To the cold tomb:
Only the actions of the just
Smell sweet and blossom in their dust.

THOMAS CAREW
1595–1639?

Song

Ask me no more where Jove bestows,
When June is past, the fading rose;
For in your beauty's orient deep
These flowers, as in their causes, sleep.

Ask me no more whither do stray
The golden atoms of the day;
For, in pure love, heaven did prepare
Those powders to enrich your hair.

Ask me no more whither doth haste
The nightingale, when May is past;
For in your sweet dividing throat
She winters, and keeps warm her note.

Ask me no more where those stars light
That downwards fall in dead of night;
For in your eyes they sit, and there
Fixèd become, as in their sphere.

Ask me no more if east or west
The Phœnix builds her spicy nest;
For unto you at last she flies,
And in your fragrant bosom dies.

EDMUND WALLER
1606–1687

On a Girdle

That which her slender waist confined,
Shall now my joyful temples bind;
No monarch but would give his crown,
His arms might do what this has done.

It was my heaven's extremest sphere,
The pale which held that lovely deer,
My joy, my grief, my hope, my love,
Did all within this circle move!

A narrow compass! and yet there
Dwelt all that's good, and all that's fair!
Give me but what this ribband bound,
Take all the rest the sun goes round!

JOHN MILTON
1608–1674

On His Blindness

When I consider how my light is spent
Ere half my days in this dark world and wide,
And that one talent which is death to hide
Lodged with me useless, though my soul more bent
To serve therewith my Maker, and present
My true account, lest he returning chide,
"Doth God exact day-labour, light denied?"
I fondly ask. But Patience, to prevent
That murmur, soon replies, "God doth not need
Either man's work or his own gifts. Who best
Bear his mild yoke, they serve him best. His state
Is kingly: thousands at his bidding speed,
And post o'er land and ocean without rest;
They also serve who only stand and wait."

On Time

Fly envious Time, till thou run out thy race,
Call on the lazy leaden-stepping hours,
Whose speed is but the heavy Plummet's pace;
And glut thy self with what thy womb devours,
Which is no more than what is false and vain,
And merely mortal dross;
So little is our loss,
So little is thy gain.
For when as each thing bad thou hast entomb'd,
And last of all, thy greedy self consum'd,
Then long Eternity shall greet our bliss
With an individual kiss;
And Joy shall overtake us as a flood,
When every thing that is sincerely good
And perfectly divine,
With Truth, and Peace, and Love shall ever shine
About the supreme Throne
Of him, t'whose happy-making sight alone,
When once our heav'nly-guided soul shall climb,
Then all this Earthy grossness quit,
Attir'd with Stars, we shall for ever sit,
Triumphing over Death, and Chance, and thee O Time.

On His Deceased Wife

Methought I saw my late espousèd Saint
Brought to me like Alcestis from the grave,
Whom Jove's great Son to her glad Husband gave,
Rescued from death by force though pale and faint,
Mine as whom washed from spot of child-bed taint,
Purification in the old Law did save,
And such, as yet once more I trust to have
Full sight of her in Heaven without restraint,
Came vested all in white, pure as her mind:
Her face was veiled, yet to my fancied sight,
Love, sweetness, goodness, in her person shined
So clear, as in no face with more delight.
But O as to embrace me she inclined
I waked, she fled, and day brought back my night.

Ode on the Morning of Christ's Nativity

This is the month, and this the happy morn
Wherein the Son of Heaven's Eternal King
Of wedded maid and virgin mother born,
Our great redemption from above did bring;
For so the holy sages once did sing
That He our deadly forfeit should release,
And with His Father work us a perpetual peace.

That glorious Form, that Light unsufferable,
And that far-beaming blaze of Majesty
Wherewith He wont at Heaven's high council-table
To sit the midst of Trinal Unity,
He laid aside; and, here with us to be,
Forsook the courts of everlasting day,
And chose with us a darksome house of mortal clay.

Say, heavenly Muse, shall not thy sacred vein
Afford a present to the Infant God?
Hast thou no verse, no hymn, or solemn strain
To welcome Him to this His new abode,
Now while the heaven, by the sun's team untrod,
Hath took no print of the approaching light,
And all the spangled host keep watch in squadrons bright?

See how from far, upon the eastern road,
The star-led wizards haste with odours sweet:
O run, prevent them with thy humble ode
And lay it lowly at His blessed feet;
Have thou the honour first thy Lord to greet,
And join thy voice unto the Angel choir
From out His secret altar touch'd with hallow'd fire.

THE HYMN

It was the winter wild,
While the heaven-born Child,
All meanly wrapt in the rude manger lies;
Nature in awe to Him
Had doff'd her gaudy trim,
With her great Master so to sympathize:
It was no season then for her
To wanton with the sun, her lusty paramour.

Only with speeches fair
She woos the gentle air
To hide her guilty front with innocent snow;
And on her naked shame,
Pollute with sinful blame,
The saintly veil of maiden white to throw;
Confounded, that her Maker's eyes
Should look so near upon her foul deformities.

But He, her fears to cease,
Sent down the meek-eyed Peace;
She, crown'd with olive green, came softly sliding
Down through the turning sphere,
His ready harbinger,
With turtle wing the amorous clouds dividing,
And waving wide her myrtle wand,
She strikes a universal peace through sea and land.

No war, or battle's sound
Was heard the world around:
The idle spear and shield were high uphung;
The hookèd chariot stood
Unstain'd with hostile blood,
The trumpet spake not to the armèd throng
And kings sat still with awful eye,
As if they surely knew their sovran Lord was by.

But peaceful was the night
Wherein the Prince of Light
His reign of peace upon the earth began:
The winds, with wonder whist,
Smoothly the waters kist,
Whispering new joys to the mild ocean—
Who now hath quite forgot to rave,
While birds of calm sit brooding on the charmèd wave.

The stars, with deep amaze
Stand fix'd in steadfast gaze,
Bending one way their precious influence;
And will not take their flight,
For all the morning light,

Or Lucifer that often warn'd them thence;
But in their glimmering orbs did glow,
Until their Lord Himself bespake, and bid them go.

And though the shady gloom
Had given day her room,
The sun himself withheld his wonted speed,
And hid his head for shame,
As his inferior flame
The new-enlighten'd world no more should need;
He saw a greater Sun appear
Than his bright throne, or burning axletree could bear.

The shepherds on the lawn,
Or ere the point of dawn,
Sate simply chatting in a rustic row;
Full little thought they than
That the mighty Pan
Was kindly come to live with them below;
Perhaps their loves, or else their sheep,
Was all that did their silly thoughts so busy keep.

When such music sweet
Their hearts and ears did greet,
As never was by mortal finger strook—
Divinely-warbled voice
Answering the stringèd noise,
As all their souls in blissful rapture took:
The air, such pleasure loth to lose,
With thousand echoes still prolongs each heavenly close.

Nature, that heard such sound
Beneath the hollow round
Of Cynthia's seat the airy region thrilling,
Now was almost won
To think her part was done,
And that her reign had here its last fulfilling;
She knew such harmony alone
Could hold all Heaven and Earth in happier union.

At last surrounds their sight
A globe of circular light,
That with long beams the shamefaced night array'd;
The helmèd Cherubim
And sworded Seraphim,
Are seen in glittering ranks with wings display'd,
Harping in loud and solemn choir,
With unexpressive notes, to Heaven's new-born Heir.

Such music (as 'tis said)
Before was never made
But when of old the Sons of Morning sung,
While the Creator great
His constellations set,
And the well-balanced world on hinges hung,
And cast the dark foundations deep,
And bid the weltering waves their oozy channel keep.

Ring out, ye crystal spheres!
Once bless our human ears,
If ye have power to touch our senses so;
And let your silver chime
Move in melodious time;
And let the bass of Heaven's deep organ blow;
And with your ninefold harmony
Make up full consort to the angelic symphony.

For if such holy song
Enwrap our fancy long,
Time will run back, and fetch the age of gold,
And speckled Vanity
Will sicken soon and die,
And leprous Sin will melt from earthly mould,
And Hell itself will pass away,
And leave her dolorous mansions to the peering day.

Yea, Truth, and Justice then
Will down return to men,
Orb'd in a rainbow; and, like glories wearing,
Mercy will sit between
Throned in celestial sheen,

With radiant feet the tissued clouds down steering;
And Heaven, as at some festival,
Will open wide the gates of her high palace hall.

But wisest Fate says No;
This must not yet be so;
The Babe yet lies in smiling infancy,
That on the bitter cross
Must redeem our loss;
So both Himself and us to glorify:
Yet first, to those ychain'd in sleep,
The wakeful trump of doom must thunder through the deep.

With such a horrid clang
As on Mount Sinai rang
While the red fire and smouldering clouds outbrake:
The aged Earth aghast
With terror of that blast,
Shall from the surface to the centre shake;
When, at the world's last sessiòn,
The dreadful Judge in middle air shall spread His throne.

And then at last our bliss
Full and perfect is,
But now begins; for from this happy day
Th' old Dragon under ground
In straiter limits bound,
Not half so far casts his usurpèd sway,
And wroth to see his kingdom fail,
Swings the scaly horror of his folded tail.

The Oracles are dumb;
No voice or hideous hum
Runs through the archèd roof in words deceiving.
Apollo from his shrine
Can no more divine,
With hollow shriek the steep of Delphos leaving.
No nightly trance or breathèd spell,
Inspires the pale-eyed priest from the prophetic cell.

The lonely mountains o'er,
And the resounding shore,
A voice of weeping heard, and loud lament:
From haunted spring and dale
Edged with poplar pale,
The parting Genius is with sighing sent;
With flower-inwoven tresses torn
The Nymphs in twilight shade of tangled thickets mourn.

In consecrated earth,
And on the holy hearth,
The Lars and Lemures moan with midnight plaint,
In urns, and altars round,
A drear and dying sound
Affrights the Flamens at their service quaint;
And the chill marble seems to sweat,
While each peculiar Power forgoes his wonted seat.

Peor and Baalim
Forsake their temples dim,
With that twice-batter'd god of Palestine,
And moonèd Ashtaroth
Heaven's queen and mother both,
Now sits not girt with tapers' holy shine;
The Lybic Hammon shrinks his horn,
In vain the Tyrian maids their wounded Thammuz mourn.

And sullen Moloch, fled,
Hath left in shadows dread,
His burning idol all of blackest hue,
In vain with cymbals' ring,
They call the grisly king,
In dismal dance about the furnace blue;
The brutish gods of Nile as fast,
Isis, and Orus, and the dog Anubis haste.

Nor is Osiris seen
In Memphian grove, or green,
Trampling the unshower'd grass with lowings loud:
Nor can he be at rest
Within his sacred chest,

Nought but profoundest Hell can be his shroud,
In vain with timbrell'd anthems dark
The sable-stolèd sorcerers bear his worship't ark.

He feels from Juda's land
The dreaded Infant's hand,
The rays of Bethlehem blind his dusky eyn;
Nor all the gods beside,
Longer dare abide,
Not Typhon huge ending in snaky twine:
Our Babe, to show His Godhead true,
Can in His swaddling bands control the damnèd crew.

So, when the sun in bed,
Curtain'd with cloudy red,
Pillows his chin upon an orient wave,
The flocking shadows pale,
Troop to the infernal jail,
Each fetter'd ghost slips to his several grave;
And the yellow-skirted fays,
Fly after the night-steeds leaving their moon-loved maze.

But see! the Virgin blest,
Hath laid her Babe to rest;
Time is, our tedious song should here have ending;
Heaven's youngest-teemèd star
Hath fix'd her polish'd car,
Her sleeping Lord with hand-maid lamp attending:
And all about the courtly stable,
Bright-harness'd Angels sit in order serviceable.

The Blindness of Samson

O loss of sight, of thee I most complain!
Blind among enemies, O worse than chains,
Dungeon, or beggary, or decrepit age!
Light, the prime work of God, to me is extinct,
And all her various objects of delight
Annulled, which might in part my grief have eased,
Inferior to the vilest now become
Of man or worm; the vilest here excel me,
They creep, yet see, I dark in light exposed

To daily fraud, contempt, abuse and wrong,
Within doors, or without, still as a fool,
In power of others, never in my own;
Scarce half I seem to live, dead more than half.
O dark, dark, dark, amid the blaze of noon,
Irrecoverably dark, total eclipse
Without all hope of day!
O first created beam, and thou great Word,
Let there be light, and light was over all;
Why am I thus bereaved Thy prime decree?
The sun to me is dark
And silent as the moon,
When she deserts the night
Hid in her vacant interlunar cave.
Since light so necessary is to life,
And almost life itself, if it be true
That light is in the soul,
She all in every part; why was the sight
To such a tender ball as th' eye confined?
So obvious and so easy to be quenched,
And not as feeling through all parts diffused,
That she might look at will through every pore?
Then had I not been thus exiled from light;
As in the land of darkness yet in light,
To live a life half dead, a living death,
And buried; but O yet more miserable!
Myself, my sepulcher, a moving grave.

From *Samson Agonistes*

L'Allegro

Hence, loathèd Melancholy,
   Of Cerberus and blackest Midnight born
In Stygian cave forlorn,
   'Mongst horrid shapes, and shrieks, and sights unholy!
Find out some uncouth cell,
   Where brooding darkness spreads his jealous wings,
And the night-raven sings;
   There, under ebon shades and low-browed rocks,
As ragged as thy locks,
   In dark Cimmerian desert ever dwell.
But come, thou goddess fair and free,

In heaven yclept Euphrosyne,
And by men heart-easing Mirth;
Whom lovely Venus, at a birth,
With two sister Graces more,
To ivy-crownèd Bacchus bore;
Or whether (as some sager sing)
The frolic wind that breathes the spring,
Zephyr, with Aurora playing,
As he met her once a-Maying,
There, on beds of violets blue,
And fresh-blown roses washed in dew,
Filled her with thee, a daughter fair,
So buxom, blithe, and debonair.
Haste thee, nymph, and bring with thee
Jest and youthful Jollity,
Quips and Cranks and wanton Wiles,
Nods and Becks and wreathèd Smiles,
Such as hang on Hebe's cheek,
And love to live in dimple sleek;
Sport, that wrinkled Care derides,
And Laughter holding both his sides.
Come, and trip it, as ye go,
On the light fantastic toe;
And in thy right hand lead with thee
The mountain-nymph, sweet Liberty.
And if I give thee honor due,
Mirth, admit me of thy crew,
To live with her, and live with thee,
In unreprovèd pleasures free:
To hear the lark begin his flight,
And, singing, startle the dull night,
From his watch-tower in the skies,
Till the dappled dawn doth rise;
Then to come in spite of sorrow,
And at my window bid good morrow,
Through the sweetbriar or the vine
Or the twisted eglantine,
While the cock, with lively din,
Scatters the rear of darkness thin,
And to the stack or the barn door
Stoutly struts his dames before;

Oft listening how the hounds and horn
Cheerly rouse the slumbering morn,
From the side of some hoar hill,
Through the high wood echoing shrill;
Sometime walking, not unseen,
By hedgerow elms, on hillocks green,
Right against the eastern gate,
Where the great sun begins his state,
Robed in flames and amber light,
The clouds in thousand liveries dight;
While the ploughman, near at hand,
Whistles o'er the furrowed land,
And the milkmaid singeth blithe,
And the mower whets his scythe,
And every shepherd tells his tale
Under the hawthorn in the dale.
Straight mine eye hath caught new pleasures,
Whilst the landskip round it measures:
Russet lawns and fallows gray,
Where the nibbling flocks do stray;
Mountains on whose barren breast
The laboring clouds do often rest;
Meadows trim, with daisies pied;
Shallow brooks and rivers wide.
Towers and battlements it sees
Bosomed high in tufted trees,
Where perhaps some beauty lies,
The cynosure of neighboring eyes.
Hard by, a cottage chimney smokes
From betwixt two agèd oaks,
Where Corydon and Thyrsis, met,
Are at their savory dinner set
Of herbs and other country messes,
Which the neat-handed Phillis dresses;
And then in haste her bower she leaves,
With Thestylis to bind the sheaves,
Or, if the earlier season lead,
To the tanned haycock in the mead.
Sometimes, with secure delight,
The upland hamlets will invite,
When the merry bells ring round,

And the jocund rebecks sound
To many a youth and many a maid
Dancing in the checkered shade;
And young and old come forth to play
On a sunshine holiday,
Till the livelong daylight fail.
Then to the spicy, nut-brown ale,
With stories told of many a feat:
How faery Mab the junkets eat;
She was pinched and pulled, she said;
And he, by friar's lanthorn led,
Tells how the drudging goblin sweat
To earn his cream-bowl duly set,
When in one night, ere glimpse of morn,
His shadowy flail hath threshed the corn
That ten day-laborers could not end;
Then lies him down the lubber fiend,
And, stretched out all the chimney's length,
Basks at the fire his hairy strength,
And, crop-full, out of doors he flings
Ere the first cock his matin rings.
Thus done the tales, to bed they creep,
By whispering winds soon lulled asleep.
Towered cities please us then,
And the busy hum of men,
Where throngs of knights and barons bold,
In weeds of peace, high triumphs hold,
With store of ladies, whose bright eyes
Rain influence, and judge the prize
Of wit or arms, while both contend
To win her grace whom all commend.
There let Hymen oft appear
In saffron robe, with taper clear,
And pomp and feast and revelry,
With mask and antique pageantry;
Such sights as youthful poets dream
On summer eves by haunted stream.
Then to the well-trod stage anon,
If Jonson's learnèd sock be on,
Or sweetest Shakespeare, Fancy's child,
Warble his native wood-notes wild.

And ever, against eating cares,
Lap me in soft Lydian airs,
Married to immortal verse,
Such as the meeting soul may pierce,
In notes with many a winding bout
Of linkèd sweetness long drawn out
With wanton heed and giddy cunning,
The melting voice through mazes running,
Untwisting all the chains that tie
The hidden soul of harmony;
That Orpheus' self may heave his head
From golden slumber on a bed
Of heaped Elysian flowers, and hear
Such strains as would have won the ear
Of Pluto to have quite set free
His half-regained Eurydice.
These delights if thou canst give,
Mirth, with thee I mean to live.

Il Penseroso

Hence, vain, deluding joys,
    The brood of Folly without father bred!
How little you bestèd,
    Or fill the fixèd mind with all your toys!
Dwell in some idle brain,
    And fancies fond with gaudy shapes possess,
As thick and numberless
    As the gay motes that people the sunbeams,
Or likest hovering dreams,
    The fickle pensioners of Morpheus' train.
But hail, thou goddess sage and holy!
Hail, divinest Melancholy!
Whose saintly visage is too bright
To hit the sense of human sight,
And therefore to our weaker view
O'erlaid with black, staid Wisdom's hue;
Black, but such as in esteem
Prince Memnon's sister might beseem,
Or that starred Ethiop queen that strove
To set her beauty's praise above
The sea-nymphs, and their powers offended.

Yet thou art higher far descended:
Thee bright-haired Vesta long of yore
To solitary Saturn bore;
His daughter she (in Saturn's reign
Such mixture was not held a stain).
Oft in glimmering bowers and glades
He met her, and in secret shades
Of woody Ida's inmost grove,
Whilst yet there was no fear of Jove.
Come, pensive nun, devout and pure,
Sober, steadfast, and demure,
All in a robe of darkest grain,
Flowing with majestic train,
And sable stole of cypress lawn
Over thy decent shoulders drawn.
Come, but keep thy wonted state,
With even step and musing gait
And looks commercing with the skies,
Thy rapt soul sitting in thine eyes;
There, held in holy passion still,
Forget thyself to marble, till
With a sad, leaden, downward cast
Thou fix them on the earth as fast.
And join with thee calm Peace and Quiet,
Spare Fast, that oft with gods doth diet,
And hears the Muses in a ring
Aye round about Jove's altar sing;
And add to these retirèd Leisure,
That in trim gardens takes his pleasure;
But, first and chiefest, with thee bring
Him that yon soars on golden wing,
Guiding the fiery-wheelèd throne,
The cherub Contemplation;
And the mute Silence hist along,
'Less Philomel will deign a song,
In her sweetest, saddest plight,
Smoothing the rugged brow of night,
While Cynthia checks her dragon yoke
Gently o'er the accustomed oak.
Sweet bird, that shunn'st the noise of folly,
Most musical, most melancholy!

Thee, chauntress, oft the woods among
I woo, to hear thy even-song;
And, missing thee, I walk unseen
On the dry, smooth-shaven green,
To behold the wandering moon,
Riding near her highest noon,
Like one that had been led astray
Through the heaven's wide, pathless way,
And oft, as if her head she bowed,
Stooping through a fleecy cloud.
Oft, on a plat of rising ground,
I hear the far-off curfew sound,
Over some wide-watered shore,
Swinging slow with sullen roar;
Or, if the air will not permit,
Some still, removèd place will fit,
Where glowing embers through the room
Teach light to counterfeit a gloom,
Far from all resort of mirth,
Save the cricket on the hearth,
Or the bellman's drowsy charm
To bless the doors from nightly harm.
Or let my lamp at midnight hour
Be seen in some high, lonely tower,
Where I may oft outwatch the Bear,
With thrice-great Hermes, or unsphere
The spirit of Plato to unfold
What worlds or what vast regions hold
The immortal mind that hath forsook
Her mansion in this fleshly nook;
And of those demons that are found
In fire, air, flood, or under ground,
Whose power hath a true consent
With planet or with element.
Sometime let gorgeous Tragedy
In sceptered pall come sweeping by,
Presenting Thebes, or Pelops' line,
Or the tale of Troy divine,
Or what (though rare) of later age
Ennobled hath the buskined stage.
But, O sad virgin, that thy power

Might raise Musaeus from his bower;
Or bid the soul of Orpheus sing
Such notes as, warbled to the string,
Drew iron tears down Pluto's cheek,
And made hell grant what love did seek;
Or call up him that left half told
The story of Cambuscan bold,
Of Camball, and of Algarsife,
And who had Canace to wife,
That owned the virtuous ring and glass,
And of the wondrous horse of brass
On which the Tartar king did ride;
And if aught else great bards beside
In sage and solemn tunes have sung,
Of tourneys, and of trophies hung,
Of forests, and enchantments drear,
Where more is meant than meets the ear.
Thus, Night, oft see me in thy pale career,
Till civil-suited Morn appear,
Not tricked and frounced, as she was won
With the Attic boy to hunt,
But kerchiefed in a comely cloud,
While rocking winds are piping loud,
Or ushered with a shower still,
When the gust hath blown his fill,
Ending on the rustling leaves,
With minute-drops from off the eaves
And when the sun begins to fling
His flaring beams, me, goddess, bring
To archèd walks of twilight groves,
And shadows brown, that Sylvan loves.
Of pine or monumental oak,
Where the rude axe with heavèd stroke
Was never heard the nymphs to daunt,
Or fright them from their hallowed haunt
There in close covert by some brook,
Where no profaner eye may look,
Hide me from day's garish eye,
While the bee with honied thigh,
That at her flowery work doth sing,
And the waters murmuring,

With such consort as they keep,
Entice the dewy-feathered sleep:
And let some strange, mysterious dream
Wave at his wings, in airy stream
Of lively portraiture displayed,
Softly on my eyelids laid;
And, as I wake, sweet music breathe
Above, about, or underneath,
Sent by some spirit to mortals good,
Or the unseen genius of the wood.
But let my due feet never fail
To walk the studious cloister's pale,
And love the high embowèd roof,
With antique pillars massy proof,
And storied windows richly dight,
Casting a dim, religious light.
There let the pealing organ blow
To the full-voiced choir below,
In service high and anthems clear,
As may with sweetness, through mine ear,
Dissolve me into ecstasies,
And bring all heaven before mine eyes.
And may at last my weary age
Find out the peaceful hermitage,
The hairy gown and mossy cell,
Where I may sit and rightly spell
Of every star that heaven doth shew,
And every herb that sips the dew,
Till old experience do attain
To something like prophetic strain.
These pleasures, Melancholy, give,
And I with thee will choose to live.

Lycidas

In this Monody the Author bewails a learned Friend, unfortunately drowned in his passage
from Chester on the Irish Seas, 1637; and, by occasion, foretells the ruin of our corrupted
Clergy, then in their height.

Yet once more, O ye laurels, and once more,
Ye myrtles brown, with ivy never sere,
I come to pluck your berries harsh and crude,

And with forced fingers rude
Shatter your leaves before the mellowing year.
Bitter constraint and sad occasion dear
Compels me to disturb your season due;
For Lycidas is dead, dead ere his prime,
Young Lycidas, and hath not left his peer.
Who would not sing for Lycidas? he knew
Himself to sing, and build the lofty rhyme.
He must not float upon his watery bier
Unwept, and welter to the parching wind,
Without the meed of some melodious tear.
    Begin, then, Sisters of the sacred well
That from beneath the seat of Jove doth spring;
Begin, and somewhat loudly sweep the string.
Hence with denial vain and coy excuse:
So may some gentle Muse
With lucky words favor my destined urn,
And as he passes turn,
And bid fair peace be to my sable shroud!
    For we were nursed upon the self-same hill,
Fed the same flock, by fountain, shade, and rill;
Together both, ere the high lawns appeared
Under the opening eyelids of the Morn,
We drove a-field, and both together heard
What time the gray-fly winds her sultry horn,
Battening our flocks with the fresh dews of night,
Oft till the star that rose at evening bright
Toward heaven's descent had sloped his westering wheel
Meanwhile the rural ditties were not mute;
Tempered to the oaten flute
Rough Satyrs danced, and Fauns with cloven heel
From the glad sound would not be absent long;
And old Damœtas loved to hear our song.
    But, oh! the heavy change, now thou art gone,
Now thou art gone and never must return!
Thee, Shepherd, thee the woods and desert caves,
With wild thyme and the gadding vine o'ergrown,
And all their echoes, mourn.
The willows, and the hazel copses green,
Shall now no more be seen
Fanning their joyous leaves to thy soft lays.

As killing as the canker to the rose,
Or taint-worm to the weanling herds that graze,
Or frost to flowers that their gay wardrobe wear,
When first the white-thorn blows;
Such, Lycidas, thy loss to shepherd's ear.

  Where were ye, Nymphs, when the remorseless deep
Closed o'er the head of your loved Lycidas?
For neither were ye playing on the steep
Where your old bards, the famous Druids, lie,
Nor on the shaggy top of Mona high,
Nor yet where Deva spreads her wizard stream.
Ay me! I fondly dream,
"Had ye been there," . . . for what could that have done?
What could the Muse herself that Orpheus bore,
The Muse herself, for her enchanting son,
Whom universal nature did lament,
When, by the rout that made the hideous roar,
His gory visage down the stream was sent,
Down the swift Hebrus to the Lesbian shore?

  Alas! what boots it with uncessant care
To tend the homely, slighted, shepherd's trade,
And strictly meditate the thankless Muse?
Were it not better done, as others use,
To sport with Amaryllis in the shade,
Or with the tangles of Neæra's hair?
Fame is the spur that the clear spirit doth raise
(That last infirmity of noble mind)
To scorn delights and live laborious days;
But the fair guerdon when we hope to find,
And think to burst out into sudden blaze,
Comes the blind Fury with the abhorrèd shears
And slits the thin-spun life. "But not the praise,"
Phœbus replied, and touched my trembling ears:
"Fame is no plant that grows on mortal soil,
Nor in the glistering foil
Set off to the world, nor in broad rumor lies,
But lives and spreads aloft by those pure eyes
And perfect witness of all-judging Jove;
As he pronounces lastly on each deed,
Of so much fame in heaven expect thy meed."

  O fountain Arethuse, and thou honored flood,

Smooth-sliding Mincius, crowned with vocal reeds,
That strain I heard was of a higher mood.
But now my oat proceeds,
And listens to the Herald of the Sea
That came in Neptune's plea.
He asked the waves, and asked the felon winds,
What hard mishap hath doomed this gentle swain?
And questioned every gust of rugged wings,
That blows from off each beakèd promontory;
They knew not of his story,
And sage Hippotades their answer brings,
That not a blast was from his dungeon strayed:
The air was calm, and on the level brine
Sleek Panopé with all her sisters played.
It was that fatal and perfidious bark,
Built in the eclipse, and rigged with curses dark,
That sunk so low that sacred head of thine.
     Next, Camus, reverend sire, went footing slow,
His mantle hairy, and his bonnet sedge,
Inwrought with figures dim, and on the edge
Like to that sanguine flower inscribed with woe.
"Ah! who hath reft," quoth he, "my dearest pledge?"
Last came, and last did go,
The Pilot of the Galilean Lake;
Two massy keys he bore of metals twain
(The golden opes, the iron shuts amain).
He shook his mitred locks, and stern bespake:—
"How well could I have spared for thee, young swain,
Enow of such as, for their bellies' sake,
Creep, and intrude, and climb into the fold!
Of other care they little reckoning make
Than how to scramble at the shearers' feast
And shove away the worthy bidden guest.
Blind mouths! that scarce themselves know how to hold
A sheep-hook, or have learned ought else the least
That to the faithful herdman's art belongs!
What recks it them? What need they? They are sped;
And, when they list, their lean and flashy songs
Grate on their scrannel pipes of wretched straw;
The hungry sheep look up, and are not fed,
But, swoln with wind and the rank mist they draw,

Rot inwardly, and foul contagion spread;
Besides what the grim wolf with privy paw
Daily devours apace, and nothing said.
But that two-handed engine at the door
Stands ready to smite once, and smite no more."
   Return, Alpheus; the dread voice is past
That shrunk thy streams; return, Sicilian Muse,
And call the vales, and bid them hither cast
Their bells and flowerets of a thousand hues.
Ye valleys low, where the mild whispers use
Of shades, and wanton winds, and gushing brooks,
On whose fresh lap the swart star sparely looks,
Throw hither all your quaint enameled eyes
That on the green turf suck the honeyed showers,
And purple all the ground with vernal flowers.
Bring the rathe primrose that forsaken dies,
The tufted crow-toe, and pale jessamine,
The white pink, and the pansy freaked with jet,
The glowing violet,
The musk-rose, and the well-attired woodbine,
With cowslips wan that hang the pensive head,
And every flower that sad embroidery wears;
Bid amaranthus all his beauty shed,
And daffadillies fill their cups with tears,
To strew the laureate hearse where Lycid lies.
For so, to interpose a little ease,
Let our frail thoughts dally with false surmise.
Ay me! whilst thee the shores and sounding seas
Wash far away, where'er thy bones are hurled;
Whether beyond the stormy Hebrides,
Where thou perhaps under the whelming tide
Visit'st the bottom of the monstrous world;
Or whether thou, to our moist vows denied,
Sleep'st by the fable of Bellerus old,
Where the great Vision of the guarded mount
Looks toward Namancos and Bayona's hold.
Look homeward, Angel, now, and melt with ruth:
And, O ye dolphins, waft the hapless youth.
   Weep no more, woeful shepherds, weep no more,
For Lycidas, your sorrow, is not dead,
Sunk though he be beneath the watery floor.

So sinks the day-star in the ocean bed,
And yet anon repairs his drooping head,
And tricks his beams, and with new-spangled ore
Flames in the forehead of the morning sky:
So Lycidas sunk low, but mounted high,
Through the dear might of Him that walked the waves,
Where, other groves and other streams along,
With nectar pure his oozy locks he laves,
And hears the unexpressive nuptial song,
In the blest kingdoms meek of joy and love.
There entertain him all the Saints above,
In solemn troops, and sweet societies,
That sing, and singing in their glory move,
And wipe the tears for ever from his eyes.
Now, Lycidas, the shepherds weep no more;
Henceforth thou art the Genius of the shore,
In thy large recompense, and shalt be good
To all that wander in that perilous flood.

    Thus sang the uncouth swain to the oaks and rills,
While the still morn went out with sandals gray;
He touched the tender stops of various quills,
With eager thought warbling his Doric lay:
And now the sun had stretched out all the hills,
And now was dropped into the western bay.
At last he rose, and twitched his mantle blue:
To-morrow to fresh woods, and pastures new.

Hail, Holy Light

Hail holy light, offspring of Heav'n first-born,
Or of th' Eternal Coeternal beam
May I express thee unblam'd? since God is light,
And never but in unapproached light
Dwelt from Eternity, dwelt then in thee,
Bright effluence of bright essence increate.
Or hearest thou rather pure Ethereal stream,
Whose Fountain who shall tell? before the Sun,
Before the Heavens thou wert, and at the voice
Of God, as with a Mantle didst invest
The rising world of water dark and deep,
Won from the void and formless infinite.
Thee I re-visit now with bolder wing,
Escaped the *Stygian* Pool, though long detained

In that obscure sojourn, while in my flight
Through utter and through middle darkness borne
With other notes then to th' *Orphean* Lyre
I sung of *Chaos* and *Eternal Night*,
Taught by the heavenly Muse to venture down
The dark descent, and up to reascend,
Though hard and rare: thee I revisit safe,
And feel thy sovereign vital Lamp; but thou
Revisit'st not these eyes, that roll in vain
To find thy piercing ray, and find no dawn;
So thick a drop serene hath quenched their Orbs,
Or dim suffusion veiled. Yet not the more
Cease I to wander where the Muses haunt
Clear Spring, or shady Grove, or Sunny Hill,
Smit with the love of sacred song; but chief
Thee *Zion* and the flowery Brooks beneath
That wash thy hallowed feet, and warbling flow,
Nightly I visit: nor sometimes forget
Those other two equalled with me in Fate,
So were I equalled with them in renown,
Blind *Thamyris* and blind *Mæonides*,
And *Tiresias* and *Phineus* Prophets old.
Then feed on thoughts, that voluntary move
Harmonious numbers; as the wakeful Bird
Sings darkling, and in shadiest Covert hid
Tunes her nocturnal Note. Thus with the Year
Seasons return, but not to me returns
Day, or the sweet approach of Even or Morn,
Or sight of vernal bloom, or Summer's Rose,
Or flocks, or herds, or human face divine;
But cloud instead, and ever-during dark
Surrounds me, from the cheerful ways of men
Cut off, and for the Book of knowledge fair
Presented with a Universal blank
Of Nature's works to me expung'd and raised,
And wisdom at one entrance quite shut out.
So much the rather thou Celestial light
Shine inward, and the mind through all her powers
Irradiate, there plant eyes, all mist from thence
Purge and disperse, that I may see and tell
Of things invisible to mortal sight.

From *Paradise Lost*

SIR JOHN SUCKLING
1609–1642

The Constant Lover

Out upon it, I have loved
  Three whole days together!
And am like to love three more,
  If it prove fair weather.

Time shall moult away his wings
  Ere he shall discover
In the whole wide world again
  Such a constant lover.

But the spite on't is, no praise
  Is due at all to me:
Love with me had made no stays
  Had it any been but she.

Had it any been but she,
  And that very face,
There had been at least ere this
  A dozen dozen in her place

WILLIAM CARTWRIGHT
1611–1643

No Platonic Love

Tell me no more of minds embracing minds,
  And hearts exchang'd for hearts;
That spirits spirits meet, as winds do winds,
  And mix their subt'lest parts;
That two unbodied essences may kiss,
And then like Angels, twist and feel one Bliss.

I was that silly thing that once was wrought
  To practise this thin love;

I climb'd from sex to soul, from soul to thought;
    But thinking there to move,
Headlong I rolled from thought to soul, and then
From soul I lighted at the sex again.

As some strict down-looked men pretend to fast,
    Who yet in closets eat;
So lovers who profess they spirits taste,
    Feed yet on grosser meat;
I know they boast they souls to souls convey,
Howe'r they meet, the body is the way.

Come, I will undeceive thee, they that tread
    Those vain aerial ways,
Are like young heirs and alchemists misled
    To waste their wealth and days,
For searching thus to be for ever rich,
They only find a med'cine for the itch.

RICHARD CRASHAW

1613–1649

Wishes

TO HIS (SUPPOSED) MISTRESS

Whoe'er she be
That not impossible she
That shall command my heart and me;
Where'er she lie,
Locked up from mortal eye,
In shady leaves of destiny;
Till that ripe birth
Of studied fate stand forth
And teach her fair steps to our earth;
Till that divine
Idea take a shrine
Of crystal flesh, through which to shine;
Meet you her, my wishes,
Bespeak her to my blisses,

And be ye called my absent kisses.
I wish her beauty,
That owes not all its duty
To gaudy tire, or glistering shoo-tie;
A face that's best
By its own beauty dressed,
And can alone command the rest;
A face made up
Out of no other shop
Than what Nature's white hand sets ope;
A cheek where youth
And blood, with pen of truth
Write what the reader sweetly ru'th;
A cheek where grows
More than a morning rose,
Which to no box its being owes;
Lips where all day
A lover's kiss may play,
Yet carry nothing thence away;
Looks that oppress
Their richest tires, but dress
And clothe their simplest nakedness;
Eyes that displace
The neighbour diamond and outface
That sun-shine by their own sweet grace;
Tresses that wear
Jewels, but to declare
How much themselves more precious are.
Whose native ray
Can tame the wanton day
Of gems that in their bright shades play;
Each ruby there
Or pearl that dares appear,
Be its own blush, be its own tear;
A well-tamed heart,
For whose more noble smart
Love may be long choosing a dart;
Eyes that bestow
Full quivers on Love's bow,
Yet pay less arrows than they owe;
Smiles that can warm

The blood, yet teach a charm
That chastity shall take no harm;
Blushes that bin
The burnish of no sin,
Nor flames of aught too hot within;
Joys that confess
Virtue their mistress,
And have no other head to dress;
Days that need borrow
No part of their good morrow
From a fore-spent night of sorrow;
I wish her store
Of worth may leave her poor
Of wishes; and I wish—no more.
Her that dares be
What these lines wish to see:
I seek no further, it is she.
'Tis she: and here
Lo! I unclothe and clear
My wishes' cloudy character.
May she enjoy it
Whose merit dares apply it
But modesty dares still deny it.
Such worth as this is
Shall fix my flying wishes,
And determine them to kisses.
Let her full glory,
My fancies, fly before ye;
Be ye my fictions, but her story.

The Tear

What bright soft thing is this,
    Sweet Mary, thy fair eyes' expense?
A moist spark it is,
    A watery diamond; from whence
The very term, I think, was found,
The water of a diamond.

Oh! 'tis not a tear,
    'Tis a star about to drop
From thine eye, its sphere;

The Sun will stoop and take it up.
Proud will his sister be to wear
This thine eye's jewel in her ear.

Oh! 'tis a tear,
    Too true a tear; for no sad eyne,
How sad soe'er,
    Rain so true a tear as thine;
Each drop, leaving a place so dear,
Weeps for itself, is its own tear.

Such a pearl as this is,
    (Slipped from Aurora's dewy breast)
The rose-bud's sweet lip kisses;
    And such the rose itself, when vexèd
With ungentle flames, does shed,
Sweating in too warm a bed.

Such the maiden gem
    By the wanton Spring put on,
Peeps from her parent stem,
    And blushes on the manly Sun:
This wat'ry blossom of thy eyne,
Ripe, will make the richer wine.

Fair drop, why quak'st thou so?
    'Cause thou straight must lay thy head
In the dust? Oh no;
    The dust shall never be thy bed:
A pillow for thee will I bring,
Stuffed with down of angel's wing.

Thus carried up on high,
    (For to heaven thou must go)
Sweetly shalt thou lie,
    And in soft slumbers bathe thy woe;
Till the singing orbs awake thee,
And one of their bright chorus make thee.

There thyself shalt be
    An eye, but not a weeping one;

Yet I doubt of thee,
   Whether th'hadst rather there have shone
An eye of Heaven; or still shine here
In th' Heaven of Mary's eye, a tear.

RICHARD LOVELACE
1618–1658

To Lucasta
ON GOING TO THE WARS

Tell me not, Sweet, I am unkind
   That from the nunnery
Of thy chaste breast, and quiet mind,
   To war and arms I fly.

True, a new mistress now I chase,
   The first foe in the field;
And with a stronger faith embrace
   A sword, a horse, a shield.

Yet this inconstancy is such
   As you too shall adore;
I could not love thee, Dear, so much,
   Loved I not honour more

To Althea from Prison

When Love with unconfinèd wings
   Hovers within my gates,
And my divine Althea brings
   To whisper at the grates;
When I lie tangled in her hair
   And fetter'd to her eye,
The birds that wanton in the air
   Know no such liberty.

When flowing cups run swiftly round
   With no allaying Thames,
Our careless heads with roses bound,

Our hearts with loyal flames;
When thirsty grief in wine we steep,
When healths and draughts go free—
Fishes that tipple in the deep
Know no such liberty.

When, like committed linnets, I
With shriller throat shall sing
The sweetness, mercy, majesty,
And glories of my King;
When I shall voice aloud how good
He is, how great should be,
Enlargèd winds, that curl the flood,
Know no such liberty.

Stone walls do not a prison make,
Nor iron bars a cage;
Minds innocent and quiet take
That for an hermitage;
If I have freedom in my love
And in my soul am free,
Angels alone, that soar above,
Enjoy such liberty.

ABRAHAM COWLEY
1618–1667

Beauty

Beauty, thou wild fantastic ape,
Who dost in ev'ry country change thy shape!
Here black, there brown, here tawny, and there white;
Thou flatt'rer which compli'st with every sight!
Thou babel which confound'st the eye
With unintelligible variety!
Who hast no certain what, nor where,
But vary'st still, and dost thy self declare
Inconstant, as thy she-professors are.

Beauty, love's scene and masquerade,
So gay by well-plac'd lights, and distance made;
False coin, with which th' impostor cheats us still;
The stamp and colour good, but metal ill!
  Which light, or base we find, when we
Weigh by enjoyment, and examine thee!
  For though thy being be but show,
'Tis chiefly night which men to thee allow:
And choose t'enjoy thee, when thou least art thou.

Beauty, thou active, passive ill!
Which diest thy self as fast as thou dost kill!
Thou tulip, who thy stock in paint dost waste,
Neither for physic good, nor smell, nor taste.
  Beauty, whose flames but meteors are,
Short-liv'd and low, though thou wouldst seem a star,
  Who dar'st not thine own home descry,
Pretending to dwell richly in the eye,
When thou, alas, dost in the fancy lie.

Beauty, whose conquests still are made
O'er hearts by cowards kept, or else betray'd!
Weak victor! who thy self destroy'd must be
When sickness storms, or time besieges thee!
  Thou'unwholesome thaw to frozen age!
Thou strong wine, which youth's fever dost enrage,
  Thou tyrant which leav'st no man free!
Thou subtle thief, from whom nought safe can be!
Thou murth'rer which hast kill'd, and devil which
    wouldst damn me.

ANDREW MARVELL
1621–1678

To His Coy Mistress

Had we but world enough, and time,
This coyness, lady, were no crime.
We would sit down, and think which way
To walk, and pass our long love's day.

Thou by the Indian Ganges' side
Should'st rubies find: I by the tide
Of Humber would complain. I would
Love you ten years before the Flood,
And you should, if you please, refuse
Till the conversion of the Jews.
My vegetable love should grow
Vaster than empires, and more slow.
An hundred years should go to praise
Thine eyes, and on thy forehead gaze:
Two hundred to adore each breast:
But thirty thousand to the rest;
An age at least to every part,
And the last age should show your heart.
For, lady, you deserve this state,
Nor would I love at lower rate.

   But at my back I always hear
Time's wingèd chariot hurrying near:
And yonder all before us lie
Deserts of vast eternity.
Thy beauty shall no more be found;
Nor, in thy marble vault, shall sound
My echoing song: then worms shall try
That long-preserved virginity,
And your quaint honour turn to dust,
And into ashes all my lust.
The grave's a fine and private place,
But none, I think, do there embrace.

   Now, therefore, while the youthful hue
Sits on thy skin like morning dew,
And while thy willing soul transpires
At every pore with instant fires,
Now let us sport us while we may;
And now, like amorous birds of prey,
Rather at once our Time devour,
Than languish in his slow-chapt power.
Let us roll all our strength and all
Our sweetness up into one ball,
And tear our pleasures with rough strife
Thorough the iron gates of life.
Thus, though we cannot make our sun
Stand still, yet we will make him run.

The Garden

How vainly men themselves amaze
To win the palm, the oak, or bays;
And their incessant labours see
Crowned from some single herb, or tree,
Whose short and narrow-vergèd shade
Does prudently their toils upbraid;
While all flowers and all trees do close
To weave the garlands of repose!

Fair Quiet, have I found thee here,
And Innocence, thy sister dear?
Mistaken long, I sought you then
In busy companies of men.
Your sacred plants, if here below,
Only among the plants will grow;
Society is all but rude
To this delicious solitude.

No white nor red was ever seen
So amorous as this lovely green.
Fond lovers, cruel as their flame,
Cut in these trees their mistress' name:
Little, alas! they know or heed
How far these beauties hers exceed!
Fair trees! wheres'e'er your barks I wound
No name shall but your own be found.

When we have run our passion's heat,
Love hither makes his best retreat.
The gods, that mortal beauty chase,
Still in a tree did end their race;
Apollo hunted Daphne so,
Only that she might laurel grow;
And Pan did after Syrinx speed,
Not as a nymph, but for a reed.

What wondrous life is this I lead!
Ripe apples drop about my head;
The luscious clusters of the vine
Upon my mouth do crush their wine;

The nectarine, and curious peach,
Into my hands themselves do reach;
Stumbling on melons, as I pass,
Ensnared with flowers, I fall on grass.

Meanwhile, the mind, from pleasure less,
Withdraws into its happiness:
The mind, that ocean where each kind
Does straight its own resemblance find;
Yet it creates, transcending these,
Far other worlds, and other seas;
Annihilating all that's made
To a green thought in a green shade.

Here at the fountain's sliding foot,
Or at some fruit-tree's mossy root,
Casting the body's vest aside,
My soul into the boughs does glide:
There like a bird it sits, and sings,
Then whets and combs its silver wings;
And, till prepared for longer flight,
Waves in its plumes the various light.

Such was that happy garden-state,
While man there walked without a mate:
After a place so pure and sweet,
What other help could yet be meet?
But 'twas beyond a mortal's share
To wander solitary there:
Two paradises 'twere in one,
To live in paradise alone.

How well the skillful gardener drew
Of flowers, and herbs, this dial new;
Where, from above, the milder sun
Does through a fragrant zodiac run;
And, as it works, the industrious bee
Computes its time as well as we.
How could such sweet and wholesome hours
Be reckoned but with herbs and flowers!

The Definition of Love

My love is of a birth as rare
As 'tis for object strange and high:
It was begotten by Despair
Upon Impossibility.

Magnanimous Despair alone
Could show me so divine a thing,
Where feeble Hope could ne'er have flown
But vainly flapped its tinsel wing.

And yet I quickly might arrive
Where my extended soul is fixed,
But Fate does iron wedges drive,
And always crowds itself betwixt.

For Fate with jealous eye does see
Two perfect loves, nor lets them close:
Their union would her ruin be,
And her tyrannic power depose.

And therefore her decrees of steel
Us as the distant poles have placed,
(Though love's whole world on us doth wheel)
Not by themselves to be embraced,

Unless the giddy heaven fall,
And earth some new convulsion tear,
And, us to join, the world should all
Be cramped into a planisphere.

As lines, so loves oblique may well
Themselves in every angle greet;
But ours, so truly parallel,
Though infinite, can never meet.

Therefore the love which us doth bind,
But fate so enviously debars,
Is the conjunction of the mind,
And opposition of the stars.

HENRY VAUGHAN
1621–1695

The World

I saw Eternity the other night,
Like a great ring of pure and endless light,
    All calm, as it was bright;
And round beneath it, Time in hours, days, years,
    Driven by the spheres
Like a vast shadow moved; in which the world
    And all her train were hurled.
The doting lover in his quaintest strain
    Did there complain;
Near him, his lute, his fancy, and his flights,
    Wit's sour delights;
With gloves, and knots, the silly snares of pleasure,
    Yet his dear treasure,
All scattered lay, while he his eyes did pour
    Upon a flower.

The darksome statesman, hung with weights and woe,
Like a thick midnight-fog, moved there so slow,
    He did not stay, nor go;
Condemning thoughts—like sad eclipses—scowl
    Upon his soul,
And clouds of crying witnesses without
    Pursued him with one shout.
Yet digged the mole, and lest his ways be found,
    Worked underground,
Where he did clutch his prey; but one did see
    That policy.
Churches and altars fed him; perjuries
    Were gnats and flies;
It rained about him blood and tears, but he
    Drank them as free.

The fearful miser on a heap of rust
Sat pining all his life there, did scarce trust
    His own hands with the dust,
Yet would not place one piece above, but lives

In fear of thieves.
Thousands there were as frantic as himself,
    And hugged each one his pelf;
The downright epicure placed heav'n in sense,
    And scorned pretence;
While others, slipped into a wide excess,
    Said little less;
The weaker sort slight, trivial wares enslave,
    Who think them brave;
And poor, despisèd Truth sat counting by
    Their victory.

Yet some, who all this while did weep and sing,
And sing and weep, soared up into the ring;
    But most would use no wing.
Oh, fools—said I—thus to prefer dark night
    Before true light!
To live in grots and caves, and hate the day
    Because it shows the way;
The way, which from this dead and dark abode
    Leads up to God;
A way where you might tread the sun, and be
    More bright than he!
But as I did their madness so discuss,
    One whispered thus,
"This ring the Bridegroom did for none provide,
    But for His bride."

They Are All Gone

They are all gone into the world of light!
    And I alone sit lingering here;
Their very memory is fair and bright,
    And my sad thoughts doth clear.

It glows and glitters in my cloudy breast,
    Like stars upon some gloomy grove,
Or those faint beams in which this hill is dressed,
    After the sun's remove.

I see them walking in an air of glory,
    Whose light doth trample on my days;

My days, which are at best but dull and hoary,
    Mere glimmering and decays.

O holy Hope! and high Humility!
   High as the heavens above!
These are your walks, and you have showed them me,
    To kindle my cold love.

Dear beauteous Death! the jewel of the just,
   Shining nowhere but in the dark;
What mysteries do lie beyond thy dust,
    Could man outlook that mark!

He that hath found some fledged bird's nest may know
   At first sight if the bird be flown;
But what fair well or grove he sings in now,
    That is to him unknown.

And yet, as angels in some brighter dreams
   Call to the soul when man doth sleep,
So some strange thoughts transcend our wonted themes,
    And into glory peep.

If a star were confined into a tomb,
   Her captive flames must needs burn there;
But when the hand that locked her up gives room,
    She'll shine through all the sphere.

O Father of eternal life, and all
   Created glories under Thee!
Resume Thy spirit from this world of thrall
    Into true liberty.

Either disperse these mists, which blot and fill
   My perspective still as they pass;
Or else remove me hence unto that hill
    Where I shall need no glass.

The Retreat

Happy those early days, when I
Shin'd in my Angel-infancy!
Before I understood this place
Appointed for my second race,
Or taught my soul to fancy aught
But a white celestial thought:
When yet I had not walk'd above
A mile or two from my first Love,
And looking back—at that short space—
Could see a glimpse of His bright face:
When on some gilded cloud, or flow'r,
My gazing soul would dwell an hour,
And in those weaker glories spy
Some shadows of eternity:
Before I taught my tongue to wound
My Conscience with a sinful sound,
Or had the black art to dispense
A several sin to ev'ry sense,
But felt through all this fleshly dress
Bright shoots of everlastingness.
     O how I long to travel back,
And tread again that ancient track!
That I might once more reach that plain
Where first I left my glorious train;
From whence th' enlightened spirit sees
That shady City of Palm-trees.
But ah! my soul with too much stay
Is drunk, and staggers in the way!
Some men a forward motion love,
But I by backward steps would move;
And when this dust falls to the urn,
In that state I came, return.

JOHN DRYDEN
1631–1700

All, All of a Piece

All, all of a piece throughout:
Thy chase had a beast in view;
Thy wars brought nothing about;
Thy lovers were all untrue.
'Tis well an old age is out,
And time to begin a new.

From *The Secular Masque*

A Song for St. Cecilia's Day

From harmony, from heavenly harmony,
    This universal frame began:
When nature underneath a heap
    Of jarring atoms lay,
    And could not heave her head,
The tuneful voice was heard from high,
    "Arise, ye more than dead!"
Then cold, and hot, and moist, and dry,
    In order to their stations leap,
    And Music's power obey.
From harmony, from heavenly harmony,
    This universal frame began:
    From harmony to harmony
Through all the compass of the notes it ran,
The diapason closing full in Man.

What passion cannot Music raise and quell?
    When Jubal struck the corded shell,
His listening brethren stood around,
    And, wondering, on their faces fell
To worship that celestial sound:
Less than a God they thought there could not dwell
    Within the hollow of that shell,
    That spoke so sweetly, and so well.
What passion cannot Music raise and quell?

    The trumpet's loud clangour
      Excites us to arms,

With shrill notes of anger,
    And mortal alarms.
The double double double beat
    Of the thundering drum
    Cries Hark! the foes come;
Charge, charge, 'tis too late to retreat!

    The soft complaining flute,
    In dying notes, discovers
    The woes of hopeless lovers,
Whose dirge is whisper'd by the warbling lute.

    Sharp violins proclaim
Their jealous pangs and desperation,
Fury, frantic indignation,
Depth of pains, and height of passion,
    For the fair, disdainful dame.

    But O, what art can teach,
    What human voice can reach,
        The sacred organ's praise?
    Notes inspiring holy love,
Notes that wing their heavenly ways
    To mend the choirs above.

Orpheus could lead the savage race;
And trees unrooted left their place,
    Sequacious of the lyre;
But bright Cecilia rais'd the wonder higher:
When to her organ vocal breath was given,
    An angel heard, and straight appear'd
    Mistaking Earth for Heaven.

GRAND CHORUS

As from the power of sacred lays
    The spheres began to move,
And sung the great Creator's praise
    To all the Blest above;
So when the last and dreadful hour
This crumbling pageant shall devour,
The trumpet shall be heard on high,
The dead shall live, the living die,
And Music shall untune the sky!

THOMAS TRAHERNE
1637?–1674

On Leaping Over the Moon

I saw new Worlds beneath the Water lie,
New People; yea, another Sky
And Sun, which seen by Day
Might things more clear display.
Just such another
Of late my Brother
Did in his Travel see, and saw by Night,
A much more strange and wondrous Sight:
Nor could the World exhibit such another,
So Great a Sight, but in a Brother.

Adventure strange! No such in Story we,
New or old, true or feigned, see.
On Earth he seem'd to move
Yet Heaven went above;
Up in the Skies
His body flies
In open, visible, yet Magic, sort:
As he along the Way did sport,
Over the Flood he takes his nimble Course
Without the help of feigned Horse.

As he went tripping o'er the King's high-way,
A little pearly river lay
O'er which, without a wing
Or Oar, he dar'd to swim,
Swim through the air
On body fair;
He would not use nor trust *Icarian* wings
Lest they should prove deceitful things;
For had he fall'n, it had been wondrous high,
Not from, but from above, the sky:
He might have dropt through that thin element
Into a fathomless descent;
Unto the nether sky
That did beneath him lie,
And there might tell

What wonders dwell
On earth above. Yet doth he briskly run,
  And bold the danger overcome;
Who, as he leapt, with joy related soon
  How *happy* he o'er-leapt the Moon.

What wondrous things upon the Earth are done
  Beneath, and yet above the sun?
    Deeds all appear again
    In higher spheres; remain
      In clouds as yet:
      But there they get
Another light, and in another way
  Themselves to us *above* display.
The skies themselves this earthly globe surround;
  W'are even here within them found.

On heav'nly ground within the skies we walk,
  And in this middle centre talk:
    Did we but wisely move,
    On earth in heav'n above,
      Then soon should we
      Exalted be
Above the sky: from whence whoever falls,
  Through a long dismal precipice,
Sinks to the deep abyss where *Satan* crawls
  Where horrid Death and Despair lies.

As much as others thought themselves to lie
Beneath the moon, so much more high
    Himself he thought to fly
    Above the starry sky,
      As *that* he spied
      Below the tide.
Thus did he yield me in the shady night
  A wondrous and instructive light,
Which taught me that under our feet there is,
  As o'er our heads, a place of bliss.

To the same purpose; he, not long before
  Brought home from nurse, going to the door
    To do some little thing

He must not do within,
    With wonder cries,
        As in the skies
He saw the moon, *O yonder is the moon*
    Newly come after me to town,
That shin'd at Lugwardin but yesternight,
    Where I enjoy'd the self-same light.

As if it had ev'n twenty thousand faces,
    It shines at once in many places;
        To all the earth so wide
        God doth the stars divide
            With so much art
            The moon impart,
They serve us all; serve wholly ev'ry one
    As if they served him alone.
While every single person hath such store,
    'Tis want of sense that makes us poor.

Wonder

How like an angel came I down!
    How bright are all things here!
When first among his works I did appear,
    Oh, how their glory did me crown!
The world resembled his eternity,
        In which my soul did walk;
    And ev'rything that I did see
        Did with me talk.

The skies in their magnificence,
    The lovely lively air,
Oh, how divine, how soft, how sweet, how fair!
The stars did entertain my sense,
And all the works of God so bright and pure,
    So rich and great, did seem,
    As if they ever must endure
        In my esteem.

A native health and innocence
    Within my bones did grow,
And while my God did all his glories show,
    I felt a vigour in my sense

That was all spirit; I within did flow
        With seas of life like wine;
    I nothing in the world did know,
        But 'twas divine.

    Harsh rugged objects were concealed;
        Oppressions, tears, and cries,
Sins, griefs, complaints, dissensions, weeping eyes,
        Were hid, and only things revealed
Which heavenly spirits and the angels prize:
        The state of innocence
        And bliss, not trades and poverties,
          Did fill my sense.

    The streets seemed paved with golden stones,
        The boys and girls all mine—
To me how did their lovely faces shine!
        The sons of men all holy ones,
In joy and beauty then appeared to me;
        And ev'rything I found,
        While like an angel I did see,
        Adorned the ground.

    Rich diamonds, and pearl, and gold
        Might ev'rywhere be seen;
Rare colours, yellow, blue, red, white, and green,
        Mine eyes on ev'ry side behold;
All that I saw a wonder did appear,
        Amazement was my bliss,
        That and my wealth met ev'rywhere;
        No joy to this!

    Cursed, ill-devised properties,
        With envy, avarice,
And fraud, those fiends that spoil ev'n paradise,
        Were not the object of mine eyes;
Nor hedges, ditches, limits, narrow bounds,
        I dreamt not aught of those,
        But in surveying all men's grounds
        I found repose.

For property itself was mine,
And hedges, ornaments,
Walls, houses, coffers, and their rich contents,
To make me rich combine.
Clothes, costly jewels, laces, I esteemed
My wealth, by others worn,
For me they all to wear them seemed,
When I was born.

WILLIAM DOUGLAS
1672–1748

Annie Laurie

Maxwelton's braes are bonnie
Where early fa's the dew,
And it's there that Annie Laurie
Gie'd me her promise true;
Gie'd me her promise true,
Which ne'er forgot will be;
And for bonnie Annie Laurie
I'd lay me doun and dee.

Her brow is like the snaw drift;
Her throat is like the swan;
Her face it is the fairest
That e'er the sun shone on—
That e'er the sun shone on—
And dark blue is her ee;
And for bonnie Annie Laurie
I'd lay me doun and dee.

Like dew on the gowan lying
Is the fa' o' her fairy feet;
And like the winds in summer sighing,
Her voice is low and sweet—
Her voice is low and sweet—
And she's a' the world to me;
And for bonnie Annie Laurie
I'd lay me doun and dee.

GEORGE BERKELEY
1685–1753

On the Prospect of Planting Arts and Learning in America

The Muse, disgusted at an age and clime
    Barren of every glorious theme,
In distant lands now waits a better time,
    Producing subjects worthy fame:

In happy climes where from the genial sun
    And virgin earth such scenes ensue,
The force of art by nature seems outdone,
    And fancied beauties by the true:

In happy climes, the seat of innocence,
    Where nature guides and virtue rules,
Where men shall not impose for truth and sense
    The pedantry of courts and schools:

There shall be sung another golden age,
    The rise of empire and of arts,
The good and great inspiring epic rage,
    The wisest heads and noblest hearts.

Not such as Europe breeds in her decay;
    Such as she bred when fresh and young,
When heavenly flame did animate her clay,
    By future poets shall be sung.

Westward the course of empire takes its way;
    The four first acts already past,
A fifth shall close the drama with the day;
    Time's noblest offspring is the last.

JOHN GAY
1685–1732

To a Lady on Her Passion for Old China

What ecstasies her bosom fire!
How her eyes languish with desire!
How blest, how happy should I be,
Were that fond glance bestow'd on me!
New doubts and fears within me war:
What rival's near? a china jar.

China's the passion of her soul;
A cup, a plate, a dish, a bowl,
Can kindle wishes in her breast,
Inflame with joy, or break her rest.

Some gems collect; some medals prize,
And view the rust with lover's eyes;
Some court the stars at midnight hours;
Some dote on Nature's charms in flowers!
But ev'ry beauty I can trace
In Laura's mind, in Laura's face;
My stars are in this brighter sphere,
My lily and my rose is here.

Philosophers more grave than wise
Hunt science down in butterflies;
Or fondly poring on a spider
Stretch human contemplation wider;
Fossils give joy to Galen's soul,
He digs for knowledge, like a mole;
In shells so learn'd, that all agree
No fish that swims knows more than he!
In such pursuits if wisdom lies,
Who, Laura, shall thy taste despise?

When I some antique jar behold,
Or white, or blue, or speck'd with gold,
Vessels so pure, and so refined,
Appear the types of woman-kind:
Are they not valued for their beauty,
Too fair, too fine, for household duty?
With flowers and gold and azure dyed,
Of ev'ry house the grace and pride?

How white, how polish'd is their skin,
And valued most when only seen!
She who before was highest prized,
Is for a crack or flaw despised;
I grant they're frail, yet they're so rare,
The treasure cannot cost too dear!
But man is made of coarser stuff,
And serves convenience well enough;
He's a strong earthen vessel made,
For drudging, labour, toil, and trade;
And when wives lose their other self,
With ease they bear the loss of delf.

   Husbands more covetous than sage
Condemn this china-buying rage;
They count that woman's prudence little,
Who sets her heart on things so brittle.
But are those wise men's inclinations
Fixt on more strong, more sure foundations?
If all that's frail we must despise,
No human view or scheme is wise.
Are not ambition's hopes as weak?
They swell like bubbles, shine and break.
A courtier's promise is so slight,
'Tis made at noon, and broke at night.
What pleasure's sure? The miss you keep
Breaks both your fortune and your sleep,
The man who loves a country life,
Breaks all the comforts of his wife;
And if he quit his farm and plough,
His wife in town may break her vow.
Love, Laura, love, while youth is warm,
For each new winter breaks a charm,
And woman's not like china sold,
But cheaper grows in growing old;
Then quickly choose the prudent part,
Or else you break a faithful heart.

ALEXANDER POPE
1688–1744

Solitude

Happy the man, whose wish and care
A few paternal acres bound,
Content to breathe his native air
    In his own ground.

Whose herds with milk, whose fields with bread,
Whose flocks supply him with attire;
Whose trees in summer yield him shade,
    In winter, fire.

Blest, who can unconcernedly find
Hours, days, and years slide soft away
In health of body, peace of mind;
    Quiet by day,

Sound sleep by night; study and ease
Together mixed, sweet recreation,
And innocence, which most does please
    With meditation.

Thus let me live, unseen, unknown;
Thus unlamented let me die,
Steal from the world, and not a stone
    Tell where I lie.

Know Then Thyself

Know then thyself, presume not God to scan,
The proper study of Mankind is Man.
Plac'd on this isthmus of a middle state,
A Being darkly wise, and rudely great:
With too much knowledge for the Sceptic side,
With too much weakness for the Stoic's pride,
He hangs between; in doubt to act, or rest;
In doubt to deem himself a God, or Beast;
In doubt his Mind or Body to prefer;
Born but to die, and reas'ning but to err;

Alike in ignorance, his reason such,
Whether he thinks too little, or too much:
Chaos of Thought and Passion, all confus'd;
Still by himself abus'd, or disabus'd;
Created half to rise, and half to fall;
Great lord of all things, yet a prey to all;
Sole judge of truth, in endless error hurl'd:
The glory, jest, and riddle of the world!

   Self-love, the spring of motion, acts the soul;
Reason's comparing balance rules the whole.
Man, but for that, no action could attend,
And, but for this, were active to no end:
Fix'd like a plant on his peculiar spot,
To draw nutrition, propagate, and rot;
Or, meteor-like, flame lawless through the void,
Destroying others, by himself destroy'd.

   Most strength the moving principle requires;
Active its task, it prompts, impels, inspires.
Sedate and quiet the comparing lies,
Form'd but to check, delib'rate, and advise.
Self-love still stronger, as its objects nigh;
Reason's at distance, and in prospect lie:
That sees immediate good by present sense;
Reason, the future and the consequence.
Thicker than arguments, temptations throng,
At best more watchful this, but that more strong.
The action of the stronger to suspend
Reason still use, to reason still attend.
Attention, habit and experience gains;
Each strengthens reason, and self-love restrains.

   Vice is a monster of so frightful mien,
As, to be hated, needs but to be seen;
Yet seen too oft, familiar with her face,
We first endure, then pity, then embrace.
But where th' extreme of vice, was ne'er agreed:
Ask where's the north? at York, 'tis on the Tweed;
In Scotland, at the Orcades; and there,
At Greenland, Zembla, or the Lord knows where.
No creature owns it in the first degree,

But thinks his neighbour farther gone than he;
Ev'n those who dwell beneath its very zone,
Or never feel the rage, or never own;
What happier natures shrink at with affright,
The hard inhabitant contends is right.

Honor and shame from no condition rise;
Act well your part, there all the honour lies.
Fortune in men has some small diff'rence made,
One flaunts in rags, one flutters in brocade;
The cobbler apron'd, and the parson gown'd,
The friar hooded, and the monarch crown'd.
"What differ more," you cry, "than crown and cowl?"
I'll tell you, friend! a wise man and a fool.
You'll find, if once the monarch acts the monk,
Or, cobbler-like, the parson will be drunk,
Worth makes the man, and want of it, the fellow;
The rest is all but leather or prunella.

From *An Essay on Man*

Vital Spark of Heavenly Flame

Vital spark of heavenly flame!
Quit, O quit this mortal frame:
    Trembling, hoping, lingering, flying,
    O the pain, the bliss of dying!
Cease, fond Nature, cease thy strife,
And let me languish into life.

    Hark! they whisper; angels say,
    Sister Spirit, come away!
    What is this absorbs me quite?
    Steals my senses, shuts my sight,
Drowns my spirits, draws my breath?
Tell me, my soul, can this be death?

    The world recedes; it disappears!
    Heav'n opens on my eyes! my ears
        With sounds seraphic ring!
    Lend, lend your wings! I mount! I fly!
    O Grave! where is thy victory?
        O Death! where is thy sting?

A Little Learning

A little learning is a dang'rous thing;
Drink deep, or taste not the Pierian spring:
There shallow draughts intoxicate the brain,
And drinking largely sobers us again.
Fir'd at first sight with what the Muse imparts,
In fearless youth we tempt the heights of Arts,
While from the bounded level of our mind,
Short views we take, nor see the lengths behind;
But more advanc'd, behold with strange surprise
New distant scenes of endless science rise!
    So pleas'd at first the tow'ring Alps we try,
Mount o'er the vales, and seem to tread the sky,
Th' eternal snows appear already past,
And the first clouds and mountains seem the last:
But, those attain'd, we tremble to survey
The growing labours of the lengthen'd way,
Th' increasing prospect tires our wand'ring eyes.
Hills peep o'er hills, and Alps on Alps arise!
    A perfect Judge will read each work of Wit
With the same spirit that its author writ:
Survey the Whole, nor seek slight faults to find
Where nature moves, and rapture warms the mind;
Nor lose, for that malignant dull delight,
The gen'rous pleasure to be charm'd with wit.
But in such lays as neither ebb, nor flow,
Correctly cold, and regularly low,
That shunning faults, one quiet tenour keep;
We cannot blame indeed—but we may sleep.
In Wit, as Nature, what affects our hearts
Is not th' exactness of peculiar parts;
'Tis not a lip, or eye, we beauty call,
But the joint force and full result of all.
Thus when we view some well-proportion'd dome
(The world's just wonder, and ev'n thine, O Rome!)
No single parts unequally surprise,
All comes united to th' admiring eyes;
No monstrous height, or breadth, or length appear;
The Whole at once is bold, and regular.

From *An Essay on Criticism*

Engraved on the Collar of a Dog, Which I Gave to His Royal Highness

I am his Highness' dog at Kew;
Pray tell me, sir, whose dog are you?

The Coxcomb Bird

The coxcomb bird, so talkative and grave,
That from his cage cries Cuckold, Whore, and Knave,
Though many a passenger he rightly call,
You hold him no Philosopher at all.

From *Moral Essays*

The Rape of the Lock

CANTO I

What dire offense from am'rous causes springs,
What mighty contests rise from trivial things,
I sing—This verse to Caryl, Muse! is due:
This, even Belinda may vouchsafe to view:
Slight is the subject, but not so the praise,
If She inspire, and He approve my lays.

Say what strange motive, Goddess! could compel
A well-bred Lord t' assault a gentle Belle?
O say what stranger cause, yet unexplored,
Could make a gentle Belle reject a Lord?
In tasks so bold, can little men engage,
And in soft bosoms dwells such mighty Rage?

Sol through white curtains shot a tim'rous ray,
And oped those eyes that must eclipse the day:
Now lap-dogs give themselves the rousing shake,
And sleepless lovers, just at twelve, awake:
Thrice rung the bell, the slipper knocked the ground,
And the pressed watch returned a silver sound.
Belinda still her downy pillow prest,
Her guardian Sylph prolonged the balmy rest:
'Twas He had summoned to her silent bed
The morning-dream that hovered o'er her head;
A Youth more glitt'ring than a Birth-night Beau,
(That even in slumber caused her cheek to glow)
Seemed to her ear his winning lips to lay,
And thus in whispers said, or seemed to say.

"Fairest of mortals, thou distinguished care
Of thousand bright Inhabitants of Air!
If e'er one vision touched thy infant thought,
Of all the Nurse and all the Priest have taught;
Of airy Elves by moonlight shadows seen,
The silver token, and the circled green,
Or virgins visited by Angel-powers,
With golden crowns and wreaths of heav'nly flowers;
Hear and believe! thy own importance know,
Nor bound thy narrow views to things below.
Some secret truths, from learnèd pride concealed,
To Maids alone and Children are revealed:
What though no credit doubting Wits may give?
The Fair and Innocent shall still believe.
Know, then, unnumbered Spirits round thee fly,
The light Militia of the lower sky:
These, though unseen, are ever on the wing,
Hang o'er the Box, and hover round the Ring.
Think what an equipage thou hast in Air,
And view with scorn two Pages and a Chair.
As now your own, our beings were of old,
And once inclosed in Woman's beauteous mould;
Thence, by a soft transition, we repair
From earthly Vehicles to these of air.
Think not, when Woman's transient breath is fled,
That all her vanities at once are dead;
Succeeding vanities she still regards,
And though she plays no more, o'erlooks the cards
Her joy in gilded Chariots, when alive,
And love of Ombre, after death survive.
For when the Fair in all their pride expire,
To their first Elements their Souls retire:
The Sprites of fiery Termagants in Flame
Mount up, and take a Salamander's name.
Soft yielding minds to Water glide away,
And sip, with Nymphs, their elemental Tea.
The graver Prude sinks downward to a Gnome,
In search of mischief still on Earth to roam.
The light Coquettes in Sylphs aloft repair,
And sport and flutter in the fields of Air.
    Know further yet; whoever fair and chaste

Rejects mankind, is by some Sylph embraced:
For Spirits, freed from mortal laws, with ease
Assume what sexes and what shapes they please.
What guards the purity of melting Maids,
In courtly balls, and midnight masquerades,
Safe from the treach'rous friend, the daring spark,
The glance by day, the whisper in the dark,
When kind occasion prompts their warm desires,
When music softens, and when dancing fires?
'Tis but their Sylph, the wise Celestials know,
Though Honor is the word with Men below.

Some nymphs there are, too conscious of their face,
For life predestined to the Gnomes' embrace.
These swell their prospects and exalt their pride,
When offers are disdained, and love denied:
Then gay Ideas crowd the vacant brain,
While Peers, and Dukes, and all their sweeping train,
And Garters, Stars, and Coronets appear,
And in soft sounds, 'Your Grace' salutes their ear.
'Tis these that early taint the female soul,
Instruct the eyes of young Coquettes to roll,
Teach Infant-cheeks a bidden blush to know,
And little hearts to flutter at a Beau.

Oft, when the world imagine women stray,
The Sylphs through mystic mazes guide their way,
Through all the giddy circle they pursue,
And old impertinence expel by new.
What tender maid but must a victim fall
To one man's treat, but for another's ball?
When Florio speaks what virgin could withstand,
If gentle Damon did not squeeze her hand?
With varying vanities, from every part,
They shift the moving Toyshop of their heart;
Where wigs with wigs, with sword-knots sword-knots strive,
Beaux banish beaux, and coaches coaches drive.
This erring mortals Levity may call;
Oh blind to truth! the Sylphs contrive it all.

Of these am I, who thy protection claim,
A watchful sprite, and Ariel is my name.
Late, as I ranged the crystal wilds of air,
In the clear Mirror of thy ruling Star

I saw, alas! some dread event impend,
Ere to the main this morning sun descend,
But heaven reveals not what, or how, or where:
Warned by the Sylph, oh pious maid, beware!
This to disclose is all thy guardian can:
Beware of all, but most beware of Man!"

He said; when Shock, who thought she slept too long,
Leaped up, and waked his mistress with his tongue.
'Twas then, Belinda, if report say true,
Thy eyes first opened on a Billet-doux;
Wounds, Charms, and Ardors were no sooner read,
But all the Vision vanished from thy head.

And now, unveiled, the Toilet stands displayed,
Each silver Vase in mystic order laid.
First, robed in white, the Nymph intent adores,
With head uncovered, the Cosmetic powers.
A heav'nly image in the glass appears,
To that she bends, to that her eyes she rears;
Th' inferior Priestess, at her altar's side,
Trembling, begins the sacred rites of Pride.
Unnumbered treasures ope at once, and here
The various off'rings of the world appear;
From each she nicely culls with curious toil,
And decks the Goddess with the glitt'ring spoil.
This casket India's glowing gems unlocks,
And all Arabia breathes from yonder box.
The Tortoise here and Elephant unite,
Transformed to combs, the speckled, and the white.
Here files of pins extend their shining rows,
Puffs, Powders, Patches, Bibles, Billet-doux.
Now awful Beauty puts on all its arms;
The fair each moment rises in her charms,
Repairs her smiles, awakens every grace,
And calls forth all the wonders of her face;
Sees by degrees a purer blush arise,
And keener lightnings quicken in her eyes.
The busy Sylphs surround their darling care,
These set the head, and those divide the hair,
Some fold the sleeve, whilst others plait the gown;
And Betty's praised for labors not her own.

CANTO II

Not with more glories, in th' etherial plain,
The Sun first rises o'er the purpled main,
Than, issuing forth, the rival of his beams
Launched on the bosom of the silver Thames.
Fair Nymphs, and well-drest Youths around her shone,
But every eye was fixed on her alone.
On her white breast a sparkling Cross she wore,
Which Jews might kiss, and Infidels adore.
Her lively looks a sprightly mind disclose,
Quick as her eyes, and as unfixed as those:
Favors to none, to all she smiles extends;
Oft she rejects, but never once offends.
Bright as the sun, her eyes the gazers strike,
And, like the sun, they shine on all alike.
Yet graceful ease, and sweetness void of pride,
Might hide her faults, if Belles had faults to hide:
If to her share some female errors fall,
Look on her face, and you'll forget 'ém all.

  This Nymph, to the destruction of mankind,
Nourished two Locks, which graceful hung behind
In equal curls, and well conspired to deck
With shining ringlets the smooth iv'ry neck.
Love in these labyrinths his slaves detains,
And mighty hearts are held in slender chains.
With hairy springes we the birds betray,
Slight lines of hair surprise the finny prey,
Fair tresses man's imperial race ensnare,
And beauty draws us with a single hair.

  Th' advent'rous Baron the bright locks admired;
He saw, he wished, and to the prize aspired.
Resolved to win, he meditates the way,
By force to ravish, or by fraud betray;
For when success a Lover's toil attends,
Few ask, if fraud or force attained his ends.

  For this, ere Phœbus rose, he had implored
Propitious heaven, and every power adored,
But chiefly Love—to Love an Altar built,
Of twelve vast French Romances, neatly gilt.
There lay three garters, half a pair of gloves;
And all the trophies of his former loves;

With tender Billet-doux he lights the pyre,
And breathes three am'rous sighs to raise the fire.
Then prostrate falls, and begs with ardent eyes
Soon to obtain, and long possess the prize:
The powers gave ear, and granted half his prayer,
The rest, the winds dispersed in empty air.

But now secure the painted vessel glides,
The sun-beams trembling on the floating tides:
While melting music steals upon the sky,
And softened sounds along the waters die;
Smooth flow the waves, the Zephyrs gently play,
Belinda smiled, and all the world was gay.
All but the Sylph—with careful thoughts opprest,
Th' impending woe sat heavy on his breast.
He summons strait his Denizens of air;
The lucid squadrons round the sails repair:
Soft o'er the shrouds aërial whispers breathe,
That seemed but Zephyrs to the train beneath.
Some to the sun their insect-wings unfold,
Waft on the breeze, or sink in clouds of gold;
Transparent forms, too fine for mortal sight,
Their fluid bodies half dissolved in light,
Loose to the wind their airy garments flew,
Thin glitt'ring textures of the filmy dew,
Dipt in the richest tincture of the skies,
Where light disports in ever-mingling dyes,
While every beam new transient colors flings,
Colors that change whene'er they wave their wings.
Amid the circle, on the gilded mast,
Superior by the head, was Ariel placed;
His purple pinions opening to the sun,
He raised his azure wand, and thus begun.

"Ye Sylphs and Sylphids, to your chief give ear!
Fays, fairies, Genii, Elves, and Dæmons, hear!
Ye know the spheres and various tasks assigned
By laws eternal to th' aërial kind.
Some in the fields of purest Æther play,
And bask and whiten in the blaze of day.
Some guide the course of wand'ring orbs on high,
Or roll the planets through the boundless sky.
Some less refined, beneath the moon's pale light

Pursue the stars that shoot athwart the night,
Or suck the mists in grosser air below,
Or dip their pinions in the painted bow,
Or brew fierce tempests on the wintry main,
Or o'er the glebe distil the kindly rain.
Others on earth o'er human race preside,
Watch all their ways, and all their actions guide:
Of these the chief the care of Nations own,
And guard with Arms divine the British Throne.

    Our humbler province is to tend the Fair,
Not a less pleasing, though less glorious care;
To save the powder from too rude a gale,
Nor let th' imprisoned essences exhale;
To draw fresh colors from the vernal flowers;
To steal from rainbows ere they drop in showers
A brighter wash; to curl their waving hairs,
Assist their blushes, and inspire their airs;
Nay oft, in dreams, invention we bestow,
To change a Flounce, or add a Furbelow.

    This day, black Omens threat the brightest Fair,
That e'er deserved a watchful spirit's care;
Some dire disaster, or by force, or slight;
But what, or where, the fates have wrapt in night.
Whether the nymph shall break Diana's law,
Or some frail China jar receive a flaw;
Or stain her honor or her new brocade;
Forget her prayers, or miss a masquerade;
Or lose her heart, or necklace, at a ball;
Or whether Heaven has doomed that Shock must fall.
Haste, then, ye spirits! to your charge repair:
The flutt'ring fan be Zephyretta's care;
The drops to thee, Brillante, we consign;
And, Momentilla, let the watch be thine;
Do thou, Crispissa, tend her fav'rite Lock;
Ariel himself shall be the guard of Shock.

    To fifty chosen Sylphs, of special note,
We trust th' important charge, the Petticoat:
Oft have we known that seven-fold fence to fail,
Though stiff with hoops, and armed with ribs of whale;
Form a strong line about the silver bound,
And guard the wide circumference around.

Whatever spirit, careless of his charge,
His post neglects, or leaves the fair at large,
Shall feel sharp vengeance soon o'ertake his sins,
Be stopped in vials, or transfixed with pins;
Or plunged in lakes of bitter washes lie,
Or wedged whole ages in a bodkin's eye:
Gums and Pomatums shall his flight restrain,
While clogged he beats his silken wings in vain;
Or Alum styptics with contracting power
Shrink his thin essence like a riveled flower:
Or, as Ixion fixed, the wretch shall feel
The giddy motion of the whirling Mill,
In fumes of burning Chocolate shall glow,
And tremble at the sea that froths below!"
    He spoke; the spirits from the sails descend;
Some, orb in orb, around the nymph extend;
Some thrid the mazy ringlets of her hair;
Some hang upon the pendants of her ear:
With beating hearts the dire event they wait,
Anxious, and trembling for the birth of Fate.

CANTO III

Close by those meads, forever crowned with flowers,
Where Thames with pride surveys his rising towers,
There stands a structure of majestic frame,
Which from the neighb'ring Hampton takes its name.
Here Britain's statesmen oft the fall foredoom
Of foreign Tyrants and of Nymphs at home;
Here thou, great Anna! whom three realms obey,
Dost sometimes counsel take—and sometimes Tea.
    Hither the heroes and the nymphs resort,
To taste awhile the pleasures of a Court;
In various talk th' instructive hours they past,
Who gave the ball, or paid the visit last;
One speaks the glory of the British Queen,
And one describes a charming Indian screen;
A third interprets motions, looks, and eyes;
At every word a reputation dies.
Snuff, or the fan, supply each pause of chat,
With singing, laughing, ogling, *and all that.*
    Meanwhile, declining from the noon of day,
The sun obliquely shoots his burning ray;

The hungry Judges soon the sentence sign,
And wretches hang that jury-men may dine;
The merchant from th' Exchange returns in peace,
And the long labors of the Toilet cease.
Belinda now, whom thirst of fame invites,
Burns to encounter two advent'rous Knights,
At Ombre singly to decide their doom;
And swells her breast with conquests yet to come.
Straight the three bands prepare in arms to join,
Each band the number of the sacred nine.
Soon as she spreads her hand, th' aërial guard
Descend, and sit on each important card:
First Ariel perched upon a Matadore,
Then each, according to the rank they bore;
For Sylphs, yet mindful of their ancient race,
Are, as when women, wondrous fond of place.

Behold, four Kings in majesty revered,
With hoary whiskers and a forky beard;
And four fair Queens whose hands sustain a flower,
Th' expressive emblem of their softer power;
Four Knaves in garbs succinct, a trusty band,
Caps on their heads, and halberts in their hand;
And particolored troops, a shining train,
Draw forth to combat on the velvet plain.

The skilful Nymph reviews her force with care:
"Let Spades be trumps!" she said, and trumps they were.

Now move to war her sable Matadores,
In show like leaders of the swarthy Moors.
Spadillio first, unconquerable Lord!
Led off two captive trumps, and swept the board.
As many more Manillio forced to yield,
And marched a victor from the verdant field.
Him Basto followed, but his fate more hard
Gained but one trump and one Plebeian card.
With his broad sabre next, a chief in years,
The hoary Majesty of Spades appears,
Puts forth one manly leg, to sight revealed,
The rest, his many-colored robe concealed.
The rebel Knave, who dares his prince engage,
Proves the just victim of his royal rage.
Even mighty Pam, that Kings and Queens o'erthrew

And mowed down armies in the fights of Lu,
Sad chance of war! now destitute of aid,
Falls undistinguished by the victor spade!
   Thus far both armies to Belinda yield;
Now to the Baron fate inclines the field.
His warlike Amazon her host invades,
Th' imperial consort of the crown of Spades.
The Club's black Tyrant first her victim dyed,
Spite of his haughty mien, and barb'rous pride:
What boots the regal circle on his head,
His giant limbs, in state unwieldy spread;
That long behind he trails his pompous robe,
And, of all monarchs, only grasps the globe?
   The Baron now his Diamonds pours apace;
Th' embroidered King who shows but half his face,
And his refulgent Queen, with powers combined
Of broken troops an easy conquest find.
Clubs, Diamonds, Hearts, in wild disorder seen,
With throngs promiscuous strow the level green.
Thus when dispersed a routed army runs,
Of Asia's troops, and Afric's sable sons,
With like confusion different nations fly,
Of various habit, and of various dye,
The pierced battalions dis-united fall,
In heaps on heaps; one fate o'erwhelms them all.
   The Knave of Diamonds tries his wily arts,
And wins (oh shameful chance!) the Queen of Hearts.
At this, the blood the virgin's cheek forsook,
A livid paleness spreads o'er all her look;
She sees, and trembles at th' approaching ill,
Just in the jaws of ruin, and Codille.
And now (as oft in some distempered State)
On one nice Trick depends the general fate.
An Ace of Hearts steps forth: The King unseen
Lurked in her hand, and mourned his captive Queen:
He springs to Vengeance with an eager pace,
And falls like thunder on the prostrate Ace.
The nymph exulting fills with shouts the sky;
The walls, the woods, and long canals reply.
   Oh thoughtless mortals! ever blind to fate,
Too soon dejected, and too soon elate.

Sudden, these honors shall be snatched away,
And cursed for ever this victorious day.

    For lo! the board with cups and spoons is crowned,
The berries crackle, and the mill turns round;
On shining Altars of Japan they raise
The silver lamp; the fiery spirits blaze:
From silver spouts the grateful liquors glide,
While China's earth receives the smoking tide:
At once they gratify their scent and taste,
And frequent cups prolong the rich repast.
Straight hover round the Fair her airy band;
Some, as she sipped, the fuming liquor fanned,
Some o'er her lap their careful plumes displayed,
Trembling, and conscious of the rich brocade.
Coffee, (which makes the politician wise,
And see through all things with his half-shut eyes)
Sent up in vapors to the Baron's brain
New Stratagems, the radiant Lock to gain.
Ah cease, rash youth! desist ere 'tis too late,
Fear the just Gods, and think of Scylla's Fate!
Changed to a bird, and sent to flit in air,
She dearly pays for Nisus' injured hair!

    But when to mischief mortals bend their will,
How soon they find fit instruments of ill!
Just then, Clarissa drew with tempting grace
A two-edged weapon from her shining case:
So Ladies in Romance assist their Knight,
Present the spear, and arm him for the fight.
He takes the gift with rev'rence, and extends
The little engine on his fingers' ends;
This just behind Belinda's neck he spread,
As o'er the fragrant steams she bends her head.
Swift to the Lock a thousand Sprites repair,
A thousand wings, by turns, blow back the hair;
And thrice they twitched the diamond in her ear;
Thrice she looked back, and thrice the foe drew near.
Just in that instant, anxious Ariel sought
The close recesses of the Virgin's thought;
As on the nosegay in her breast reclined,
He watched th' Ideas rising in her mind,
Sudden he viewed, in spite of all her art,

An earthly Lover lurking at her heart.
Amazed, confused, he found his power expired,
Resigned to fate, and with a sigh retired.
   The Peer now spreads the glitt'ring Forfex wide,
T' inclose the Lock; now joins it, to divide.
Even then, before the fatal engine closed,
A wretched Sylph too fondly interposed;
Fate urged the shears, and cut the Sylph in twain,
(But airy substance soon unites again)
The meeting points the sacred hair dissever
From the fair head, forever, and forever!
   Then flashed the living lightning from her eyes,
And screams of horror rend th' affrighted skies.
Not louder shrieks to pitying heaven are cast,
When husbands, or when lap-dogs breathe their last;
Or when rich China vessels fall'n from high,
In glitt'ring dust and painted fragments lie!
   "Let wreaths of triumph now my temples twine,"
(The victor cried) "the glorious Prize is mine!
While fish in streams, or birds delight in air,
Or in a coach and six the British Fair,
As long as Atalantis shall be read,
Or the small pillow grace a Lady's bed,
While visits shall be paid on solemn days,
When num'rous wax-lights in bright order blaze,
While nymphs take treats, or assignations give,
So long my honor, name, and praise shall live!
What Time would spare, from Steel receives its date,
And monuments, like men, submit to fate!
Steel could the labor of the Gods destroy,
And strike to dust th' imperial towers of Troy;
Steel could the works of mortal pride confound,
And hew triumphal arches to the ground.
What wonder then, fair nymph! thy hairs should feel,
The conq'ring force of unresisted steel?"

CANTO IV

But anxious cares the pensive nymph oppressed,
And secret passions labored in her breast.
Not youthful kings in battle seized alive,
Not scornful virgins who their charms survive,
Not ardent lovers robbed of all their bliss,

Not ancient ladies when refused a kiss,
Not tyrants fierce that unrepenting die,
Not Cynthia when her manteau's pinned awry,
E'er felt such rage, resentment, and despair,
As thou, sad Virgin! for thy ravished Hair.

  For, that sad moment, when the Sylphs withdrew
And Ariel weeping from Belinda flew,
Umbriel, a dusky, melancholy sprite,
As ever sullied the fair face of light,
Down to the central earth, his proper scene,
Repaired to search the gloomy Cave of Spleen.

  Swift on his sooty pinions flits the Gnome,
And in a vapor reached the dismal dome.
No cheerful breeze this sullen region knows,
The dreaded East is all the wind that blows.
Here in a grotto, sheltered close from air,
And screened in shades from day's detested glare,
She sighs forever on her pensive bed,
Pain at her side, and Megrim at her head.

  Two handmaids wait the throne: alike in place,
But diff'ring far in figure and in face.
Here stood Ill-nature like an ancient maid,
Her wrinkled form in black and white arrayed;
With store of prayers, for mornings, nights, and noons,
Her hand is filled; her bosom with lampoons.

  There Affectation, with a sickly mien,
Shows in her cheek the roses of eighteen,
Practised to lisp, and hang the head aside,
Faints into airs, and languishes with pride,
On the rich quilt sinks with becoming woe,
Wrapt in a gown, for sickness, and for show.
The fair one feels such maladies as these,
When each new night-dress gives a new disease.

  A constant Vapor o'er the palace flies;
Strange phantoms rising as the mists arise;
Dreadful, as hermit's dreams in haunted shades,
Or bright, as visions of expiring maids.
Now glaring fields, and snakes on rolling spires,
Pale specters, gaping tombs, and purple fires:
Now lakes of liquid gold, Elysian scenes,
And crystal domes, and angels in machines.

Unnumbered throngs on every side are seen,
Of bodies changed to various forms by Spleen.
Here living Tea-pots stand, one arm held out,
One bent; the handle this, and that the spout:
A Pipkin there, like Homer's Tripod walks;
Here sighs a Jar, and there a Goose-pie talks;
Men prove with child, as powerful fancy works,
And maids turned bottles, call aloud for corks.

Safe past the Gnome through this fantastic band,
A branch of healing Spleenwort in his hand.
Then thus addressed the power: "Hail, wayward Queen!
Who rule the sex to fifty from fifteen:
Parent of vapors and of female wit,
Who give th' hysteric or poetic fit,
On various tempers act by various ways,
Make some take physic, others scribble plays;
Who cause the proud their visits to delay,
And send the godly in a pet to pray.
A nymph there is, that all thy power disdains,
And thousands more in equal mirth maintains.
But oh! if e'er thy Gnome could spoil a grace,
Or raise a pimple on a beauteous face,
Like Citron-waters matrons' cheeks inflame,
Or change complexions at a losing game;
If e'er with airy horns I planted heads,
Or rumpled petticoats, or tumbled beds,
Or caus'd suspicion when no soul was rude,
Or discomposed the head-dress of a Prude,
Or e'er to costive lap-dog gave disease,
Which not the tears of brightest eyes could ease:
Hear me, and touch Belinda with chagrin,
That single act gives half the world the spleen."

The Goddess with a discontented air
Seems to reject him, though she grants his prayer.
A wondrous Bag with both her hands she binds,
Like that where once Ulysses held the winds;
There she collects the force of female lungs,
Sighs, sobs, and passions, and the war of tongues.
A Vial next she fills with fainting fears,
Soft sorrows, melting griefs, and flowing tears.
The Gnome rejoicing bears her gifts away,

Spreads his black wings, and slowly mounts to day.
   Sunk in Thalestris' arms the nymph he found,
Her eyes dejected and her hair unbound.
Full o'er their heads the swelling bag he rent,
And all the Furies issued at the vent.
Belinda burns with more than mortal ire,
And fierce Thalestris fans the rising fire,
"Oh wretched maid!" she spread her hands, and cried,
(While Hampton's echoes, "Wretched maid!" replied)
"Was it for this you took such constant care
The bodkin, comb, and essence to prepare?
For this your locks in paper durance bound,
For this with torturing irons wreathed around?
For this with fillets strained your tender head,
And bravely bore the double loads of lead?
Gods! shall the ravisher display your hair,
While the Fops envy, and the Ladies stare!
Honor forbid! at whose unrivaled shrine
Ease, pleasure, virtue, all our sex resign.
Methinks already I your tears survey,
Already hear the horrid things they say,
Already see you a degraded toast,
And all your honor in a whisper lost!
How shall I, then, your helpless fame defend?
'Twill then be infamy to seem your friend!
And shall this prize, th' inestimable prize,
Exposed through crystal to the gazing eyes,
And heightened by the diamond's circling rays,
On that rapacious hand forever blaze?
Sooner shall grass in Hyde-park Circus grow,
And wits take lodgings in the sound of Bow;
Sooner let earth, air, sea, to Chaos fall,
Men, monkeys, lap-dogs, parrots, perish all!"

   She said; then raging to Sir Plume repairs,
And bids her Beau demand the precious hairs:
(Sir Plume of amber snuff-box justly vain,
And the nice conduct of a clouded cane)
With earnest eyes, and round unthinking face,
He first the snuff-box opened, then the case,
And thus broke out—"My Lord, why, what the devil?
Z—ds! damn the lock! 'fore Gad, you must be civil!

Plague on't! 'tis past a jest—nay prithee, pox!
Give her the hair"—he spoke, and rapped his box.
   "It grieves me much" (replied the Peer again)
"Who speaks so well should ever speak in vain.
But by this Lock, this sacred Lock I swear,
(Which never more shall join its parted hair;
Which never more its honors shall renew,
Clipped from the lovely head where late it grew)
That while my nostrils draw the vital air,
This hand, which won it, shall for ever wear."
He spoke, and speaking, in proud triumph spread
The long-contended honors of her head.

   But Umbriel, hateful Gnome! forbears not so;
He breaks the Vial whence the sorrows flow.
Then see! the nymph in beauteous grief appears,
Her eyes half-languishing, half-drowned in tears;
On her heaved bosom hung her drooping head,
Which, with a sigh, she raised; and thus she said.
   "Forever cursed be this detested day,
Which snatched my best, my fav'rite curl away!
Happy! ah ten times happy had I been,
If Hampton-Court these eyes had never seen!
Yet am not I the first mistaken maid,
By love of Courts to numerous ills betrayed.
Oh had I rather un-admired remained
In some lone isle, or distant Northern land;
Where the gilt Chariot never marks the way,
Where none learn Ombre, none e'er taste Bohea!
There kept my charms concealed from mortal eye,
Like roses, that in deserts bloom and die.
What moved my mind with youthful Lords to roam?
Oh had I stayed, and said my prayers at home!
'Twas this, the morning omens seemed to tell,
Thrice from my trembling hand the patch-box fell;
The tott'ring China shook without a wind,
Nay, Poll sat mute, and Shock was most unkind!
A Sylph too warned me of the threats of fate,
In mystic visions, now believed too late!
See the poor remnants of these slighted hairs!
My hands shall rend what even thy rapine spares:
These in two sable ringlets taught to break,

Once gave new beauties to the snowy neck;
The sister-lock now sits uncouth, alone,
And in its fellow's fate foresees its own;
Uncurled it hangs, the fatal shears demands,
And tempts once more, thy sacrilegious hands.
Oh hadst thou, cruel! been content to seize
Hairs less in sight, or any hairs but these!"

CANTO V

She said: the pitying audience melt in tears.
But Fate and Jove had stopped the Baron's ears.
In vain Thalestris with reproach assails,
For who can move when fair Belinda fails?
Not half so fixed the Trojan could remain,
While Anna begged and Dido raged in vain.
Then grave Clarissa graceful waved her fan;
Silence ensued, and thus the nymph began.
    "Say why are Beauties praised and honored most,
The wise man's passion, and the vain man's toast?
Why decked with all that land and sea afford,
Why Angels called, and Angel-like adored?
Why round our coaches crowd the white-gloved Beaux,
Why bows the side-box from its inmost rows;
How vain are all these glories, all our pains,
Unless good sense preserve what beauty gains:
That men may say, when we the front-box grace:
'Behold the first in virtue as in face!'
Oh! if to dance all night, and dress all day,
Charmed the small-pox, or chased old-age away;
Who would not scorn what housewife's cares produce,
Or who would learn one earthly thing of use?
To patch, nay ogle, might become a Saint,
Nor could it sure be such a sin to paint.
But since, alas! frail beauty must decay,
Curled or uncurled, since Locks will turn to grey;
Since painted, or not painted, all shall fade,
And she who scorns a man, must die a maid;
What then remains but well our power to use,
And keep good-humor still whate'er we lose?
And trust me, dear! good-humor can prevail,
When airs, and flights, and screams, and scolding fail.
Beauties in vain their pretty eyes may roll;

Charms strike the sight, but merit wins the soul."
   So spoke the Dame, but no applause ensued;
Belinda frowned, Thalestris called her Prude.
"To arms, to arms!" the fierce Virago cries,
And swift as lightning to the combat flies.
All side in parties, and begin th' attack;
Fans clap, silks rustle, and tough whalebones crack;
Heroes' and Heroines' shouts confus'dly rise,
And bass and treble voices strike the skies.
No common weapons in their hands are found,
Like Gods they fight, nor dread a mortal wound.
   So when bold Homer makes the Gods engage,
And heavenly breasts with human passions rage;
'Gainst Pallas, Mars; Latona, Hermes arms;
And all Olympus rings with loud alarms:
Jove's thunder roars, heaven trembles all around,
Blue Neptune storms, the bellowing deeps resound:
Earth shakes her nodding towers, the ground gives way,
And the pale ghosts start at the flash of day!
   Triumphant Umbriel on a sconce's height
Clapped his glad wings, and sat to view the fight:
Propped on their bodkin spears, the Sprites survey
The growing combat, or assist the fray.
   While through the press enraged Thalestris flies,
And scatters death around from both her eyes,
A Beau and Witling perished in the throng,
One died in metaphor, and one in song.
"O cruel nymph! a living death I bear,"
Cried Dapperwit, and sunk beside his chair.
A mournful glance Sir Fopling upwards cast,
"Those eyes are made so killing"—was his last.
Thus on Mæander's flowery margin lies
Th' expiring Swan, and as he sings he dies.
   When bold Sir Plume had drawn Clarissa down,
Chloe stepped in, and killed him with a frown;
She smiled to see the doughty hero slain,
But, at her smile, the Beau revived again.
   Now Jove suspends his golden scales in air,
Weighs the Men's wits against the Lady's hair;
The doubtful beam long nods fom side to side;
At length the wits mount up, the hairs subside.

See, fierce Belinda on the Baron flies,
With more than usual lightning in her eyes:
Nor feared the Chief th' unequal fight to try,
Who sought no more than on his foe to die.
But this bold Lord with manly strength endued,
She with one finger and a thumb subdued:
Just where the breath of life his nostrils drew,
A charge of Snuff the wily virgin threw;
The Gnomes direct, to every atom just,
The pungent grains of titillating dust.
Sudden, with starting tears each eye o'erflows,
And the high dome re-echoes to his nose.

    "Now meet thy fate," incensed Belinda cried,
And drew a deadly bodkin from her side.
(The same, his ancient personage to deck,
Her great great grandsire wore about his neck,
In three seal-rings; which after, melted down,
Formed a vast buckle for his widow's gown:
Her infant grandame's whistle next it grew,
The bells she jingled, and the whistle blew;
Then in a bodkin graced her mother's hairs,
Which long she wore, and now Belinda wears.)

    "Boast not my fall" (he cried) "insulting foe!
Thou by some other shalt be laid as low;
Nor think, to die dejects my lofty mind:
All that I dread is leaving you behind!
Rather than so, ah let me still survive,
And burn in Cupid's flames—but burn alive."

    "Restore the Lock!" she cries; and all around
"Restore the Lock!" the vaulted roofs rebound.
Not fierce Othello in so loud a strain
Roared for the handkerchief that caused his pain.
But see how oft ambitious aims are crossed,
And chiefs contend till all the prize is lost!
The Lock, obtained with guilt, and kept with pain,
In every place is sought, but sought in vain:
With such a prize no mortal must be blest,
So heaven decrees! with heaven who can contest?

    Some thought it mounted to the Lunar sphere,
Since all things lost on earth are treasured there.
There Heroes' wits are kept in pond'rous vases,

And beaux' in snuff-boxes and tweezer-cases.
There broken vows and death-bed alms are found,
And lovers' hearts with ends of riband bound,
The courtier's promises, and sick man's prayers,
The smiles of harlots, and the tears of heirs,
Cages for gnats, and chains to yoke a flea,
Dried butterflies, and tomes of casuistry.

But trust the Muse—she saw it upward rise,
Though marked by none but quick, poetic eyes:
(So Rome's great founder to the heavens withdrew,
To Proculus alone confessed in view)
A sudden Star, it shot through liquid air,
And drew behind a radiant trail of hair.
Not Berenice's Locks first rose so bright,
The heavens bespangling with disheveled light.
The Sylphs behold it kindling as it flies,
And pleased pursue its progress through the skies.

This the Beau monde shall from the Mall survey,
And hail with music its propitious ray.
This the blest Lover shall for Venus take,
And send up vows from Rosamonda's lake.
This Partridge soon shall view in cloudless skies,
When next he looks through Galileo's eyes;
And hence th' egregious wizard shall foredoom
The fate of Louis, and the fall of Rome.

Then cease, bright Nymph! to mourn thy ravished hair,
Which adds new glory to the shining sphere!
Not all the tresses that fair head can boast,
Shall draw such envy as the Lock you lost.
For, after all the murders of your eye,
When, after millions slain, yourself shall die:
When those fair suns shall set, as set they must,
And all those tresses shall be laid in dust,
This Lock, the Muse shall consecrate to fame,
And 'midst the stars inscribe Belinda's name.

WILLIAM OLDYS
1696–1761

On a Fly Drinking Out of His Cup

Busy, curious, thirsty fly!
Drink with me and drink as I:
Freely welcome to my cup,
Couldst thou sip and sip it up:
Make the most of life you may,
Life is short and wears away.

Both alike are mine and thine
Hastening quick to their decline:
Thine's a summer, mine's no more,
Though repeated to threescore.
Threescore summers, when they're gone,
Will appear as short as one!

THOMAS GRAY
1716–1771

Elegy Written in a Country Churchyard

The curfew tolls the knell of parting day,
   The lowing herd wind slowly o'er the lea,
The plowman homeward plods his weary way,
   And leaves the world to darkness and to me.

Now fades the glimmering landscape on the sight,
   And all the air a solemn stillness holds,
Save where the beetle wheels his droning flight,
   And drowsy tinklings lull the distant folds;

Save that from yonder ivy-mantled tow'r
   The moping owl does to the moon complain
Of such as, wand'ring near her secret bow'r,
   Molest her ancient solitary reign.

Beneath those rugged elms, that yew-tree's shade,
　　Where heaves the turf in many a mould'ring heap.
Each in his narrow cell for ever laid,
　　The rude Forefathers of the hamlet sleep.

The breezy call of incense-breathing morn,
　　The swallow twitt'ring from the straw-built shed
The cock's shrill clarion, or the echoing horn,
　　No more shall rouse them from their lowly bed.

For them no more the blazing hearth shall burn,
　　Or busy housewife ply her evening care:
No children run to lisp their sire's return,
　　Or climb his knees the envied kiss to share.

Oft did the harvest to their sickle yield,
　　Their furrow oft the stubborn glebe has broke:
How jocund did they drive their team afield!
　　How bow'd the woods beneath their sturdy stroke!

Let not Ambition mock their useful toil,
　　Their homely joys, and destiny obscure;
Nor Grandeur hear with a disdainful smile
　　The short and simple annals of the poor.

The boast of heraldry, the pomp of pow'r,
　　And all that beauty, all that wealth e'er gave,
Awaits alike th' inevitable hour:
　　The paths of glory lead but to the grave.

Nor you, ye Proud, impute to these the fault,
　　If Memory o'er their tomb no trophies raise,
Where through the long-drawn aisle and fretted vault
　　The pealing anthem swells the note of praise.

Can storied urn or animated bust
　　Back to its mansion call the fleeting breath?
Can Honour's voice provoke the silent dust,
　　Or Flatt'ry soothe the dull cold ear of death?

Perhaps in this neglected spot is laid
　　Some heart once pregnant with celestial fire;

Hands, that the rod of empire might have sway'd,
  Or waked to ecstasy the living lyre.

But Knowledge to their eyes her ample page
  Rich with the spoils of time did ne'er unroll;
Chill Penury repress'd their noble rage,
  And froze the genial current of the soul.

Full many a gem of purest ray serene
  The dark unfathom'd caves of ocean bear:
Full many a flower is born to blush unseen,
  And waste its sweetness on the desert air.

Some village Hampden that with dauntless breast
  The little tyrant of his fields withstood,
Some mute inglorious Milton, here may rest,
  Some Cromwell guiltless of his country's blood.

Th' applause of list'ning senates to command,
  The threats of pain and ruin to despise,
To scatter plenty o'er a smiling land,
  And read their history in a nation's eyes,

Their lot forbade: nor circumscribed alone
  Their growing virtues, but their crimes confined;
Forbade to wade through slaughter to a throne,
  And shut the gates of mercy on mankind,

The struggling pangs of conscious truth to hide,
  To quench the blushes of ingenuous shame,
Or heap the shrine of Luxury and Pride
  With incense kindled at the Muse's flame.

Far from the madding crowd's ignoble strife
  Their sober wishes never learn'd to stray;
Along the cool sequester'd vale of life
  They kept the noiseless tenor of their way.

Yet ev'n these bones from insult to protect
  Some frail memorial still erected nigh,
With uncouth rhymes and shapeless sculpture deck'd
  Implores the passing tribute of a sigh.

Their name, their years, spelt by th' unletter'd muse,
    The place of fame and elegy supply:
And many a holy text around she strews,
    That teach the rustic moralist to die.

For who, to dumb Forgetfulness a prey,
    This pleasing anxious being e'er resign'd,
Left the warm precincts of the cheerful day,
    Nor cast one longing ling'ring look behind?

On some fond breast the parting soul relies,
    Some pious drops the closing eye requires;
E'en from the tomb the voice of Nature cries,
    E'en in our ashes live their wonted fires.

For thee, who, mindful of th' unhonour'd dead,
    Dost in these lines their artless tale relate;
If chance, by lonely contemplation led,
    Some kindred spirit shall inquire thy fate,

Haply some hoary-headed Swain may say,
    "Oft have we seen him at the peep of dawn
Brushing with hasty steps the dews away
    To meet the sun upon the upland lawn.

"There at the foot of yonder nodding beech
    That wreathes its old fantastic roots so high,
His listless length at noontide would be stretch,
    And pore upon the brook that babbles by.

"Hard by yon wood, now smiling as in scorn,
    Mutt'ring his wayward fancies he would rove,
Now drooping, woeful wan, like one forlorn,
    Or crazed with care, or cross'd in hopeless love.

"One morn I miss'd him on the custom'd hill,
    Along the heath and near his fav'rite tree;
Another came, nor yet beside the rill,
    Nor up the lawn, nor at the wood was he;

"The next with dirges due in sad array
  Slow through the church-way path we saw him borne.
Approach and read (for thou canst read) the lay
  Graved on the stone beneath yon aged thorn."

THE EPITAPH

Here rests his head upon the lap of Earth
  A Youth to Fortune and to Fame unknown.
Fair Science frown'd not on his humble birth,
  And Melancholy mark'd him for her own.

Large was his bounty, and his soul sincere,
  Heav'n did a recompense as largely send:
He gave to Mis'ry all he had, a tear,
  He gain'd from Heav'n ('twas all he wish'd) a friend.

No farther seek his merits to disclose,
  Or draw his frailties from their dread abode,
(There they alike in trembling hope repose,)
  The bosom of his Father and his God.

Ode on a Distant Prospect of Eton College

Ye distant spires, ye antique towers
  That crown the watery glade,
Where grateful Science still adores
  Her Henry's holy shade;
And ye, that from the stately brow
Of Windsor's heights th' expanse below
Of grove, of lawn, of mead survey,
Whose turf, whose shade, whose flowers among
Wanders the hoary Thames along
  His silver-winding way:

Ah happy hills! ah pleasing shade!
  Ah fields beloved in vain!
Where once my careless childhood stray'd,
  A stranger yet to pain!
I feel the gales that from ye blow
A momentary bliss bestow,
As waving fresh their gladsome wing
My weary soul they seem to soothe,

And, redolent of joy and youth,
　To breathe a second spring.

Say, Father Thames, for thou hast seen
　Full many a sprightly race
Disporting on thy margent green
　The paths of pleasure trace;
Who foremost now delight to cleave
With pliant arm, thy glassy wave?
The captive linnet which enthral?
What idle progeny succeed
To chase the rolling circle's speed,
　Or urge the flying ball?

While some on earnest business bent
　Their murmuring labours ply
'Gainst graver hours that bring constraint
　To sweeten liberty:
Some bold adventurers disdain
The limits of their little reign
And unknown regions dare descry:
Still as they run they look behind,
They hear a voice in every wind,
　And snatch a fearful joy.

Gay hope is theirs by fancy fed,
　Less pleasing when possest;
The tear forgot as soon as shed,
　The sunshine of the breast:
Theirs buxom health, of rosy hue,
Wild wit, invention ever new,
And lively cheer, of vigour born;
The thoughtless day, the easy night,
The spirits pure, the slumbers light
　That fly th' approach of morn.

Alas! regardless of their doom
　The little victims play;
No sense have they of ills to come,
　Nor care beyond to-day:
Yet see how all around 'em wait

The ministers of human fate
And black Misfortune's baleful train!
Ah show them where in ambush stand
To seize their prey, the murderous band!
   Ah, tell them they are men!

These shall the fury Passions tear
   The vultures of the mind,
Disdainful Anger, pallid Fear,
   And Shame that skulks behind;
Or pining Love shall waste their youth,
Or Jealousy with rankling tooth,
That inly gnaws the secret heart,
And Envy wan, and faded Care,
Grim-visaged comfortless Despair,
   And Sorrow's piercing dart.

Ambition this shall tempt to rise,
   Then whirl the wretch from high,
To bitter Scorn a sacrifice
   And grinning Infamy.
The stings of Falsehood those shall try
And hard Unkindness' alter'd eye,
That mocks the tear it forced to flow;
And keen Remorse with blood defiled,
And moody Madness laughing wild
   Amid severest woe.

Lo, in the vale of years beneath
   A griesly troop are seen,
The painful family of Death,
   More hideous than their queen:
This racks the joints, this fires the veins,
That every labouring sinew strains,
Those in the deeper vitals rage:
Lo! Poverty, to fill the band,
That numbs the soul with icy hand,
   And slow-consuming Age.

To each his sufferings: all are men,
   Condemn'd alike to groan;

The tender for another's pain,
  Th' unfeeling for his own.
Yet, ah! why should they know their fate.
Since sorrow never comes too late,
And happiness too swiftly flies?
Thought would destroy their paradise.
No more;—where ignorance is bliss
  'Tis folly to be wise.

WILLIAM COLLINS
1721–1759

Ode to Evening

If aught of oaten stop, or pastoral song,
May hope, chaste Eve, to soothe thy modest ear,
  Like thy own solemn springs,
  Thy springs, and dying gales,
O Nymph reserved, while now the bright-haired sun
Sits in yon western tent, whose cloudy skirts,
  With brede ethereal wove,
  O'erhang his wavy bed:
Now air is hushed, save where the weak-eyed bat
With short shrill shriek flits by on leathern wing;

  Or where the beetle winds
  His small but sullen horn,
As oft he rises midst the twilight path,
Against the pilgrim borne in heedless hum:
  Now teach me, maid composed,
  To breathe some softened strain,
Whose numbers, stealing through thy darkening vale,
May not unseemly with its stillness suit,
  As, musing slow, I hail
  Thy genial loved return.

For when thy folding-star arising shows
His paly circlet, at his warning lamp
  The fragrant Hours, and Elves

Who slept in flowers the day,
And many a Nymph who wreathes her brows with sedge,
And sheds the freshening dew, and, lovelier still,
    The pensive Pleasures sweet,
    Prepare thy shadowy car;
Then let me rove some wild and heathy scene;
Or find some ruin, midst its dreary dells,
    Whose walls more awful nod
    By thy religious gleams.
Or, if chill blustering winds, or driving rain,
Prevent my willing feet, be mine the hut,
    That, from the mountain's side,
    Views wilds, and swelling floods,
And hamlets brown, and dim-discovered spires;
And hears their simple bell, and marks o'er all
    Thy dewy fingers draw
    The gradual dusky veil.

While Spring shall pour his showers, as oft he wont,
And bathe thy breathing tresses, meekest Eve!
    While Summer loves to sport
    Beneath thy lingering light;
While sallow Autumn fills thy lap with leaves,
Or Winter, yelling through the troublous air,
    Affrights thy shrinking train,
    And rudely rends thy robes,
So long sure found beneath thy sylvan shed,
Shall Fancy, Friendship, Science, rose-lipped Health,
    Thy gentlest influence own,
    And hymn thy favourite name!

CHRISTOPHER SMART
1722–1770

A Song to David

O Thou, that sitt'st upon a throne,
With harp of high, majestic tone,
    To praise the King of kings:

And voice of heaven-ascending swell,
Which, while its deeper notes excel,
   Clear as a clarion rings;

To bless each valley, grove, and coast,
And charm the cherubs to the post
   Of gratitude in throngs;
To keep the days on Zion's Mount,
And send the Year to his account,
   With dances and with songs:

O servant of God's holiest charge,
The minister of praise at large,
   Which thou mayst now receive;
From thy blest mansion hail and hear,
From topmost eminence appear
   To this the wreath I weave.

Great, valiant, pious, good, and clean,
Sublime, contemplative, serene,
   Strong, constant, pleasant, wise!
Bright effluence of exceeding grace;
Best man! the swiftness and the race,
   The peril and the prize!

Great—from the lustre of his crown,
From Samuel's horn, and God's renown,
   Which is the people's voice;
For all the host, from rear to van,
Applauded and embraced the man—
   The man of God's own choice.

Valiant—the word, and up he rose:
The fight—he triumphed o'er the foes
   Whom God's just laws abhor;
And, armed in gallant faith, he took
Against the boaster, from the brook,
   The weapons of the war.

Pious—magnificent and grand,
'Twas he the famous temple plann'd,

(The seraph in his soul:)
Foremost to give the Lord his dues,
Foremost to bless the welcome news,
   And foremost to condole.

Good—from Jehudah's genuine vein,
From God's best nature, good in grain,
   His aspect and his heart:
To pity, to forgive, to save,
Witness En-gedi's conscious cave,
   And Shimei's blunted dart.

Clean—if perpetual prayer be pure,
And love, which could itself inure
   To fasting and to fear—
Clean in his gestures, hands and feet,
To smite the lyre, the dance complete,
   To play the sword and spear.

Sublime—invention ever young,
Of vast conception, tow'ring tongue,
   To God the eternal theme;
Notes from yon exaltations caught,
Unrivall'd royalty of thought,
   O'er meaner strains supreme.

Contemplative—on God to fix
His musings, and above the six
   The Sabbath-day he blessed;
'Twas then his thoughts self-conquest pruned,
And heavenly melancholy tuned,
   To bless and bear the rest.

Serene—to sow the seeds of peace,
Remembering, when he watched the fleece,
   How sweetly Kidron purled—
To further knowledge, silence vice,
And plant perpetual paradise,
   When God had calmed the world.

Strong—in the Lord, who could defy
Satan, and all his powers that lie

In sempiternal night;
And hell, and horror, and despair
Were as the lion and the bear
    To his undaunted might.

Constant—in love to God, THE TRUTH,
Age, manhood, infancy, and youth:
    To Jonathan his friend
Constant, beyond the verge of death;
And Ziba, and Mephibosheth,
    His endless fame attend.

Pleasant—and various as the year;
Man, soul, and angel without Peer,
    Priest, champion, sage, and boy;
In armour or in ephod clad,
His pomp, his piety was glad;
    Majestic was his joy.

Wise—in recovery from his fall,
Whence rose his eminence o'er all,
    Of all the most reviled;
The light of Israel in his ways,
Wise are his precepts, prayer, and praise,
    And counsel to his child.

His muse, bright angel of his verse,
Gives balm for all the thorns that pierce,
    For all the pangs that rage:
Blest light, still gaining on the gloom,
The more than Michal of his bloom,
    The Abishag of his age.

He sang of God—the mighty source
Of all things—the stupendous force
    On which all strength depends;
From Whose right arm, beneath Whose eyes,
All period, power, and enterprise
    Commences, reigns, and ends.

Angels—their ministry and meed,
Which to and fro with blessings speed,

Or with their citterns wait;
Where Michael, with his millions, bows,
Where dwells the seraph and his spouse,
   The cherub and her mate.

Of man—the semblance and effect
Of God and love—the saint elect
   For infinite applause—
To rule the land, and briny broad,
To be laborious in his laud,
   And heroes in his cause.

The world—the clustering spheres He made,
The glorious light, the soothing shade,
   Dale, champaign, grove, and hill;
The multitudinous abyss,
Where Secrecy remains in bliss,
   And Wisdom hides her skill.

Trees, plants, and flowers—of virtuous root;
Gem yielding blossom, yielding fruit,
   Choice gums and precious balm;
Bless ye the nosegay in the vale,
And with the sweetness of the gale
   Enrich the thankful psalm.

Of fowl—even every beak and wing
Which cheer the winter, hail the spring,
   That live in peace or prey;
They that make music, or that mock,
The quail, the brave domestic cock,
   The raven, swan, and jay.

Of fishes—every size and shape,
Which nature frames of light escape,
   Devouring man to shun:
The shells are in the wealthy deep,
The shoals upon the surface leap,
   And love the glancing sun.

Of beasts—the beaver plods his task;
While the sleek tigers roll and bask,

Nor yet the shades arouse;
Her cave the mining coney scoops;
Where o'er the mead the mountain stoops,
   The kids exult and browse.

Of gems—their virtue and their price,
Which, hid in earth from man's device,
   Their darts of lustre sheathe;
The jasper of the master's stamp,
The topaz blazing like a lamp,
   Among the mines beneath.

Blest was the tenderness he felt,
When to his graceful harp he knelt,
   And did for audience call;
When Satan with his hand he quelled,
And in serene suspense he held
   The frantic throes of Saul.

His furious foes no more maligned
As he such melody divined,
   And sense and soul detained;
Now striking strong, now soothing soft,
He sent the godly sounds aloft,
   Or in delight refrained.

When up to heaven his thoughts he piled
From fervent lips fair Michal smiled,
   As blush to blush she stood;
And chose herself the queen, and gave
Her utmost from her heart—"so brave,
   And plays his hymns so good."

The pillars of the Lord are seven,
Which stand from earth to topmost heaven;
   His wisdom drew the plan;
His Word accomplished the design,
From brightest gem to deepest mine,
   From CHRIST enthroned to Man.

Alpha, the cause of causes, first
In station, fountain, whence the burst

Of light and blaze of day;
Whence bold attempt, and brave advance,
Have motion, life, and ordinance,
    And heaven itself its stay.

Gamma supports the glorious arch
On which angelic legions march,
    And is with sapphires paved;
Thence the fleet clouds are sent adrift,
And thence the painted folds that lift
    The crimson veil, are waved.

Eta with living sculpture breathes,
With verdant carvings, flowery wreaths,
    Of never-wasting bloom;
In strong relief his goodly base
All instruments of labour grace,
    The trowel, spade, and loom.

Next Theta stands to the Supreme—
Who formed in number, sign, and scheme,
    The illustrious lights that are;
And one addressed his saffron robe,
And one, clad in a silver globe,
    Held rule with every star.

Iota's tuned to choral hymns
Of those that fly, while he that swims
    In thankful safety lurks;
And foot, and chapiter, and niche,
The various histories enrich
    Of God's recorded works.

Sigma presents the social droves
With him that solitary roves,
    And man of all the chief;
Fair on whose face, and stately frame,
Did God impress His hallowed name,
    For ocular belief.

OMEGA! GREATEST and the BEST,
Stands sacred to the day of rest,

For gratitude and thought;
Which blessed the world upon his pole,
And gave the universe his goal,
    And closed the infernal draught.

O DAVID, scholar of the Lord!
Such is thy science, whence reward,
    And infinite degree;
O strength, O sweetness, lasting ripe!
God's harp thy symbol, and thy type
    The lion and the bee!

There is but One who ne'er rebelled,
But One by passion unimpelled,
    By pleasures unenticed;
He from himself hath semblance sent,
Grand object of his own content,
    And saw the God in CHRIST.

Tell them, I AM, JEHOVAH said
To MOSES; while earth heard in dread,
    And, smitten to the heart,
At once above, beneath, around,
All Nature, without voice or sound,
    Replied, "O LORD, THOU ART."

Thou art—to give and to confirm,
For each his talent and his term;
    All flesh thy bounties share:
Thou shalt not call thy brother fool:
The porches of the Christian school
    Are meekness, peace, and prayer.

Open and naked of offence,
Man's made of mercy, soul, and sense:
    God armed the snail and wilk;
Be good to him that pulls thy plough:
Due food and care, due rest allow
    For her that yields thee milk.

Rise up before the hoary head,
And God's benign commandment dread,

Which says thou shalt not die:
"Not as I will, but as Thou wilt,"
Prayed He, whose conscience knew no guilt;
   With Whose blessed pattern vie.

Use all thy passions! love is thine,
And joy, and jealousy divine;
   Thine hope's eternal fort,
And care thy leisure to disturb
With fear concupiscence to curb,
   And rapture to transport.

Act simply, as occasion asks;
Put mellow wine in seasoned casks;
   Till not with ass and bull:
Remember thy baptismal bond;
Keep from commixtures foul and fond,
   Nor work thy flax with wool.

Distribute; pay the Lord His tithe,
And make the widow's heart-strings blithe;
   Resort with those that weep:
As you from all and each expect,
For all and each thy love direct,
   And render as you reap.

The slander and its bearer spurn,
And propagating praise sojourn,
   To make thy welcome last;
Turn from old Adam to the New:
By hope futurity pursue:
   Look upwards to the past.

Control thine eye, salute success,
Honour the wiser, happier bless,
   And for their neighbour feel:
Grutch not of mammon and his leaven,
Work emulation up to heaven
   By knowledge and by zeal.

O David, highest in the list
Of worthies, on God's ways insist,

The genuine word repeat!
Vain are the documents of men,
And vain the flourish of the pen
    That keeps the fool's conceit.

Praise above all—for praise prevails;
Heap up the measure, load the scales,
    And good to goodness add:
The generous soul her Saviour aids,
But peevish obloquy degrades;
    The Lord is great and glad.

For ADORATION all the ranks
Of Angels yield eternal thanks,
    And David in the midst:
With God's good poor, which, last and least
In man's esteem, Thou to Thy feast,
    O blessèd Bridegroom, bidst.

For ADORATION seasons change,
And order, truth, and beauty range,
    Adjust, attract, and fill:
The grass the polyanthus checks;
And polished porphyry reflects,
    By the descending rill.

Rich almonds colour to the prime
For ADORATION; tendrils climb,
    And fruit-trees pledge their gems;
And Ivis, with her gorgeous vest,
Builds for her eggs her cunning nest,
    And bell-flowers bow their stems.

With vinous syrup cedars spout;
From rocks pure honey gushing out,
    For ADORATION springs:
All scenes of painting crowd the map
Of nature; to the mermaid's pap
    The scalèd infant clings.

The spotted ounce and playsome cubs
Run rustling 'mong the flowering shrubs,

And lizards feed the moss;
For ADORATION beasts embark,
While waves upholding halcyon's ark
  No longer roar and toss.

While Israel sits beneath his fig,
With coral root and amber sprig
  The weaned adventurer sports;
Where to the palm the jasmine cleaves,
For ADORATION 'mong the leaves
  The gale his peace reports.

Increasing days their reign exalt,
Nor in the pink and mottled vault
  The opposing spirits tilt;
And by the coasting reader spied,
The silverlings and crusions glide
  For ADORATION gilt.

For ADORATION ripening canes,
And cocoa's purest milk detains
  The western pilgrim's staff;
Where rain in clasping boughs enclosed,
And vines with oranges disposed,
  Embower the social laugh.

Now labour his reward receives,
For ADORATION counts his sheaves,
  To peace, her bounteous prince;
The nect'rine his strong tint imbibes,
And apples of ten thousand tribes,
  And quick peculiar quince.

The wealthy crops of whitening rice
'Mongst thyine woods and groves of spice,
  For ADORATION grow;
And, marshalled in the fencèd land,
The peaches and pomegranates stand,
  Where wild carnations blow.

The laurels with the winter strive;
The crocus burnishes alive

Upon the snow-clad earth;
For ADORATION myrtles stay
To keep the garden from dismay,
    And bless the sight from dearth.

The pheasant shows his pompous neck;
And ermine, jealous of a speck,
    With fear eludes offence:
The sable, with his glossy pride,
For ADORATION is descried,
    Where frosts the waves condense.

The cheerful holly, pensive yew,
And holy thorn, their trim renew;
    The squirrel hoards his nuts;
All creatures batten o'er their stores,
And careful nature all her doors
    For ADORATION shuts.

For ADORATION, DAVID's Psalms
Lift up the heart to deeds of alms;
    And he, who kneels and chants,
Prevails his passions to control,
Finds meat and medicine to the soul,
    Which for translation pants.

For ADORATION, beyond match,
The scholar bullfinch aims to catch
    The soft flute's ivory touch;
And, careless, on the hazel spray
The daring redbreast keeps at bay
    The damsel's greedy clutch.

For ADORATION, in the skies,
The Lord's philosopher espies
    The dog, the ram, and rose;
The planet's ring, Orion's sword;
Nor is his greatness less adored
    In the vile worm that glows.

For ADORATION, on the strings
The western breezes work their wings,

The captive ear to soothe—
Hark! 'tis a voice—how still, and small—
That makes the cataracts to fall,
    Or bids the sea be smooth!

For ADORATION, incense comes
From bezoar, and Arabian gums,
    And from the civet's fur:
But as for prayer, or e'er it faints,
Far better is the breath of saints
    Than galbanum or myrrh.

For ADORATION, from the down
Of damsons to th' anana's crown,
    God sends to tempt the taste;
And while the luscious zest invites
The sense, that in the scene delights,
    Commands desire be chaste.

For ADORATION, all the paths
Of grace are open, all the baths,
    Of purity refresh;
And all the rays of glory beam
To deck the man of God's esteem,
    Who triumphs o'er the flesh.

For ADORATION, in the dome
Of CHRIST, the sparrows find a home;
    And on his olives perch;
The swallow also dwells with thee,
O man of GOD's humility,
    Within his Saviour's CHURCH.

Sweet is the dew that falls betimes,
And drops upon the leafy limes;
    Sweet, Hermon's fragrant air:
Sweet is the lily's silver bell,
And sweet the wakeful tapers' smell
    That watch for early prayer.

Sweet the young nurse, with love intense,
Which smiles o'er sleeping innocence;

Sweet when the lost arrive:
Sweet the musician's ardour beats,
While his vague mind's in quest of sweets,
   The choicest flowers to hive.

Sweeter, in all the strains of love,
The language of thy turtle-dove,
   Paired to thy swelling chord;
Sweeter, with every grace endued,
The glory of thy gratitude
   Respired unto the Lord.

Strong is the horse upon his speed;
Strong in pursuit the rapid glede,
   Which makes at once his game:
Strong the tall ostrich on the ground;
Strong through the turbulent profound
   Shoots Xiphias to his aim.

Strong is the lion—like a coal
His eyeball—like a bastion's mole
   His chest against the foes:
Strong the gier-eagle on his sail,
Strong against tide the enormous whale
   Emerges as he goes.

But stronger still in earth and air,
And in the sea, the man of prayer,
   And far beneath the tide:
And in the seat to faith assigned,
Where ask is have, where seek is find,
   Where knock is open wide.

Beauteous the fleet before the gale;
Beauteous the multitudes in mail,
   Ranked arms, and crested heads;
Beauteous the garden's umbrage mild,
Walk, water, meditated wild,
   And all the bloomy beds.

Beauteous the moon full on the lawn;
And beauteous when the veil's withdrawn,

The virgin to her spouse:
Beauteous the temple, decked and filled,
When to the heaven of heavens they build
Their heart-directed vows.

Beauteous, yea beauteous more than these,
The Shepherd King upon his knees,
    For his momentous trust;
With wish of infinite conceit,
For man, beast, mute, the small and great,
    And prostrate dust to dust.

Precious the bounteous widow's mite;
And precious, for extreme delight,
    The largess from the churl:
Precious the ruby's blushing blaze,
And alba's blest imperial rays,
    And pure cerulean pearl.

Precious the penitential tear;
And precious is the sigh sincere;
    Acceptable to God:
And precious are the winning flowers,
In gladsome Israel's feast of bowers,
    Bound on the hallowed sod.

More precious that diviner part
Of David, even the Lord's own heart,
    Great, beautiful, and new;
In all things where it was intent,
In all extremes, in each event,
    Proof—answering true to true.

Glorious the sun in mid career;
Glorious th' assembled fires appear;
    Glorious the comet's train:
Glorious the trumpet and alarm;
Glorious th' Almighty's stretched-out arm;
    Glorious th' enraptured main:

Glorious the northern lights a-stream;
Glorious the song, when God's the theme;

Glorious the thunder's roar:
Glorious Hosannah from the den;
Glorious the catholic Amen;
   Glorious the martyr's gore:

Glorious,—more glorious, is the crown
Of Him that brought salvation down,
   By meekness called thy Son:
Thou that stupendous truth believed;—
And now the matchless deed's achieved,
DETERMINED, DARED, and DONE.

OLIVER GOLDSMITH
1728–1774

Woman

When lovely woman stoops to folly,
   And finds too late that men betray,
What charm can soothe her melancholy?
   What art can wash her tears away?

The only art her guilt to cover,
   To hide her shame from ev'ry eye,
To give repentance to her lover,
   And wring his bosom is—to die.

The Deserted Village

Sweet Auburn! loveliest village of the plain,
Where health and plenty cheered the laboring swain,
Where smiling spring its earliest visit paid,
And parting summer's lingering blooms delayed;
Dear lovely bowers of innocence and ease,
Seats of my youth, when every sport could please,
How often have I loitered o'er thy green,
Where humble happiness endeared each scene!
How often have I paused on every charm,
The sheltered cot, the cultivated farm,
The never-failing brook, the busy mill,

The decent church that topped the neighboring hill,
The hawthorn bush, with seats beneath the shade,
For talking age and whispering lovers made!
How often have I blessed the coming day,
When toil remitting lent its turn to play,
And all the village train, from labor free,
Led up their sports beneath the spreading tree;
While many a pastime circled in the shade,
The young contending as the old surveyed;
And many a gambol frolicked o'er the ground,
And sleights of art and feats of strength went round;
And still, as each repeated pleasure tired,
Succeeding sports and mirthful hand inspired;
The dancing pair that simply sought renown,
By holding out to tire each other down;
The swain mistrustless of his smutted face,
While secret laughter tittered round the place;
The bashful virgin's sidelong looks of love,
The matron's glance that would those looks reprove:
These were thy charms, sweet village! sports like these,
With sweet succession taught even toil to please;
These round thy bowers their cheerful influence shed;
These were thy charms—but all these charms are fled.

Sweet smiling village, loveliest of the lawn,
Thy sports are fled and all thy charms withdrawn;
Amidst thy bowers the tyrant's hand is seen,
And desolation saddens all thy green;
One only master grasps the whole domain,
And half a tillage stints thy smiling plain;
No more thy glassy brook reflects the day,
But choked with sedges works its weedy way;
Along thy glades, a solitary guest,
The hollow-sounding bittern guards its nest;
Amidst thy desert walks the lapwing flies,
And tires their echoes with unvaried cries.
Sunk are thy bowers in shapeless ruin all,
And the long grass o'ertops the moldering wall;
And, trembling, shrinking from the spoiler's hand,
Far, far away, thy children leave the land.

Ill fares the land, to hastening ills a prey,
Where wealth accumulates and men decay;

Princes and lords may flourish or may fade;
A breath can make them as a breath has made:
But a bold peasantry, their country's pride,
When once destroyed, can never be supplied.

A time there was, ere England's griefs began,
When every rood of ground maintained its man;
For him light labor spread her wholesome store,
Just gave what life required, but gave no more:
His best companions, innocence and health;
And his best riches, ignorance of wealth.

But times are altered; trade's unfeeling train
Usurp the land, and dispossess the swain;
Along the lawn, where scattered hamlets rose,
Unwieldy wealth and cumbrous pomp repose;
And every want to opulence allied,
And every pang that folly pays to pride.
Those gentle hours that plenty bade to bloom,
Those calm desires that asked but little room,
Those helpful sports that graced the peaceful scene,
Lived in each look, and brightened all the green—
These, far departing, seek a kinder shore,
And rural mirth and manners are no more.

Sweet Auburn! parent of the blissful hour,
Thy glades forlorn confess the tyrant's power.
Here, as I take my solitary rounds
Amidst thy tangling walks and ruined grounds,
And, many a year elapsed, return to view
Where once the cottage stood, the hawthorn grew,
Remembrance wakes with all her busy train,
Swells at my breast, and turns the past to pain.

In all my wanderings round this world of care,
In all my griefs—and God has given my share—
I still had hopes, my latest hours to crown,
Amidst these humble bowers to lay me down;
To husband out life's taper at the close,
And keep the flame from wasting by repose.
I still had hopes, for pride attends us still,
Amidst the swains to show my book-learned skill,
Around my fire an evening group to draw,
And tell of all I felt, and all I saw;
And, as a hare whom hounds and horns pursue,

Pants to the place from whence at first she flew,
I still had hopes, my long vexations past,
Here to return—and die at home at last.

O blessed retirement, friend to life's decline,
Retreats from care, that never must be mine,
How happy he who crowns in shades like these
A youth of labor with an age of ease;
Who quits a world where strong temptations try,
And, since 'tis hard to combat, learns to fly!
For him no wretches, born to work and weep,
Explore the mine, or tempt the dangerous deep;
No surly porter stands in guilty state,
To spurn imploring famine from the gate;
But on he moves to meet his latter end,
Angels around befriending virtue's friend;
Bends to the grave with unperceived decay,
While resignation gently slopes the way;
And, all his prospects brightening to the last,
His heaven commences ere the world be past.

Sweet was the sound, when oft at evening's close
Up yonder hill the village murmur rose;
There, as I passed with careless steps and slow,
The mingling notes came softened from below;
The swain responsive as the milkmaid sung,
The sober herd that lowed to meet their young,
The noisy geese that gabbled o'er the pool,
The playful children just let loose from school,
The watch-dog's voice that bayed the whispering wind,
And the loud laugh that spoke the vacant mind:
These all in sweet confusion sought the shade,
And filled each pause the nightingale had made.
But now the sounds of population fail,
No cheerful murmurs fluctuate in the gale,
No busy steps the grass-grown footway tread,
For all the bloomy flush of life is fled;
All but yon widowed, solitary thing,
That feebly bends beside the plashy spring;
She, wretched matron, forced in age, for bread,
To strip the brook with mantling cresses spread,
To pick her wintry fagot from the thorn,
To seek her nightly shed, and weep till morn—

She only left of all the harmless train,
The sad historian of the pensive plain.

  Near yonder copse, where once the garden smiled,
And still where many a garden flower grows wild,
There, where a few torn shrubs the place disclose,
The village preacher's modest mansion rose.
A man he was to all the country dear,
And passing rich with forty pounds a year;
Remote from towns he ran his godly race,
Nor e'er had changed, nor wished to change his place;
Unpractised he to fawn, or seek for power,
By doctrines fashioned to the varying hour;
Far other aims his heart had learned to prize,
More skilled to raise the wretched than to rise.
His house was known to all the vagrant train;
He chid their wanderings, but relieved their pain;
The long-remembered beggar was his guest,
Whose beard descending swept his aged breast;
The ruined spendthrift, now no longer proud,
Claimed kindred there, and had his claims allowed;
The broken soldier, kindly bade to stay,
Sat by his fire and talked the night away;
Wept o'er his wounds, or, tales of sorrow done,
Shouldered his crutch and showed how fields were won.
Pleased with his guests, the good man learned to glow,
And quite forgot their vices in their woe;
Careless their merits or their faults to scan,
His pity gave ere charity began.

  Thus to relieve the wretched was his pride,
And e'en his failings leaned to virtue's side;
But in his duty prompt at every call,
He watched and wept, he prayed and felt for all:
And, as a bird each fond endearment tries
To tempt its new-fledged offspring to the skies,
He tried each art, reproved each dull delay,
Allured to brighter worlds, and led the way.

  Beside the bed where parting life was laid,
And sorrow, guilt, and pain by turns dismayed,
The reverend champion stood. At his control
Despair and anguish fled the struggling soul;
Comfort came down the trembling wretch to raise,

And his last faltering accents whispered praise.
　　At church, with meek and unaffected grace,
His looks adorned the venerable place;
Truth from his lips prevailed with double sway,
And fools who came to scoff remained to pray.
The service past, around the pious man,
With steady zeal, each honest rustic ran;
Even children followed, with endearing wile,
And plucked his gown, to share the good man's smile.
His ready smile a parent's warmth expressed,
Their welfare pleased him and their cares distressed;
To them his heart, his love, his griefs were given,
But all his serious thoughts had rest in Heaven.
As some tall cliff, that lifts its awful form,
Swells from the vale, and midway leaves the storm,
Though round its breast the rolling clouds are spread,
Eternal sunshine settles on its head.

　　Beside yon straggling fence that skirts the way,
With blossomed furze unprofitably gay,
There, in his noisy mansion, skilled to rule,
The village master taught his little school.
A man severe he was, and stern to view;
I knew him well, and every truant knew;
Well had the boding tremblers learned to trace
The day's disasters in his morning face;
Full well they laughed with counterfeited glee
At all his jokes, for many a joke had he;
Full well the busy whisper, circling round,
Conveyed the dismal tidings when he frowned;
Yet he was kind, or, if severe in aught,
The love he bore to learning was in fault;
The village all declared how much he knew;
'Twas certain he could write, and cipher too;
Lands he could measure, terms and tides presage,
And even the story ran that he could gauge:
In arguing, too, the parson owned his skill,
For even though vanquished, he could argue still;
While words of learned length and thundering sound
Amazed the gazing rustics ranged around;
And still they gazed, and still the wonder grew
That one small head could carry all he knew.

But past is all his fame. The very spot
Where many a time he triumphed is forgot.
Near yonder thorn that lifts its head on high,
Where once the sign-post caught the passing eye,
Low lies that house where nut-brown draughts inspired,
Where graybeard mirth and smiling toil retired,
Where village statesmen talked with looks profound,
And news much older than their ale went round.
Imagination fondly stoops to trace
The parlor splendors of that festive place;
The whitewashed wall, the nicely sanded floor,
The varnished clock that clicked behind the door;
The chest contrived a double debt to pay,
A bed by night, a chest of drawers by day;
The pictures placed for ornament and use,
The twelve good rules, the royal game of goose;
The hearth, except when winter chilled the day,
With aspen boughs and flowers and fennel gay;
While broken teacups, wisely kept for show,
Ranged o'er the chimney, glistened in a row.

   Vain transitory splendors! Could not all
Reprieve the tottering mansion from its fall?
Obscure it sinks, nor shall it more impart
An hour's importance to the poor man's heart;
Thither no more the peasant shall repair
To sweet oblivion of his daily care;
No more the farmer's news, the barber's tale,
No more the woodman's ballad shall prevail;
No more the smith his dusky brow shall clear,
Relax his ponderous strength, and lean to hear;
The host himself no longer shall be found
Careful to see the mantling bliss go round;
Nor the coy maid, half willing to be pressed,
Shall kiss the cup to pass it to the rest.

   Yes! let the rich deride, the proud disdain,
These simple blessings of the lowly train;
To me more dear, congenial to my heart,
One native charm, than all the gloss of art;
Spontaneous joys, where nature has its play,
The soul adopts, and owns their first-born sway;
Lightly they frolic o'er the vacant mind,

Unenvied, unmolested, unconfined.
But the long pomp, the midnight masquerade,
With all the freaks of wanton wealth arrayed,—
In these, ere triflers half their wish obtain,
The toiling pleasure sickens into pain;
And e'en while fashion's brightest arts decoy,
The heart distrusting asks if this be joy.

Ye friends to truth, ye statesmen, who survey
The rich man's joys increase, the poor's decay,
'Tis yours to judge how wide the limits stand
Between a splendid and an happy land.
Proud swells the tide with loads of freighted ore,
And shouting Folly hails them from her shore;
Hoards even beyond the miser's wish abound,
And rich men flock from all the world around.
Yet count our gains: this wealth is but a name
That leaves our useful products still the same.
Not so the loss: the man of wealth and pride
Takes up a space that many poor supplied;
Space for his lake, his park's extended bounds,
Space for his horses, equipage, and hounds;
The robe that wraps his limbs in silken sloth
Has robbed the neighboring fields of half their growth;
His seat, where solitary sports are seen,
Indignant spurns the cottage from the green;
Around the world each needful product flies,
For all the luxuries the world supplies;
While thus the land, adorned for pleasure all,
In barren splendor feebly waits the fall.

As some fair female, unadorned and plain,
Secure to please while youth confirms her reign,
Slights every borrowed charm that dress supplies,
Nor shares with art the triumph of her eyes;
But when those charms are past, for charms are frail,
When time advances and when lovers fail,
She then shines forth, solicitous to bless,
In all the glaring impotence of dress:
Thus fares the land, by luxury betrayed,
In nature's simplest charms at first arrayed;
But verging to decline, its splendors rise,
Its vistas strike, its palaces surprise;

While, scourged by famine from the smiling land,
The mournful peasant leads his humble band;
And while he sinks, without one arm to save,
The country blooms—a garden and a grave.

　Where then, ah where, shall poverty reside,
To 'scape the pressure of contiguous pride?
If to some common's fenceless limits strayed,
He drives his flock to pick the scanty blade,
Those fenceless fields the sons of wealth divide,
And even the bare-worn common is denied.

　If to the city sped—what waits him there?
To see profusion that he must not share;
To see ten thousand baneful arts combined
To pamper luxury, and thin mankind;
To see those joys the sons of pleasure know
Extorted from his fellow-creature's woe.
Here while the courtier glitters in brocade,
There the pale artist plies the sickly trade;
Here while the proud their long-drawn pomps display,
There the black gibbet glooms beside the way;
The dome where Pleasure holds her midnight reign,
Here, richly decked, admits the gorgeous train;
Tumultuous grandeur crowds the blazing square,
The rattling chariots clash, the torches glare.
Sure scenes like these no troubles e'er annoy!
Sure these denote one universal joy!
Are these thy serious thoughts?—Ah, turn thine eyes
Where the poor houseless shivering female lies.
She once, perhaps, in village plenty blessed,
Has wept at tales of innocence distressed;
Her modest looks the cottage might adorn,
Sweet as the primrose peeps beneath the thorn;
Now lost to all—her friends, her virtue fled—
Near her betrayer's door she lays her head,
And, pinched with cold, and shrinking from the shower,
With heavy heart deplores that luckless hour,
When idly first, ambitious of the town,
She left her wheel and robes of country brown.

　Do thine, sweet Auburn, thine, the loveliest train—
Do thy fair tribes participate her pain?
E'en now, perhaps, by cold and hunger led,

At proud men's doors they ask a little bread.
    Ah, no! To distant climes, a dreary scene,
Where half the convex world intrudes between,
Through torrid tracts with fainting steps they go,
Where wild Altama murmurs to their woe.
Far different there from all that charmed before,
The various terrors of that horrid shore;
Those blazing suns that dart a downward ray,
And fiercely shed intolerable day;
Those matted woods where birds forget to sing,
But silent bats in drowsy clusters cling;
Those poisonous fields with rank luxuriance crowned,
Where the dark scorpion gathers death around;
Where at each step the stranger fears to wake
The rattling terrors of the vengeful snake;
Where crouching tigers wait their hapless prey,
And savage men more murderous still than they;
While oft in whirls the mad tornado flies,
Mingling the ravaged landscape with the skies.
Far different these from every former scene,
The cooling brook, the grassy-vested green,
The breezy covert of the warbling grove,
That only sheltered thefts of harmless love.
    Good Heaven! what sorrows gloomed that parting day
That called them from their native walks away;
When the poor exiles, every pleasure past,
Hung round their bowers, and fondly looked their last,
And took a long farewell, and wished in vain
For seats like these beyond the western main;
And, shuddering still to face the distant deep,
Returned and wept, and still returned to weep.
The good old sire the first prepared to go
To new-found worlds, and wept for others' woe;
But for himself, in conscious virtue brave,
He only wished for worlds beyond the grave.
His lovely daughter, lovelier in her tears,
The fond companion of his helpless years,
Silent went next, neglectful of her charms,
And left a lover's for a father's arms.
With louder plaints the mother spoke her woes,
And blessed the cot where every pleasure rose,

And kissed her thoughtless babes with many a tear,
And clasped them close, in sorrow doubly dear;
Whilst her fond husband strove to lend relief
In all the silent manliness of grief.

O Luxury! thou cursed by Heaven's decree,
How ill exchanged are things like these for thee!
How do thy potions, with insidious joy,
Diffuse their pleasures only to destroy!
Kingdoms by thee, to sickly greatness grown,
Boast of a florid vigor not their own:
At every draught more large and large they grow,
A bloated mass of rank, unwieldy woe;
Till, sapped their strength, and every part unsound,
Down, down they sink, and spread a ruin round.
E'en now the devastation is begun.
And half the business of destruction done;

E'en now, methinks, as pondering here I stand,
I see the rural virtues leave the land:
Down where yon anchoring vessel spreads the sail,
That idly waiting flaps with every gale,
Downward they move, a melancholy band,
Pass from the shore, and darken all the strand.
Contented Toil, and hospitable Care,
And kind connubial Tenderness are there;
And Piety with wishes placed above,
And steady Loyalty, and faithful Love.
And thou, sweet Poetry, thou loveliest maid,
Still first to fly where sensual joys invade,
Unfit, in these degenerate times of shame,
To catch the heart, or strike for honest fame;
Dear charming nymph, neglected and decried,
My shame in crowds, my solitary pride;
Thou source of all my bliss and all my woe,
That found'st me poor at first, and keep'st me so;
Thou guide by which the nobler arts excel,
Thou nurse of every virtue, fare thee well!
Farewell, and O! where'er thy voice be tried,
On Torno's cliffs, or Pambamarca's side,
Whether where equinoctial fervors glow,
Or winter wraps the polar world in snow,
Still let thy voice, prevailing over time,

Redress the rigors of the inclement clime;
Aid slighted truth with thy persuasive train;
Teach erring man to spurn the rage of gain;
Teach him, that states of native strength possessed,
Though very poor, may still be very blessed;
That trade's proud empire hastes to swift decay,
As ocean sweeps the labored mole away;
While self-dependent power can time defy,
As rocks resist the billows and the sky.

WILLIAM COWPER
1731–1800

Light Shining Out of Darkness

God moves in a mysterious way,
   His wonders to perform;
He plants his footsteps in the sea,
   And rides upon the storm.

Deep in unfathomable mines
   Of never failing skill,
He treasures up his bright designs,
   And works his sovereign will.

Ye fearful saints fresh courage take;
   The clouds ye so much dread
Are big with mercy, and shall break
   In blessings on your head.

Judge not the Lord by feeble sense,
   But trust him for his grace;
Behind a frowning providence,
   He hides a smiling face.

His purposes will ripen fast,
   Unfolding every hour:
The bud may have a bitter taste,
   But sweet will be the flower.

Blind unbelief is sure to err,
    And scan his work in vain;
God is his own interpreter,
    And he will make it plain.

THOMAS CHATTERTON
1752–1770

O Sing unto My Roundelay

O sing unto my roundelay,
O drop the briny tear with me;
Dance no more at holyday,
Like a running river be:
    My love is dead,
        Gone to his death-bed
All under the willow-tree.

Black his cryne as the winter night,
White his rode as the summer snow,
Red his face as the morning light,
Cold he lies in the grave below:
    My love is dead,
        Gone to his death-bed
All under the willow-tree.

Sweet his tongue as the throstle's note,
Quick in dance as thought can be,
Deft his tabor, cudgel stout;
O he lies by the willow-tree!
    My love is dead,
        Gone to his death-bed
All under the willow-tree.

Hark! the raven flaps his wing
In the brier'd dell below;
Hark! the death-owl loud doth sing
To the nightmares, as they go:
    My love is dead,

Gone to his death-bed
All under the willow-tree.

See! the white moon shines on high;
Whiter is my true-love's shroud:
Whiter than the morning sky,
Whiter than the evening cloud:
    My love is dead,
      Gone to his death-bed
All under the willow-tree.

Here upon my true-love's grave
Shall the barren flowers be laid;
Not one holy saint to save
All the coldness of a maid:
    My love is dead,
      Gone to his death-bed
All under the willow-tree.

With my hands I'll dent the briers
Round his holy corse to gre:
Ouph and fairy, light your fires,
Here my body still shall be:
    My love is dead,
      Gone to his death-bed
All under the willow-tree.

Come, with acorn-cup and thorn,
Drain my heartès blood away;
Life and all its good I scorn,
Dance by night, or feast by day:
    My love is dead,
      Gone to his death-bed
All under the willow-tree.

WILLIAM BLAKE
1757–1827

Reeds of Innocence

Piping down the valleys wild,
   Piping songs of pleasant glee,
On a cloud I saw a child,
   And he laughing said to me:

"Pipe a song about a Lamb!"
   So I piped with merry cheer.
"Piper, pipe that song again;"
   So I piped: he wept to hear.

"Drop thy pipe, thy happy pipe;
   Sing thy songs of happy cheer!"
So I sung the same again,
   While he wept with joy to hear.

"Piper, sit thee down and write
   In a book that all may read."
So he vanish'd from my sight;
   And I pluck'd a hollow reed,

And I made a rural pen,
   And I stain'd the water clear,
And I wrote my happy songs
   Every child may joy to hear.

The Lamb

  Little Lamb, who made thee?
  Dost thou know who made thee?
Gave thee life, and bid thee feed,
By the stream and o'er the mead;
Gave thee clothing of delight,
Softest clothing, woolly, bright;
Gave thee such a tender voice,
Making all the vales rejoice?
Little Lamb, who made thee?
Dost thou know who made thee?

Little Lamb, I'll tell thee,
Little Lamb, I'll tell thee:
He is callèd by thy name,
For He calls Himself a Lamb.
He is meek, and He is mild;
He became a little child.
I a child, and thou a lamb,
We are callèd by His name.
Little Lamb, God bless thee!
Little Lamb, God bless thee!

Auguries of Innocence

To see a World in a grain of sand,
And a Heaven in a wild flower,
Hold Infinity in the palm of your hand,
And Eternity in an hour.
A robin redbreast in a cage
Puts all Heaven in a rage.
A dove-house fill'd with doves and pigeons
Shudders Hell thro' all its regions.
A dog starv'd at his master's gate
Predicts the ruin of the State.
A horse misus'd upon the road
Calls to Heaven for human blood.
Each outcry of the hunted hare
A fibre from the brain does tear.
A skylark wounded in the wing,
A cherubim does cease to sing.
The game-cock clipt and arm'd for fight
Does the rising sun affright.
Every wolf's and lion's howl
Raises from Hell a Human soul.
The wild deer, wandering here and there,
Keeps the Human soul from care.
The lamb misus'd breeds public strife,
And yet forgives the butcher's knife.
The bat that flits at close of eve
Has left the brain that won't believe.
The owl that calls upon the night
Speaks the unbeliever's fright.
He who shall hurt the little wren

Shall never be belov'd by men.
He who the ox to wrath has mov'd
Shall never be by woman lov'd.
The wanton boy that kills the fly
Shall feel the spider's enmity.
He who torments the chafer's sprite
Weaves a bower in endless night.
The caterpillar on the leaf
Repeats to thee thy mother's grief.
Kill not the moth nor butterfly,
For the Last Judgment draweth nigh.
He who shall train the horse to war
Shall never pass the polar bar.
The beggar's dog and widow's cat,
Feed them, and thou wilt grow fat.
The gnat that sings his summer's song
Poison gets from Slander's tongue.
The poison of the snake and newt
Is the sweat of Envy's foot.
The poison of the honey-bee
Is the artist's jealousy.
The prince's robes and beggar's rags
Are toadstools on the miser's bags.
A truth that's told with bad intent
Beats all the lies you can invent.
It is right it should be so;
Man was made for joy and woe;
And when this we rightly know,
Thro' the world we safely go.
Joy and woe are woven fine,
A clothing for the soul divine;
Under every grief and pine
Runs a joy with silken twine.
The babe is more than swaddling-bands;
Throughout all these human lands
Tools were made, and born were hands,
Every farmer understands.
Every tear from every eye
Becomes a babe in Eternity;
This is caught by Females bright,
And return'd to its own delight.

The bleat, the bark, bellow, and roar
Are waves that beat on Heaven's shore.
The babe that weeps the rod beneath
Writes revenge in realms of death.
The beggar's rags, fluttering in air,
Does to rags the heavens tear.
The soldier, arm'd with sword and gun,
Palsied strikes the summer's sun.
The poor man's farthing is worth more
Than all the gold on Afric's shore.
One mite wrung from the labourer's hands
Shall buy and sell the miser's lands:
Or, if protected from on high,
Does that whole nation sell and buy.
He who mocks the infant's faith
Shall be mock'd in Age and Death.
He who shall teach the child to doubt
The rotting grave shall ne'er get out.
He who respects the infant's faith
Triumphs over Hell and Death.
The child's toys and the old man's reasons
Are the fruits of the two seasons.
The questioner, who sits so sly,
Shall never know how to reply.
He who replies to words of Doubt
Doth put the light of knowledge out.
The strongest poison ever known
Came from Caesar's laurel crown.
Nought can deform the human race
Like to the armour's iron brace.
When gold and gems adorn the plough
To peaceful arts shall Envy bow.
A riddle, or the cricket's cry,
Is to Doubt a fit reply.
The emmet's inch and eagle's mile
Make lame Philosophy to smile.
He who doubts from what he sees
Will ne'er believe, do what you please.
If the Sun and Moon should doubt,
They'd immediately go out.
To be in a passion you good may do,

But no good if a passion is in you.
The whore and gambler, by the state
Licensed, build that nation's fate.
The harlot's cry from street to street
Shall weave Old England's winding-sheet.
The winner's shout, the loser's curse,
Dance before dead England's hearse.
Every night and every morn
Some to misery are born.
Every morn and every night
Some are born to sweet delight.
Some are born to sweet delight,
Some are born to endless night.
We are led to believe a lie
When we see not thro' the eye,
Which was born in a night, to perish in a night,
When the Soul slept in beams of light.
God appears, and God is Light,
To those poor souls who dwell in Night;
But does a Human Form display
To those who dwell in realms of Day.

I Saw a Chapel All of Gold

I saw a Chapel all of gold
That none did dare to enter in,
And many weeping stood without,
Weeping, mourning, worshipping.

I saw a Serpent rise between
The white pillars of the door,
And he forc'd and forc'd and forc'd;
Down the golden hinges tore,

And along the pavement sweet,
Set with pearls and rubies bright,
All his shining length he drew,
Till upon the altar white

Vomiting his poison out
On the Bread and on the Wine.
So I turned into a sty,
And laid me down among the swine.

The Angel

I asked a thief to steal me a peach:
He turn'd up his eyes.
I ask'd a lithe lady to lie her down:
Holy and meek she cries.

As soon as I went an angel came:
He wink'd at the thief
And smil'd at the dame,
And without one word spoke
Had a peach from the tree,
And 'twixt earnest and joke
Enjoy'd the Lady.

The Scoffers

Mock on, mock on, Voltaire, Rousseau,
    Mock on, mock on; 'tis all in vain;
You throw the sand against the wind
    And the wind blows it back again.

And every sand becomes a gem
    Reflected in the beams divine;
Blown back, they blind the mocking eye,
    But still in Israel's paths they shine.

The atoms of Democritus
    And Newton's particles of light
Are sands upon the Red Sea shore,
    Where Israel's tents do shine so bright.

Song

How sweet I roam'd from field to field
And tasted all the summer's pride,
Till I the Prince of Love beheld
Who in the sunny beams did glide!

He show'd me lilies for my hair,
And blushing roses for my brow;
He led me through his gardens fair
Where all his golden pleasures grow.

With sweet May dews my wings were wet,
And Phoebus fir'd my vocal rage;
He caught me in his silken net,
And shut me in his golden cage.

He loves to sit and hear me sing,
Then, laughing, sports and plays with me;
Then stretches out my golden wing,
And mocks my loss of liberty.

A Poison Tree

I was angry with my friend,
I told my wrath, my wrath did end;
I was angry with my foe,
I told it not, my wrath did grow.

And I water'd it in fears,
Night and morning with my tears;
And I sunned it with smiles,
And with soft deceitful wiles.

And it grew both day and night,
Till it bore an apple bright;
And my foe beheld it shine,
And he knew that it was mine,

And into my garden stole
When the night had veil'd the pole:
In the morning glad I see
My foe outstretch'd beneath the tree.

The New Jerusalem

And did those feet in ancient time
  Walk upon England's mountains green?
And was the holy Lamb of God
  On England's pleasant pastures seen?

And did the Countenance Divine
  Shine forth upon our clouded hills?
And was Jerusalem builded here
  Among these dark Satanic Mills?

Bring me my bow of burning gold!
  Bring me my arrows of desire!
Bring me my spear! O clouds, unfold!
  Bring me my chariot of fire!

I will not cease from mental fight,
  Nor shall my sword sleep in my hand
Till we have built Jerusalem
  In England's green and pleasant land.

The Tiger

Tiger, tiger, burning bright
In the forests of the night,
What immortal hand or eye
Could frame thy fearful symmetry?

In what distant deeps or skies
Burnt the fire of thine eyes?
On what wings dare he aspire?
What the hand dare seize the fire?

And what shoulder and what art
Could twist the sinews of thy heart?
And, when thy heart began to beat,
What dread hand and what dread feet?

What the hammer? What the chain?
In what furnace was thy brain?
What the anvil? What dread grasp
Dare its deadly terrors clasp?

When the stars threw down their spears,
And water'd heaven with their tears,
Did He smile His work to see?
Did He who made the lamb make thee?

Tiger, tiger, burning bright
In the forests of the night,
What immortal hand or eye
Dare frame thy fearful symmetry?

Eternity

He who bends to himself a joy
Does the winged life destroy;
But he who kisses the joy as it flies
Lives in eternity's sunrise.

Ah, Sun-flower

Ah, Sun-flower! weary of time,
Who countest the steps of the Sun;
Seeking after that sweet golden clime,
Where the traveler's journey is done;

Where the Youth pined away with desire,
And the pale Virgin shrouded in snow,
Arise from their graves, and aspire
Where my Sun-flower wishes to go!

To the Muses

Whether on Ida's shady brow
    Or in the chambers of the East,
The chambers of the Sun, that now
    From ancient melody have ceased;

Whether in heaven ye wander fair,
    Or the green corners of the earth,
Or the blue regions of the air
    Where the melodious winds have birth;

Whether on crystal rocks ye rove,
    Beneath the bosom of the sea,
Wandering in many a coral grove;
    Fair Nine, forsaking Poetry;

How have you left the ancient love
    That bards of old enjoy'd in you!
The languid strings do scarcely move,
    The sound is forced, the notes are few.

Epilogue

(TO THE ACCUSER WHO IS THE GOD OF THIS WORLD)

Truly, my Satan, thou art but a dunce,
And dost not know the garment from the man;
Every harlot was a virgin once,
Nor can'st thou ever change Kate into Nan.

Tho' thou art worshipped by the names divine
Of Jesus and Jehovah, thou art still
The son of morn in weary night's decline,
The lost traveller's dream under the hill.

ROBERT BURNS
1759–1796

A Red, Red Rose

O, my luve is like a red, red rose,
  That's newly sprung in June.
O my luve is like the melodie
  That's sweetly played in tune.

As fair art thou, my bonnie lass,
  So deep in luve am I,
And I will luve thee still, my dear,
  Till a' the seas gang dry.

Till a' the seas gang dry, my dear,
  And the rocks melt wi' the sun!
And I will luve thee still, my dear,
  While the sands o' life shall run.

And fare thee weel, my only luve,
  And fare thee weel awhile!
And I will come again, my luve,
  Though it were ten thousand mile!

Gang, go.

Flow Gently, Sweet Afton

Flow gently, sweet Afton, among thy green braes!
Flow gently, I'll sing thee a song in thy praise!
My Mary's asleep by thy murmuring stream—
Flow gently, sweet Afton, disturb not her dream!

Thou stock dove whose echo resounds through the glen,
Ye wild whistling blackbirds in yon thorny den,
Thou green-crested lapwing, thy screaming forbear—
I charge you, disturb not my slumbering fair!

How lofty, sweet Afton, thy neighboring hills,
Far marked with the courses of clear winding rills!
There daily I wander, as noon rises high,
My flocks and my Mary's sweet cot in my eye.

How pleasant thy banks and green valleys below,
Where wild in the woodlands the primroses blow;
There oft, as mild Evening weeps over the lea,
The sweet-scented birk shades my Mary and me.

Thy crystal stream, Afton, how lovely it glides,
And winds by the cot where my Mary resides!
How wanton thy waters her snowy feet lave,
As, gathering sweet flowerets, she stems thy clear wave!

Flow gently, sweet Afton, among thy green braes!
Flow gently, sweet river, the theme of my lays!
My Mary's asleep by thy murmuring stream—
Flow gently, sweet Afton, disturb not her dream!

Braes, slopes;
birk, birch.

My Heart's in the Highlands

Farewell to the Highlands, farewell to the North,
The birth-place of valor, the country of worth!
Wherever I wander, wherever I rove,
The hills of the Highlands for ever I love.

My heart's in the Highlands, my heart is not here,
My heart's in the Highlands a-chasing the deer,

A-chasing the wild deer and following the roe—
My heart's in the Highlands, wherever I go.

Farewell to the mountains high-covered with snow,
Farewell to the straths and green valleys below,
Farewell to the forests and wild-hanging woods,
Farewell to the torrents and loud-pouring floods!

My heart's in the Highlands, my heart is not here;
My heart's in the Highlands a-chasing the deer,
A-chasing the wild deer and following the roe—
My heart's in the Highlands, wherever I go!

John Anderson My Jo

John Anderson my jo, John,
    When we were first acquent,
Your locks were like the raven,
    Your bonnie brow was brent;
But now your brow is beld, John,
    Your locks are like the snaw,
But blessings on your frosty pow,
    John Anderson my jo!

John Anderson my jo, John,
    We clamb the hill thegither,
And monie a cantie day, John,
    We've had wi' ane anither;
Now we maun totter down, John,
    And hand in hand we'll go,
And sleep thegither at the foot,
    John Anderson my jo!

Straths, wide valleys; *jo*, joy, sweetheart;
acquent, acquainted; *brent*, smooth;
beld, bald; *pow*, head;
cantie, cheerful; *maun*, must.

Song: Green Grow the Rashes

Green grow the rashes, O;
Green grow the rashes, O;
The sweetest hours that e'er I spend,
    Are spent amang the lasses, O.

There's nought but care on every han',
   In every hour that passes, O:
What signifies the life o' man,
   An 'twere na for the lasses, O.

The war'ly race may riches chase,
   An' riches still may fly them, O;
An' though at last they catch them fast,
   Their hearts can ne'er enjoy them, O.

But gie me a cannie hour at e'en,
   My arms about my dearie, O,
An' war'ly cares, an' war'ly men
   May a' gae tapsalteerie, O!

For you sae douce, ye sneer at this;
   Ye're nought but senseless asses, O;
The wisest man the warl' e'er saw,
   He dearly loved the lasses, O.

Auld Nature swears, the lovely dears
   Her noblest work she classes, O:
Her 'prentice han' she tried on man,
   An' then she made the lasses, O.

War'ly, worldly; *cannie*, cozy;
tapsalteerie, topsy-turvy; *douce*, sober.

A Man's a Man for A' That

Is there for honest poverty
   That hangs his head, an' a' that;
The coward slave—we pass him by,
   We dare be poor for a' that!
For a' that, an' a' that,
   Our toils obscure an' a' that,
The rank is but the guinea's stamp,
   The man's the gowd for a' that.
What though on hamely fare we dine,
   Wear hoddin grey, an' a' that?
Gie fools their silks, and knaves their wine,
   A man's a man for a' that.
For a' that, an' a' that,

Their tinsel show an' a' that,
The honest man, tho' e'er sae poor,
  Is king o' men for a' that.
Ye see yon birkie ca'd a lord,
  Wha struts, an' stares, an' a' that;
Tho' hundreds worship at his word,
  He's but a coof for a' that,
For a' that, an' a' that,
  His ribband, star, an' a' that,
The man o' independent mind
  He looks an' laughs at a' that.
A prince can mak a belted knight,
  A marquis, duke, an' a' that;
But an honest man's aboon his might,
  Gude faith, he maunna fa' that!
For a' that, an' a' that,
  Their dignities an' a' that,
The pith o' sense, an' pride o' worth,
  Are higher rank than a' that.
Then let us pray that come it may,
  (As come it will for a' that,)
That Sense and Worth, o'er a' the earth,
  Shall bear the gree, an' a' that.
For a' that, an' a' that,
  It's coming yet for a' that,
That man to man, the world o'er,
  Shall brithers be for a' that.

Gowd, gold; *hoddin*, plodding;
birkie, fellow; *coof*, fool; *fa'*, obtain;
gree, prize; *brithers*, brothers.

Auld Lang Syne

Should auld acquaintance be forgot,
  And never brought to mind?
Should auld acquaintance be forgot,
  And auld lang syne?

Cho.—For auld lang syne, my dear,
  For auld lang syne,
We'll tak a cup o' kindness yet
  For auld lang syne!

And surely ye'll be your pint-stowp,
  And surely I'll be mine,
And we'll tak a cup o' kindness yet
  For auld lang syne!

We twa hae run about the braes
  And pou'd the gowans fine,
But we've wandered monie a weary fit
  Sin' auld lang syne.

We two hae paidl'd in the burn
  Frae morning sun till dine,
But seas between us braid hae roared
  Sin' auld lang syne.

Auld, old; *syne*, since; *pint-stowp*, pint-cup;
gowans, daisies; *fit*, foot; *paidl'd*, paddled;
burn, stream; *dine*, dinner.

To a Mouse

ON TURNING HER UP IN HER NEST WITH THE PLOUGH

Wee, sleekit, cow'rin', tim'rous beastie,
O what a panic's in thy breastie!
Thou need na start awa sae hasty,
        Wi' bickering brattle!
I wad be laith to rin an' chase thee
        Wi' murd'ring pattle!

I'm truly sorry man's dominion
Has broken Nature's social union,
An' justifies that ill opinion
        Which makes thee startle
At me, thy poor earth-born companion,
        An' fellow-mortal!

I doubt na, whiles, but thou may thieve;
What then? poor beastie, thou maun live!
A daimen-icker in a thrave
        'S a sma' request:
I'll get a blessin' wi' the lave,
        And never miss 't!

Thy wee bit housie, too, in ruin!
Its silly wa's the win's are strewin'!
An' naething, now, to big a new ane
      O' foggage green!
An' bleak December's winds ensuin',
      Baith snell an' keen!

Thou saw the fields laid bare and waste,
An' weary winter comin' fast,
An' cozie here, beneath the blast,
      Thou thought to dwell,
Till crash! the cruel coulter past
      Out-thro' thy cell.

That wee bit heap o' leaves an' stibble
Has cost thee mony a weary nibble!
Now thou's turn'd out, for a' thy trouble,
      But house or hald,
To thole the winter's sleety dribble,
      An' cranreuch cauld!

But, Mousie, thou art no thy lane,
In proving foresight may be vain:
The best laid schemes o' mice an' men
      Gang aft a-gley,
An' lea'e us nought but grief an' pain
      For promis'd joy.

Still thou art blest compar'd wi' me!
The present only toucheth thee:
But oh! I backward cast my e'e
      On prospects drear!
An' forward tho' I canna see,
      I guess an' fear!

Sleekit, sleek; *pattle*, plow-staff;
a daimen-icker in a thrave, an occasional ear in twenty-four sheaves;
big, build; *snell*, bitter; *thole*, endure; *cranreuch*, hoar-frost;
no thy lane, not alone; *a-gley*, astray.

Tam O' Shanter

When chapman billies leave the street,
And drouthy neibors neibors meet,
As market-days are wearing late,
An' folk begin to tak the gate;
While we sit bousing at the nappy,
An' getting fou and unco happy,
We think na on the lang Scots miles,
The mosses, waters, slaps, and styles,
That lie between us and our hame,
Whare sits our sulky sullen dame,
Gathering her brows like gathering storm,
Nursing her wrath to keep it warm.

This truth fand honest Tam o' Shanter,
As he frae Ayr ae night did canter—
(Auld Ayr, wham ne'er a town surpasses
For honest men and bonnie lasses).

O Tam! hadst thou but been sae wise
As ta'en thy ain wife Kate's advice!
She tauld thee weel thou was a skellum,
A bletherin', blusterin', drunken blellum;
That frae November till October,
Ae market-day thou was na sober;
That ilka melder wi' the miller
Thou sat as lang as thou had siller;
That every naig was ca'd a shoe on,
The smith and thee gat roarin' fou on;
That at the Lord's house, even on Sunday,
Thou drank wi' Kirkton Jean till Monday.
She prophesied that, late or soon,
Thou would be found deep drown'd in Doon;
Or catch'd wi' warlocks in the mirk
By Alloway's auld haunted kirk.

Ah, gentle dames! it gars me greet
To think how mony counsels sweet,
How mony lengthen'd sage advices,
The husband frae the wife despises!

But to our tale: Ae market night,
Tam had got planted unco right,
Fast by an ingle, bleezing finely,
Wi' reaming swats, that drank divinely;

And at his elbow, Souter Johnny,
His ancient, trusty, drouthy crony;
Tam lo'ed him like a very brither;
They had been fou for weeks thegither.
The night drave on wi' sangs and clatter,
And aye the ale was growing better:
The landlady and Tam grew gracious,
Wi' favours secret, sweet, and precious;
The souter tauld his queerest stories;
The landlord's laugh was ready chorus:
The storm without might rair and rustle
Tam did na mind the storm a whistle.

   Care, mad to see a man sae happy,
E'en drown'd himsel amang the nappy.
As bees flee hame wi' lades o' treasure,
The minutes wing'd their way wi' pleasure;
Kings may be blest, but Tam was glorious,
O'er a' the ills o' life victorious!

   But pleasures are like poppies spread—
You seize the flow'r, its bloom is shed;
Or like the snow falls in the river—
A moment white, then melts for ever;
Or like the borealis race,
That flit ere you can point their place;
Or like the rainbow's lovely form
Evanishing amid the storm.
Nae man can tether time or tide;
The hour approaches Tam maun ride;
That hour, o' night's black arch the key-stane,
That dreary hour, he mounts his beast in;
And sic a night he taks the road in,
As ne'er poor sinner was abroad in.

   The wind blew as 'twad blawn its last;
The rattling show'rs rose on the blast;
The speedy gleams the darkness swallow'd;
Loud, deep, and lang, the thunder bellow'd:
That night, a child might understand,
The Deil had business on his hand.

   Weel mounted on his gray mare, Meg,
A better never lifted leg,
Tam skelpit on thro' dub and mire,

Despising wind, and rain, and fire;
Whiles holding fast his gude blue bonnet;
Whiles crooning o'er some auld Scots sonnet;
Whiles glow'ring round wi' prudent cares,
Lest bogles catch him unawares.
Kirk-Alloway was drawing nigh,
Whare ghaists and houlets nightly cry.

　　By this time he was cross the ford,
Whare in the snaw the chapman smoor'd;
And past the birks and meikle stane,
Whare drunken Charlie brak's neck-bane;
And thro' the whins, and by the cairn,
Whare hunters fand the murder'd bairn;
And near the thorn, aboon the well,
Whare Mungo's mither hang'd hersel.
Before him Doon pours all his floods;
The doubling storm roars thro' the woods;
The lightnings flash from pole to pole;
Near and more near the thunders roll:
When, glimmering thro' the groaning trees,
Kirk-Alloway seem'd in a bleeze;
Thro' ilka bore the beams were glancing;
And loud resounded mirth and dancing.

　　Inspiring bold John Barleycorn!
What dangers thou canst make us scorn!
Wi' tippenny, we fear nae evil;
Wi' usquabae, we'll face the devil!
The swats sae ream'd in Tammie's noddle,
Fair play, he car'd na deils a boddle!
But Maggie stood right sair astonish'd,
Till, by the heel and hand admonish'd,
She ventur'd forward on the light;
And, vow! Tam saw an unco sight!
Warlocks and witches in a dance!
Nae cotillon brent new frae France,
But hornpipes, jigs, strathspeys, and reels,
Put life and mettle in their heels.
A winnock-bunker in the east,
There sat auld Nick, in shape o' beast—
A touzie type, black, grim, and large!
To gie them music was his charge:

He screw'd the pipes and gart them skirl,
Till roof and rafters a' did dirl.
Coffins stood round like open presses,
That shaw'd the dead in their last dresses;
And by some devilish cantraip sleight
Each in its cauld hand held a light,
By which heroic Tam was able
To note upon the haly table
A murderer's banes in gibbet-airns;
Twa span-lang, wee, unchristen'd bairns;
A thief new-cutted frae a rape—
Wi' his last gasp his gab did gape;
Five tomahawks, wi' blude red-rusted;
Five scymitars, wi' murder crusted;
A garter, which a babe had strangled;
A knife, a father's throat had mangled,
Whom his ain son o' life bereft—
The gray hairs yet stack to the heft;
Wi' mair of horrible and awefu',
Which even to name wad be unlawfu'.

As Tammie glowr'd, amaz'd, and curious,
The mirth and fun grew fast and furious:
The piper loud and louder blew;
The dancers quick and quicker flew;
They reel'd, they set, they cross'd, they cleekit,
Till ilka carlin swat and reekit,
And coost her duddies to the wark,
And linkit at it in her sark!

Now Tam, O Tam! had thae been queans,
A' plump and strapping in their teens;
Their sarks, instead o' creeshie flannen,
Been snaw-white seventeen hunder linen!
Thir breeks o' mine, my only pair,
That ance were plush, o' gude blue hair,
I wad hae gi'en them off my hurdies,
For ae blink o' the bonnie burdies!

But wither'd beldams, auld and droll,
Rigwoodie hags wad spean a foal,
Louping and flinging on a crummock,
I wonder didna turn thy stomach.

But Tam kent what was what fu' brawlie

There was ae winsome wench and wawlie
That night enlisted in the core,
Lang after kent on Carrick shore!
(For mony a beast to dead she shot,
And perish'd mony a bonnie boat,
And shook baith meikle corn and bear,
And kept the country-side in fear.)
Her cutty sark, o' Paisley harn,
That while a lassie she had worn,
In longitude tho' sorely scanty,
It was her best, and she was vauntie.—
Ah! little kent thy reverend grannie
That sark she coft for her wee Nannie
Wi' twa pund Scots ('twas a' her riches)
Wad ever grac'd a dance of witches!

But here my Muse her wing maun cour;
Sic flights are far beyond her pow'r—
To sing how Nannie lap and flang,
(A souple jade she was, and strang),
And how Tam stood, like ane bewitch'd,
And thought his very een enrich'd;
Even Satan glowr'd, and fidg'd fu' fain,
And hotch'd and blew wi' might and main:
Till first ae caper, syne anither,
Tam tint his reason a' thegither,
And roars out "Weel done, Cutty-sark!"
And in an instant all was dark!
And scarcely had he Maggie rallied,
When out the hellish legion sallied.

As bees bizz out wi' angry fyke
When plundering herds assail their byke,
As open pussie's mortal foes
When pop! she starts before their nose,
As eager runs the market-crowd,
When "Catch the thief!" resounds aloud,
So Maggie runs; the witches follow,
Wi' money an eldritch skriech and hollow.
Ah, Tam! ah, Tam! thou'll get thy fairin'!
In hell they'll roast thee like a herrin'!
In vain thy Kate awaits thy comin'!
Kate soon will be a woefu' woman!

Now do thy speedy utmost, Meg,
And win the key-stane of the brig:
There at them thou thy tail may toss,
A running stream they darena cross.
But ere the key-stane she could make,
The fient a tail she had to shake!
For Nannie, far before the rest,
Hard upon noble Maggie prest,
And flew at Tam wi' furious ettle;
But little wist she Maggie's mettle!
Ae spring brought off her master hale,
But left behind her ain gray tail:
The carlin claught her by the rump,
And left poor Maggie scarce a stump.

   Now, wha this tale o' truth shall read,
Ilk man and mother's son, take heed;
Whene'er to drink you are inclin'd,
Or cutty-sarks run in your mind,
Think! ye may buy the joys o'er dear;
Remember Tam o' Shanter's mare.

WILLIAM WORDSWORTH
1770–1850

She Was a Phantom of Delight

She was a Phantom of delight
When first she gleamed upon my sight;
A lovely Apparition, sent
To be a moment's ornament;
Her eyes as stars of Twilight fair;
Like Twilight's, too, her dusky hair;
But all things else about her drawn
From May-time and the cheerful Dawn;
A dancing Shape, an Image gay,
To haunt, to startle, and way-lay.

I saw her upon nearer view,
A Spirit, yet a Woman too!

Her household motions light and free,
And steps of virgin-liberty;
A countenance in which did meet
Sweet records, promises as sweet;
A Creature not too bright or good
For human nature's daily food;
For transient sorrows, simple wiles,
Praise, blame, love, kisses, tears, and smiles.

And now I see with eye serene
The very pulse of the machine;
A Being breathing thoughtful breath,
A Traveller between life and death;
The reason firm, the temperate will,
Endurance, foresight, strength, and skill;
A perfect Woman, nobly planned,
To warn, to comfort, and command;
And yet a Spirit still, and bright
With something of angelic light.

Daffodils

I wandered lonely as a cloud
    That floats on high o'er vales and hills,
When all at once I saw a crowd,
    A host, of golden daffodils;
Beside the lake, beneath the trees,
Fluttering and dancing in the breeze.

Continuous as the stars that shine
    And twinkle on the Milky Way,
They stretched in never-ending line
    Along the margin of a bay:
Ten thousand saw I at a glance,
Tossing their heads in sprightly dance.

The waves beside them danced, but they
    Out-did the sparkling waves in glee:
A poet could not but be gay,
    In such a jocund company:
I gazed—and gazed—but little thought
What wealth the show to me had brought:

For oft, when on my couch I lie
In vacant or in pensive mood,
They flash upon that inward eye
Which is the bliss of solitude;
And then my heart with pleasure fills,
And dances with the daffodils.

She Dwelt Among the Untrodden Ways

She dwelt among the untrodden ways
Beside the springs of Dove,
A maid whom there were none to praise
And very few to love:

A violet by a mossy stone
Half hidden from the eye!
—Fair as a star, when only one
Is shining in the sky.

She lived unknown, and few could know
When Lucy ceased to be;
But she is in her grave, and, oh,
The difference to me!

A Slumber Did My Spirit Seal

A slumber did my spirit seal;
I had no human fears;
She seemed a thing that could not feel
The touch of earthly years.

No motion has she now, no force;
She neither hears nor sees;
Rolled round in earth's diurnal course,
With rocks, and stones, and trees.

My Heart Leaps Up

My heart leaps up when I behold
A rainbow in the sky;
So was it when my life began;
So is it now I am a man;
So be it when I shall grow old.

Or let me die!
The Child is father of the Man;
And I could wish my days to be
Bound each to each by natural piety.

Composed Upon Westminster Bridge

Earth has not anything to show more fair:
Dull would he be of soul who could pass by
A sight so touching in its majesty:
This city now doth like a garment wear
The beauty of the morning; silent, bare,
Ships, towers, domes, theaters, and temples lie
Open unto the fields, and to the sky;
All bright and glittering in the smokeless air.

Never did sun more beautifully steep
In his first splendor valley, rock, or hill;
Ne'er saw I, never felt, a calm so deep!
The river glideth at his own sweet will:
Dear God! the very houses seem asleep;
And all that mighty heart is lying still!

It Is a Beauteous Evening

It is a beauteous evening, calm and free,
The holy time is quiet as a Nun
Breathless with adoration: the broad sun
Is sinking down in its tranquillity;
The gentleness of heaven broods o'er the Sea:
Listen! the mighty Being is awake,
And doth with his eternal motion make
A sound like thunder—everlastingly.

Dear Child! dear Girl! that walkest with me here,
If thou appear untouched by solemn thought,
Thy nature is not therefore less divine:
Thou liest in Abraham's bosom all the year,
And worship'st at the Temple's inner shrine,
God being with thee when we know it not.

The Solitary Reaper

Behold her, single in the field,
  Yon solitary Highland lass!
Reaping and singing by herself;
  Stop here, or gently pass!
Alone she cuts and binds the grain,
And sings a melancholy strain;
O listen! for the vale profound
Is overflowing with the sound.

No nightingale did ever chaunt
  More welcome notes to weary bands
Of travelers in some shady haunt,
  Among Arabian sands:
A voice so thrilling ne'er was heard
In spring-time from the cuckoo-bird,
Breaking the silence of the seas
Among the farthest Hebrides.

Will no one tell me what she sings?—
  Perhaps the plaintive numbers flow
For old, unhappy, far-off things,
  And battles long ago:
Or is it some more humble lay,
Familiar matter of to-day?
Some natural sorrow, loss, or pain,
That has been, and may be again?

Whate'er the theme, the maiden sang
  As if her song could have no ending;
I saw her singing at her work,
  And o'er the sickle bending;—
I listened, motionless and still;
And, as I mounted up the hill,
The music in my heart I bore,
Long after it was heard no more.

Ode to Duty

Stern Daughter of the Voice of God!
O Duty! if that name thou love,
Who art a light to guide, a rod

To check the erring, and reprove;
Thou, who art victory and law
When empty terrors overawe;
From vain temptations dost set free;
And calm'st the weary strife of frail humanity!

There are who ask not if thine eye
Be on them; who, in love and truth,
Where no misgiving is, rely
Upon the genial sense of youth:
Glad Hearts! without reproach or blot
Who do thy work, and know it not:
O if through confidence misplaced
They fail, thy saving arms, dread Power, around them cast.

Serene will be our days and bright,
And happy will our nature be,
When love is an unerring light,
And joy its own security.
And they a blissful course may hold
Even now, who, not unwisely bold,
Live in the spirit of this creed;
Yet seek thy firm support, according to their need.

I, loving freedom, and untried;
No sport of every random gust,
Yet being to myself a guide,
Too blindly have reposed my trust:
And oft, when in my heart was heard
Thy timely mandate, I deferred
The task, in smoother walks to stray;
But thee I now would serve more strictly, if I may.

Through no disturbance of my soul,
Or strong compunction in me wrought,
I supplicate for thy control;
But in the quietness of thought:
Me this unchartered freedom tires;
I feel the weight of chance-desires:
My hopes no more must change their name,
I long for a repose that ever is the same.

Stern Lawgiver! yet thou dost wear
The Godhead's most benignant grace;
Nor know we anything so fair
As is the smile upon thy face:
Flowers laugh before thee on their beds
And fragrance in thy footing treads;
Thou dost preserve the stars from wrong;
And the most ancient heavens, through Thee, are fresh and strong.

To humbler functions, awful Power!
I call thee: I myself commend
Unto thy guidance from this hour;
Oh, let my weakness have an end!
Give unto me, made lowly wise,
The spirit of self-sacrifice;
The confidence of reason give;
And in the light of truth thy Bondman let me live!

Tintern Abbey

Five years have past; five summers, with the length
Of five long winters! and again I hear
These waters, rolling from their mountain-springs
With a soft inland murmur.—Once again
Do I behold these steep and lofty cliffs,
That on a wild secluded scene impress
Thoughts of more deep seclusion, and connect
The landscape with the quiet of the sky.
The day is come when I again repose
Here, under this dark sycamore, and view

These plots of cottage-ground, these orchard-tufts,
Which at this season, with their unripe fruits,
Are clad in one green hue, and lose themselves
'Mid groves and copses. Once again I see
These hedge-rows, hardly hedge-rows, little lines
Of sportive wood run wild: these pastoral farms,
Green to the very door; and wreaths of smoke
Sent up, in silence, from among the trees!
With some uncertain notice, as might seem
Of vagrant dwellers in the houseless woods,
Or of some Hermit's cave, where by his fire
The Hermit sits alone.

These beauteous forms,
Through a long absence, have not been to me
As is a landscape to a blind man's eye:
But oft, in lonely rooms, and 'mid the din
Of towns and cities, I have owed to them
In hours of weariness, sensations sweet,
Felt in the blood, and felt along the heart;
And passing even into my purer mind,
With tranquil restoration:—feelings too
Of unremembered pleasure: such, perhaps,
As have no slight or trivial influence
On that best portion of a good man's life,
His little, nameless, unremembered acts
Of kindness and of love. Nor less, I trust,
To them I may have owed another gift,
Of aspect more sublime; that blessed mood,
In which the burden of the mystery,
In which the heavy and the weary weight
Of all this unintelligible world,
Is lightened:—that serene and blessed mood,
In which the affections gently lead us on,—
Until, the breath of this corporeal frame
And even the motion of our human blood
Almost suspended, we are laid asleep
In body, and become a living soul:
While with an eye made quiet by the power
Of harmony, and the deep power of joy,
We see into the life of things.
                                   If this
Be but a vain belief, yet, oh! how oft—
In darkness and amid the many shapes
Of joyless daylight; when the fretful stir
Unprofitable, and the fever of the world,
Have hung upon the beatings of my heart—
How oft, in spirit, have I turned to thee,
O sylvan Wye! thou wanderer thro' the woods,
How often has my spirit turned to thee!

    And now, with gleams of half extinguished thought,
With many recognitions dim and faint,
And somewhat of a sad perplexity,
The picture of the mind revives again:
While here I stand, not only with the sense

Of present pleasure, but with pleasing thoughts
That in this moment there is life and food
For future years. And so I dare to hope,
Though changed, no doubt, from what I was when first
I came among these hills; when like a roe
I bounded o'er the mountains, by the sides
Of the deep rivers, and the lonely streams,
Wherever nature led: more like a man
Flying from something that he dreads, than one
Who sought the thing he loved. For nature then
(The coarser pleasures of my boyish days,
And their glad animal movements all gone by)
To me was all in all.—I cannot paint
What then I was. The sounding cataract
Haunted me like a passion: the tall rock,
The mountain, and the deep and gloomy wood,
Their colours and their forms, were then to me
An appetite; a feeling and a love,
That had no need of a remoter charm,
By thought supplied, nor any interest
Unborrowed from the eye.—That time is past,
And all its aching joys are now no more,
And all its dizzy raptures. Not for this
Faint I, nor mourn nor murmur; other gifts
Have followed; for such loss, I would believe,
Abundant recompense. For I have learned
To look on nature, not as in the hour
Of thoughtless youth; but hearing oftentimes
The still, sad music of humanity,
Nor harsh nor grating, though of ample power
To chasten and subdue. And I have felt
A presence that disturbs me with the joy
Of elevated thoughts; a sense sublime
Of something far more deeply interfused,
Whose dwelling is the light of setting suns,
And the round ocean, and the living air,
And the blue sky, and in the mind of man;
A motion and a spirit, that impels
All thinking things, all objects of all thought,
And rolls through all things. Therefore am I still
A lover of the meadows and the woods,

And mountains; and of all that we behold
From this green earth; of all the mighty world
Of eye, and ear,—both what they half create,
And what perceive; well pleased to recognize
In nature and the language of the sense,
The anchor of my purest thoughts, the nurse,
The guide, the guardian of my heart, and soul
Of all my moral being.
                              Nor perchance,
If I were not thus taught, should I the more
Suffer my genial spirits to decay:
For thou art with me here upon the banks
Of this fair river; thou my dearest Friend,
My dear, dear Friend; and in thy voice I catch
The language of my former heart, and read
My former pleasures in the shooting lights
Of thy wild eyes. Oh! yet a little while
May I behold in thee what I was once,
My dear, dear Sister! and this prayer I make,
Knowing that Nature never did betray
The heart that loved her; 'tis her privilege,
Through all the years of this our life, to lead
From joy to joy: for she can so inform
The mind that is within us, so impress
With quietness and beauty, and so feed
With lofty thoughts, that neither evil tongues,
Rash judgments, nor the sneers of selfish men,
Nor greetings where no kindness is, nor all
The dreary intercourse of daily life,
Shall e'er prevail against us, or disturb
Our cheerful faith that all which we behold
Is full of blessings. Therefore let the moon
Shine on thee in thy solitary walk;
And let the misty mountain-winds be free
To blow against thee: and, in after years,
When these wild ecstasies shall be matured
Into a sober pleasure; when thy mind
Shall be a mansion for all lovely forms,
Thy memory be as a dwelling-place
For all sweet sounds and harmonies; oh! then,
If solitude, or fear, or pain, or grief,

Should be thy portion, with what healing thoughts
Of tender joy wilt thou remember me,
And these my exhortations! Nor, perchance—
If I should be where I no more can hear
Thy voice, nor catch from thy wild eyes these gleams
Of past existence—wilt thou then forget
That on the banks of this delightful stream
We stood together; and that I, so long
A worshipper of Nature, hither came
Unwearied in that service: rather say
With warmer love—oh! with far deeper zeal
Of holier love. Nor wilt thou then forget,
That after many wanderings, many years
Of absence, these steep woods and lofty cliffs,
And this green pastoral landscape, were to me
More dear, both for themselves and for thy sake!

The World Is Too Much with Us

The world is too much with us; late and soon,
Getting and spending, we lay waste our powers:
Little we see in Nature that is ours;
We have given our hearts away, a sordid boon!
This Sea that bares her bosom to the moon;
The winds that will be howling at all hours,
And are up-gathered now like sleeping flowers;
For this, for everything, we are out of tune;
It moves us not.—Great God! I'd rather be
A Pagan suckled in a creed outworn;
So might I, standing on this pleasant lea,
Have glimpses that would make me less forlorn;
Have sight of Proteus rising from the sea;
Or hear old Triton blow his wreathèd horn.

Ode

INTIMATIONS OF IMMORTALITY FROM
RECOLLECTIONS OF EARLY CHILDHOOD

The Child is father of the Man;
And I could wish my days to be
Bound each to each by natural piety.

I

There was a time when meadow, grove, and stream,
The earth, and every common sight,
    To me did seem
    Apparelled in celestial light,
The glory and the freshness of a dream.
It is not now as it hath been of yore;—
    Turn wheresoe'er I may,
        By night or day,
The things which I have seen I now can see no more.

II

    The Rainbow comes and goes,
    And lovely is the Rose,
    The Moon doth with delight
Look round her when the heavens are bare,
    Waters on a starry night
    Are beautiful and fair;
    The sunshine is a glorious birth;
    But yet I know, where'er I go,
That there hath past away a glory from the earth.

III

Now, while the birds thus sing a joyous song,
    And while the young lambs bound
        As to the tabor's sound,
To me alone there came a thought of grief:
A timely utterance gave that thought relief,
        And I again am strong:
The cataracts blow their trumpets from the steep;
No more shall grief of mine the season wrong;
I hear the Echoes through the mountains throng,
The Winds come to me from the fields of sleep,
        And all the earth is gay;
            Land and sea
        Give themselves up to jollity,
            And with the heart of May
        Doth every beast keep holiday;—
            Thou Child of Joy,
Shout round me, let me hear thy shouts, thou happy Shepherd-boy!

IV

Ye blessèd Creatures, I have heard the call
    Ye to each other make; I see
The heavens laugh with you in your jubilee;
      My heart is at your festival,
      My head hath its coronal,
The fullness of your bliss, I feel—I feel it all.
      Oh evil day! if I were sullen
      While Earth herself is adorning,
        This sweet May-morning,
      And the children are culling
        On every side,
    In a thousand valleys far and wide,
    Fresh flowers; while the sun shines warm,
And the Babe leaps up on his mother's arm:—
      I hear, I hear, with joy I hear!
      —But there's a Tree, of many, one,
A single Field which I have looked upon,
Both of them speak of something that is gone:
      The Pansy at my feet
      Doth the same tale repeat:
Whither is fled the visionary gleam?
Where is it now, the glory and the dream?

V

Our birth is but a sleep and a forgetting:
The Soul that rises with us, our life's Star,
      Hath had elsewhere its setting,
        And cometh from afar:
      Not in entire forgetfulness,
      And not in utter nakedness,
But trailing clouds of glory do we come
      From God, who is our home:
Heaven lies about us in our infancy!
Shades of the prison-house begin to close
      Upon the growing Boy,
But he beholds the light, and whence it flows,
      He sees it in his joy;
The Youth, who daily farther from the east
      Must travel, still is Nature's priest,
      And by the vision splendid
      Is on his way attended;

At length the Man perceives it die away,
And fade into the light of common day.

VI

Earth fills her lap with pleasures of her own;
Yearnings she hath in her own natural kind,
And, even with something of a mother's mind,
     And no unworthy aim,
The homely nurse doth all she can
To make her Foster-child, her inmate Man,
     Forget the gloriess he hath known,
And that imperial palace whence he came.

VII

Behold the Child among his new-born blisses,
A six years' darling of a pigmy size!
See, where 'mid work of his own hand he lies,
Fretted by sallies of his mother's kisses,
With light upon him from his father's eyes!
See, at his feet, some little plan or chart,
Some fragment from his dream of human life,
Shaped by himself with newly-learnèd art;
     A wedding or a festival,
     A mourning or a funeral;
       And this hath now his heart,
       And unto this he frames his song:
        Then will he fit his tongue
To dialogues of business, love, or strife;
       But it will not be long
       Ere this be thrown aside,
       And with new joy and pride
The little Actor cons another part;
Filling from time to time his "humorous stage"
With all the Persons, down to palsied Age,
That Life brings with her in her equipage;
       As if his whole vocation
       Were endless imitation.

VIII

Thou, whose exterior semblance doth belie
     Thy soul's immensity;

Thou best philosopher, who yet dost keep
Thy heritage, thou eye among the blind,
That, deaf and silent, read'st the Eternal Deep,
Haunted forever by the Eternal Mind,—
      Mighty prophet! seer blest!
      On whom those truths do rest,
Which we are toiling all our lives to find,
In darkness lost, the darkness of the grave;
Thou, over whom thy Immortality
Broods like the Day, a master o'er a slave,
A Presence which is not to be put by;
Thou little Child, yet glorious in the might
Of heaven-born freedom on thy being's height,
Why with such earnest pains dost thou provoke
The years to bring the inevitable yoke,
Thus blindly with thy blessedness at strife?
Full soon thy Soul shall have her earthly freight,
And custom lie upon thee with a weight,
Heavy as frost, and deep almost as life!

IX

      O joy! that in our embers
      Is something that doth live,
      That nature yet remembers
      What was so fugitive!
The thought of our past years in me doth breed
Perpetual benediction; not indeed
For that which is most worthy to be blest;
Delight and liberty, the simple creed
Of childhood, whether busy or at rest,
With new-fledged hope still fluttering in his breast:—
      Not for these I raise
      The song of thanks and praise;
      But for those obstinate questionings
      Of sense and outward things,
      Fallings from us, vanishings;
      Blank misgivings of a Creature
Moving about in worlds not realized,
High instincts before which our mortal nature
Did tremble like a guilty thing surprised:
      But for those first affections,
      Those shadowy recollections,

Which, be they what they may,
Are yet the fountain-light of all our day,
Are yet a master-light of all our seeing;
Uphold us, cherish, and have power to make
Our noisy years seem moments in the being
Of the Eternal Silence: truths that wake,
　　　To perish never:
Which neither listlessness, nor mad endeavor,
　　　Nor man nor boy,
Nor all that is at enmity with joy,
Can utterly abolish or destroy!
　　　Hence in a season of calm weather
　　　Though inland far we be,
Our souls have sight of that immortal sea
　　　Which brought us hither,
　　　Can in a moment travel thither,
And see the children sport upon the shore,
And hear the mighty waters rolling evermore.

X

Then sing, ye Birds, sing, sing a joyous song!
　　　And let the young Lambs bound
　　　As to the tabor's sound!
We in thought will join your throng,
　　　Ye that pipe and ye that play,
　　　Ye that through your hearts to-day
　　　Feel the gladness of the May!
What though the radiance which was once so bright
Be now forever taken from my sight,
　　　Though nothing can bring back the hour
Of splendor in the grass, of glory in the flower;
　　　We will grieve not, rather find
　　　Strength in what remains behind;
　　　In the primal sympathy
　　　Which having been must ever be;
　　　In the soothing thoughts that spring
　　　Out of human suffering;
　　　In the faith that looks through death,
In years that bring the philosophic mind.

XI

And O, ye Fountains, Meadows, Hills, and Groves,
Forebode not any severing of our loves!

Yet in my heart of hearts I feel your might;
I only have relinquished one delight
To live beneath your more habitual sway.
I love the Brooks which down their channels fret,
Even more than when I tripped lightly as they;
The innocent brightness of a new-born Day
   Is lovely yet;
The Clouds that gather round the setting sun
Do take a sober coloring from an eye
That hath kept watch o'er man's mortality;
Another race hath been, and other palms are won.
Thanks to the human heart by which we live,
Thanks to its tenderness, its joys, and fears,
To me the meanest flower that blows can give
Thoughts that do often lie too deep for tears.

SAMUEL TAYLOR COLERIDGE
1772–1839

Kubla Khan

In Xanadu did Kubla Khan
A stately pleasure-dome decree:
Where Alph, the sacred river, ran
Through caverns measureless to man
 Down to a sunless sea.
So twice five miles of fertile ground
With walls and towers were girdled round:
And there were gardens bright with sinuous rills,
Where blossomed many an incense-bearing tree;
And here were forests ancient as the hills,
Enfolding sunny spots of greenery.

But oh! that deep romantic chasm which slanted
Down the green hill athwart a cedarn cover!
A savage place! as holy and enchanted
As e'er beneath a waning moon was haunted
By woman wailing for her demon-lover!

And from this chasm, with ceaseless turmoil seething,
As if this earth in fast thick pants were breathing,
A mighty fountain momently was forced:
Amid whose swift half-intermitted burst
Huge fragments vaulted like rebounding hail,
Or chaffy grain beneath the thresher's flail:
And 'mid these dancing rocks at once and ever
It flung up momently the sacred river.
Five miles meandering with a mazy motion
Through wood and dale the sacred river ran,
Then reached the caverns measureless to man,
And sank in tumult to a lifeless ocean:
And 'mid this tumult Kubla heard from far
Ancestral voices prophesying war!
    The shadow of the dome of pleasure
    Floated midway on the waves;
    Where was heard the mingled measure
    From the fountain and the caves.
It was a miracle of rare device,
A sunny pleasure-dome with caves of ice!

    A damsel with a dulcimer
    In a vision once I saw:
    It was an Abyssinian maid,
    And on her dulcimer she played,
      Singing of Mount Abora.
    Could I revive within me
      Her symphony and song,
      To such a deep delight 'twould win me,
That with music loud and long,
I would build that dome in air,
That sunny dome! those caves of ice!
And all who heard should see them there,
And all should cry, Beware! Beware!
His flashing eyes, his floating hair!
Weave a circle round him thrice,
And close your eyes with holy dread,
For he on honey-dew hath fed,
And drunk the milk of Paradise.

Epigram

Sir, I admit your general rule,
That every poet is a fool,
But you yourself may serve to show it,
That every fool is not a poet.

The Rime of the Ancient Mariner

PART I

It is an ancient Mariner,
And he stoppeth one of three.
"By thy long grey beard and glittering eye,
Now wherefore stopp'st thou me?

An ancient Mariner meeteth three gallants bidden to a wedding feast, and detaineth one.

The Bridegroom's doors are open'd wide,
And I am next of kin;
The guests are met, the feast is set:
May'st hear the merry din."

He holds him with his skinny hand,
"There was a ship," quoth he.
"Hold off! Unhand me, grey-beard loon!"
Eftsoons his hand dropt he.

The Wedding-Guest is spellbound by the eye of the old seafaring man, and constrained to hear his tale.

He holds him with his glittering eye—
The Wedding-Guest stood still,
And listens like a three years' child:
The Mariner hath his will.

The Wedding-Guest sat on a stone:
He cannot choose but hear;
And thus spake on that ancient man,
The bright-eyed Mariner.

The Mariner tells how the ship sailed southward with a good wind and fair weather, till it reached the Line.

"The ship was cheer'd, the harbour clear'd,
Merrily did we drop
Below the kirk, below the hill,
Below the lighthouse top.

The Sun came up upon the left,
Out of the sea came he!

And he shone bright, and on the right
Went down into the sea.

Higher and higher every day,
Till over the mast at noon—"
The Wedding-Guest here beat his breast,
For he heard the loud bassoon.

*The Wedding-
Guest heareth
the bridal music;
but the Mariner
continueth his tale.*

The bride hath paced into the hall,
Red as a rose is she;
Nodding their heads before her goes
The merry minstrelsy.

The Wedding-Guest he beat his breast,
Yet he cannot choose but hear;
And thus spake on that ancient man,
The bright-eyed Mariner.

*The skip driven by
a storm toward the
South Pole.*

"And now the Storm-blast came, and he
Was tyrannous and strong:
He struck with his o'ertaking wings,
And chased us south along.

With sloping masts and dipping prow,
As who pursued with yell and blow
Still treads the shadow of his foe,
And forward bends his head,
The ship drove fast, loud roar'd the blast,
And southward aye we fled.

And now there came both mist and snow,
And it grew wondrous cold:
And ice, mast-high, came floating by,
As green as emerald.

*The land of ice, and
of fearful sounds,
where no living
thing was to be
seen.*

And through the drifts the snowy clifts
Did send a dismal sheen:
Nor shapes of men nor beasts we ken—
The ice was all between.

The ice was here, the ice was there,
The ice was all around:

It crack'd and growl'd, and roar'd and howled,
Like noises in a swound!

At length did cross an Albatross,
Through the fog it came;
As if it had been a Christian soul,
We hail'd it in God's name.

It ate the food it ne'er had eat,
And round and round it flew.
The ice did split with a thunder-fit;
The helmsman steer'd us through!

And a good south wind sprung up behind;
The Albatross did follow,
And every day, for food or play,
Came to the mariners' hollo!

In mist or cloud, on mast or shroud,
It perch'd for vespers nine;
Whiles all the night, through fog-smoke white,
Glimmer'd the white moonshine."

"God save thee, ancient Mariner,
From the fiends, that plague thee thus!—
Why look'st thou so?"—"With my crossbow
I shot the Albatross.

*Till a great
sea-bird, called
the Albatross,
came through the
snow-fog, and was
received with great
joy and hospitality.*

*And lo! the
Albatross proveth a
bird of good omen,
and followeth the
ship as it returned
north ward through
fog and floating ice.*

*The ancient
Mariner
inhospitably killeth
the pious bird of
good omen.*

PART II

"The Sun now rose upon the right:
Out of the sea came he,
Still hid in mist, and on the left
Went down into the sea.

And the good south wind still blew behind,
But no sweet bird did follow,
Nor any day for food or play
Came to the mariners' hollo!

And I had done an hellish thing,
And it would work 'em woe:
For all averr'd I had kill'd the bird

*His shipmates cry
out against the
ancient Mariner for
killing the bird of
good luck.*

That made the breeze to blow.
Ah wretch! said they, the bird to slay,
That made the breeze to blow!

Nor dim nor red, like God's own head,
The glorious Sun uprist:
Then all averr'd I had kill'd the bird
That brought the fog and mist.
'Twas right, said they, such birds to slay,
That bring the fog and mist.

The fair breeze blew, the white foam flew,
The furrow follow'd free;
We were the first that ever burst
Into that silent sea.

Down dropt the breeze, the sails dropt down,
'Twas sad as sad could be;
And we did speak only to break
The silence of the sea!

All in a hot and copper sky,
The bloody Sun, at noon,
Right up above the mast did stand,
No bigger than the Moon.

Day after day, day after day,
We stuck, nor breath nor motion;
As idle as a painted ship
Upon a painted ocean.

Water, water, everywhere,
And all the boards did shrink;
Water, water, everywhere,
Nor any drop to drink.

The very deep did rot: O Christ!
That ever this should be!
Yea, slimy things did crawl with legs
Upon the slimy sea.

But when the fog cleared off, they justify the same, and thus make themselves accomplices in the crime.

The fair breeze continues; the ship enters the Pacific Ocean, and sails northward, even till it reaches the Line.

The ship hath been suddenly becalmed.

And the Albatross begins to be avenged.

About, about, in reel and rout
The death-fires danced at night;
The water, like a witch's oils,
Burnt green, and blue, and white.

And some in dreams assurèd were
Of the Spirit that plagued us so;
Nine fathom deep he had follow'd us
From the land of mist and snow.

A Spirit had followed them, one of the invisible inhabitants of this planet, neither departed souls nor angels; concerning whom the learned Jew, Josephus, and the Platonic Constantinopolitan, Michael Psellus, may be consulted. They are very numerous, and there is no climate or element without one or more.

And every tongue, through utter drought,
Was wither'd at the root;
We could not speak, no more than if
We had been choked with soot.

Ah! well a-day! what evil looks
Had I from old and young!
Instead of the cross, the Albatross
About my neck was hung.

The shipmates, in their sore distress, would fain throw the whole guilt on the ancient Mariner: in sign whereof they hang the dead sea-bird round his neck.

PART III

"There passed a weary time. Each throat
Was parch'd, and glazed each eye.
A weary time! a weary time!
How glazed each weary eye!
When, looking westward, I beheld
A something in the sky.

The ancient Mariner beholdeth a sign in the element afar off.

At first it seem'd a little speck,
And then it seem'd a mist;
It moved and moved, and took at last
A certain shape, I wist.

A speck, a mist, a shape, I wist!
And still it near'd and near'd:
As if it dodged a water-sprite,
It plunged, and tack'd and veer'd.

With throats unslaked, with black lips baked,
We could nor laugh nor wail;
Through utter drought all dumb we stood!

I bit my arm, I suck'd the blood,
And cried, A sail! a sail!

At its nearer approach, it seemeth him to be a ship; and at a dear ransom he freeth his speech from the bonds of thirst.

With throats unslaked, with black lips baked,
Agape they heard me call:
Gramercy! they for joy did grin,
And all at once their breath drew in,
As they were drinking all.

A flash of joy;

See! see! (I cried) she tacks no more!
Hither to work us weal—
Without a breeze, without a tide,
She steadies with upright keel!

And horror follows. For can it be a ship that comes onward without wind or tide?

The western wave was all aflame,
The day was wellnigh done!
Almost upon the western wave
Rested the broad, bright Sun;
When that strange shape drove suddenly
Betwixt us and the Sun.

And straight the Sun was fleck'd with bars
(Heaven's Mother send us grace!),
As if through a dungeon-grate he peer'd
With broad and burning face.

It seemeth him but the skeleton of a ship.

Alas! (thought I, and my heart beat loud)
How fast she nears and nears!
Are those her sails that glance in the Sun,
Like restless gossameres?

Are those her ribs through which the Sun
Did peer, as through a grate?
And is that Woman all her crew
Is that a Death? and are there two?
Is Death that Woman's mate?

And its ribs are seen as bars on the face of the setting Sun. The Spectre-Woman and her Deathmate, and no other, on board the skeleton ship. Like vessel, like crew!

Her lips were red, her looks were free,
Her locks were yellow as gold:
Her skin was as white as leprosy,

The Nightmare Life-in-Death was she,
Who thicks man's blood with cold.

The naked hulk alongside came,
And the twain were casting dice;
"The game is done! I've won! I've won!"
Quoth she, and whistles thrice.

Death and Life-in-Death have diced for the ship's crew and she (the latter) winneth the ancient Mariner.

The Sun's rim dips; the stars rush out:
At one stride comes the dark;
With far-heard whisper, o'er the sea,
Off shot the spectre-bark.

No twilight within the courts of the Sun.

We listen'd and look'd sideways up!
Fear at my heart, as at a cup,
My life-blood seem'd to sip!
The stars were dim, and thick the night,
The steersman's face by his lamp gleam'd white;
From the sails the dew did drip—
Till clomb above the eastern bar
The hornèd Moon, with one bright star
Within the nether tip.

At the rising of the Moon,

One after another,

One after one, by the star-dogg'd Moon,
Too quick for groan or sigh,
Each turn'd his face with a ghastly pang,
And cursed me with his eye.

Four times fifty living men
(And I heard nor sigh nor groan),
With heavy thump, a lifeless lump,
They dropp'd down one by one.

His shipmates drop down dead.

The souls did from their bodies fly—
They fled to bliss or woe!
And every soul, it pass'd me by
Like the whizz of my crossbow!"

But Life-in-Death begins her work on the ancient Mariner.

Part IV

"I fear thee, ancient Mariner!
I fear thy skinny hand!

And thou art long, and lank, and brown,
As is the ribb'd sea-sand.

*The Wedding-Guest
feareth that a spirit
is talking to him.*

I fear thee and thy glittering eye,
And thy skinny hand so brown."—
"Fear not, fear not, thou Wedding-Guest!
This body dropt not down.

*But the ancient
Mariner assureth
him of his bodily
life, and proceedeth
to relate his
horrible penance.*

Alone, alone, all, all alone,
Alone on a wide, wide sea!
And never a saint took pity on
My soul in agony.

The many men, so beautiful!
And they all dead did lie:
And a thousand thousand slimy things
Lived on; and so did I.

*He despiseth the
creatures of the
calm.*

I look'd upon the rotting sea,
And drew my eyes away;
I look'd upon the rotting deck,
And there the dead men lay.

*And envieth that
they should live,
and so many lie
dead.*

I look'd to heaven, and tried to pray;
But or ever a prayer had gusht,
A wicked whisper came, and made
My heart as dry as dust.

I closed my lids, and kept them close,
And the balls like pulses beat;
But the sky and the sea, and the sea and the sky,
Lay like a load on my weary eye,
And the dead were at my feet.

The cold sweat melted from their limbs,
Nor rot nor reek did they:
The look with which they look'd on me
Had never pass'd away.

*But the curse liveth
for him in the eye of
the dead men.*

An orphan's curse would drag to hell
A spirit from on high;
But oh! more horrible than that

Is the curse in a dead man's eye!
Seven days, seven nights, I saw that curse,
And yet I could not die.

The moving Moon went up the sky,
And nowhere did abide;
Softly she was going up,
And a star or two beside,—

*In his loneliness and fixedness
he yearneth towards the
journeying Moon, and the stars
that still sojourn, yet still move
onward; and everywhere the
blue sky belongs to them, and is
their appointed rest and their
native country and their own
natural homes, which they
enter unannounced, as lords
that are certainly expected,
and yet there is a silent joy at
their arrival.*

Her beams bemock'd the sultry main,
Like April hoar-frost spread;
But where the ship's huge shadow lay,
The charmèd water burnt alway
A still and awful red.

Beyond the shadow of the ship,
I watch'd the water-snakes:
They moved in tracks of shining white
And when they rear'd, the elfish light
Fell off in hoary flakes.

*By the light of the Moon he
beholdeth God's creatures of
the great calm.*

Within the shadow of the ship
I watch'd their rich attire:
Blue, glossy green, and velvet black,
They coil'd and swam; and every track
Was a flash of golden fire.

O happy living things! no tongue
Their beauty might declare:
A spring of love gush'd from my heart,
And I bless'd them unaware:
Sure my kind saint took pity on me,
And I bless'd them unaware.

*Their beauty and their
happiness.*

He blesseth them in his heart.

The selfsame moment I could pray;
And from my neck so free
The Albatross fell off, and sank
Like lead into the sea.

The spell begins to break.

Part V

"O sleep! it is a gentle thing,
Beloved from pole to pole!

To Mary Queen the praise be given!
She sent the gentle sleep from Heaven,
That slid into my soul.

The silly buckets on the deck,
That had so long remain'd,
I dreamt that they were fill'd with dew;
And when I awoke, it rain'd.

*By grace of the
holy Mother, the
ancient Mariner is
refreshed with rain.*

My lips were wet, my throat was cold,
My garments all were dank;
Sure I had drunken in my dreams,
And still my body drank.

I moved, and could not feel my limbs:
I was so light—almost
I thought that I had died in sleep,
And was a blessèd ghost.

And soon I heard a roaring wind:
It did not come anear;
But with its sound it shook the sails,
That were so thin and sere.

*He heareth
sounds and seeth
strange sights and
commotions in
the sky and the
element.*

The upper air burst into life;
And a hundred fire-flags sheen;
To and fro they were hurried about!
And to and fro, and in and out,
The wan stars danced between.

And the coming wind did roar more loud,
And the sails did sigh like sedge;
And the rain pour'd down from one black cloud;
The Moon was at its edge.

The thick black cloud was cleft, and still
The Moon was at its side;
Like waters shot from some high crag,
The lightning fell with never a jag,
A river steep and wide.

The loud wind never reach'd the ship,
Yet now the ship moved on!
Beneath the lightning and the Moon
The dead men gave a groan.

They groan'd, they stirr'd, they all uprose,
Nor spake, nor moved their eyes;
It had been strange, even in a dream,
To have seen those dead men rise.

The helmsman steer'd, the ship moved on;
Yet never a breeze up-blew;
The mariners all 'gan work the ropes,
Where they were wont to do;
They raised their limbs like lifeless tools—
We were a ghastly crew.

The body of my brother's son
Stood by me, knee to knee:
The body and I pull'd at one rope,
But he said naught to me."

"I fear thee, ancient Mariner!"
"Be calm, thou Wedding-Guest:
'Twas not those souls that fled in pain,
Which to their corses came again,
But a troop of spirits blest:

For when it dawn'd—they dropp'd their arms,
And cluster'd round the mast;
Sweet sounds rose slowly through their mouths,
And from their bodies pass'd.

Around, around, flew each sweet sound,
Then darted to the Sun;
Slowly the sounds came back again,
Now mix'd, now one by one.

Sometimes a-dropping from the sky
I heard the skylark sing;
Sometimes all little birds that are,

The bodies of the ship's crew are inspired, and the ship moves on;

But not by the souls of the men, nor by demons of earth or middle air, but by a blessed troop of angelic spirits, sent down by the invocation of the guardian saint.

How they seem'd to fill the sea and air
With their sweet jargoning!

And now 'twas like all instruments,
Now like a lonely flute;
And now it is an angel's song,
That makes the Heavens be mute.

It ceased; yet still the sails made on
A pleasant noise till noon,
A noise like of a hidden brook
In the leafy month of June,
That to the sleeping woods all night
Singeth a quiet tune.

Till noon we quietly sail'd on,
Yet never a breeze did breathe:
Slowly and smoothly went the ship,
Moved onward from beneath.

Under the keel nine fathom deep,
From the land of mist and snow,
The Spirit slid: and it was he
That made the ship to go.
The sails at noon left off their tune,
And the ship stood still also.

The lonesome Spirit from the South Pole carries on the ship as far as the Line, in obedience to the angelic troop, but still requireth vengeance.

The Sun, right up above the mast,
Had fix'd her to the ocean:
But in a minute she 'gan stir,
With a short uneasy motion—
Backwards and forwards half her length
With a short uneasy motion.

Then like a pawing horse let go,
She made a sudden bound:
It flung the blood into my head,
And I fell down in a swound.

How long in that same fit I lay,
I have not to declare;

But ere my living life return'd,
I heard, and in my soul discern'd
Two voices in the air.

"Is it he?" quoth one, "is this the man?
By Him who died on cross,
With his cruel bow he laid full low
The harmless Albatross.

The Spirit who bideth by himself
In the land of mist and snow,
He loved the bird that loved the man
Who shot him with his bow."

The other was a softer voice,
As soft as honey-dew:
Quoth he, "The man hath penance done,
And penance more will do."

*The Polar Spirit's
fellow demons,
the invisible
inhabitants of the
element, take part
in his wrong; and
two of them relate,
one to the other,
that penance long
and heavy for the
ancient Mariner
hath been accorded
to the Polar Spirit,
who returneth
southward.*

PART VI

First Voice:
"But tell me, tell me! speak again,
Thy soft response renewing—
What makes that ship drive on so fast?
What is the Ocean doing?"

Second Voice:
"Still as a slave before his lord,
The Ocean hath no blast;
His great bright eye most silently
Up to the Moon is cast—

If he may know which way to go;
For she guides him smooth or grim.
See, brother, see! how graciously
She looketh down on him."

First Voice:
"But why drives on that ship so fast,
Without or wave or wind?"

*The Mariner hath
been cast into a
trance; for the
angelic power
causeth the vessel
to drive northward
faster than human
life could endure.*

Second Voice:
"The air is cut away before,
And closes from behind.

Fly, brother, fly! more high, more high!
Or we shall be belated:
For slow and slow that ship will go,
When the Mariner's trance is abated."

I woke, and we were sailing on
As in a gentle weather:
'Twas night, calm night, the Moon was high;
The dead men stood together.

The supernatural motion is retarded; the Mariner awakes, and his penance begins anew.

All stood together on the deck,
For a charnel-dungeon fitter:
All fix'd on me their stony eyes,
That in the Moon did glitter.

The pang, the curse, with which they died,
Had never pass'd away:
I could not draw my eyes from theirs,
Nor turn them up to pray.

And now this spell was snapt: once more
I viewed the ocean green,
And look'd far forth, yet little saw
Of what had else been seen—

The curse is finally expiated.

Like one that on a lonesome road
Doth walk in fear and dread,
And having once turn'd round, walks on,
And turns no more his head;
Because he knows a frightful fiend
Doth close behind him tread.

But soon there breathed a wind on me,
Nor sound nor motion made:
Its path was not upon the sea,
In ripple or in shade.

It raised my hair, it fann'd my cheek
Like a meadow-gale of spring—
It mingled strangely with my fears,
Yet it felt like a welcoming.

Swiftly, swiftly flew the ship,
Yet she sail'd softly too:
Sweetly, sweetly blew the breeze—
On me alone it blew.

O dream of joy! is this indeed
The lighthouse top I see?
Is this the hill? is this the kirk?
Is this mine own countree?

And the ancient Mariner beholdeth his native country.

We drifted o'er the harbour-bar,
And I with sobs did pray—
O let me be awake, my God!
Or let me sleep alway.

The harbour-bay was clear as glass,
So smoothly it was strewn!
And on the bay the moonlight lay,
And the shadow of the Moon.

The rock shone bright, the kirk no less
That stands above the rock:
The moonlight steep'd in silentness
The steady weathercock.

And the bay was white with silent light
Till rising from the same,
Full many shapes, that shadows were,
In crimson colours came.

The angelic spirits leave the dead bodies.

A little distance from the prow
Those crimson shadows were:
I turn'd my eyes upon the deck—
O Christ! what saw I there!

And appear in their own forms of light.

Each corse lay flat, lifeless and flat,
And, by the holy rood!

A man all light, a seraph-man,
On every corse there stood.

This seraph-band, each waved his hand:
It was a heavenly sight!
They stood as signals to the land,
Each one a lovely light;

This seraph-band, each waved his hand,
No voice did they impart—
No voice; but O, the silence sank
Like music on my heart.

But soon I heard the dash of oars,
I heard the Pilot's cheer;
My head was turn'd perforce away,
And I saw a boat appear.

The Pilot and the Pilot's boy,
I heard them coming fast:
Dear Lord in Heaven! it was a joy
The dead men could not blast.

I saw a third—I heard his voice:
It is the Hermit good!
He singeth loud his godly hymns
That he makes in the wood.
He'll shrieve my soul, he'll wash away
The Albatross's blood."

Part VII

"This Hermit good lives in that wood   *The Hermit of the*
Which slopes down to the sea.   *Wood*
How loudly his sweet voice he rears!
He loves to talk with marineres
That come from a far countree.

He kneels at morn, and noon, and eve—
He hath a cushion plump.
It is the moss that wholly hides
The rotted old oak-stump.

The skiff-boat near'd: I heard them talk,
"Why, this is strange, I trow!
Where are those lights so many and fair,
That signal made but now?"

"Strange, by my faith!" the Hermit said—   *Approacheth the*
"And they answer'd not our cheer!   *ship with wonder.*
The planks look warp'd! and see those sails,
How thin they are and sere!
I never saw aught like to them,
Unless perchance it were

Brown skeletons of leaves that lag
My forest-brook along;
When the ivy-tod is heavy with snow,
And the owlet whoops to the wolf below,
That eats the she-wolf's young."

"Dear Lord! it hath a fiendish look—
(The Pilot made reply)
I am a-fear'd."—"Push on, push on!"
Said the Hermit cheerily.

The boat came closer to the ship,
But I nor spake nor stirr'd;
The boat came close beneath the ship,
And straight a sound was heard.

Under the water it rumbled on   *The ship suddenly*
Still louder and more dread: *sinketh.*
It reach'd the ship, it split the bay;
The ship went down like lead.

Stunn'd by that loud and dreadful sound,   *The ancient*
Which sky and ocean smote,   *Mariner is saved in*
Like one that hath been seven days drown'd   *the Pilot's boat.*
My body lay afloat;
But swift as dreams, myself I found
Within the Pilot's boat.

Upon the whirl, where sank the ship,
The boat spun round and round;

And all was still, save that the hill
Was telling of the sound.

I moved my lips—the Pilot shriek'd
And fell down in a fit;
The holy Hermit raised his eyes,
And pray'd where he did sit.

I took the oars: the Pilot's boy,
Who now doth crazy go,
Laugh'd loud and long, and all the while
His eyes went to and fro.
"Ha! ha!" quoth he, "full plain I see
The Devil knows how to row."

And now, all in my own countree,
I stood on the firm land!
The Hermit stepp'd forth from the boat,
And scarcely he could stand.

The ancient Mariner earnestly entreateth the Hermit to shrieve him; and the penance of life falls on him.

"O shrieve me, shrieve me, holy man!"
The Hermit cross'd his brow.
"Say quick," quoth he, "I bid thee say—
What manner of man art thou?"

Forthwith this frame of mine was wrench'd
With a woeful agony,
Which forced me to begin my tale;
And then it left me free.

And ever and anon throughout his future life an agony constraineth him to travel from land to land;

Since then, at an uncertain hour,
That agony returns:
And till my ghastly tale is told,
This heart within me burns.

I pass, like night, from land to land;
I have strange power of speech;
That moment that his face I see,
I know the man that must hear me:
To him my tale I teach.

What loud uproar bursts from that door!
The wedding-guests are there:
But in the garden-bower the bride
And bride-maids singing are:
And hark, the little vesper bell,
Which biddeth me to prayer!

O Wedding-Guest! this soul hath been
Alone on a wide, wide sea:
So lonely 'twas, that God Himself
Scarce seemèd there to be.

O sweeter than the marriage-feast,
'Tis sweeter far to me,
To walk together to the kirk
With a goodly company!—

To walk together to the kirk,
And all together pray,
While each to his great Father bends,
Old men, and babes, and loving friends,
And youths and maidens gay!

Farewell, farewell! but this I tell   *And to teach, by his*
To thee, thou Wedding-Guest!   *own example, love*
He prayeth well, who loveth well   *and reverence to*
Both man and bird and beast.   *all things that God*
                                                                 made and loveth.

He prayeth best, who loveth best
All things both great and small;
For the dear God who loveth us,
He made and loveth all."

The Mariner, whose eye is bright,
Whose beard with age is hoar,
Is gone: and now the Wedding-Guest
Turn'd from the bridegroom's door.

He went like one that hath been stunn'd,
And is of sense forlorn:
A sadder and a wiser man
He rose the morrow morn.

THOMAS CAMPBELL
1774—1844

The River of Life

The more we live, more brief appear
    Our life's succeeding stages:
A day to childhood seems a year,
    And years like passing ages.

The gladsome current of our youth,
    Ere passion yet disorders,
Steals lingering like a river smooth
    Along its grassy borders.

But as the care-worn cheek grows wan,
    And sorrow's shafts fly thicker,
Ye stars, that measure life to man,
    Why seem your courses quicker?

When joys have lost their bloom and breath
    And life itself is vapid,
Why, as we reach the Falls of Death,
    Feel we its tide more rapid?

It may be strange—yet who would change
    Time's course to slower speeding,
When one by one our friends have gone
    And left our bosoms bleeding?

Heaven gives our years of fading strength
    Indemnifying fleetness;
And those of youth, a seeming length,
    Proportion'd to their sweetness.

WALTER SAVAGE LANDOR
1775–1864

Rose Aylmer

Ah what avails the sceptred race,
　　Ah what the form divine!
What every virtue, every grace!
　　Rose Aylmer, all were thine.

Rose Aylmer, whom these wakeful eyes
　　May weep, but never see,
A night of memories and of sighs
　　I consecrate to thee.

THOMAS MOORE
1779–1852

Believe Me, If All Those Endearing Young Charms

Believe me, if all those endearing young charms,
　　Which I gaze on so fondly today,
Were to change by tomorrow, and fleet in my arms,
　　Like fairy-gifts fading away,
Thou wouldst still be adored, as this moment thou art,
　　Let thy loveliness fade as it will,
And around the dear ruin each wish of my heart
　　Would entwine itself verdantly still.

It is not while beauty and youth are thine own,
　　And thy cheeks unprofaned by a tear,
That the fervour and faith of a soul can be known,
　　To which time will but make thee more dear;
No, the heart that has truly loved never forgets,
　　But as truly loves on to the close,
As the sunflower turns on her god, when he sets,
　　The same look which she turned when he rose.

LEIGH HUNT
1784–1859

Jenny Kiss'd Me

Jenny kiss'd me when we met,
    Jumping from the chair she sat in;
Time, you thief, who love to get
    Sweets into your list, put that in!
Say I'm weary, say I'm sad,
    Say that health and wealth have miss'd me,
Say I'm growing old, but add,
    Jenny kiss'd me.

GEORGE GORDON, LORD BYRON
1788–1824

She Walks in Beauty

She walks in beauty, like the night
    Of cloudless climes and starry skies;
And all that's best of dark and bright
    Meet in her aspect and her eyes:
Thus mellowed to that tender light
    Which heaven to gaudy day denies.

One shade the more, one ray the less,
    Had half impaired the nameless grace
Which waves in every raven tress,
    Or softly lightens o'er her face;
Where thoughts serenely sweet express
    How pure, how dear their dwelling-place.

And on that cheek, and o'er that brow,
    So soft, so calm, yet eloquent,
The smiles that win, the tints that glow,
    But tell of days in goodness spent,
A mind at peace with all below,
    A heart whose love is innocent!

So, We'll Go No More A-Roving

So, we'll go no more a-roving
　　So late into the night,
Though the heart be still as loving,
　　And the moon be still as bright.

For the sword outwears its sheath,
　　And the soul wears out the breast,
And the heart must pause to breathe,
　　And Love itself have rest.

Though the night was made for loving,
　　And the day returns too soon,
Yet we'll go no more a-roving
　　By the light of the moon.

The Sea

There is a pleasure in the pathless woods,
There is a rapture on the lonely shore,
There is society where none intrudes
By the deep sea, and music in its roar:
I love not man the less, but nature more,
From these our interviews, in which I steal
From all I may be, or have been before,
To mingle with the universe, and feel
What I can ne'er express, yet cannot all conceal.

Roll on, thou deep and dark blue Ocean,—roll!
Ten thousand fleets sweep over thee in vain;
Man marks the earth with ruin,—his control
Stops with the shore;—upon the watery plain
The wrecks are all thy deed, nor doth remain
A shadow of man's ravage, save his own,
When, for a moment, like a drop of rain,
He sinks into thy depths with bubbling groan,
Without a grave, unknelled, uncoffined, and unknown.

His steps are not upon thy paths,—thy fields
Are not a spoil for him,—thou dost arise
And shake him from thee; the vile strength he wields
For earth's destruction thou dost all despise,

Spurning him from thy bosom to the skies,
And send'st him, shivering in thy playful spray
And howling, to his gods, where haply lies
His petty hope in some near port or bay,
And dashest him again to earth:—there let him lay.

The armaments which thunderstrike the walls
Of rock-built cities, bidding nations quake
And monarchs tremble in their capitals,
The oak leviathans, whose huge ribs make
Their clay creator the vain title take
Of lord of thee and arbiter of war,—
These are thy toys, and, as the snowy flake,
They melt into thy yeast of waves, which mar
Alike the Armada's pride or spoils of Trafalgar.

Thy shores are empires, changed in all save thee;
Assyria, Greece, Rome, Carthage, what are they?
Thy waters wasted them while they were free,
And many a tyrant since; their shores obey
The stranger, slave, or savage; their decay
Has dried up realms to deserts: not so thou;
Unchangeable save to thy wild waves' play,
Time writes no wrinkles on thine azure brow;
Such as creation's dawn beheld, thou rollest now.

Thou glorious mirror, where the Almighty's form
Glasses itself in tempests; in all time,
Calm or convulsed,—in breeze, or gale, or storm,
Icing the pole, or in the torrid clime
Dark-heaving; boundless, endless, and sublime,
The image of Eternity,—the throne
Of the Invisible! even from out thy slime
The monsters of the deep are made; each zone
Obeys thee; thou goest forth, dread, fathomless, alone.

And I have loved thee, Ocean! and my joy
Of youthful sports was on thy breast to be
Borne, like thy bubbles, onward; from a boy
I wantoned with thy breakers,—they to me
Were a delight; and if the freshening sea

Made them a terror, 'twas a pleasing fear;
For I was as it were a child of thee,
And trusted to thy billows far and near,
And laid my hand upon thy mane,—as I do here.

From *Childe Harold's Pilgrimage*

PERCY BYSSHE SHELLEY
1792–1822

The World's Great Age

The world's great age begins anew,
   The golden years return,
The earth doth like a snake renew
   Her winter weeds outworn:
Heaven smiles, and faiths and empires gleam,
Like wrecks of a dissolving dream.

A brighter Hellas rears its mountains
   From waves serener far;
A new Peneus rolls his fountains
   Against the morning star.
Where fairer Tempes bloom, there sleep
Young Cyclads on a sunnier deep.

A loftier Argo cleaves the main,
   Fraught with a later prize;
Another Orpheus sings again,
   And loves, and weeps, and dies.
A new Ulysses leaves once more
Calypso for his native shore.

Oh, write no more the tale of Troy,
   If earth Death's scroll must be!
Nor mix with Laian rage the joy
   Which dawns upon the free:
Although a subtler Sphinx renew
Riddles of death Thebes never knew.

Another Athens shall arise,
  And to remoter time
Bequeath, like sunset to the skies,
  The splendor of its prime;
And leave, if naught so bright may live,
All earth can take or Heaven can give.

Saturn and Love their long repose
  Shall burst, more bright and good
Than all who fell, than One who rose,
  Than many unsubdued:
Not gold, not blood, their altar dowers,
But votive tears and symbol flowers.

Oh, cease! must hate and death return?
  Cease! must men kill and die?
Cease! drain not to its dregs the urn
  Of bitter prophecy.
The world is weary of the past,
Oh, might it die or rest at last!

From *Hellas*

Ozymandias

I met a traveler from an antique land
Who said: Two vast and trunkless legs of stone
Stand in the desert. Near them, on the sand,
Half sunk, a shattered visage lies, whose frown,
And wrinkled lip, and sneer of cold command,
Tell that its sculptor well those passions read
Which yet survive, stamped on these lifeless things,
The hand that mocked them and the heart that fed;
And on the pedestal these words appear:
"My name is Ozymandias, king of kings:
Look on my works, ye Mighty, and despair!"
Nothing beside remains. Round the decay
Of that colossal wreck, boundless and bare
The lone and level sands stretch far away.

One Word Is Too Often Profaned

One word is too often profaned
   For me to profane it;
One feeling too falsely disdain'd
   For thee to disdain it;
One hope is too like despair
   For prudence to smother;
And pity from thee more dear
   Than that from another.

I can give not what men call love:
   But wilt thou accept not
The worship the heart lifts above
   And the heavens reject not,
The desire of the moth for the star,
   Of the night for the morrow,
The devotion to something afar
   From the sphere of our sorrow?

The Indian Serenade

I arise from dreams of thee
In the first sweet sleep of night,
When the winds are breathing low,
And the stars are shining bright:
I arise from dreams of thee,
And a spirit in my feet
Hath led me—who knows how?
To thy chamber window, Sweet!

The wandering airs they faint
On the dark, the silent stream—
The Champak odors fail
Like sweet thoughts in a dream;
The nightingale's complaint,
It dies upon her heart;—
As I must on thine,
Oh, belovèd as thou art!

Oh lift me from the grass!
I die! I faint! I fail!
Let thy love in kisses rain

On my lips and eyelids pale.
My cheek is cold and white, alas!
My heart beats loud and fast;—
Oh! press it to thine own again,
Where it will break at last.

Ode to the West Wind

O wild West Wind, thou breath of Autumn's being,
Thou, from whose unseen presence the leaves dead
Are driven, like ghosts from an enchanter fleeing,

Yellow, and black, and pale, and hectic red,
Pestilence-stricken multitudes: O thou
Who chariotest to their dark wintry bed

The wingéd seeds, where they lie cold and low,
Each like a corpse within its grave, until
Thine azure sister of the Spring shall blow

Her clarion o'er the dreaming earth, and fill
(Driving sweet buds like flocks to feed in air)
With living hues and odours plain and hill:

Wild Spirit, which art moving everywhere;
Destroyer and Preserver; Hear, oh, hear!

Thou on whose stream, 'mid the steep sky's commotion,
Loose clouds like earth's decaying leaves are shed,
Shook from the tangled boughs of Heaven and Ocean,

Angels of rain and lightning; there are spread
On the blue surface of thine airy surge,
Like the bright hair uplifted from the head

Of some fierce Maenad, ev'n from the dim verge
Of the horizon to the zenith's height—
The locks of the approaching storm. Thou dirge

Of the dying year, to which this closing night
Will be the dome of a vast sepulchre,
Vaulted with all thy congregated might

Of vapours, from whose solid atmosphere
Black rain, and fire, and hail, will burst; oh, hear!

Thou who didst waken from his summer-dreams
The blue Mediterranean, where he lay,
Lull'd by the coil of his crystalline streams,

Beside a pumice isle in Baiae's bay,

And saw in sleep old palaces and towers
Quivering within the wave's intenser day,
All overgrown with azure moss and flowers
So sweet, the sense faints picturing them! Thou
For whose path the Atlantic's level powers
Cleave themselves into chasms, while far below
The sea-blooms and the oozy woods which wear
The sapless foliage of the ocean, know
Thy voice, and suddenly grow grey with fear
And tremble and despoil themselves: oh, hear!

If I were a dead leaf thou mightest bear;
If I were a swift cloud to fly with thee;
A wave to pant beneath thy power, and share
The impulse of thy strength, only less free
Than thou, O uncontrollable! If even
I were as in my boyhood, and could be
The comrade of thy wanderings over heaven,
As then, when to outstrip thy skiey speed
Scarce seem'd a vision, I would ne'er have striven
As thus with thee in prayer in my sore need.
Oh, lift me as a wave, a leaf, a cloud!
I fall upon the thorns of life! I bleed!
A heavy weight of hours has chain'd and bow'd
One too like thee: tameless, and swift, and proud.

Make me thy lyre, ev'n as the forest is:
What if my leaves are falling like its own?
The tumult of thy mighty harmonies
Will take from both a deep autumnal tone,
Sweet though in sadness. Be thou, Spirit fierce,
My spirit! be thou me, impetuous one!
Drive my dead thoughts over the universe
Like wither'd leaves to quicken a new birth;
And, by the incantation of this verse,
Scatter, as from an unextinguish'd hearth
Ashes and sparks, my words among mankind!
Be through my lips to unawaken'd earth
The trumpet of a prophecy! O Wind,
If Winter comes, can Spring be far behind?

Hymn to Intellectual Beauty

The awful shadow of some unseen Power
   Floats though unseen among us,—visiting
   This various world with as inconstant wing
As summer winds that creep from flower to flower;
Like moonbeams that behind some piny mountain shower,
     It visits with inconstant glance
     Each human heart and countenance:
Like hues and harmonies of evening,—
     Like clouds in starlight widely spread,—
     Like memory of music fled,—
     Like aught that for its grace may be
Dear, and yet dearer for its mystery.

Spirit of Beauty, that dost consecrate
   With thine own hues all thou dost shine upon
   Of human thought or form,—where art thou gone?
Why dost thou pass away and leave our state,
This dim vast vale of tears, vacant and desolate?
     Ask why the sunlight not forever
     Weaves rainbows o'er yon mountain river,
Why aught should fail and fade that once is shown,
     Why fear and dream and death and birth
     Cast on the daylight of this earth
     Such gloom,—why man has such a scope
For love and hate, despondency and hope?

No voice from some sublimer world hath ever
   To sage or poet these responses given—
   Therefore the names of Daemon, Ghost, and Heaven,
Remain the records of their vain endeavor,
Frail spells—whose uttered charm might not avail to sever,
     From all we hear and all we see,
     Doubt, chance, and mutability.
Thy light alone—like mist o'er mountains driven,
     Or music by the night wind sent
     Through strings of some still instrument,
     Or moonlight on a midnight stream,
Gives grace and truth to life's unquiet dream.

Love, Hope, and Self-esteem, like clouds depart
   And come, for some uncertain moments lent.

Man were immortal, and omnipotent,
Didst thou, unknown and awful as thou art,
Keep with thy glorious train firm state within his heart.
    Thou messenger of sympathies,
    That wax and wane in lovers' eyes—
Thou—that to human thought art nourishment,
    Like darkness to a dying flame!
    Depart not as thy shadow came,
    Depart not—lest the grave should be,
Like life and fear, a dark reality.

While yet a boy I sought for ghosts, and sped
    Through many a listening chamber, cave and ruin,
    And starlight wood, with fearful steps pursuing
Hopes of high talk with the departed dead.
I called on poisonous names with which our youth is fed;
    I was not heard—I saw them not—
    When musing deeply on the lot
Of life, at that sweet time when winds are wooing
    All vital things that wake to bring
    News of birds and blossoming,—
    Sudden, thy shadow fell on me;
I shrieked, and clasped my hands in ecstasy!

I vowed that I would dedicate my powers
    To thee and thine—have I not kept the vow?
    With beating heart and streaming eyes, even now
I call the phantoms of a thousand hours
Each from his voiceless grave: they have in visioned bowers
    Of studious zeal or love's delight
    Outwatched with me the envious night—
They know that never joy illumed my brow
    Unlinked with hope that thou wouldst free
    This world from its dark slavery,
    That thou—O awful Loveliness,
Wouldst give whate'er these words cannot express.

The day becomes more solemn and serene
    When noon is past—there is a harmony
    In autumn, and a lustre in its sky,
Which through the summer is not heard or seen,

As if it could not be, as if it had not been!
    Thus let thy power, which like the truth
    Of nature on thy passive youth
Descended, to my onward life supply
    Its calm—to one who worships thee,
    And every form containing thee,
    Whom, Spirit fair, thy spells did bind
To fear himself, and love all human kind.

When the Lamp Is Shatter'd

    When the lamp is shatter'd
The light in the dust lies dead—
    When the cloud is scatter'd,
The rainbow's glory is shed.
    When the lute is broken,
Sweet tones are remember'd not;
    When the lips have spoken,
Loved accents are soon forgot.

    As music and splendour
Survive not the lamp and the lute,
    The heart's echoes render
No song when the spirit is mute—
    No song but sad dirges,
Like the wind through a ruin'd cell,
    Or the mournful surges
That ring the dead seaman's knell.

    When hearts have once mingled,
Love first leaves the well-built nest;
    The weak one is singled
To endure what it once possess'd.
    O Love! who bewailest
The frailty of all things here,
    Why choose you the frailest
For your cradle, your home, and your bier?

    Its passions will rock thee
As the storms rock the ravens on high;
    Bright reason will mock thee
Like the sun from a wintry sky.

From thy nest every rafter
Will rot, and thine eagle home
Leave thee naked to laughter,
When leaves fall and cold winds come.

Music, When Soft Voices Die

Music, when soft voices die,
Vibrates in the memory—
Odours, when sweet violets sicken,
Live within the sense they quicken.
Rose leaves, when the rose is dead,
Are heap'd for the beloved's bed;
And so thy thoughts, when thou art gone,
Love itself shall slumber on.

To a Skylark

Hail to thee, blithe spirit!
  Bird thou never wert—
That from heaven or near it
  Pourest thy full heart
In profuse strains of unpremeditated art.

Higher still and higher
  From the earth thou springest,
Like a cloud of fire;
  The blue deep thou wingest,
And singing still dost soar, and soaring ever singest.

In the golden light'ning
  Of the sunken sun,
O'er which clouds are bright'ning,
  Thou dost float and run,
Like an unbodied joy whose race is just begun.

The pale purple even
  Melts around thy flight;
Like a star of heaven,
  In the broad daylight
Thou art unseen, but yet I hear thy shrill delight—

Keen as are the arrows
  Of that silver sphere

Whose intense lamp narrows
    In the white dawn clear,
Until we hardly see, we feel that it is there.

All the earth and air
    With thy voice is loud,
As, when night is bare,
    From one lonely cloud
The moon rains out her beams, and heaven is overflow'd.

What thou art we know not;
    What is most like thee?
From rainbow clouds there flow not
    Drops so bright to see,
As from thy presence showers a rain of melody:—

Like a poet hidden
    In the light of thought,
Singing hymns unbidden,
    Till the world is wrought
To sympathy with hopes and fears it heeded not:

Like a high-born maiden
    In a palace tower,
Soothing her love-laden
    Soul in secret hour
With music sweet as love, which overflows her bower:

Like a glow-worm golden
    In a dell of dew,
Scattering unbeholden
    Its aërial hue
Among the flowers and grass which screen it from the view:

Like a rose embower'd
    In its own green leaves,
By warm winds deflower'd,
    Till the scent it gives
Makes faint with too much sweet those heavy-wingèd thieves.

Sound of vernal showers
    On the twinkling grass,

Rain-awaken'd flowers—
        All that ever was
Joyous and clear and fresh—thy music doth surpass.

Teach us, sprite or bird,
        What sweet thoughts are thine:
I have never heard
        Praise of love or wine
That panted forth a flood of rapture so divine.

Chorus hymeneal,
        Or triumphal chant,
Match'd with thine would be all
        But an empty vaunt—
A thing wherein we feel there is some hidden want.

What objects are the fountains
        Of thy happy strain?
What fields, or waves, or mountains?
        What shapes of sky or plain?
What love of thine own kind? what ignorance of pain?

With thy clear keen joyance
        Languor cannot be:
Shadow of annoyance
        Never came near thee:
Thou lovest, but ne'er knew love's sad satiety.

Waking or asleep,
        Thou of death must deem
Things more true and deep
        Than we mortals dream,
Or how could thy notes flow in such a crystal stream?

We look before and after,
        And pine for what is not:
Our sincerest laughter
        With some pain is fraught;
Our sweetest songs are those that tell of saddest thought.

Yet, if we could scorn
        Hate and pride and fear,

If we were things born
        Not to shed a tear,
I know not how thy joy we ever should come near.

        Better than all measures
        Of delightful sound,
        Better than all treasures
        That in books are found,
Thy skill to poet were, thou scorner of the ground!

        Teach me half the gladness
        That thy brain must know;
        Such harmonious madness
        From my lips would flow,
The world should listen then, as I am listening now.

Adonais

I weep for Adonais—he is dead!
Oh weep for Adonais! though our tears
Thaw not the frost which binds so dear a head!
And thou, sad Hour, selected from all years
To mourn our loss, rouse thy obscure compeers,
And teach them thine own sorrow! Say: "With me
Died Adonais; till the Future dares
Forget the Past, his fate and fame shall be
An echo and a light unto Eternity!"

Where wert thou, mighty Mother, when he lay,
When thy son lay, pierced by the shaft which flies
In darkness? where was lorn Urania
When Adonais died? With veilèd eyes,
'Mid listening Echoes, in her paradise
She sate, while one, with soft enamored breath,
Rekindled all the fading melodies,
With which, like flowers that mock the corse beneath,
He had adorned and hid the coming bulk of death.

Oh, weep for Adonais—he is dead!
Wake, melancholy Mother, wake and weep!
Yet wherefore? Quench within their burning bed
Thy fiery tears, and let thy loud heart keep

Like his, a mute and uncomplaining sleep;
For he is gone, where all things wise and fair
Descend. Oh, dream not that the amorous Deep
Will yet restore him to the vital air;
Death feeds on his mute voice, and laughs at our despair.

Most musical of mourners, weep again!
Lament anew, Urania!—He died,
Who was the sire of an immortal strain,
Blind, old, and lonely, when his country's pride,
The priest, the slave, and the liberticide,
Trampled and mocked with many a loathèd rite
Of lust and blood; he went, unterrified,
Into the gulf of death; but his clear Sprite
Yet reigns o'er earth, the third among the sons of light.

Most musical of mourners, weep anew!
Not all to that bright station dared to climb;
And happier they their happiness who knew,
Whose tapers yet burn through that night of time
In which suns perished; others more sublime,
Struck by the envious wrath of man or God,
Have sunk, extinct in their refulgent prime;
And some yet live, treading the thorny road,
Which leads, through toil and hate, to Fame's serene abode.

But now, thy youngest, dearest one has perished,
The nursling of thy widowhood, who grew,
Like a pale flower by some sad maiden cherished,
And fed with true-love tears instead of dew;
Most musical of mourners, weep anew!
Thy extreme hope, the loveliest and the last,
The bloom, whose petals nipped before they blew,
Died on the promise of the fruit, is waste;
The broken lily lies—the storm is overpast.

To that high Capital, where kingly Death
Keeps his pale court in beauty and decay,
He came; and bought, with price of purest breath,
A grave among the eternal.—Come away!
Haste, while the vault of blue Italian day

Is yet his fitting charnel-roof! while still
He lies, as if in dewy sleep he lay;
Awake him not! surely he takes his fill
Of deep and liquid rest, forgetful of all ill.

He will awake no more, oh, never more!
Within the twilight chamber spreads apace
The shadow of white Death, and at the door
Invisible Corruption waits to trace
His extreme way to her dim dwelling-place;
The eternal Hunger sits, but pity and awe
Soothe her pale rage, nor dares she to deface
So fair a prey, till darkness, and the law
Of change, shall o'er his sleep the mortal curtain draw.

Oh, weep for Adonais!—The quick Dreams,
The passion-wingèd ministers of thought,
Who were his flocks, whom near the living streams
Of his young spirit he fed, and whom he taught
The love which was its music, wander not,—
Wander no more, from kindling brain to brain,
But droop there, whence they sprung; and mourn their lot
Round the cold heart, where, after their sweet pain,
They ne'er will gather strength, or find a home again.

And one with trembling hands clasps his cold head,
And fans him with her moonlight wings, and cries;
"Our love, our hope, our sorrow, is not dead;
See, on the silken fringe of his faint eyes,
Like dew upon a sleeping flower, there lies
A tear some Dream has loosened from his brain."
Lost Angel of a ruined paradise!
She knew not 'twas her own; as with no stain
She faded, like a cloud which had outwept its rain.

One from a lucid urn of starry dew
Washed his light limbs as if embalming them;
Another clipped her profuse locks, and threw
The wreath upon him, like an anadem,
Which frozen tears instead of pearls begem;
Another in her wilful grief would break

Her bow and winged reeds, as if to stem
A greater loss with one which was more weak;
And dull the barbèd fire against his frozen cheek.

Another Splendor on his mouth alit,
That mouth, whence it was wont to draw the breath
Which gave it strength to pierce the guarded wit,
And pass into the panting heart beneath
With lightning and with music: the damp death
Quenched its caress upon his icy lips;
And, as a dying meteor stains a wreath
Of moonlight vapor, which the cold night clips,
It flushed through his pale limbs, and passed to its eclipse.

And others came—Desires and Adorations,
Wingèd Persuasions and veiled Destinies,
Splendors, and Glooms, and glimmering Incarnations
Of hopes and fears, and twilight Fantasies;
And Sorrow, with her family of Sighs,
And Pleasure, blind with tears, led by the gleam
Of her own dying smile instead of eyes,
Came in slow pomp;—the moving pomp might seem
Like pageantry of mist on an autumnal stream.

All he had loved, and molded into thought,
From shape, and hue, and odor, and sweet sound,
Lamented Adonais. Morning sought
Her eastern watch-tower, and her hair unbound,
Wet with the tears which should adorn the ground,
Dimmed the aërial eyes that kindle day;
Afar the melancholy thunder moaned,
Pale Ocean in unquiet slumber lay,
And the wild winds flew round, sobbing in their dismay.

Lost Echo sits amid the voiceless mountains,
And feeds her grief with his remembered lay,
And will no more reply to winds or fountains,
Or amorous birds perched on the young green spray,
Or herdsmen's horn, or bell at closing day;
Since she can mimic not his lips, more dear
Than those for whose disdain she pined away

Into a shadow of all sounds:—a drear
Murmur, between their songs, is all the woodmen hear.

Grief made the young Spring wild, and she threw down
Her kindling buds, as if she Autumn were,
Or they dead leaves; since her delight is flown,
For whom should she have waked the sullen year?
To Phœbus was not Hyacinth so dear
Nor to himself Narcissus, as to both
Thou, Adonais: wan they stand and sere
Amid the faint companions of their youth,
With dew all turned to tears; odor, to sighing ruth.

Thy spirit's sister, the lorn nightingale
Mourns not her mate with such melodious pain;
Not so the eagle, who like thee could scale
Heaven, and could nourish in the sun's domain
Her mighty youth with morning, doth complain,
Soaring and screaming round her empty nest,
As Albion wails for thee: the curse of Cain
Light on his head who pierced thy innocent breast,
And scared the angel soul that was its earthly guest!

Ah, woe is me! Winter is come and gone,
But grief returns with the revolving year;
The airs and streams renew their joyous tone;
The ants, the bees, the swallows reappear;
Fresh leaves and flowers deck the dead Seasons' bier;
The amorous birds now pair in every brake,
And build their mossy homes in field and brere;
And the green lizard, and the golden snake,
Like unimprisoned flames, out of their trance awake.

Through wood and stream and field and hill and ocean
A quickening life from the Earth's heart has burst
As it has ever done, with change and motion,
From the great morning of the world when first
God dawned on Chaos; in its stream immersed,
The lamps of Heaven flash with a softer light;
All baser things pant with life's sacred thirst;
Diffuse themselves; and spend in love's delight,
The beauty and the joy of their renewèd might.

The leprous corpse, touched by this spirit tender,
Exhales itself in flowers of gentle breath;
Like incarnations of the stars, when splendor
Is changed to fragrance, they illumine death
And mock the merry worm that wakes beneath;
Nought we know dies. Shall that alone which knows
Be as a sword consumed before the sheath
By sightless lightning?—the intense atom glows
A moment, then is quenched in a most cold repose.

Alas! that all we loved of him should be,
But for our grief, as if it had not been,
And grief itself be mortal! Woe is me!
Whence are we, and why are we? of what scene
The actors or spectators? Great and mean
Meet massed in death, who lends what life must borrow.
As long as skies are blue, and fields are green,
Evening must usher night, night urge the morrow,
Month follow month with woe, and year wake year to sorrow.

He will awake no more, oh, never more!
"Wake thou," cried Misery, "childless Mother, rise
Out of thy sleep, and slake, in thy heart's core,
A wound more fierce than his, with tears and sighs."
And all the Dreams that watched Urania's eyes,
And all the Echoes whom their sister's song
Had held in holy silence, cried: "Arise!"
Swift as a Thought by the snake Memory stung,
From her ambrosial rest the fading Splendor sprung.

She rose like an autumnal Night, that springs
Out of the East, and follows wild and drear
The golden Day, which, on eternal wings,
Even as a ghost abandoning a bier,
Had left the Earth a corpse;—sorrow and fear
So struck, so roused, so rapt Urania;
So saddened round her like an atmosphere
Of stormy mist; so swept her on her way
Even to the mournful place where Adonais lay.

Out of her secret paradise she sped.
Through camps and cities rough with stone, and steel,

And human hearts, which to her airy tread
Yielding not, wounded the invisible
Palms of her tender feet where'er they fell:
And barbèd tongues, and thoughts more sharp than they.
Rent the soft Form they never could repel,
Whose sacred blood, like the young tears of May,
Paved with eternal flowers that undeserving way.

In the death-chamber for a moment Death,
Shamed by the presence of that living Might,
Blushed to annihilation, and the breath
Revisited those lips, and Life's pale light
Flashed through those limbs, so late her dear delight.
"Leave me not wild and drear and comfortless,
As silent lightning leaves the starless night!
Leave me not!" cried Urania: her distress
Roused Death: Death rose and smiled, and met her vain caress.

"Stay yet awhile! speak to me once again;
Kiss me, so long but as a kiss may live;
And in my heartless breast and burning brain
That word, that kiss, shall all thoughts else survive,
With food of saddest memory kept alive,
Now thou art dead, as if it were a part
Of thee, my Adonais! I would give
All that I am to be as thou now art!
But I am chained to Time, and cannot thence depart!

"O gentle child, beautiful as thou wert,
Why didst thou leave the trodden paths of men
Too soon, and with weak hands though mighty heart
Dare the unpastured dragon in his den?
Defenseless as thou wert, oh, where was then
Wisdom the mirrored shield, or scorn the spear?
Or hadst thou waited the full cycle when
Thy spirit should have filled its crescent sphere,
The monsters of life's waste had fled from thee like deer.

"The herded wolves, bold only to pursue;
The obscene ravens, clamorous o'er the dead;
The vultures to the conqueror's banner true
Who feed where Desolation first has fed,

And whose wings rain contagion;—how they fled,
When, like Apollo, from his golden bow
The Pythian of the age one arrow sped
And smiled!—The spoilers tempt no second blow,
They fawn on the proud feet that spurn them lying low.

"The sun comes forth, and many reptiles spawn;
He sets, and each ephemeral insect then
Is gathered into death without a dawn,
And the immortal stars awake again;
So is it in the world of living men:
A godlike mind soars forth, in its delight
Making earth bare and veiling heaven, and when
It sinks, the swarms that dimmed or shared its light
Leave to its kindred lamps the spirit's awful night."

Thus ceased she: and the mountain shepherds came,
Their garlands sere, their magic mantles rent;
The Pilgrim of Eternity, whose fame
Over his living head like Heaven is bent,
An early but enduring monument,
Came, veiling all the lightnings of his song
In sorrow; from her wilds Ierne sent
The sweetest lyrist of her saddest wrong,
And love taught grief to fall like music from his tongue.

Midst others of less note, came one frail Form,
A phantom among men; companionless
As the last cloud of an expiring storm
Whose thunder is its knell; he, as I guess,
Had gazed on Nature's naked loveliness,
Actæon-like, and now he fled astray
With feeble steps o'er the world's wilderness,
And his own thoughts, along that rugged way,
Pursued, like raging hounds, their father and their prey.

A pardlike Spirit beautiful and swift—
A Love in desolation masked;—a Power
Girt round with weakness;—it can scarce uplift
The weight of the superincumbent hour;
It is a dying lamp, a falling shower,

A breaking billow;—even whilst we speak
Is it not broken? On the withering flower
The killing sun smiles brightly: on a cheek
The life can burn in blood, even while the heart may break.

His head was bound with pansies overblown,
And faded violets, white, and pied, and blue;
And a light spear topped with a cypress cone,
Round whose rude shaft dark ivy-tresses grew
Yet dripping with the forest's noonday dew,
Vibrated, as the ever-beating heart
Shook the weak hand that grasped it; of that crew
He came the last, neglected and apart;
A herd-abandoned deer struck by the hunter's dart.

All stood aloof, and at his partial moan
Smiled through their tears; well knew that gentle band
Who in another's fate now wept his own,
As in the accents of an unknown land
He sung new sorrow; sad Urania scanned
The stranger's mien, and murmured: "Who art thou?"
He answered not, but with a sudden hand
Made bare his branded and ensanguined brow,
Which was like Cain's or Christ's—oh! that it should be so!

What softer voice is hushed over the dead?
Athwart what brow is that dark mantle thrown?
What form leans sadly o'er the white death-bed,
In mockery of monumental stone,
The heavy heart heaving without a moan?
If it be he, who, gentlest of the wise,
Taught, soothed, loved, honored the departed one,
Let me not vex, with inharmonious sighs,
The silence of that heart's accepted sacrifice.

Our Adonais has drunk poison—oh,
What deaf and viperous murderer could crown
Life's early cup with such a draught of woe?
The nameless worm would now itself disown:
It felt, yet could escape, the magic tone
Whose prelude held all envy, hate, and wrong,

But what was howling in one breast alone,
Silent with expectation of the song,
Whose master's hand is cold, whose silver lyre unstrung.

Live thou, whose infamy is not thy fame!
Live! fear no heavier chastisement from me,
Thou noteless blot on a remembered name!
But be thyself, and know thyself to be!
And ever at thy season be thou free
To spill the venom when thy fangs o'erflow:
Remorse and Self-Contempt shall cling to thee;
Hot Shame shall burn upon thy secret brow,
And like a beaten hound tremble thou shalt—as now.

Nor let us weep that our delight is fled
Far from these carrion kites that scream below;
He wakes or sleeps with the enduring dead;
Thou canst not soar where he is sitting now.—
Dust to the dust! but the pure spirit shall flow
Back to the burning fountain whence it came,
A portion of the Eternal, which must glow
Through time and change, unquenchably the same,
Whilst thy cold embers choke the sordid hearth of shame.

Peace, peace! he is not dead, he doth not sleep—
He hath awakened from the dream of life—
'Tis we, who, lost in stormy visions, keep
With phantoms an unprofitable strife,
And in mad trance, strike with our spirit's knife
Invulnerable nothings. *We* decay
Like corpses in a charnel; fear and grief
Convulse us and consume us day by day,
And cold hopes swarm like worms within our living clay.

He has outsoared the shadow of our night;
Envy and calumny and hate and pain,
And that unrest which men miscall delight,
Can touch him not and torture not again;
From the contagion of the world's slow stain
He is secure, and now can never mourn
A heart grown cold, a head grown gray in vain;

Nor, when the spirit's self has ceased to burn,
With sparkless ashes load an unlamented urn.

He lives, he wakes—'tis Death is dead, not he;
Mourn not for Adonais—Thou young Dawn,
Turn all thy dew to splendor, for from thee
The spirit thou lamentest is not gone;
Ye caverns and ye forests, cease to moan!
Cease, ye faint flowers and fountains, and thou air,
Which like a mourning veil thy scarf hadst thrown
O'er the abandoned Earth, now leave it bare
Even to the joyous stars which smile on its despair!

He is made one with Nature: there is heard
His voice in all her music, from the moan
Of thunder, to the song of night's sweet bird;
He is a presence to be felt and known
In darkness and in light, from herb and stone,
Spreading itself where'er that Power may move
Which has withdrawn his being to its own;
Which wields the world with never-wearied love,
Sustains it from beneath, and kindles it above.

He is a portion of the loveliness
Which once he made more lovely: he doth bear
His part, while the one Spirit's plastic stress
Sweeps through the dull dense world, compelling there
All new successions to the forms they wear,
Torturing the unwilling dross that checks its flight
To its own likeness, as each mass may bear;
And bursting in its beauty and its might
From trees and beasts and men into the Heaven's light.

The splendors of the firmament of time
May be eclipsed, but are extinguished not;
Like stars to their appointed height they climb,
And death is a low mist which cannot blot
The brightness it may veil. When lofty thought
Lifts a young heart above its mortal lair,
And love and life contend in it for what
Shall be its earthly doom, the dead live there
And move like winds of light on dark and stormy air.

The inheritors of unfulfilled renown
Rose from their thrones, built beyond mortal thought,
Far in the Unapparent. Chatterton
Rose pale,—his solemn agony had not
Yet faded from him; Sidney, as he fought
And as he fell and as he lived and loved
Sublimely mild, a Spirit without spot,
Arose; and Lucan, by his death approved:
Oblivion as they rose shrank like a thing reproved.

And many more, whose names on earth are dark,
But whose transmitted effluence cannot die
So long as fire outlives the parent spark,
Rose, robed in dazzling immortality.
"Thou art become as one of us," they cry,
"It was for thee yon kingless sphere has long
Swung blind in unascended majesty,
Silent alone amid an heaven of song.
Assume thy wingèd throne, thou Vesper of our throng!"

Who mourns for Adonais? Oh, come forth,
Fond wretch! and know thyself and him aright.
Clasp with thy panting soul the pendulous earth;
As from a center, dart by thy spirit's light
Beyond all worlds, until its spacious might
Satiate the void circumference: then shrink
Even to a point within our day and night;
And keep thy heart light lest it make thee sink
When hope has kindled hope, and lured thee to the brink.

Or go to Rome, which is the sepulcher,
Oh, not of him, but of our joy: 'tis nought
That ages, empires, and religious there
Lie buried in the ravage they have wrought;
For such as he can lend,—they borrow not
Glory from those who made the world their prey;
And he is gathered to the kings of thought
Who waged contention with their time's decay,
And of the past are all that cannot pass away.

Go thou to Rome,—at once the Paradise,
The grave, the city, and the wilderness;

And where its wrecks like shattered mountains rise,
And flowering weeds and fragrant copses dress
The bones of Desolation's nakedness,
Pass, till the Spirit of the spot shall lead
Thy footsteps to a slope of green access
Where, like an infant's smile, over the dead
A light of laughing flowers along the grass is spread;

And gray walls molder round, on which dull Time
Feeds, like slow fire, upon a hoary brand;
And one keen pyramid with wedge sublime,
Pavilioning the dust of him who planned
This refuge for his memory, doth stand
Like flame transformed to marble; and beneath,
A field is spread, on which a newer band
Have pitched in Heaven's smile their camp of death,
Welcoming him we lose with scarce extinguished breath.

Here pause: these graves are all too young as yet
To have outgrown the sorrow which consigned
Its charge to each; and if the seal is set,
Here, on one fountain of a mourning mind,
Break it not thou! too surely shalt thou find
Thine own well full, if thou returnest home,
Of tears and gall. From the world's bitter wind
Seek shelter in the shadow of the tomb.
What Adonais is, why fear we to become?

The One remains, the many change and pass;
Heaven's light forever shines, Earth's shadows fly;
Life, like a dome of many-colored glass,
Stains the white radiance of Eternity,
Until Death tramples it to fragments.—Die,
If thou wouldst be with that which thou dost seek!
Follow where all is fled!—Rome's azure sky,
Flowers, ruins, statues, music, words, are weak
The glory they transfuse with fitting truth to speak.

Why linger, why turn back, why shrink, my heart?
Thy hopes are gone before: from all things here
They have departed; thou shouldst now depart!

A light is passed from the revolving year,
And man, and woman; and what still is dear
Attracts to crush, repels to make thee wither.
The soft sky smiles,—the low wind whispers near:
'Tis Adonais calls! oh, hasten thither,
No more let Life divide what Death can join together.

That Light whose smile kindles the Universe,
That Beauty in which all things work and move,
That Benediction which the eclipsing Curse
Of birth can quench not, that sustaining Love
Which through the web of being blindly wove
By man and beast and earth and air and sea,
Burns bright or dim, as each are mirrors of
The fire for which all thirst; now beams on me,
Consuming the last clouds of cold mortality.

The breath whose might I have invoked in song
Descends on me; my spirit's bark is driven,
Far from the shore, far from the trembling throng
Whose sails were never to the tempest given;
The massy earth and spherèd skies are riven!
I am borne darkly, fearfully, afar:
Whilst, burning through the inmost veil of Heaven,
The soul of Adonais, like a star,
Beacons from the abode where the Eternal are.

WILLIAM CULLEN BRYANT
1794–1878

To a Waterfowl

Whither, 'midst falling dew,
While glow the heavens with the last steps of day,
Far, through their rosy depths, dost thou pursue
Thy solitary way!

Vainly the fowler's eye
Might mark thy distant flight to do thee wrong,
As, darkly painted on the crimson sky,
 Thy figure floats along.

Seek'st thou the plashy brink
Of weedy lake, or marge of river wide,
Or where the rocking billows rise and sink
 On the chafed ocean side?

There is a power whose care
Teaches thy way along that pathless coast,—
The desert and illimitable air,—
 Lone wandering, but not lost.

All day thy wings have fanned,
At that far height, the cold, thin atmosphere,
Yet stoop not, weary, to the welcome land,
 Though the dark night is near.

And soon that toil shall end;
Soon shalt thou find a summer home, and rest,
And scream among thy fellows; reeds shall bend,
 Soon, o'er thy sheltered nest.

Thou'rt gone, the abyss of heaven
Hath swallowed up thy form; yet, on my heart
Deeply hath sunk the lesson thou hast given,
 And shall not soon depart.

He who, from zone to zone,
Guides through the boundless sky thy certain flight.
In the long way that I must tread alone,
 Will lead my steps aright.

JOHN KEATS
1795–1821

On First Looking into Chapman's Homer

Much have I travelled in the realms of gold,
And many goodly states and kingdoms seen;
Round many western islands have I been
Which bards in fealty to Apollo hold.
Oft of one wide expanse had I been told
That deep-browed Homer ruled as his demesne;
Yet did I never breathe its pure serene
Till I heard Chapman speak out loud and bold.

Then felt I like some watcher of the skies
When a new planet swims into his ken;
Or like stout Cortez when with eagle eyes
He stared at the Pacific—and all his men
Looked at each other with a wild surmise—
Silent, upon a peak in Darien.

Ode to a Nightingale

My heart aches, and a drowsy numbness pains
    My sense, as though of hemlock I had drunk,
Or emptied some dull opiate to the drains
    One minute past, and Lethe-wards had sunk:
'Tis not through envy of thy happy lot,
    But being too happy in thine happiness—
        That thou, light-wingèd Dryad of the trees,
            In some melodious plot
Of beechen green, and shadows numberless,
    Singest of summer in full-throated ease.

O for a draught of vintage! that hath been
    Cooled a long age in the deep delvèd earth,
Tasting of Flora and the country green,
    Dance, and Provençal song, and sunburnt mirth!
O for a beaker full of the warm South,
    Full of the true, the blushful Hippocrene,
        With beaded bubbles winking at the brim,
            And purple-stainèd mouth;

That I might drink, and leave the world unseen,
   And with thee fade away into the forest dim:

Fade away, dissolve, and quite forget
   What thou among the leaves hast never known,
The weariness, the fever, and the fret
   Here, where men sit and hear each other groan;
Where palsy shakes a few, sad, last gray hairs,
   Where youth grows pale, and specter-thin, and dies;
     Where but to think is to be full of sorrow
      And leaden-eyed despairs,
Where Beauty cannot keep her lustrous eyes,
   Or new Love pine at them beyond to-morrow.

Away! away! for I will fly to thee,
   Not charioted by Bacchus and his pards,
But on the viewless wings of Poesy,
   Though the dull brain perplexes and retards:
Already with thee! tender is the night,
   And haply the Queen-Moon is on her throne,
     Clustered around by all her starry Fays;
      But here there is no light,
Save what from heaven is with the breezes blown
     Through verdurous glooms and winding mossy ways.

I cannot see what flowers are at my feet,
   Nor what soft incense hangs upon the boughs,
But, in embalmèd darkness, guess each sweet
   Wherewith the seasonable month endows
The grass, the thicket, and the fruit-tree wild;
   White hawthorn, and the pastoral eglantine;
     Fast-fading violets covered up in leaves;
      And mid-May's eldest child,
The coming musk-rose, full of dewy wine,
     The murmurous haunt of flies on summer eves.

Darkling I listen; and for many a time
   I have been half in love with easeful Death,
Called him soft names in many a musèd rhyme,
   To take into the air my quiet breath;
Now more than ever seems it rich to die,

To cease upon the midnight with no pain,
   While thou art pouring forth thy soul abroad
     In such an ecstasy!
   Still wouldst thou sing, and I have ears in vain—
     To thy high requiem become a sod.

Thou wast not born for death, immortal Bird!
   No hungry generations tread thee down;
The voice I hear this passing night was heard
   In ancient days by emperor and clown:
Perhaps the self-same song that found a path
   Through the sad heart of Ruth, when, sick for home,
     She stood in tears amid the alien corn;
       The same that oft-times hath
   Charmed magic casements, opening on the foam
     Of perilous seas, in faery lands forlorn.

Forlorn! the very word is like a bell
   To toll me back from thee to my sole self!
Adieu! the fancy cannot cheat so well
   As she is famed to do, deceiving elf.
Adieu! adieu! thy plaintive anthem fades
   Past the near meadows, over the still stream,
     Up the hill-side; and now 'tis buried deep
       In the next valley-glades:
   Was it a vision, or a waking dream?
     Fled is that music:—Do I wake or sleep?

On the Grasshopper and the Cricket

   The poetry of earth is never dead:
   When all the birds are faint with the hot sun,
   And hide in cooling trees, a voice will run
   From hedge to hedge about the new-mown mead;
   That is the Grasshopper's—he takes the lead
   In summer luxury,—he has never done
   With his delights; for when tired out with fun
   He rests at ease beneath some pleasant weed.
   The poetry of earth is ceasing never:
   On a lone winter evening, when the frost
   Has wrought a silence, from the stove there shrills
   The Cricket's song, in warmth increasing ever,

And seems to one in drowsiness half lost,
The Grasshopper's among some grassy hills.

Ode on a Grecian Urn

Thou still unravished bride of quietness,
 Thou foster-child of silence and slow time,
Sylvan historian, who canst thus express
 A flowery tale more sweetly than our rhyme:
What leaf-fringed legend haunts about thy shape
 Of deities or mortals, or of both,
  In Tempe or the dales of Arcady?
What men or gods are these? What maidens loth?
 What mad pursuit? What struggle to escape?
  What pipes and timbrels? What wild ecstasy?

Heard melodies are sweet, but those unheard
 Are sweeter; therefore, ye soft pipes, play on;
Not to the sensual ear, but, more endeared,
 Pipe to the spirit ditties of no tone:
Fair youth, beneath the trees, thou canst not leave
 Thy song, nor ever can those trees be bare;
  Bold Lover, never, never canst thou kiss,
Though winning near the goal—yet, do not grieve;
 She cannot fade, though thou hast not thy bliss,
  For ever wilt thou love, and she be fair!

Ah, happy, happy boughs! that cannot shed
 Your leaves, nor ever bid the Spring adieu;
And, happy melodist, unwearièd,
 For ever piping songs for ever new;
More happy love! more happy, happy love!
 For ever warm and still to be enjoyed,
  For ever panting, and for ever young;
All breathing human passion far above,
 That leaves a heart high-sorrowful and cloyed,
  A burning forehead, and a parching tongue.

Who are these coming to the sacrifice?
 To what green altar, O mysterious priest,
Lead'st thou that heifer lowing at the skies,
 And all her silken flanks with garlands dressed?

What little town by river or sea shore,
　Or mountain-built with peaceful citadel,
　　Is emptied of its folk, this pious morn?
And, little town, thy streets for evermore
　Will silent be; and not a soul, to tell
　　Why thou art desolate, can e'er return.

O Attic shape! Fair attitude! with brede
　Of marble men and maidens overwrought,
With forest branches and the trodden weed;
　Thou, silent form, dost tease us out of thought
As doth eternity: Cold Pastoral!
　When old age shall this generation waste,
　　Thou shalt remain, in midst of other woe
Than ours, a friend to man, to whom thou say'st,
　"Beauty is truth, truth beauty,"—that is all
　　Ye know on earth, and all ye need to know.

To Autumn

Season of mists and mellow fruitfulness,
　Close bosom-friend of the maturing sun:
Conspiring with him how to load and bless
　　With fruit the vines that round the thatch-eves run;
To bend with apples the mossed cottage-trees,
　And fill all fruit with ripeness to the core;
　　To swell the gourd, and plump the hazel shells
With a sweet kernel; to set budding more,
　And still more, later flowers for the bees,
　Until they think warm days will never cease,
　　For Summer has o'er-brimmed their clammy cells.

Who hath not seen thee oft amid thy store?
　Sometimes whoever seeks abroad may find
Thee sitting careless on a granary floor,
　Thy hair soft-lifted by the winnowing wind;
Or on a half-reaped furrow sound asleep,
　Drowsed with the fume of poppies, while thy hook
　　Spares the next swath and all its twinèd flowers:
And sometimes like a gleaner thou dost keep
　Steady thy laden head across a brook;
　Or by a cider-press, with patient look,
　　Thou watchest the last oozings hours by hours.

Where are the songs of Spring? Ay, where are they?
    Think not of them, thou hast thy music too,—
While barrèd clouds bloom the soft-dying day,
And touch the stubble-plains with rosy hue;
Then in a wailful choir the small gnats mourn
    Among the river sallows, borne aloft
      Or sinking as the light wind lives or dies;
And full-grown lambs loud bleat from hilly bourn;
    Hedge-crickets sing; and now with treble soft
    The red-breast whistles from a garden-croft;
And gathering swallows twitter in the skies.

La Belle Dame sans Merci

O what can ail thee, knight-at-arms,
    Alone and palely loitering?
The sedge has withered from the lake,
    And no birds sing.

O what can ail thee, knight-at-arms,
    So haggard and so woe-begone?
The squirrel's granary is full,
    And the harvest's done.

I see a lily on thy brow
    With anguish moist and fever dew,
And on thy cheek a fading rose
    Fast withereth too.

I met a lady in the meads,
    Full beautiful—a faery's child;
Her hair was long, her foot was light,
    And her eyes were wild.

I made a garland for her head,
    And bracelets too, and fragrant zone;
She looked at me as she did love,
    And made sweet moan.

I set her on my pacing steed,
    And nothing else saw all day long,
For sidelong would she bend, and sing
    A faery's song.

She found me roots of relish sweet,
   And honey wild, and manna dew,
And sure in language strange she said—
   "I love thee true!"

She took me to her elfin grot,
   And there she wept and sighed full sore,
And there I shut her wild wild eyes
   With kisses four.

And there she lullèd me asleep,
   And there I dreamed—ah! woe betide!
The latest dream I ever dreamed
   On the cold hill's side.

I saw pale kings and princes too,
   Pale warriors, death-pale were they all;
They cried—"La Belle Dame sans Merci
   Hath thee in thrall!"

I saw their starved lips in the gloam,
   With horrid warning gapèd wide,
And I awoke and found me here,
   On the cold hill's side.

And this is why I sojourn here,
   Alone and palely loitering,
Though the sedge is withered from the lake
   And no birds sing.

When I Have Fears That I May Cease to Be

When I have fears that I may cease to be
Before my pen has gleaned my teeming brain,
Before high-pilèd books, in charact'ry,
Hold like rich garners the full-ripened grain;
When I behold, upon the night's starred face,
Huge cloudy symbols of a high romance,
And think that I may never live to trace
Their shadows, with the magic hand of chance;

And when I feel, fair creature of an hour!
That I shall never look upon thee more,
Never have relish in the faery power
Of unreflecting love;—then on the shore
Of the wide world I stand alone, and think,
Till Love and Fame to nothingness do sink.

On Seeing the Elgin Marbles

My spirit is too weak—mortality
Weighs heavily on me like unwilling sleep,
And each imagined pinnacle and steep
Of godlike hardship, tells me I must die
Like a sick Eagle looking at the sky.
Yet 'tis a gentle luxury to weep
That I have not the cloudy winds to keep,
Fresh for the opening of the morning's eye.

Such dim-conceivèd glories of the brain
Bring round the heart an undescribable feud;
So do these wonders a most dizzy pain,
That mingles Grecian grandeur with the rude
Wasting of old Time—with a billowy main—
A sun—a shadow of a magnitude.

To One Who Has Been Long in City Pent

To one who has been long in city pent,
'Tis very sweet to look into the fair
And open face of heaven,—to breathe a prayer
Full in the smile of the blue firmament.
Who is more happy, when, with heart's content,
Fatigued he sinks into some pleasant lair
Of wavy grass, and reads a debonair
And gentle tale of love and languishment?

Returning home at evening, with an ear
Catching the notes of Philomel,—an eye
Watching the sailing cloudlet's bright career,
He mourns that day so soon has glided by,
E'en like the passage of an angel's tear
That falls through the clear ether silently.

Bright Star! Would I Were Steadfast as Thou Art

Bright star! would I were steadfast as thou art—
Not in lone splendour hung aloft the night,
And watching, with eternal lids apart,
Like Nature's patient sleepless Eremite,
The moving waters at their priestlike task
Of pure ablution round earth's human shores,
Or gazing on the new soft-fallen mask
Of snow upon the mountains and the moors—

No—yet still steadfast, still unchangeable,
Pillowed upon my fair love's ripening breast,
To feel for ever its soft fall and swell,
Awake for ever in a sweet unrest,
Still, still to hear her tender-taken breath,
And so live ever—or else swoon to death.

A Thing of Beauty

A thing of beauty is a joy for ever:
Its loveliness increases; it will never
Pass into nothingness; but still will keep
A bower quiet for us, and a sleep
Full of sweet dreams, and health, and quiet breathing.
Therefore, on every morrow, are we wreathing
A flowery band to bind us to the earth,
Spite of despondence, of the inhuman dearth
Of noble natures, of the gloomy days,
Of all the unhealthy and o'er-darkened ways
Made for our searching: yes, in spite of all,
Some shape of beauty moves away the pall
From our dark spirits. Such the sun, the moon,
Trees old and young, sprouting a shady boon
For simple sheep; and such are daffodils
With the green world they live in; and clear rills
That for themselves a cooling covert make
'Gainst the hot season; the mid-forest brake,
Rich with a sprinkling of fair musk-rose blooms:
And such too is the grandeur of the dooms
We have imagined for the mighty dead,
All lovely tales that we have heard or read:
An endless fountain of immortal drink,

Pouring unto us from the heaven's brink.
Nor do we merely feel these essences
For one short hour; no, even as the trees
That whisper round a temple become soon
Dear as the temple's self, so does the moon,
The passion poesy, glories infinite,
Haunt us till they become a cheering light
Unto our souls, and bound to us so fast,
That, whether there be shine, or gloom o'ercast,
They always must be with us, or we die.

From *Endymion*

Ode on Melancholy

No, no, go not to Lethe, neither twist
    Wolfs-bane, tight-rooted, for its poisonous wine;
Nor suffer thy pale forehead to be kiss'd
    By nightshade, ruby grape of Proserpine;
Make not your rosary of yew-berries,
    Nor let the beetle, nor the death-moth be
        Your mournful Psyche, nor the downy owl
A partner in your sorrow's mysteries;
    For shade to shade will come too drowsily,
        And drown the wakeful anguish of the soul.

But when the melancholy fit shall fall
    Sudden from heaven like a weeping cloud,
That fosters the droop-headed flowers all,
    And hides the green hill in an April shroud;
Then glut thy sorrow on a morning rose,
    Or on the rainbow of the salt sand-wave,
        Or on the wealth of the globèd peonies;
Or if thy mistress some rich anger shows,
    Emprison her soft hand, and let her rave,
        And feed deep, deep upon her peerless eyes.

She dwells with Beauty—Beauty that must die;
    And Joy, whose hand is ever at his lips
Bidding adieu; and aching Pleasure nigh,
    Turning to poison while the bee-mouth sips:
Ay, in the very temple of Delight
    Veil'd Melancholy has her sovereign shrine,

Though seen of none save him whose strenuous tongue
Can burst Joy's grape against his palate fine;
His soul shall taste the sadness of her might,
And be among her cloudy trophies hung.

The Eve of St. Agnes

St. Agnes' Eve—Ah, bitter chill it was!
The owl, for all his feathers, was a-cold;
The hare limp'd trembling through the frozen grass,
And silent was the flock in woolly fold:
Numb were the beadsman's fingers, while he told
His rosary, and while his frosted breath,
Like pious incense from a censer old,
Seem'd taking flight for heaven, without a death,
Past the sweet Virgin's picture, while his prayer he saith.

His prayer he saith, this patient, holy man;
Then takes his lamp, and riseth from his knees,
And back returneth, meager, barefoot, wan,
Along the chapel aisle by slow degrees:
The sculptur'd dead, on each side, seem to freeze,
Emprison'd in black, purgatorial rails:
Knights, ladies, praying in dumb orat'ries,
He passeth by; and his weak spirit fails
To think how they may ache in icy hoods and mails.

Northward he turneth through a little door,
And scarce three steps, ere Music's golden tongue
Flatter'd to tears this aged man and poor;
But no—already had his deathbell rung:
The joys of all his life were said and sung:
His was harsh penance on St. Agnes' Eve:
Another way he went, and soon among
Rough ashes sat he for his soul's reprieve,
And all night kept awake, for sinners' sake to grieve.

That ancient beadsman heard the prelude soft;
And so it chanc'd, for many a door was wide,
From hurry to and fro. Soon, up aloft,
The silver, snarling trumpets 'gan to chide:
The level chambers, ready with their pride,

Were glowing to receive a thousand guests:
The carved angels, ever eager-eyed,
Star'd, where upon their heads the cornice rests,
With hair blown back, and wings put cross-wise on their breasts.

At length burst in the argent revelry,
With plume, tiara, and all rich array,
Numerous as shadows haunting fairily
The brain, new stuff'd, in youth, with triumphs gay
Of old romance. These let us wish away,
And turn, sole-thoughted, to one lady there,
Whose heart had brooded, all that wintry day,
On love, and wing'd St. Agnes' saintly care,
As she had heard old dames full many times declare.

They told her how, upon St. Agnes' Eve,
Young virgins might have visions of delight,
And soft adorings from their loves receive
Upon the honey'd middle of the night,
If ceremonies due they did aright;
As, supperless to bed they must retire,
And couch supine their beauties, lily white;
Nor look behind, nor sideways, but require
Of Heaven with upward eyes for all that they desire.

Full of this whim was thoughtful Madeline:
The music, yearning like a god in pain,
She scarcely heard: her maiden eyes divine,
Fix'd on the floor, saw many a sweeping train
Pass by—she heeded not at all: in vain
Came many a tiptoe, amorous cavalier,
And back retir'd; not cool'd by high disdain,
But she saw not: her heart was otherwhere:
She sigh'd for Agnes' dreams, the sweetest of the year.

She danc'd along with vague, regardless eyes,
Anxious her lips, her breathing quick and short:
The hallow'd hour was near at hand: she sighs
Amid the timbrels, and the throng'd resort
Of whisperers in anger, or in sport;
'Mid looks of love, defiance, hate, and scorn,

Hoodwink'd with faery fancy; all amort,
Save to St. Agnes and her lambs unshorn,
And all the bliss to be before tomorrow morn.

So, purposing each moment to retire,
She linger'd still. Meantime, across the moors,
Had come young Porphyro, with heart on fire
For Madeline. Beside the portal doors,
Buttress'd from moonlight, stands he, and implores
All saints to give him sight of Madeline,
But for one moment in the tedious hours,
That he might gaze and worship all unseen;
Perchance speak, kneel, touch, kiss—in sooth such things have been.

He ventures in: let no buzz'd whisper tell:
All eyes be muffled, or a hundred swords
Will storm his heart, Love's fev'rous citadel:
For him, those chambers held barbarian hordes,
Hyena foemen, and hot-blooded lords,
Whose very dogs would execrations howl
Against his lineage: not one breast affords
Him any mercy, in that mansion foul,
Save one old beldame, weak in body and in soul.

Ah, happy chance! the aged creature came,
Shuffling along with ivory-headed wand,
To where he stood, hid from the torch's flame,
Behind a broad hall-pillar, far beyond
The sound of merriment and chorus bland:
He startled her; but soon she knew his face,
And grasp'd his fingers in her palsied hand,
Saying, "Mercy, Porphyro! hie thee from this place:
They are all here tonight, the whole blood-thirsty race!

"Get hence! get hence! there's dwarfish Hildebrand;
He had a fever late, and in the fit
He cursed thee and thine, both house and land:
Then there's that old Lord Maurice, not a whit
More tame for his gray hairs—Alas me! flit!
Flit like a ghost away."—"Ah, gossip dear,
We're safe enough; here in this armchair sit,

And tell me how"—"Good Saints! not here, not here;
Follow me, child, or else these stones will be thy bier."

He follow'd through a lowly arched way,
Brushing the cobwebs with his lofty plume,
And as she mutter'd "Well-a—well-a-day!"
He found him in a little moonlight room,
Pale, lattic'd, chill, and silent as a tomb.
"Now tell me where is Madeline," said he,
"O tell me, Angela, by the holy loom
Which none but secret sisterhood may see,
When they St. Agnes' wool are weaving piously."

"St. Agnes! Ah! it is St. Agnes' Eve—
Yet men will murder upon holy days:
Thou must hold water in a witch's sieve,
And be liege-lord of all the elves and fays,
To venture so: it fills me with amaze
To see thee, Porphyro!—St. Agnes' Eve!
God's help! my lady fair the conjuror plays
This very night: good angels her deceive!
But let me laugh awhile, I've mickle time to grieve."

Feebly she laugheth in the languid moon,
While Porphyro upon her face doth look,
Like puzzled urchin on an aged crone
Who keepeth clos'd a wond'rous riddle-book,
As spectacled she sits in chimney nook.
But soon his eyes grew brilliant, when she told
His lady's purpose; and he scare could brook
Tears, at the thought of those enchantments cold,
And Madeline asleep in lap of legends old.

Sudden a thought came like a full-blown rose,
Flushing his brow, and in his pained heart
Made purple riot: then doth he propose
A stratagem, that makes the beldame start:
"A cruel man and impious thou art:
Sweet lady, let her pray, and sleep, and dream
Alone with her good angels, far apart
From wicked men like thee. Go, go!—I deem
Thou canst not surely be the same that thou didst seem."

"I will not harm her, by all saints I swear,"
Quoth Porphyro: "O may I ne'er find grace
When my weak voice shall whisper its last prayer,
If one of her soft ringlets I displace,
Or look with ruffian passion in her face:
Good Angela, believe me by these tears;
Or I will, even in a moment's space,
Awake, with horrid shout, my foemen's ears,
And beard them, though they be more fang'd than wolves and bears."

"Ah! why wilt thou affright a feeble soul?
A poor, weak, palsy-stricken, churchyard thing,
Whose passing-bell may ere the midnight toll;
Whose prayers for thee, each morn and evening,
Were never miss'd."—Thus plaining, doth she bring
A gentler speech from burning Porphyro;
So woful, and of such deep sorrowing,
That Angela gives promise she will do
Whatever he shall wish, betide her weal or woe.

Which was, to lead him, in close secrecy,
Even to Madeline's chamber, and there hide
Him in a closet, of such privacy
That he might see her beauty unespied,
And win perhaps that night a peerless bride,
While legion'd fairies pac'd the coverlet,
And pale enchantment held her sleepy-eyed.
Never on such a night have lovers met,
Since Merlin paid his demon all the monstrous debt.

"It shall be as thou wishest," said the dame:
"All cates and dainties shall be stored there
Quickly on this feast-night: by the tambour frame
Her own lute thou wilt see: no time to spare,
For I am slow and feeble, and scarce dare
On such a catering trust my dizzy head.
Wait here, my child, with patience; kneel in prayer
The while. Ah! thou must needs the lady wed,
Or may I never leave my grave among the dead."

So saying, she hobbled off with busy fear.
The lover's endless minutes slowly pass'd;

The dame return'd, and whisper'd in his ear
To follow her; with aged eyes aghast
From fright of dim espial. Safe at last,
Through many a dusky gallery, they gain
The maiden's chamber, silken, hush'd, and chaste;
Where Porphyro took covert, pleas'd amain.
His poor guide hurried back with agues in her brain.

Her falt'ring hand upon the balustrade,
Old Angela was feeling for the stair,
When Madeline, St. Agnes' charmed maid,
Rose, like a mission'd spirit, unaware:
With silver taper's light, and pious care,
She turn'd, and down the aged gossip led
To a safe level matting. Now prepare,
Young Porphyro, for gazing on that bed;
She comes, she comes again, like ringdove fray'd and fled.

Out went the taper as she hurried in;
Its little smoke, in pallid moonshine, died:
She clos'd the door, she panted, all akin
To spirits of the air, and visions wide:
No uttered syllable, or, woe betide!
But to her heart, her heart was voluble,
Paining with eloquence her balmy side;
As though a tongueless nightingale should swell
Her throat in vain, and die, heart-stifled, in her dell.

A casement high and triple-arch'd there was,
All garlanded with carven imag'ries
Of fruits, and flowers, and bunches of knot-grass,
And diamonded with panes of quaint device,
Innumerable of stains and splendid dyes,
As are the tiger-moth's deep-damask'd wings;
And in the midst, 'mid thousand heraldries,
And twilight saints, and dim emblazonings,
A shielded scutcheon blush'd with blood of queens and kings.

Full on this casement shone the wintry moon,
And threw warm gules on Madeline's fair breast,
As down she knelt for heaven's grace and boon;

Rose-bloom, fell on her hands, together prest,
And on her silver cross soft amethyst,
And on her hair a glory, like a saint:
She seem'd a splendid angel, newly drest,
Save wings, for heaven:—Porphyro grew faint:
She knelt, so pure a thing, so free from mortal taint.

Anon his heart revives: her vespers done,
Of all its wreathed pearls her hair she frees;
Unclasps her warmed jewels one by one;
Loosens her fragrant bodice; by degrees
Her rich attire creeps rustling to her knees:
Half-hidden, like a mermaid in sea-weed,
Pensive awhile she dreams awake, and sees
In fancy, fair St. Agnes in her bed,
But dares not look behind, or all the charm is fled.

Soon, trembling in her soft and chilly nest,
In sort of wakeful swoon, perplex'd she lay,
Until the poppied warmth of sleep oppress'd
Her soothed limbs, and soul fatigued away;
Flown, like a thought, until the morrow-day;
Blissfully haven'd both from joy and pain;
Clasp'd like a missal where swart Paynims pray;
Blinded alike from sunshine and from rain,
As though a rose should shut, and be a bud again.

Stol'n to this paradise, and so entranced,
Porphyro gazed upon her empty dress,
And listen'd to her breathing, if it chanced
To wake into a slumbrous tenderness;
Which when he heard, that minute did he bless,
And breath'd himself: then from the closet crept,
Noiseless as fear in a wide wilderness,
And over the hush'd carpet, silent, stept,
And 'tween the curtain peep'd, where, lo!—how fast she slept.

Then by the bed-side, where the faded moon
Made a dim, silver twilight, soft he set
A table, and, half anguish'd, threw thereon
A cloth of woven crimson, gold, and jet:—

O for some drowsy Morphean amulet!
The boisterous, midnight, festive clarion,
The kettle-drum, and far-heard clarinet,
Affray his ears, though but in dying tone:—
The hall door shuts again, and all the noise is gone.

And still she slept an azure-lidded sleep,
In blanched linen, smooth, and lavender'd,
While he from forth the closet brought a heap
Of candied apple, quince, and plum, and gourd;
With jellies soother than the creamy curd,
And lucent syrups, tinct with cinnamon;
Manna and dates, in argosy transferr'd
From Fez; and spiced dainties, every one,
From silken Samarcand to cedar'd Lebanon.

These delicacies he heap'd with glowing hand
On golden dishes and in baskets bright
Of wreathed silver, sumptuous they stand
In the retired quiet of the night,
Filling the chilly room with perfume light.—
"And now, my love, my seraph fair, awake!
Thou art my heaven, and I thine eremite:
Open thine eyes, for meek St. Agnes' sake,
Or I shall drowse beside thee, so my soul doth ache."

Thus whispering, his warm, unnerved arm
Sank in her pillow. Shaded was her dream
By the dusk curtains:—'twas a midnight charm
Impossible to melt as iced stream:
The lustrous salvers in the moonlight gleam;
Broad golden fringe upon the carpet lies:
It seem'd he never, never could redeem
From such a steadfast spell his lady's eyes;
So mus'd awhile, entoil'd in woofed phantasies.

Awakening up, he took her hollow lute,—
Tumultuous,—and, in chords that tenderest be,
He play'd an ancient ditty, long since mute,
In Provence call'd, "La belle dame sans mercy:"
Close to her ear touching the melody;—

Wherewith disturb'd, she utter'd a soft moan:
He ceased—she panted quick—and suddenly
Her blue affrayed eyes wide open shone:
Upon his knees he sank, pale as smooth-sculptured stone.

Her eyes were open, but she still beheld,
Now wide awake, the vision of her sleep:
There was a painful change, that nigh expell'd
The blisses of her dream so pure and deep
At which fair Madeline began to weep,
And moan forth witless words with many a sigh;
While still her gaze on Porphyro would keep;
Who knelt, with joined hands and piteous eye,
Fearing to move or speak, she look'd so dreamingly.

"Ah, Porphyro!" said she, "but even now
Thy voice was at sweet tremble in mine ear,
Made tuneable with every sweetest vow;
And those sad eyes were spiritual and clear:
How chang'd thou art! how pallid, chill, and drear!
Give me that voice again, my Porphyro,
Those looks immortal, those complainings dear!
Oh leave me not in this eternal woe,
For if thou diest, my love, I know not where to go."

Beyond a mortal man impassion'd far
At these voluptuous accents, he arose,
Ethereal, flush'd, and like a throbbing star
Seen mid the sapphire heaven's deep repose;
Into her dream he melted, as the rose
Blendeth its odor with the violet,—
Solution sweet: meantime the frostwind blows
Like Love's alarum pattering the sharp sleet
Against the window-panes; St. Agnes' moon hath set.

'Tis dark: quick pattereth the flaw-blown sleet:
"This is no dream, my bride, my Madeline!"
'Tis dark: the iced gusts still rave and beat:
"No dream, alas! alas! and woe is mine!
Porphyro will leave me here to fade and pine.—
Cruel! what traitor could thee hither bring?

I curse not, for my heart is lost in thine,
    Though thou forsakest a deceived thing;—
A dove forlorn and lost with sick unpruned wing."

    "My Madeline! sweet dreamer! lovely bride!
    Say, may I be for aye thy vassal blest?
    Thy beauty's shield, heart-shap'd and vermeil-dyed?
    Ah, silver shrine, here will I take my rest
    After so many hours of toil and quest,
    A famish'd pilgrim,—sav'd by miracle.
    Though I have found, I will not rob thy nest
    Saving of thy sweet self; if thou think'st well
To trust, fair Madeline, to no rude infidel.

    "Hark! 'tis an elfin-storm from faery land,
    Of haggard seeming, but a boon indeed:
    Arise—arise! the morning is at hand;—
    The bloated wassaillers will never heed:—
    Let us away, my love, with happy speed;
    There are no ears to hear, or eyes to see,—
    Drown'd all in Rhenish and the sleepy mead:
    Awake! arise! my love, and fearless be,
For o'er the southern moors I have a home for thee."

    She hurried at his words, beset with fears,
    For there were sleeping dragons all around,
    At glaring watch, perhaps, with ready spears—
    Down the wide stairs a darkling way they found.—
    In all the house was heard no human sound.
    A chain-droop'd lamp was flickering by each door;
    The arras, rich with horseman, hawk, and hound,
    Flutter'd in the besieging wind's uproar;
And the long carpets rose along the gusty floor.

    They glide, like phantoms, into the wide hall;
    Like phantoms, to the iron porch, they glide;
    Where lay the porter in uneasy sprawl,
    With a huge empty flagon by his side:
    The wakeful bloodhound rose, and shook his hide,
    But his sagacious eye an inmate owns:
    By one and one, the bolts full easy slide:—

The chains lie silent on the footworn stones;—
The key turns, and the door upon its hinges groans.

And they are gone: aye, ages long ago
These lovers fled away into the storm.
That night the Baron dreamt of many a woe,
And all his warrior-guests, with shade and form
Of witch, and demon, and large coffin-worm,
Were long be-nightmar'd. Angela the old
Died palsy-twitch'd, with meager face deform;
The beadsman after thousand aves told,
For aye unsought-for slept among his ashes cold.

THOMAS HOOD
1798–1845

Autumn

I saw old Autumn in the misty morn
Stand shadowless like Silence, listening
To silence, for no lonely bird would sing
Into his hollow ear from woods forlorn,
Nor lowly hedge nor solitary thorn;—
Shaking his languid locks all dewy bright
With tangled gossamer that fell by night,
    Pearling his coronet of golden corn.

Where are the songs of Summer?—With the sun,
Oping the dusky eyelids of the South,
Till shade and silence waken up as one,
And Morning sings with a warm odorous mouth.
Where are the merry birds?—Away, away,
On panting wings through the inclement skies,
    Lest owls should prey
    Undazzled at noonday,
And tear with horny beak their lustrous eyes.

Where are the blooms of Summer?—In the West,
Blushing their last to the last sunny hours,

When the mild Eve by sudden Night is prest
Like tearful Proserpine, snatch'd from her flow'rs
   To a most gloomy breast.
Where is the pride of Summer,—the green prime,—
The many, many leaves all twinkling?—Three
On the moss'd elm; three on the naked lime
Trembling,—and one upon the old oak-tree!
   Where is the Dryad's immortality?—
Gone into mournful cypress and dark yew,
Or wearing the long gloomy Winter through
   In the smooth holly's green eternity.

The squirrel gloats on his accomplish'd hoard,
The ants have brimm'd their garners with ripe grain,
     And honey bees have stored
   The sweets of Summer in their luscious cells;
   The swallows all have wing'd across the main;
   But here the autumn Melancholy dwells,
     And sighs her tearful spells
   Amongst the sunless shadows of the plain.
    Alone, alone,
    Upon a mossy stone,
She sits and reckons up the dead and gone
With the last leaves for a love-rosary,
Whilst all the wither'd world looks drearily,
Like a dim picture of the drownèd past
In the hush'd mind's mysterious far away,
Doubtful what ghostly thing will steal the last
Into that distance, grey upon the grey.

O go and sit with her, and be o'ershaded
Under the languid downfall of her hair!
She wears a coronal of flowers faded
Upon her forehead, and a face of care;—
There is enough of wither'd everywhere
To make her bower,—and enough of gloom;
There is enough of sadness to invite,
If only for the rose that died, whose doom
Is Beauty's,—she that with the living bloom
Of conscious cheeks most beautifies the light:
There is enough of sorrowing, and quite

Enough of bitter fruits the earth doth bear,—
Enough of chilly droppings for her bowl;
Enough of fear and shadowy despair,
To frame her cloudy prison for the soul!

I Remember, I Remember

I remember, I remember,
The house where I was born,
The little window where the sun
Came peeping in at morn;
He never came a wink too soon,
Nor brought too long a day,
But now, I often wish the night
Had borne my breath away!

I remember, I remember,
The roses, red and white,
The violets, and the lily-cups,
Those flowers made of light!
The lilacs where the robin built
And where my brother set
The laburnum on his birthday,—
The tree is living yet!

I remember, I remember,
Where I was used to swing,
And thought the air must rush as fresh
To swallows on the wing;
My spirit flew in feathers then
That is so heavy now,
And summer pools could hardly cool
The fever on my brow!

I remember, I remember,
The fir trees dark and high,
I used to think their slender tops
Were close against the sky:
It was a childish ignorance,
But now 'tis little joy
To know I'm farther off from heaven
Than when I was a boy.

RALPH WALDO EMERSON
1803–1882

Brahma

If the red slayer think he slays,
　Or if the slain think he is slain,
They know not well the subtle ways
　I keep, and pass, and turn again.

Far or forgot to me is near;
　Shadow and sunlight are the same;
The vanished gods to me appear;
　And one to me are shame and fame.

They reckon ill who leave me out;
　When me they fly, I am the wings;
I am the doubter and the doubt,
　And I the hymn the Brahmin sings.

The strong gods pine for my abode,
　And pine in vain the sacred Seven;
But thou, meek lover of the good!
　Find me, and turn thy back on heaven.

Fable

The mountain and the squirrel
Had a quarrel;
And the former called the latter "Little Prig."
Bun replied,
"You are doubtless very big;
But all sorts of things and weather
Must be taken in together
To make up a year
And a sphere.

And I think it's no disgrace
To occupy my place.
If I'm not so large as you,
You are not so small as I,
And not half so spry.

I'll not deny you make
A very pretty squirrel track;
Talents differ: all is well and wisely put;
If I cannot carry forests on my back,
Neither can you crack a nut."

THOMAS LOVELL BEDDOES
1803–1849

Song

How many times do I love thee, dear?
Tell me how many thoughts there be
In the atmosphere
Of a new-fall'n year,
Whose white and sable hours appear
The latest flake of Eternity:—
So many times do I love thee, dear.

How many times do I love again?
Tell me how many beads there are
In a silver chain
Of evening rain,
Unravelled from the tumbling main,
And threading the eye of a yellow star:—
So many times do I love again.

ELIZABETH BARRETT BROWNING
1806–1861

How Do I Love Thee?

How do I love thee? Let me count the ways.
I love thee to the depth and breadth and height
My soul can reach, when feeling out of sight
For the ends of Being and ideal Grace.

I love thee to the level of everyday's
Most quiet need, by sun and candle-light.
I love thee freely, as men strive for Right;
I love thee purely, as they turn from Praise.
I love thee with the passion put to use
In my old griefs, and with my childhood's faith.
I love thee with a love I seemed to lose
With my lost saints—I love thee with the breath,
Smiles, tears, of all my life!—and, if God choose,
I shall but love thee better after death.

JOHN GREENLEAF WHITTIER
1807—1892

The Saddest Words

. . . . Of all sad words of tongue or pen,
The saddest are these: "It might have been!"

From *Maud Muller*

HENRY WADSWORTH LONGFELLOW
1807–1882

The Tide Rises, the Tide Falls

The tide rises, the tide falls,
The twilight darkens, the curlew calls;
Along the sea-sands damp and brown
The traveller hastens toward the town,
    And the tide rises, the tide falls.

Darkness settles on roofs and walls,
But the sea, the sea in the darkness calls;
The little waves, with their soft, white hands,
Efface the footprints in the sands,
    And the tide rises, the tide falls.

The morning breaks; the steeds in their stalls
Stamp and neigh, as the hostler calls;
The day returns, but nevermore
Returns the traveller to the shore,
    And the tide rises, the tide falls.

EDWARD FITZGERALD
1809–1883

Rubáiyát of Omar Khayyám of Naishápúr

Wake! For the Sun who scattered into flight
The Stars before him from the Field of Night,
    Drives Night along with them from Heav'n, and strikes
The Sultán's Turret with a Shaft of Light.

Before the phantom of False morning died,
Methought a Voice within the Tavern cried,
    "When all the Temple is prepared within,
Why nods the drowsy Worshipper outside?"

And, as the Cock crew, those who stood before
The Tavern shouted—"Open then the door!
    You know how little while we have to stay,
And, once departed, may return no more."

Now the New Year reviving old Desires,
The thoughtful Soul to Solitude retires,
    Where the WHITE HAND OF MOSES on the Bough
Puts out, and Jesus from the Ground suspires.

Iram indeed is gone with all his Rose,
And Jamshyd's Sev'n-ringed Cup where no one knows;
    But still a Ruby kindles in the Vine,
And many a Garden by the Water blows.

And David's lips are lockt; but in divine
High-piping Pehleví, with "Wine! Wine! Wine!
    Red Wine!"—the Nightingale cries to the Rose
That sallow cheek of hers to incarnadine.

Come, fill the Cup, and in the fire of Spring
Your Winter-garment of Repentance fling:
   The Bird of Time has but a little way
To flutter—and the Bird is on the Wing.

Whether at Naishápúr or Babylon,
Whether the Cup with sweet or bitter run,
   The Wine of Life keeps oozing drop by drop,
The Leaves of Life keep falling one by one.

Each Morn a thousand Roses brings, you say;
Yes, but where leaves the Rose of Yesterday?
   And this first Summer month that brings the Rose
Shall take Jamshyd and Kaikobád away.

Well, let it take them! What have we to do
With Kaikobád the Great, or Kaikhosrú?
   Let Zál and Rustum bluster as they will,
Or Hátim call to Supper—heed not you.

With me along the strip of Herbage strown
That just divides the desert from the sown,
   Where name of Slave and Sultán is forgot—
And Peace to Mahmúd on his golden Throne!

A Book of Verses underneath the Bough,
A Jug of Wine, a Loaf of Bread—and Thou
   Beside me singing in the Wilderness—
Oh, Wilderness were Paradise enow!

Some for the Glories of This World; and some
Sigh for the Prophet's Paradise to come;
   Ah, take the Cash, and let the Credit go,
Nor heed the rumble of a distant Drum!

Look to the blowing Rose about us—"Lo,
Laughing," she says, "into the world I blow,
   At once the silken tassel of my Purse
Tear, and its Treasure on the Garden throw."

And those who husbanded the Golden grain,
And those who flung it to the winds like Rain,

Alike to no such aureate Earth are turned
As, buried once, Men want dug up again.

The Worldly Hope men set their Hearts upon
Turns Ashes—or it prospers; and anon,
   Like Snow upon the Desert's dusty Face,
Lighting a little hour or two—is gone.

Think, in this battered Caravanserai
Whose Portals are alternate Night and Day,
   How Sultán after Sultán with his Pomp
Abode his destined Hour, and went his way.

They say the Lion and the Lizard keep
The Courts where Jamshyd gloried and drank deep:
   And Bahrám, that great Hunter—the Wild Ass
Stamps o'er his Head, but cannot break his Sleep.

I sometimes think that never blows so red
The Rose as where some buried Cæsar bled;
   That every Hyacinth the Garden wears
Dropt in her Lap from some once lovely Head.

And this reviving Herb whose tender Green
Fledges the River-Lip on which we lean—
   Ah, lean upon it lightly! for who knows
From what once lovely Lip it springs unseen!

Ah, my Belovéd, fill the cup that clears
TO-DAY of past regrets and future Fears:
   To-morrow!—Why, To-morrow I may be
Myself with Yesterday's Sev'n thousand Years.

For some we loved, the loveliest and the best
That from his Vintage rolling Time hath prest,
   Have drunk their Cup a Round or two before,
And one by one crept silently to rest.

And we, that now make merry in the Room
They left, and Summer dresses in new bloom,
   Ourselves must we beneath the Couch of Earth
Descend—ourselves to make a Couch—for whom?

Ah, make the most of what we yet may spend,
Before we too into the Dust descend;
   Dust into Dust, and under Dust, to lie,
Sans Wine, sans Song, sans Singer, and—sans End!

Alike for those who for TO-DAY prepare,
And those that after some TO-MORROW stare,
   A Muezzín from the Tower of Darkness cries,
"Fools! Your reward is neither Here nor There."

Why, all the Saints and Sages who discussed
Of the Two Worlds so wisely—they are thrust
   Like foolish Prophets forth; their Words to Scorn
Are scatter'd, and their Mouths are stopt with Dust.

Myself when young did eagerly frequent
Doctor and Saint, and heard great argument
   About it and about: but evermore
Came out by the same door where in I went.

With them the seed of Wisdom did I sow,
And with mine own hand wrought to make it grow;
   And this was all the Harvest that I reap'd—
"I came like Water, and like Wind I go."

Into this Universe, and *Why* not knowing,
Nor *Whence*, like Water willy-nilly flowing;
   And out of it, as Wind along the Waste,
I know not *Whither*, willy-nilly blowing.

What, without asking, hither hurried *Whence*?
And, without asking, *Whither* hurried hence!
   Oh, many a Cup of this forbidden Wine
Must drown the memory of that insolence!

Up from Earth's Centre through the Seventh Gate
I rose, and on the Throne of Saturn sate;
   And many a Knot unravel'd by the Road;
But not the Master-knot of Human Fate.

There was the Door to which I found no Key;
There was the Veil through which I might not see:

Some little talk awhile of ME AND THEE
There was—and then no more of THEE AND ME.

Earth could not answer; nor the Seas that mourn
In flowing Purple, of their Lord forlorn;
   Nor rolling Heaven, with all his Signs revealed
And hidden by the sleeve of Night and Morn.

Then of the THEE IN ME who works behind
The Veil, I lifted up my hands to find
   A Lamp amid the Darkness; and I heard,
As from Without—"THE ME WITHIN THEE BLIND!"

Then to the Lip of this poor earthen Urn
I lean'd, the Secret of my Life to learn:
   And Lip to Lip it murmur'd—"While you live,
Drink!—for, once dead, you never shall return."

I think the Vessel, that with fugitive
Articulation, answer'd, once did live,
   And drink; and Ah! the passive Lip I kiss'd,
How many Kisses might it take—and give!

For I remember stopping by the way
To watch a Potter thumping his wet Clay:
   And with its all-obliterated Tongue
It murmured—"Gently, Brother, gently pray!"

And has not such a Story from of Old
Down Man's successive generations roll'd,
   Of such a clod of saturated Earth
Cast by the Maker into Human mould?

And not a drop that from our Cups we throw
For Earth to drink of, but may steal below
   To quench the fire of Anguish in some Eye
There hidden—far beneath, and long ago.

As then the Tulip from her morning sup
Of Heav'nly Vintage from the soil looks up,
   Do you devoutly do the like, till Heav'n
To Earth invert you—like an empty Cup.

Perplext no more with Human or Divine,
To-morrow's tangle to the winds resign,
    And lose your fingers in the tresses of
The Cypress-slender Minister of Wine.

And if the Wine you drink, the Lip you press,
End in what All begins and ends in—Yes;
    Think then you are TO-DAY what YESTERDAY
You were—TO-MORROW you shall not be less.

So when the Angel of the darker Drink
At last shall find you by the river-brink,
    And, offering his Cup, invite your Soul
Forth to your Lips to quaff—you shall not shrink.

Why, if the Soul can fling the Dust aside,
And naked on the Air of Heaven ride,
    Were't not a Shame—were't not a Shame for him
In this clay carcase crippled to abide?

'Tis but a Tent where takes his one-day's rest
A Sultán to the realm of Death addrest;
    The Sultán rises, and the dark Ferrásh
Strikes, and prepares it for another Guest.

And fear not lest Existence closing your
Account, and mine, should know the like no more;
    The Eternal Sákí from that Bowl has pour'd
Millions of Bubbles like us, and will pour.

When you and I behind the Veil are past,
Oh but the long, long while the World shall last,
    Which of our Coming and Departure heeds
As the SEA'S SELF should heed a pebble-cast.

A Moment's Halt—a momentary taste
Of BEING from the Well amid the Waste—
    And Lo!—the phantom Caravan has reach'd
The NOTHING it set out from—Oh, make haste!

Would you that spangle of Existence spend
About THE SECRET—quick about it, Friend!

A Hair perhaps divides the False and True—
And upon what, prithee, may Life depend?

A Hair perhaps divides the False and True;
Yes; and a single Alif were the clue—
    Could you but find it—to the Treasure-house,
And peradventure to THE MASTER too;

Whose secret Presence, through Creation's veins
Running Quicksilver-like eludes your pains;
    Taking all shapes from Máh to Máhi; and
They change and perish all—but He remains;

A moment guess'd—then back behind the Fold
Immerst of Darkness round the Drama roll'd
    Which, for the Pastime of Eternity,
He does Himself contrive, enact, behold.

But if in vain, down on the stubborn floor
Of Earth, and up to Heav'n's unopening door,
    You gaze TO-DAY, while You are You—how then
TO-MORROW, You when shall be You no more?

Waste not your Hour, nor in the vain pursuit
Of This and That endeavour and dispute;
    Better be jocund with the fruitful Grape
Than sadden after none, or bitter, Fruit.

You know, my Friends, with what a brave Carouse
I made a Second Marriage in my house;
    Divorced old barren Reason from my Bed,
And took the Daughter of the Vine to Spouse.

For "IS" and "IS-NOT" though with Rule and Line,
And "UP-AND-DOWN" by Logic I define,
    Of all that one should care to fathom, I
Was never deep in anything but—Wine.

Ah, but my Computations, People say,
Reduced the Year to better reckoning?—Nay,
    'Twas only striking from the Calendar
Unborn To-morrow, and dead Yesterday.

And lately, by the Tavern Door agape,
Came shining through the Dusk an Angel Shape
   Bearing a Vessel on his Shoulder; and
He bid me taste of it; and 'twas—the Grape!

The Grape that can with Logic absolute
The Two-and-Seventy jarring Sects confute:
   The sovereign Alchemist that in a trice
Life's leaden metal into Gold transmute:

The mighty Mahmúd, Allah-breathing Lord,
That all the misbelieving and black Horde
   Of Fears and Sorrows that infest the Soul
Scatters before him with his whirlwind Sword.

Why, be this Juice the growth of God, who dare
Blaspheme the twisted tendril as a Snare?
   A Blessing, we should use it, should we not?
And if a Curse—why, then, Who set it there?

I must abjure the Balm of Life, I must,
Scared by some After-reckoning ta'en on trust,
   Or lured with Hope of some Diviner Drink,
To fill the Cup—when crumbled into Dust!

O threats of Hell and Hopes of Paradise!
One thing at least is certain,—*This* Life flies;
   One thing is certain and the rest is Lies;
The Flower that once has blown for ever dies.

Strange, is it not? that of the myriads who
Before us passed the door of Darkness through
   Not one returns to tell us of the Road
Which to discover we must travel too.

The Revelations of Devout and Learn'd
Who rose before us, and as Prophets burn'd,
   Are all but Stories, which, awoke from Sleep
They told their fellows, and to Sleep return'd.

I sent my Soul through the Invisible,
Some letter of that After-life to spell:

And by and by my Soul return'd to me,
And answered "I Myself am Heav'n and Hell":

Heav'n but the Vision of fulfill'd Desire,
And Hell the Shadow from a Soul on fire,
    Cast on the Darkness into which Ourselves,
So late emerged from, shall so soon expire.

We are no other than a moving row
Of Magic Shadow-shapes that come and go
    Round with this Sun-illumined Lantern held
In Midnight by the Master of the Show;

But helpless Pieces of the Game He plays
Upon this Chequer-board of Nights and Days;
    Hither and thither moves, and checks, and slays,
And one by one back in the Closet lays.

The Ball no question makes of Ayes and Noes,
But Here or There as strikes the Player goes;
    And He that tossed you down into the Field,
He knows about it all—HE knows—HE knows!

The Moving Finger writes; and, having writ,
Moves on: nor all your Piety nor Wit
    Shall lure it back to cancel half a Line,
Nor all your Tears wash out a Word of it.

And that inverted Bowl they call the Sky,
Whereunder crawling coop'd we live and die,
    Lift not your hands to *It* for help—for It
As impotently rolls as you or I.

With Earth's first Clay They did the Last Man knead,
And there of the Last Harvest sowed the Seed:
    And the first Morning of Creation wrote
What the Last Dawn of Reckoning shall read.

YESTERDAY *This* Day's Madness did prepare;
TO-MORROW's Silence, Triumph, or Despair:
    Drink! for you know not whence you came, nor why:
Drink! for you know not why you go, nor where.

I tell you this—When, started from the Goal,
Over the flaming shoulders of the Foal
   Of Heav'n Parwin and Mushtarí they flung,
In my predestined Plot of Dust and Soul

The Vine had struck a fibre: which about
If clings my Being—let the Dervish flout;
   Of my Base metal may be filed a Key,
That shall unlock the Door he howls without.

And this I know: whether the one True Light
Kindle to Love, or Wrath-consume me quite,
   One Flash of It within the Tavern caught
Better than in the Temple lost outright.

What! out of senseless Nothing to provoke
A conscious Something to resent the yoke
   Of unpermitted Pleasure, under pain
Of Everlasting Penalties, if broke!

What! from his helpless Creature he repaid
Pure Gold for what he lent him dross-allayed—
   Sue for a Debt we never did contract,
And cannot answer—Oh the sorry trade!

Oh Thou, who didst with pitfall and with gin
Beset the Road I was to wander in,
   Thou wilt not with Predestined Evil round
Enmesh, and then impute my Fall to Sin!

Oh Thou, who Man of baser Earth didst make
And ev'n with Paradise devise the Snake:
   For all the Sin wherewith the Face of Man
Is blacken'd—Man's Forgiveness give—and take!

    •   •   •   •   •   •

As under cover of departing Day
Slunk hunger-stricken Ramazán away,
   Once more within the Potter's house alone
I stood, surrounded by the Shapes of Clay.

Shapes of all Sorts and Sizes, great and small,
That stood along the floor and by the wall;
   And some loquacious Vessels were; and some
Listen'd perhaps, but never talk'd at all.

Said one among them—"Surely not in vain
My substance of the common Earth was ta'en
   And to this Figure moulded, to be broke,
Or trampled back to shapeless Earth again."

Then said a Second—"Ne'er a peevish Boy
Would break the Bowl from which he drank in joy;
   And He that with his hand the Vessel made
Will surely not in after Wrath destroy."

After a momentary silence spake
Some Vessel of a more ungainly Make;
   "They sneer at me for leaning all awry:
What! did the Hand then of the Potter shake?"

Whereat some one of the loquacious Lot—
I think a Súfi pipkin—waxing hot—
   "All this of Pot and Potter—Tell me, then,
Who is the Potter, pray, and who the Pot?"

"Why," said another, "Some there are who tell
Of one who threatens he will toss to Hell
   The luckless Pots he marr'd in making—Pish!
He's a Good Fellow, and 'twill all be well."

"Well," murmur'd one, "Let whose make or buy,
My Clay with long Oblivion is gone dry:
   But fill me with the old familiar Juice,
Methinks I might recover by and by."

So while the Vessels one by one were speaking,
The little Moon look'd in that all were seeking:
   And then they jogg'd each other, "Brother! Brother!
Now for the Porter's shoulder-knot a-creaking!"

    •   •   •   •   •   •   •

Ah, with the Grape my fading Life provide,
And wash the Body whence the Life has died,
 And lay me, shrouded in the living Leaf,
By some not unfrequented Garden-side.

That ev'n my buried Ashes such a snare
Of Vintage shall fling up into the Air
 As not a True-believer passing by
But shall be overtaken unaware.

Indeed the Idols I have loved so long
Have done my credit in this World much wrong:
 Have drown'd my Glory in a shallow Cup,
And sold my Reputation for a Song.

Indeed, indeed, Repentance oft before
I swore—but was I sober when I swore?
 And then and then came Spring, and Rose-in-hand
My thread-bare Penitence apieces tore.

And much as Wine has play'd the Infidel,
And robb'd me of my Robe of Honour—Well,
 I wonder often what the Vintners buy
One half so precious as the stuff they sell.

Yet Ah, that Spring should vanish with the Rose!
That Youth's sweet-scented manuscript should close!
 The Nightingale that in the branches sang,
Ah whence, and whither flown again, who knows!

Would but the Desert of the Fountain yield
One glimpse—if dimly, yet indeed, reveal'd,
 To which the fainting Traveller might spring,
As springs the trampled herbage of the field!

Would but some wingèd Angel ere too late
Arrest the yet unfolded Roll of Fate,
 And make the stern Recorder otherwise
Enregister, or quite obliterate!

Ah Love! could you and I with Him conspire
To grasp this sorry Scheme of Things entire,

Would not we shatter it to bits—and then
Re-mould it nearer to the Heart's Desire!

.   .   .   .   .

Yon rising Moon that looks for us again—
How oft hereafter will she wax and wane;
    How oft hereafter rising look for us
Through this same Garden—and for *one* in vain!

And when like her, oh Sákí, you shall pass
Among the Guests Star-scatter'd on the Grass,
    And in your joyous errand reach the spot
Where I made One—turn down an empty Glass!

TAMÁM

EDGAR ALLAN POE
1809–1849

To Helen

Helen, thy beauty is to me
    Like those Nicæan barks of yore,
That gently, o'er a perfumed sea,
    The weary, wayworn wanderer bore
    To his own native shore.

On desperate seas long wont to roam,
    Thy hyacinth hair, thy classic face,
Thy Naiad airs have brought me home
    To the glory that was Greece
    And the grandeur that was Rome.

Lo! in yon brilliant window-niche
    How statue-like I see thee stand,
The agate lamp within thy hand!
    Ah, Psyche, from the regions which
    Are Holy Land!

Annabel Lee

It was many and many a year ago,
 In a kingdom by the sea,
That a maiden there lived whom you may know
 By the name of Annabel Lee;—
And this maiden she lived with no other thought
 Than to love and be loved by me.

I was a child and *she* was a child,
 In this kingdom by the sea,
But we loved with a love that was more than love—
 I and my Annabel Lee—
With a love that the wingèd seraphs in Heaven
 Coveted her and me.

And this was the reason that, long ago,
 In this kingdom by the sea,
A wind blew out of a cloud, chilling
 My beautiful Annabel Lee;
So that her high-born kinsmen came
 And bore her away from me,
To shut her up in a sepulcher
 In this kingdom by the sea.

The angels, not half so happy in Heaven,
 Went envying her and me:—
Yes!—that was the reason (as all men know,
 In this kingdom by the sea)
That the wind came out of the cloud, by night,
 Chilling and killing my Annabel Lee.

But our love it was stronger by far than the love
 Of those who were older than we—
 Of many far wiser than we—
And neither the angels in Heaven above,
 Nor the demons down under the sea,
Can ever dissever my soul from the soul
 Of the beautiful Annabel Lee:—

For the moon never beams without bringing me dreams
 Of the beautiful Annabel Lee;

And the stars never rise but I feel the bright eyes
  Of the beautiful Annabel Lee;
And so, all the night-tide, I lie down by the side
Of my darling,—my darling,—my life and my bride,
  In her sepulcher there by the sea—
  In her tomb by the sounding sea.

Israfel

*And the angel Israfel, whose heart-strings are a lute, and who
has the sweetest voice of all God's creatures.*—KORAN

In Heaven a spirit doth dwell
  "Whose heart-strings are a lute;"
None sing so wildly well
As the angel Israfel,
And the giddy stars (so legends tell)
Ceasing their hymns, attend the spell
  Of his voice, all mute.

Tottering above
  In her highest noon,
  The enamored moon
Blushes with love,
  While, to listen, the red levin
  (With the rapid Pleiads, even,
  Which were seven,)
  Pauses in Heaven.

And they say (the starry choir
  And the other listening things)
That Israfeli's fire
Is owing to that lyre
  By which he sits and sings—
  The trembling living wire
Of those unusual strings.

But the skies that angel trod,
  Where deep thoughts are a duty—
Where Love's a grown-up God—
  Where the Houri glances are

Imbued with all the beauty
  Which we worship in a star.

Therefore, thou art not wrong,
  Israfeli, who despisest
An unimpassioned song;
To thee the laurels belong,
  Best bard, because the wisest!
Merrily live, and long!

The ecstasies above
  With thy burning measures suit—
Thy grief, thy joy, thy hate, thy love,
  With the fervor of thy lute—
  Well may the stars be mute!
Yes, Heaven is thine; but this
  Is a world of sweets and sours;
  Our flowers are merely—flowers,
And the shadow of thy perfect bliss
  Is the sunshine of ours.

If I could dwell
Where Israfel
  Hath dwelt, and he where I,
He might not sing so wildly well
  A mortal melody,
While a bolder note than this might swell
  From my lyre within the sky.

The Conqueror Worm

Lo! 't is a gala night
  Within the lonesome latter years!
An angel throng, bewinged, bedight
  In veils, and drowned in tears,
Sit in a theatre, to see
  A play of hopes and fears,
While the orchestra breathes fitfully
  The music of the spheres.

Mimes, in the form of God on high,
  Mutter and mumble low,

And hither and thither fly—
  Mere puppets they, who come and go
At bidding of vast formless things
  That shift the scenery to and fro,
Flapping from out their Condor wings
  Invisible Woe!

That motley drama—oh, be sure
  It shall not be forgot!
With its Phantom chased for evermore,
  By a crowd that seize it not,
Through a circle that ever returneth in
  To the self-same spot,
And much of Madness, and more of Sin,
  And Horror the soul of the plot.

But see, amid the mimic rout
  A crawling shape intrude!
A blood-red thing that writhes from out
  The scenic solitude!
It writhes!—it writhes!—with mortal pangs
  The mimes become its food,
And seraphs sob at vermin fangs
  In human gore imbued.

Out—out are the lights—out all!
  And, over each quivering form,
The curtain, a funeral pall,
  Comes down with the rush of a storm,
While the angels, all pallid and wan,
  Uprising, unveiling, affirm
That the play is the tragedy, "Man,"
  And its hero the Conqueror Worm.

The Happiest Day

The happiest day—the happiest hour
  My seared and blighted heart hath known,
The highest hope of pride and power,
  I feel hath flown.

Of power! said I? Yes! such I ween
  But they have vanished long, alas!

The visions of my youth have been—
  But let them pass.

And pride, what have I now with thee?
  Another brow may ev'n inherit
The venom thou hast poured on me—
  Be still my spirit!

The happiest day—the happiest hour
  Mine eyes shall see—have even seen
The brightest glance of pride and power
  I feel have been:

But were that hope of pride and power
  Now offered with the pain
Ev'n *then* I felt—that brightest hour
  I would not live again:

For on its wings was dark alloy
  And as it fluttered—fell
An essence—powerful to destroy
  A soul that knew it well.

Ulalume

The skies they were ashen and sober;
  The leaves they were crispèd and sere,
  The leaves they were withering and sere;
It was night in the lonesome October
  Of my most immemorial year;
It was hard by the dim lake of Auber,
  In the misty mid region of Weir:
It was down by the dank tarn of Auber,
  In the ghoul-haunted woodland of Weir.

Here once, through an alley Titanic
  Of cypress, I roamed with my Soul—
  Of cypress, with Psyche, my Soul.
These were days when my heart was volcanic
  As the scoriac rivers that roll,
  As the lavas that restlessly roll
Their sulphurous currents down Yaanek

In the ultimate climes of the pole,
That groan as they roll down Mount Yaanek
In the realms of the boreal pole.

Our talk had been serious and sober,
But our thoughts they were palsied and sere,
Our memories were treacherous and sere,
For we knew not the month was October,
And we marked not the night of the year,
(Ah, night of all nights in the year!)
We noted not the dim lake of Auber
(Though once we had journeyed down here)
Remembered not the dank tarn of Auber
Nor the ghoul-haunted woodland of Weir.

And now, as the night was senescent
And star-dials pointed to morn,
As the star-dials hinted of morn,
At the end of our path a liquescent
And nebulous lustre was born,
Out of which a miraculous crescent
Arose with a duplicate horn,
Astarte's bediamonded crescent
Distinct with its duplicate horn.

And I said—"She is warmer than Dian:
She rolls through an ether of sighs,
She revels in a region of sighs:
She has seen that the tears are not dry on
These cheeks, where the worm never dies,
And has come past the stars of the Lion
To point us the path to the skies,
To the Lethean peace of the skies:
Come up, in despite of the Lion,
To shine on us with her bright eyes:
Come up through the lair of the Lion,
With love in her luminous eyes."

But Psyche, uplifting her finger,
Said—"Sadly this star I mistrust,
Her pallor I strangely mistrust:

Oh, hasten!—oh, let us not linger!
  Oh, fly!—let us fly!—for we must."
In terror she spoke, letting sink her
  Wings until they trailed in the dust;
In agony sobbed, letting sink her
  Plumes till they trailed in the dust,
  Till they sorrowfully trailed in the dust.

I replied—"This is nothing but dreaming:
  Let us on by this tremulous light!
  Let us bathe in this crystalline light!
Its sibyllic splendor is beaming
  With hope and in beauty to-night:
  See, it flickers up the sky through the night!
Ah, we safely may trust to its gleaming,
  And be sure it will lead us aright:
We safely may trust to a gleaming
  That cannot but guide us aright,
  Since it flickers up to Heaven through the night."

Thus I pacified Psyche and kissed her,
  And tempted her out of her gloom,
  And conquered her scruples and gloom;
And we passed to the end of the vista,
  But were stopped by the door of a tomb,
  By the door of a legended tomb;
And I said—"What is written, sweet sister,
  On the door of this legended tomb?"
  She replied—"Ulalume—Ulalume—
  'Tis the vault of thy lost Ulalume!"

Then my heart it grew ashen and sober
  As the leaves that were crispèd and sere,
  As the leaves that were withering and sere,
And I cried—"It was surely October
  On this very night of last year
  That I journeyed—I journeyed down here,
  That I brought a dread burden down here:
  On this night of all nights in the year,
  Ah, what demon has tempted me here?
Well I know, now, this dim lake of Auber,
  This misty mid region of Weir:

Well I know, now, this dank tarn of Auber,
This ghoul-haunted woodland of Weir."

ALFRED, LORD TENNYSON
1809–1892

Tears, Idle Tears

Tears, idle tears, I know not what they mean,
Tears from the depth of some divine despair
Rise in the heart, and gather to the eyes,
In looking on the happy autumn-fields,
And thinking of the days that are no more.

Fresh as the first beam glittering on a sail,
That brings our friends up from the under-world,
Sad as the last which reddens over one
That sinks with all we love below the verge;
So sad, so fresh, the days that are no more.

Ah, sad and strange as in dark summer dawns
The earliest pipe of half-awakened birds
To dying ears, when unto dying eyes
The casement slowly grows a glimmering square;
So sad, so strange, the days that are no more.

Dear as remembered kisses after death,
And sweet as those by hopeless fancy feigned
On lips that are for others; deep as love,
Deep as first love, and wild with all regret;
O Death in Life, the days that are no more!

Blow, Bugle, Blow

The splendour falls on castle walls
    And snowy summits old in story:
The long light shakes across the lakes,
    And the wild cataract leaps in glory.
Blow, bugle, blow, set the wild echoes flying,
Blow, bugle; answer, echoes, dying, dying, dying.

O hark, O hear! how thin and clear,
    And thinner, clearer, farther going!
O sweet and far from cliff and scar
    The horns of Elfland faintly blowing!
Blow, let us hear the purple glens replying:
Blow, bugle; answer, echoes, dying, dying, dying.

O love, they die in yon rich sky,
    They faint on hill or field or river:
Our echoes roll from soul to soul,
    And grow for ever and for ever.
Blow, bugle, blow, set the wild echoes flying,
And answer, echoes, answer, dying, dying, dying.

Break, Break, Break

Break, break, break,
    On thy cold grey stones, O Sea!
And I would that my tongue could utter
    The thoughts that arise in me.

O well for the fisherman's boy,
    That he shouts with his sister at play!
O well for the sailor lad,
    That he sings in his boat on the bay!

And the stately ships go on
    To their haven under the hill;
But O for the touch of a vanished hand,
    And the sound of a voice that is still!

Break, break, break,
    At the foot of thy crags, O Sea!
But the tender grace of a day that is dead
    Will never come back to me.

Ask Me No More

Ask me no more: the moon may draw the sea;
    The cloud may stoop from heaven and take shape,
    With fold to fold, of mountain or of cape;
But O too fond, when have I answer'd thee?
    Ask me no more.

Ask me no more: what answer should I give?
  I love not hollow cheek or faded eye:
  Yet O my friend, I will not have thee die!
Ask me no more, lest I should bid thee live;
      Ask me no more.

Ask me no more: thy fate and mine are seal'd:
  I strove against the stream and all in vain:
  Let the great river take me to the main:
No more, dear love, for at a touch I yield;
      Ask me no more.

All in All

In Love, if Love be Love, if Love be ours,
Faith and unfaith can ne'er be equal powers:
Unfaith in aught is want of faith in all.

It is the little rift within the lute,
That by and by will make the music mute,
And ever widening slowly silence all.

The little rift within the lover's lute,
Or little pitted speck in garner'd fruit,
That rotting inward slowly moulders all.

It is not worth the keeping: let it go:
But shall it? answer, darling, answer, no.
And trust me not at all or all in all.

From *Merlin and Vivien*

Flower in the Crannied Wall

Flower in the crannied wall,
I pluck you out of the crannies,
I hold you here, root and all, in my hand,
Little flower—but *if* I could understand
What you are, root and all, and all in all,
I should know what God and man is.

As Thro' the Land at Eve We Went

As thro' the land at eve we went,
  And pluck'd the ripen'd ears,
We fell out, my wife and I,

O we fell out I know not why,
  And kiss'd again with tears!
And blessings on the falling out
  That all the more endears,
When we fall out with those we love
  And kiss again with tears!
For when we came where lies the child
  We lost in other years,
There above the little grave,
O there above the little grave,
  We kiss'd again with tears.

Ulysses

It little profits that an idle king,
By this still hearth, among these barren crags,
Matched with an aged wife, I mete and dole
Unequal laws unto a savage race,
That hoard, and sleep, and feed, and know not me.
I cannot rest from travel; I will drink
Life to the lees. All times I have enjoyed
Greatly, have suffered greatly, both with those
That loved me, and alone; on shore, and when
Through scudding drifts the rainy Hyades
Vexed the dim sea. I am become a name;
For always roaming with a hungry heart
Much have I seen and known—cities of men
And manners, climates, councils, governments,
Myself not least, but honoured of them all—
And drunk delight of battle with my peers,
Far on the ringing plains of windy Troy.
I am a part of all that I have met;
Yet all experience is an arch wherethrough
Gleams that untraveled world whose margin fades
Forever and forever when I move.
How dull it is to pause, to make an end,
To rust unburnished, not to shine in use!
As though to breathe were life! Life piled on life
Were all too little, and of one to me
Little remains; but every hour is saved
From that eternal silence, something more,
A bringer of new things; and vile it were
For some three suns to store and hoard myself,

And this grey spirit yearning in desire
To follow knowledge like a sinking star,
Beyond the utmost bound of human thought.

    This is my son, mine own Telemachus,
To whom I leave the scepter and the isle—
Well-loved of me, discerning to fulfill
This labour, by slow prudence to make mild
A rugged people, and through soft degrees
Subdue them to the useful and the good.
Most blameless is he, centered in the sphere
Of common duties, decent not to fail
In offices of tenderness, and pay
Meet adoration to my household gods,
When I am gone. He works his work, I mine.

    There lies the port; the vessel puffs her sail;
There gloom the dark, broad seas. My mariners,
Souls that have toiled, and wrought, and thought with me—
That ever with a frolic welcome took
The thunder and the sunshine, and opposed
Free hearts, free foreheads—you and I are old;
Old age hath yet his honour and his toil.
Death closes all; but something ere the end,
Some work of noble note, may yet be done,
Not unbecoming men that strove with gods.
The lights begin to twinkle from the rocks;
The long day wanes; the slow moon climbs; the deep
Moans round with many voices. Come, my friends,
'Tis not too late to seek a newer world.
Push off, and sitting well in order smite
The sounding furrows; for my purpose holds
To sail beyond the sunset, and the baths
Of all the western stars, until I die.
It may be that the gulfs will wash us down;
It may be we shall touch the Happy Isles,
And see the great Achilles, whom we knew.
Though much is taken, much abides; and though
We are not now that strength which in old days
Moved earth and heaven, that which we are, we are—
One equal temper of heroic hearts,
Made weak by time and fate, but strong in will
To strive, to seek, to find, and not to yield.

Choric Song of the Lotos-Eaters

There is sweet music here that softer falls
Than petals from blown roses on the grass,
Or night-dews on still waters between walls
Of shadowy granite, in a gleaming pass;
Music that gentlier on the spirit lies,
Than tired eyelids upon tired eyes;
Music that brings sweet sleep down from the blissful skies.
Here are cool mosses deep,
And through the moss the ivies creep,
And in the stream the long-leaved flowers weep,
And from the craggy ledge the poppy hangs in sleep.

Why are we weighed upon with heaviness,
And utterly consumed with sharp distress,
While all things else have rest from weariness?
All things have rest; why should we toil alone,
We only toil, who are the first of things,
And make perpetual moan,
Still from one sorrow to another thrown;
Nor ever fold our wings,
And cease from wanderings,
Nor steep our brows in slumber's holy balm;
Nor harken what the inner spirit sings,
"There is no joy but calm!"—
Why should we only toil, the roof and crown of things?

Lo! in the middle of the wood,
The folded leaf is wooed from out the bud
With winds upon the branch, and there
Grows green and broad, and takes no care,
Sun-steeped at noon, and in the moon
Nightly dew-fed; and turning yellow
Falls, and floats adown the air.
Lo! sweetened with the summer light,
The full-juiced apple, waxing over-mellow,
Drops in a silent autumn night.
All its allotted length of days
The flower ripens in its place,
Ripens and fades, and falls, and hath no toil,
Fast-rooted in the fruitful soil.

Hateful is the dark-blue sky,
Vaulted o'er the dark-blue sea.
Death is the end of life; ah, why
Should life all labour be?
Let us alone. Time driveth onward fast,
And in a little while our lips are dumb.
Let us alone. What is it that will last?
All things are taken from us, and become
Portions and parcels of the dreadful past.
Let us alone. What pleasure can we have
To war with evil? Is there any peace
In ever climbing up the climbing wave?
All things have rest, and ripen toward the grave
In silence—ripen, fall, and cease;
Give us long rest or death, dark death, or dreamful ease.

How sweet it were, hearing the downward stream
With half-shut eyes ever to seem
Falling asleep in a half-dream!
To dream and dream, like yonder amber light,
Which will not leave the myrrh-bush on the height;
To hear each other's whispered speech;
Eating the Lotos day by day,
To watch the crisping ripples on the beach,
And tender curving lines of creamy spray;
To lend our hearts and spirits wholly
To the influence of mild-minded melancholy;
To muse and brood and live again in memory,
With those old faces of our infancy
Heaped over with a mound of grass,
Two handfuls of white dust, shut in an urn of brass!

Dear is the memory of our wedded lives,
And dear the last embraces of our wives
And their warm tears; but all hath suffered change;
For surely now our household hearths are cold,
Our sons inherit us, our looks are strange,
And we should come like ghosts to trouble joy.
Or else the island princes over-bold
Have eat our substance, and the minstrel sings
Before them of the ten years' war in Troy,

And our great deeds, as half-forgotten things.
Is there confusion in the little isle?
Let what is broken so remain.
The gods are hard to reconcile;
'Tis hard to settle order once again.
There *is* confusion worse than death,
Trouble on trouble, pain on pain,
Long labour unto aged breath,
Sore task to hearts worn out by many wars
And eyes grown dim with gazing on the pilot-stars.
But, propped on beds of amaranth and moly,
How sweet—while warm airs lull us, blowing lowly—
With half-dropped eyelid still,
Beneath a heaven dark and holy,
To watch the long bright river drawing slowly
His waters from the purple hill—
To hear the dewy echoes calling
From cave to cave through the thick-twined vine—
To watch the emerald-coloured water falling
Through many a woven acanthus-wreath divine!
Only to hear and see the far-off sparkling brine,
Only to hear were sweet, stretched out beneath the pine.

The Lotos blooms below the barren peak,
The Lotos blows by every winding creek;
All day the wind breathes low with mellower tone;
Through every hollow cave and alley lone
Round and round the spicy downs the yellow Lotos-dust is blown.
We have had enough of action, and of motion we,
Rolled to starboard, rolled to larboard, when the surge was seething free,
Where the wallowing monster spouted his foam-fountains in the sea.
Let us swear an oath, and keep it with an equal mind,
In the hollow Lotos-land to live and lie reclined
On the hills like gods together, careless of mankind.
For they lie beside their nectar, and the bolts are hurled
Far below them in the valleys, and the clouds are lightly curled
Round their golden houses, girdled with the gleaming world;
Where they smile in secret, looking over wasted lands,
Blight and famine, plague and earthquake, roaring deeps and fiery sands,
Clanging fights, and flaming towns, and sinking ships, and praying hands.
But they smile, they find a music centered in a doleful song

Steaming up, a lamentation and an ancient tale of wrong,
Like a tale of little meaning though the words are strong;
Chanted from an ill-used race of men that cleave the soil,
Sow the seed, and reap the harvest with enduring toil,
Storing yearly little dues of wheat, and wine and oil;
Till they perish and they suffer—some, 'tis whispered—down in hell
Suffer endless anguish, others in Elysian valleys dwell,
Resting weary limbs at last on beds of asphodel.
Surely, surely, slumber is more sweet than toil, the shore
Than labour in the deep mid-ocean, wind and wave and oar;
O rest ye, brother mariners, we will not wander more.

Tithonus

The woods decay, the woods decay and fall,
The vapours weep their burthen to the ground;
Man comes and tills the field and lies beneath,
And after many a summer dies the swan.
Me only cruel immortality
Consumes; I wither slowly in thine arms,
Here at the quiet limit of the world,
A white-haired shadow roaming like a dream
The ever-silent spaces of the East,
Far-folded mists, and gleaming halls of morn.
 Alas! for this grey shadow, once a man—
So glorious in his beauty and thy choice,
Who madest him thy chosen, that he seemed
To his great heart none other than a god!
I asked thee, "Give me immortality."
Then didst thou grant mine asking with a smile,
Like wealthy men who care not how they give.
But thy strong Hours indignant worked their wills,
And beat me down and marred and wasted me,
And though they could not end me, left me maimed
To dwell in presence of immortal youth,
Immortal age beside immortal youth,
And all I was in ashes. Can thy love,
Thy beauty, make amends, though even now,
Close over us, the silver star, thy guide,
Shines in those tremulous eyes that fill with tears
To hear me? Let me go; take back thy gift.
Why should a man desire in any way

To vary from the kindly race of men,
Or pass beyond the goal of ordinance
Where all should pause, as is most meet for all?
   A soft air fans the cloud apart; there comes
A glimpse of that dark world where I was born.
Once more the old mysterious glimmer steals
From thy pure brows, and from thy shoulders pure,
And bosom beating with a heart renewed.
Thy cheek begins to redden through the gloom,
Thy sweet eyes brighten slowly close to mine,
Ere yet they blind the stars, and the wild team
Which love thee, yearning for thy yoke, arise,
And shake the darkness from their loosened manes,
And beat the twilight into flakes of fire.
   Lo! ever thus thou growest beautiful
In silence; then, before thine answer given,
Departest, and thy tears are on my cheek.
   Why wilt thou ever scare me with thy tears,
And make me tremble lest a saying learnt,
In days far-off, on that dark earth, be true?
"The gods themselves cannot recall their gifts."
   Ay me! ay me! with what another heart
In days far-off, and with what other eyes
I used to watch—if I be he that watched—
The lucid outline forming round thee; saw
The dim curls kindle into sunny rings;
Changed with thy mystic change, and felt my blood
Glow with the glow that slowly crimsoned all
Thy presence and thy portals, while I lay,
Mouth, forehead, eyelids, growing dewy-warm
With kisses balmier than half-opening buds
Of April, and could hear the lips that kissed
Whispering I knew not what of wild and sweet,
Like that strange song I heard Apollo sing,
While Ilion like a mist rose into towers.
   Yet hold me not forever in thine East;
How can my nature longer mix with thine?
Coldly thy rosy shadows bathe me, cold
Are all thy lights, and cold my wrinkled feet
Upon thy glimmering thresholds, when the steam
Floats up from those dim fields about the homes

Of happy men that have the power to die,
And grassy barrows of the happier dead.
Release me, and restore me to the ground.
Thou seest all things, thou wilt see my grave;
Thou wilt renew thy beauty morn by morn,
I earth in earth forget these empty courts,
And thee returning on thy silver wheels.

Locksley Hall

Comrades, leave me here a little, while as yet 'tis early morn:
Leave me here, and when you want me, sound upon the bugle horn.
'Tis the place, and all around it, as of old, the curlews call,
Dreary gleams about the moorland flying over Locksley Hall;
Locksley Hall, that in the distance overlooks the sandy tracts,
And the hollow ocean-ridges roaring into cataracts.

Many a night from yonder ivied casement, ere I went to rest,
Did I look on great Orion sloping slowly to the West.
Many a night I saw the Pleiads, rising thro' the mellow shade,
Glitter like a swarm of fire-flies tangled in a silver braid.
Here about the beach I wander'd, nourishing a youth sublime
With the fairy tales of science, and the long result of Time;
When the centuries behind me like a fruitful land reposed;
When I clung to all the present for the promise that it closed:
When I dipt into the future far as human eye could see;
Saw the Vision of the world, and all the wonder that would be.—

In the Spring a fuller crimson comes upon the robin's breast;
In the Spring the wanton lapwing gets himself another crest;
In the Spring a livelier iris changes on the burnish'd dove;
In the Spring a young man's fancy lightly turns to thoughts of love.

Then her cheek was pale and thinner than should be for one so young,
And her eyes on all my motions with a mute observance hung.
And I said, "My cousin Amy, speak, and speak the truth to me,
Trust me, cousin, all the current of my being sets to thee."
On her pallid cheek and forehead came a colour and a light,
As I have seen the rosy red flushing in the northern night.
And she turn'd—her bosom shaken with a sudden storm of sighs—
All the spirit deeply dawning in the dark of hazel eyes—
Saying, "I have hid my feelings, fearing they should do me wrong;"
Saying, "Dost thou love me, cousin?" weeping, "I have loved thee long."

Love took up the glass of Time, and turn'd it in his glowing hands;
Every moment, lightly shaken, ran itself in golden sands.
Love took up the harp of Life, and smote on all the chords with might;
Smote the chord of Self, that, trembling, pass'd in music out of sight.
Many a morning on the moorland did we hear the copses ring,
And her whisper throng'd my pulses with the fullness of the Spring.
Many an evening by the waters did we watch the stately ships,
And our spirits rush'd together at the touching of the lips.
O my cousin, shallow-hearted! O my Amy, mine no more!
O the dreary, dreary moorland! O the barren, barren shore!
Falser than all fancy fathoms, falser than all songs have sung,
Puppet to a father's threat, and servile to a shrewish tongue!
Is it well to wish thee happy?—having known me—to decline
On a range of lower feelings and a narrower heart than mine!
Yet it shall be: thou shalt lower to his level day by day,
What is fine within thee growing coarse to sympathize with clay.

As the husband is, the wife is: thou art mated with a clown,
And the grossness of his nature will have weight to drag thee down.
He will hold thee, when his passion shall have spent its novel force,
Something better than his dog, a little dearer than his horse.
What is this? his eyes are heavy: think not they are glazed with wine.
Go to him: it is thy duty: kiss him: take his hand in thine.
It may be my lord is weary, that his brain is over-wrought:
Soothe him with thy finer fancies, touch him with thy lighter thought.

He will answer to the purpose, easy things to understand—
Better thou wert dead before me, tho' I slew thee with my hand!
Better thou and I were lying, hidden from the heart's disgrace,
Roll'd in one another's arms, and silent in a last embrace.
Cursed be the social wants that sin against the strength of youth!
Cursed be the social lies that warp us from the living truth!
Cursed be the sickly forms that err from honest Nature's rule!
Cursed be the gold that gilds the straiten'd forehead of the fool!

Well—'tis well that I should bluster!—Hadst thou less unworthy proved—
Would to God—for I had loved thee more than ever wife was loved.
Am I mad, that I should cherish that which bears but bitter fruit?
I will pluck it from my bosom, tho' my heart be at the root.
Never, tho' my mortal summers to such length of years should come
As the many-winter'd crow that leads the clanging rookery home.

Where is comfort? in division of the records of the mind?
Can I part her from herself, and love her, as I knew her, kind?

I remember one that perish'd: sweetly did she speak and move:
Such a one do I remember, whom to look at was to love.
Can I think of her as dead, and love her for the love she bore?
No—she never loved me truly: love is love for evermore.
Comfort? comfort scorn'd of devils! this is truth the poet sings,
That a sorrow's crown of sorrow is remembering happier things.

Drug thy memories, lest thou learn it, lest thy heart be put to proof,
In the dead unhappy night, and when the rain is on the roof.
Like a dog, he hunts in dreams, and thou art staring at the wall,
Where the dying night-lamp flickers, and the shadows rise and fall.
Then a hand shall pass before thee, pointing to his drunken sleep,
To thy widow'd marriage-pillows, to the tears that thou wilt weep.
Thou shalt hear the "Never, never," whisper'd by the phantom years,
And a song from out the distance in the ringing of thine ears;
And an eye shall vex thee, looking ancient kindness on thy pain.
Turn thee, turn thee on thy pillow: get thee to thy rest again.

Nay, but Nature brings thee solace; for a tender voice will cry.
'Tis a purer life than thine; a lip to drain thy trouble dry.
Baby lips will laugh me down: my latest rival brings thee rest.
Baby fingers, waxen touches, press me from the mother's breast.
O, the child too clothes the father with a dearness not his due.
Half is thine and half is his: it will be worthy of the two.

O, I see thee old and formal, fitted to thy petty part,
With a little hoard of maxims preaching down a daughter's heart.
"They were dangerous guides the feelings—she herself was not exempt—
Truly, she herself had suffer'd"—Perish in thy self-contempt!
Overlive it—lower yet—be happy! wherefore should I care?
I myself must mix with action, lest I wither by despair.
What is that which I should turn to, lighting upon days like these?
Every door is barr'd with gold, and opens but to golden keys.
Every gate is throng'd with suitors, all the markets overflow.
I have but an angry fancy: what is that which I should do?

I had been content to perish, falling on the foeman's ground,
When the ranks are roll'd in vapour, and the winds are laid with sound.

But the jingling of the guinea helps the hurt that Honour feels,
And the nations do but murmur, snarling at each other's heels.
Can I but relive in sadness? I will turn that earlier page.
Hide me from my deep emotion, O thou wondrous Mother-Age!

Make me feel the wild pulsation that I felt before the strife,
When I heard my days before me, and the tumult of my life;
Yearning for the large excitement that the coming years would yield,
Eager-hearted as a boy when first he leaves his father's field,
And at night along the dusky highway near and nearer drawn,
Sees in heaven the light of London flaring like a dreary dawn;
And his spirit leaps within him to be gone before him then,
Underneath the light he looks at, in among the throngs of men;
Men, my brothers, men the workers, ever reaping something new:
That which they have done but earnest of the things that they shall do:
For I dipt into the future, far as human eye could see,
Saw the Vision of the world, and all the wonder that would be;
Saw the heavens fill with commerce, argosies of magic sails,
Pilots of the purple twilight, dropping down with costly bales;
Heard the heavens fill with shouting, and there rain'd a ghastly dew
From the nations' airy navies grappling in the central blue;
Far along the world-wide whisper of the south-wind rushing warm,
With the standards of the peoples plunging thro' the thunder storm;
Till the war-drum throbb'd no longer, and the battle flags were furl'd
In the Parliament of man, the Federation of the world.
There the common sense of most shall hold a fretful realm in awe,
And the kindly earth shall slumber, lapt in universal law.

So I triumphed, ere my passion sweeping thro' me left me dry,
Left me with the palsied heart, and left me with the jaundiced eye;
Eye, to which all order festers, all things here are out of joint,
Science moves, but slowly slowly, creeping on from point to point:
Slowly comes a hungry people, as a lion, creeping nigher,
Glares at one that nods and winks behind a slowly-dying fire.
Yet I doubt not thro' the ages one increasing purpose runs,
And the thoughts of men are widen'd with the process of the suns.

What is that to him that reaps not harvest of his youthful joys,
Tho' the deep heart of existence beat for ever like a boy's?
Knowledge comes, but wisdom lingers, and I linger on the shore,
And the individual withers, and the world is more and more.

Knowledge comes, but wisdom lingers, and he bears a laden breast,
Full of sad experience, moving toward the stillness of his rest.

Hark, my merry comrades call me, sounding on the buglehorn,
They to whom my foolish passion were a target for their scorn:
Shall it not be scorn to me to harp on such a moulder'd string?
I am shamed thro' all my nature to have loved so slight a thing.
Weakness to be wroth with weakness! woman's pleasure, woman's pain—
Nature made them blinder motions bounded in a shallower brain:
Woman is the lesser man, and all thy passions, match'd with mine,
Are as moonlight unto sunlight, and as water unto wine—

Here at least, where nature sickens, nothing. Ah, for some retreat
Deep in yonder shining Orient, where my life began to beat;
Where in wild Mahratta-battle fell my father evil-starr'd;—
I was left a trampled orphan, and a selfish uncle's ward.
Or to burst all links of habit—there to wander far away,
On from island unto island at the gateways of the day.
Larger constellations burning, mellow moons and happy skies,
Breadths of tropic shade and palms in cluster, knots of Paradise.
Never comes the trader, never floats an European flag,
Slides the bird o'er lustrous woodland, swings the trailer from the crag;
Droops the heavy-blossom'd bower, hangs the heavy-fruited tree—
Summer isles of Eden lying in dark-purple spheres of sea.

There methinks would be enjoyment more than in this march of mind,
In the steamship, in the railway, in the thoughts that shake mankind.
There the passions cramp'd no longer shall have scope and breathing-space;
I will take some savage woman, she shall rear my dusky race.
Iron-jointed, supple-sinew'd, they shall dive, and they shall run,
Catch the wild goat by the hair, and hurl their lances in the sun;
Whistle back the parrot's call, and leap the rainbows of the brooks,
Not with blinded eyesight poring over miserable books—

Fool, again the dream, the fancy! but I *know* my words are wild,
But I count the gray barbarian lower than the Christian child.
I, to herd with narrow foreheads, vacant of our glorious gains,
Like a beast with lower pleasures, like a beast with lower pains!
Mated with a squalid savage—what to me were sun or clime?
I the heir of all the ages, in the foremost files of time—
I that rather held it better men should perish one by one,
Than that earth should stand at gaze like Joshua's moon in Ajalon!

Not in vain the distance beacons. Forward, forward let us range.
Let the great world spin for ever down the ringing grooves of change.
Thro' the shadow of the globe we swept into the younger day:
Better fifty years of Europe than a cycle of Cathay.
Mother-Age (for mine I knew not) help me as when life begun:
Rift the hills, and roll the waters, flash the lightnings, weigh the Sun—
O, I see the crescent promise of my spirit hath not set.
Ancient founts of inspiration well thro' all my fancy yet.
Howsoever these things be, a long farewell to Locksley Hall!
Now for me the woods may wither, now for me the rooftree fall.
Comes a vapour from the margin, blackening over heath and holt,
Cramming all the blast before it, in its breast a thunderbolt.
Let it fall on Locksley Hall, with rain or hail, or fire or snow;
For the mighty wind arises, roaring seaward, and I go.

NINE POEMS FROM "IN MEMORIAM"

Oh Yet We Trust

Oh yet we trust that somehow good
    Will be the final goal of ill,
    To pangs of nature, sins of will,
Defects of doubt, and taints of blood;

That nothing walks with aimless feet;
    That not one life shall be destroyed,
    Or cast as rubbish to the void,
When God hath made the pile complete;

That not a worm is cloven in vain;
    That not a moth with vain desire
    Is shrivelled in a fruitless fire,
Or but subserves another's gain.

Behold, we know not anything;
    I can but trust that good shall fall
    At last—far off—at last, to all,
And every winter change to spring.

So runs my dream: but what am I?
  An infant crying in the night:
  An infant crying for the light:
And with no language but a cry.

Dark House

Dark house, by which once more I stand
  Here in the long unlovely street,
  Doors, where my heart was used to beat
So quickly, waiting for a hand,

A hand that can be clasp'd no more—
  Behold me, for I cannot sleep,
  And like a guilty thing I creep
At earliest morning to the door.

He is not here; but far away
  The noise of life begins again,
  And ghastly thro' the drizzling rain
On the bald street breaks the blank day.

I Cannot See the Features Right

I cannot see the features right
  When on the gloom I strive to paint
  The face I know; the hues are faint
And mix with hollow masks of night;

Cloud-towers by ghostly masons wrought,
  A gulf that ever shuts and gapes,
  A hand that points, and palled shapes
In shadowy thoroughfares of thought;

And crowds that stream from yawning doors,
  And shoals of pucker'd faces drive;
  Dark bulks that tumble half alive,
And lazy lengths on boundless shores;

Till all at once beyond the will
  I hear a wizard music roll,
  And thro' a lattice on the soul
Looks thy fair face and makes it still.

To-night the Winds Begin

To-night the winds begin to rise
    And roar from yonder dropping day:
    The last red leaf is whirl'd away,
The rooks are blown about the skies;

The forest crack'd, the waters curl'd,
    The cattle huddled on the lea;
    And wildly dash'd on tower and tree
The sunbeam strikes along the world:

And but for fancies, which aver
    That all thy motions gently pass
    Athwart a plane of molten glass,
I scarce could brook the strain and stir

That make the barren branches loud;
    And but for fear it is not so,
    The wild unrest that lives in woe
Would dote and pore on yonder cloud

That rises upward always higher,
    And onward drags a labouring breast,
    And topples round the dreary west,
A looming bastion fringed with fire.

Of One Dead

If one should bring me this report,
    That thou hadst touched the land to-day,
    And I went down unto the quay,
And found thee lying in the port;

And standing, muffled round with woe,
    Should see thy passengers in rank
    Come stepping lightly down the plank,
And beckoning unto those they know;

And if along with these should come
    The man I held as half-divine;
    Should strike a sudden hand in mine,
And ask a thousand things of home;

And I should tell him all my pain,
   And how my life had droop'd of late,
   And he should sorrow o'er my state
And marvel what possess'd my brain;

And I perceived no touch of change,
   No hint of death in all his frame,
   But found him all in all the same,
I should not feel it to be strange.

I Wage Not Any Feud with Death

I wage not any feud with Death
   For changes wrought on form and face;
   No lower life that earth's embrace
May breed with him can fright my faith.

Eternal process moving on,
   From state to state the spirit walks;
   And these are but the shattered stalks,
Or ruined chrysalis of one.

Nor blame I Death, because he bare
   The use of virtue out of earth;
   I know transplanted human worth
Will bloom to profit, otherwhere.

For this alone on Death I wreak
   The wrath that garners in my heart:
   He put our lives so far apart
We cannot hear each other speak.

I Envy Not in Any Moods

I envy not in any moods
   The captive void of noble rage,
   The linnet born within the cage,
That never knew the summer woods:

I envy not the beast that takes
   His license in the field of time,
   Unfetter'd by the sense of crime,
To whom a conscience never wakes;

Nor, what may count itself as blest,
  The heart that never plighted troth
  But stagnates in the weeds of sloth,
Nor any want-begotten rest.

I hold it true, whate'er befall;
  I feel it, when I sorrow most;
  'Tis better to have loved and lost
Than never to have loved at all.

As Sometimes in a Dead Man's Face

As sometimes in a dead man's face,
  To those that watch it more and more,
  A likeness, hardly seen before,
Comes out—to someone of his race;

So, dearest, now thy brows are cold,
  I see thee what thou art, and know
  Thy likeness to the wise below,
Thy kindred with the great of old.

But there is more than I can see,
  And what I see I leave unsaid,
  Nor speak it, knowing Death has made
His darkness beautiful with thee.

Ring Out, Wild Bells

Ring out, wild bells, to the wild sky,
  The flying cloud, the frosty light:
  The year is dying in the night;
Ring out, wild bells, and let him die.

Ring out the old, ring in the new,
  Ring, happy bells, across the snow:
  The year is going, let him go;
Ring out the false, ring in the true.

Ring out the grief that saps the mind,
  For those that here we see no more;
  Ring out the feud of rich and poor,
Ring in redress to all mankind.

Ring out a slowly dying cause,
    And ancient forms of party strife;
    Ring in the nobler modes of life,
With sweeter manners, purer laws.

Ring out the want, the care, the sin,
    The faithless coldness of the times;
    Ring out, ring out my mournful rhymes,
But ring the fuller minstrel in.

Ring out false pride in place and blood,
    The civic slander and the spite;
    Ring in the love of truth and right,
Ring in the common love of good.

Ring out old shapes of foul disease,
    Ring out the narrowing lust of gold;
    Ring out the thousand wars of old,
Ring in the thousand years of peace.

Ring in the valiant man and free,
    The larger heart, the kindlier hand;
    Ring out the darkness of the land,
Ring in the Christ that is to be.

Crossing the Bar

Sunset and evening star,
  And one clear call for me!
And may there be no moaning of the bar,
  When I put out to sea,

But such a tide as moving seems asleep,
  Too full for sound and foam,
When that which drew from out the boundless deep
  Turns again home.

Twilight and evening bell,
  And after that the dark!
And may there be no sadness of farewell,
  When I embark;

For tho' from out our bourne of Time and Place
   The flood may bear me far,
   I hope to see my Pilot face to face
When I have crost the bar.

OLIVER WENDELL HOLMES
1809–1894

The Chambered Nautilus

This is the ship of pearl, which, poets feign,
   Sails the unshadowed main,—
   The venturous bark that flings
On the sweet summer wind its purpled wings
In gulfs enchanted, where the Siren sings,
   And coral reefs lie bare,
Where the cold sea-maids rise to sun their streaming hair.

Its webs of living gauze no more unfurl;
   Wrecked is the ship of pearl!
   And every chambered cell,
Where its dim dreaming life was wont to dwell,
As the frail tenant shaped his growing shell,
   Before thee lies revealed,—
Its irised ceiling rent, its sunless crypt unsealed!

Year after year beheld the silent toil
   That spread his lustrous coil;
   Still, as the spiral grew,
He left the past year's dwelling for the new,
Stole with soft step its shining archway through,
   Built up its idle door,
Stretched in his last-found home, and knew the old no more.

Thanks for the heavenly message brought by thee,
   Child of the wandering sea,
   Cast from her lap, forlorn!
From thy dead lips a clearer note is born
Than ever Triton blew from wreathèd horn!

While on mine ear it rings,
Through the deep caves of thought I hear a voice that sings:—

Build thee more stately mansions, O my soul,
  As the swift seasons roll!
  Leave thy low-vaulted past!
Let each new temple, nobler than the last,
Shut thee from heaven with a dome more vast,
  Till thou at length art free,
Leaving thine outgrown shell by life's unresting sea!

ROBERT BROWNING
1812–1889

Pippa's Song

    The year's at the spring,
    And day's at the morn;
    Morning's at seven;
    The hill-side's dew-pearl'd;
    The lark's on the wing;
    The snail's on the thorn;
    God's in His heaven—
    All's right with the world!

Home-Thoughts from Abroad

Oh, to be in England
Now that April's there,
And whoever wakes in England
Sees, some morning, unaware,
That the lowest boughs and the brush-wood sheaf
Round the elm-tree bole are in tiny leaf,
While the chaffinch sings on the orchard bough
In England—now!

And after April, when May follows,
And the whitethroat builds, and all the swallows—
Hark! where my blossomed pear-tree in the hedge
Leans to the field and scatters on the clover

Blossoms and dewdrops—at the bent-spray's edge—
That's the wise thrush; he sings each song twice over,
Lest you should think he never could recapture
The first fine careless rapture!
And though the fields look rough with hoary dew,
All will be gay when noontide wakes anew
The buttercups, the little children's dower,
—Far brighter than this gaudy melon-flower!

Parting at Morning

Round the cape of a sudden came the sea,
And the sun looked over the mountain's rim:
And straight was a path of gold for him,
And the need of a world of men for me.

Grow Old Along With Me

Grow old along with me!
The best is yet to be,
The last of life, for which the first was made:
Our times are in his hand
Who saith, "A whole I planned,
Youth shows but half; trust God: see all, nor be afraid!"

From *Rabbi Ben Ezra*

Soliloquy of the Spanish Cloister

Gr-r-r—there go, my heart's abhorrence!
  Water your damned flower-pots, do!
If hate killed men, Brother Lawrence,
  God's blood, would not mine kill you!
What? your myrtle-bush wants trimming?
  Oh, that rose has prior claims—
Needs its leaden vase filled brimming?
  Hell dry you up with its flames!

At the meal we sit together;
  Salve tibi! I must hear
Wise talk of the kind of weather,
  Sort of season, time of year:
Not a plenteous cork-crop: scarcely
  Dare we hope oak-galls, I doubt;
What's the Latin name for "parsley"?
  What's the Greek name for Swine's Snout?

Whew! We'll have our platter burnished,
   Laid with care on our own shelf!
With a fire-new spoon we're furnished,
   And a goblet for ourself,
Rinsed like something sacrificial
   Ere 'tis fit to touch our chaps—
Marked with L. for our initial!
   (He-he! There his lily snaps!)

Saint, forsooth! While brown Dolores
   Squats outside the Convent bank
With Sanchicha, telling stories,
   Steeping tresses in the tank,
Blue-black, lustrous, thick like horsehairs,
   —Can't I see his dead eye glow,
Bright as 'twere a Barbary corsair's?
   (That is, if he'd let it show!)

When he finishes refection,
   Knife and fork he never lays
Cross-wise, to my recollection,
   As do I, in Jesu's praise.
I, the Trinity illustrate,
   Drinking watered orange-pulp—
In three sips the Arian frustrate;
   While he drains his at one gulp!

Oh, those melons! if he's able
   We're to have a feast; so nice!
One goes to the Abbot's table,
   All of us get each a slice.
How go on your flowers? None double?
   Not one fruit-sort can you spy?
Strange!—And I, too, at such trouble,
   Keep them close-nipped on the sly!

There's a great text in Galatians,
   Once you trip on it, entails
Twenty-nine distinct damnations,
   One sure, if another fails;

If I trip him just a-dying,
    Sure of heaven as sure can be,
Spin him round and send him flying
    Off to hell, a Manichee?

Or, my scrofulous French novel
    On grey paper with blunt type!
Simply glance at it, you grovel
    Hand and foot in Belial's gripe;
If I double down its pages
    At the woeful sixteenth print,
When he gathers his greengages,
    Ope a sieve and slip it in't?

Or, there's Satan!—one might venture
    Pledge one's soul to him, yet leave
Such a flaw in the indenture
    As he'd miss till, past retrieve,
Blasted lay that rose-acacia
    We're so proud of! *Hy, Zy, Hine....*
'St, there's Vespers! *Plena gratia*
    Ave, Virgo! Gr-r-r—you swine!

My Last Duchess

FERRARA

That's my last Duchess painted on the wall,
Looking as if she were alive. I call
That piece a wonder, now; Frà Pandolf's hands
Worked busily a day, and there she stands.
Will 't please you sit and look at her? I said
"Frà Pandolf" by design, for never read
Strangers like you that pictured countenance,
The depth and passion of its earnest glance,
But to myself they turned (since none puts by
The curtain I have drawn for you, but I)
And seemed as they would ask me, if they durst,
How such a glance came there; so, not the first
Are you to turn and ask thus. Sir, 'twas not
Her husband's presence only, called that spot
Of joy into the Duchess' cheek; perhaps

Frà Pandolf chanced to say, "Her mantle laps
Over my lady's wrist too much," or "Paint
Must never hope to reproduce the faint
Half-flush that dies along her throat." Such stuff
Was courtesy, she thought, and cause enough
For calling up that spot of joy. She had
A heart—how shall I say?—too soon made glad,
Too easily impressed; she liked whate'er
She looked on, and her looks went everywhere.
Sir, 'twas all one! My favour at her breast,
The dropping of the daylight in the West,
The bough of cherries some officious fool
Broke in the orchard for her, the white mule
She rode with round the terrace—all and each
Would draw from her alike the approving speech,
Or blush, at least. She thanked men,—good! but thanked
Somehow—I know not how—as if she ranked
My gift of a nine-hundred-years-old-name
With anybody's gift. Who'd stoop to blame
This sort of trifling? Even had you skill
In speech—which I have not—to make your will
Quite clear to such an one, and say, "Just this
Or that in you disgusts me; here you miss,
Or there exceed the mark"—and if she let
Herself be lessoned so, nor plainly set
Her wits to yours, forsooth, and made excuse—
E'en then would be some stooping; and I choose
Never to stoop. Oh, sir, she smiled, no doubt,
Whene'er I passed her; but who passed without
Much the same smile? This grew; I gave commands;
Then all smiles stopped together. There she stands
As if alive. Will 't please you rise? We'll meet
The company below, then. I repeat,
The Count your master's known munificence
Is ample warrant that no just pretense
Of mine for dowry will be disallowed;
Though his fair daughter's self, as I avowed
At starting, is my object. Nay, we'll go
Together down, sir. Notice Neptune, though,
Taming a sea-horse, thought a rarity,
Which Claus of Innsbruck cast in bronze for me!

Prospice

Fear death? to feel the fog in my throat,
   The mist in my face,
When the snows begin, and the blasts denote
   I am nearing the place,
The power of the night, the press of the storm,
   The post of the foe;
Where he stands, the Arch Fear in a visible form,
   Yet the strong man must go:
For the journey is done and the summit attained,
   And the barriers fall,
Though a battle's to fight ere the guerdon be gained,
   The reward of it all.
I was ever a fighter, so—one fight more,
   The best and the last!
I would hate that death bandaged my eyes, and forbore,
   And bade me creep past.
No! let me taste the whole of it, fare like my peers
   The heroes of old,
Bear the brunt, in a minute pay glad life's arrears
   Of pain, darkness and cold.
For sudden the worst turns the best to the brave,
   The black minute's at end,
And the elements' rage, the fiend-voices that rave,
   Shall dwindle, shall blend,
Shall change, shall become first a peace out of pain,
   Then a light, then thy breast,
O thou soul of my soul! I shall clasp thee again,
   And with God be the rest!

EDWARD LEAR
1812–1888

The Jumblies

They went to sea in a sieve, they did;
   In a sieve they went to sea:
In spite of all their friends could say,
On a winter's morn, on a stormy day,

In a sieve they went to sea.
And when the sieve turned round and round,
And everyone cried, "You'll all be drowned!"
They called aloud, "Our sieve ain't big,
But we don't care a button; we don't care a fig:
    In a sieve we'll go to sea!"
        Far and few, far and few,
            Are the lands where the Jumblies live:
        Their heads are green, and their hands are blue;
            And they went to sea in a sieve.

They sailed away in a sieve, they did,
    In a sieve they sailed so fast,
With only a beautiful pea-green veil
Tied with a ribbon, by way of a sail,
    To a small tobacco-pipe mast.
And every one said who saw them go,
"Oh! won't they be soon upset; you know!
For the sky is dark, and the voyage is long;
And, happen what may, it's extremely wrong
    In a sieve to sail so fast."

The water it soon came in, it did;
    The water it soon came in:
So, to keep them dry, they wrapped their feet
In a pinky paper all folded neat;
    And they fastened it down with a pin.
And they passed the night in a crockery-jar;
And each of them said, "How wise we are!
Though the sky be dark, and the voyage be long,
Yet we never can think we were rash or wrong
    While round in our sieve we spin."

And all night long they sailed away;
    And, when the sun went down,
They whistled and warbled a moony song
To the echoing sound of a coppery gong,
    In the shade of the mountains brown,
        "O Timballoo! how happy we are
When we live in a sieve and crockery-jar!
And all night long, in the moonlight pale,

We sail away with a pea-green sail
In the shade of the mountains brown."

They sailed to the Western Sea, they did,—
To a land all covered with trees:
And they bought an owl, and a useful cart,
And a pound of rice, and a cranberry-tart,
And a hive of silvery bees;
And they bought a pig, and some green jackdaws,
And a lovely monkey with lollipop paws,
And forty bottles of ring-bo-ree,
And no end of Stilton cheese.

And in twenty years they all came back,—
In twenty years or more;
And every one said, "How tall they've grown!
For they've been to the Lakes, and the Torrible Zone,
And the hills of the Chankly Bore."
And they drank their health, and gave them a feast
Of dumplings made of beautiful yeast;
And every one said, "If we only live,
We, too, will go to sea in a sieve,
To the hills of the Chankly Bore."
Far and few, far and few,
Are the lands where the Jumblies live.
Their heads are green, and their hands are blue;
And they went to sea in a sieve.

EMILY BRONTË
1818–1848

Remembrance

Cold in the earth, and the deep snow piled above thee!
Far, far removed, cold in the dreary grave!
Have I forgot, my Only Love, to love thee,
Severed at last by Time's all-wearing wave?

Now, when alone, do my thoughts no longer hover
Over the mountains on Angora's shore;
Resting their wings where heath and fern-leaves cover
That noble heart for ever, ever more?

Cold in the earth, and fifteen wild Decembers
From those brown hills have melted into spring—
Faithful indeed is the spirit that remembers
After such years of change and suffering!

Sweet Love of youth, forgive if I forget thee
While the World's tide is bearing me along:
Sterner desires and darker hopes beset me,
Hopes which obscure but cannot do thee wrong.

No other Sun has lightened up my heaven;
No other Star has ever shone for me:
All my life's bliss from thy dear life was given—
All my life's bliss is in the grave with thee.

But when the days of golden dreams had perished
And even Despair was powerless to destroy,
Then did I learn how existence could be cherished,
Strengthened and fed without the aid of joy;

Then did I check the tears of useless passion,
Weaned my young soul from yearning after thine;
Sternly denied its burning wish to hasten
Down to that tomb already more than mine!

And even yet, I dare not let it languish,
Dare not indulge in Memory's rapturous pain;
Once drinking deep of that divinest anguish,
How could I seek the empty world again?

JAMES RUSSELL LOWELL
1819–1891

Not Only Around Our Infancy

Not only around our infancy
Doth heaven with all its splendors lie;
Daily, with souls that cringe and plot,
We Sinais climb and know it not.

Over our manhood bend the skies;
  Against our fallen and traitor lives
The great winds utter prophecies;
  With our faint hearts the mountain strives;
Its arms outstretched, the druid wood
  Waits with its benedicite;
And to our age's drowsy blood
  Still shouts the inspiring sea.

Earth gets its price for what Earth gives us;
  The beggar is taxed for a corner to die in,
The priest hath his fee who comes and shrives us,
  We bargain for the graves we lie in;
At the Devil's booth are all things sold,
Each ounce of dross costs its ounce of gold;
  For a cap and bells our lives we pay,
Bubbles we buy with a whole soul's tasking:
  'Tis heaven alone that is given away,
  'Tis only God may be had for the asking.

From The Vision of Sir Launfal

HERMAN MELVILLE
1819–1891

The March into Virginia

ENDING IN THE FIRST MANASSAS (JULY 1861)

Did all the lets and bars appear
  To every just or larger end,

Whence should come the trust and cheer?
   Youth must its ignorant impulse lend—
Age finds place in the rear.
    All wars are boyish, and are fought by boys,
The champions and enthusiasts of the state:
    Turbid ardours and vain joys
      Not barrenly abate—
    Stimulants to the power mature,
      Preparatives of fate.

Who here forecasteth the event?
What heart but spurns at precedent
And warnings of the wise,
Contemned foreclosures of surprise?
The banners play, the bugles call,
The air is blue and prodigal.
    No berrying party, pleasure-wooed,
No picnic party in the May,
Ever went less loth than they
    Into that leafy neighborhood.
In Bacchic glee they file toward Fate,
Moloch's uninitiate;
Expectancy, and glad surmise
Of battle's unknown mysteries.

All they feel is this: 'tis glory,
A rapture sharp, though transitory,
Yet lasting in belaurelled story.
So they gaily go to fight,
Chatting left and laughing right.

But some who this blithe mood present,
   As on in lightsome files they fare,
Shall die experienced ere three days are spent—
   Perish, enlightened by the volleyed glare;
Or shame survive, and, like to adamant,
   The throe of Second Manassas share.

WALT WHITMAN

1819–1892

O Captain! My Captain!

O Captain! my Captain! our fearful trip is done,
The ship has weather'd every rack, the prize we sought is won,
The port is near, the bells I hear, the people all exulting,
While follow eyes the steady keel, the vessel grim and daring;
But O heart! heart! heart!
O the bleeding drops of red,
Where on the deck my Captain lies,
Fallen cold and dead.

O Captain! my Captain! rise up and hear the bells;
Rise up—for you the flag is flung—for you the bugle trills,
For you bouquets and ribbon'd wreaths—for you the shores a-crowding,
For you they call, the swaying mass, their eager faces turning;
Here Captain! dear father!
The arm beneath your head!
It is some dream that on the deck,
You've fallen cold and dead.

My Captain does not answer, his lips are pale and still,
My father does not feel my arm, he has no pulse nor will,
The ship is anchor'd safe and sound, its voyage closed and done,
From fearful trip the victor ship comes in with object won;
Exult O shores, and ring O bells!
But I with mournful tread,
Walk the deck my Captain lies,
Fallen cold and dead.

A Noiseless Patient Spider

A noiseless patient spider,
I mark'd where on a little promontory it stood isolated,
Mark'd how to explore the vacant vast surrounding,
It launch'd forth filament, filament, filament, out of itself,
Ever unreeling them, ever tirelessly speeding them.

And you O my soul where you stand,
Surrounded, detached, in measureless oceans of space,

Ceaselessly musing, venturing, throwing, seeking the spheres to connect them.
Till the bridge you will need be form'd, till the ductile anchor hold,
Till the gossamer thread you fling catch somewhere, O my soul.

There Was a Child Went Forth

There was a child went forth every day,
And the first object he look'd upon, that object he became,
And that object became part of him for the day or a certain part of the day,
Or for many years or stretching cycles of years.
The early lilacs became part of this child,
And grass and white and red morning-glories, and white and red clover,
    and the song of the phœbe-bird,
And the Third-month lambs and the sow's pink-faint litter, and the mare's
    foal and cow's calf,
And the noisy brood of the barnyard or by the mire of the pond-side,
And the fish suspending themselves so curiously below there, and the
    beautiful curious liquid,
And the water-plants with their graceful flat heads, all became part of him.

The field-sprouts of Fourth-month and Fifth-month became part of him,
Winter-grain sprouts and those of the light-yellow corn, and the esculent
    roots of the garden,
And the apple-trees cover'd with blossoms and the fruit afterward, and
    wood-berries, and the commonest weeds by the road,
And the old drunkard staggering home from the out-house of the tavern
    whence he had lately risen,
And the schoolmistress that pass'd on her way to the school,
And the friendly boys that pass'd, and the quarrelsome boys,
And the tidy and fresh-cheek'd girls, and the barefoot Negro boy and girl,
And all the changes of city and country wherever he went.
His own parents, he that had father'd him and she that had conceiv'd him in
    her womb and birth'd him,
They gave this child more of themselves than that,
They gave him afterward every day, they became part of him.

The mother at home quietly placing the dishes on the supper-table,
The mother with mild words, clean her cap and gown, a wholesome odor
    falling off her person and clothes as she walks by,
The father, strong, self-sufficient, manly, mean, anger'd, unjust,
The blow, the quick loud word, the tight bargain, the crafty lure,
The family usages, the language, the company, the furniture, the yearning
    and swelling heart,

Affection that will not be gainsay'd, the sense of what is real, the thought if
    after all it should prove unreal,
The doubts of day-time and the doubts of night-time, the curious whether
    and how,
Whether that which appears so is so, or is it all flashes and specks?
Men and women crowding fast in the streets, if they are not flashes and
    specks what are they?
The streets themselves and the façades of houses, and goods in the windows,
Vehicles, teams, the heavy-plank'd wharves, the huge crossing at the ferries,
The village on the highland seen from afar at sunset, the river between,
Shadows, aureola and mist, the light falling on roofs and gables of white or
    brown two miles off,
The schooner near by sleepily dropping down the tide, the little boat slack-
    tow'd astern,
The hurrying tumbling waves, quick-broken crests, slapping,
The strata of color'd clouds, the long bar of maroon-tint away solitary by
    itself, the spread of purity it lies motionless in,
The horizon's edge, the flying sea-crow, the fragrance of salt marsh and
    shore mud,
These became part of that child who went forth every day, and who now
    goes, and will always go forth every day.

Out of the Cradle Endlessly Rocking

Out of the cradle endlessly rocking,
Out of the mocking-bird's throat, the musical shuttle,
Out of the Ninth-month midnight,
Over the sterile sands and the fields beyond, where the child leaving his bed
    wandered alone, bareheaded, barefoot,
Down from the showered halo,
Up from the mystic play of shadows twining and twisting as if they were alive,
Out from the patches of briers and blackberries,
From the memories of the bird that chanted to me,
From your memories, sad brother, from the fitful risings and fallings I heard,
From under that yellow half-moon late-risen and swollen as if with tears,
From those beginning notes of yearning and love there in the mist,
From the thousand responses of my heart never to cease,
From the myriad thence-aroused words,
From the word stronger and more delicious than any,
From such as now they start the scene revisiting,
As a flock, twittering, rising, or overhead passing,
Borne hither, ere all eludes me, hurriedly,

A man, yet by these tears a little boy again,
Throwing myself on the sand, confronting the waves,
I, chanter of pains and joys, uniter of here and hereafter,
Taking all hints to use them, but swiftly leaping beyond them,
A reminiscence sing.

Once Paumanok,
When the lilac-scent was in the air and Fifth-month grass was growing,
Up this seashore in some briers,
Two feathered guests from Alabama, two together,
And their nest, and four light-green eggs spotted with brown,
And every day the he-bird to and fro near at hand,
And every day the she-bird crouched on her nest, silent, with bright eyes,
And every day I, a curious boy, never too close, never disturbing them,
Cautiously peering, absorbing, translating.

Shine! shine! shine!
Pour down your warmth, great sun!
While we bask, we two together.
Two together!
Winds blow south, or winds blow north,
Day come white, or night come black,
Home, or rivers and mountains from home,
Singing all time, minding no time,
While we two keep together.

Till of a sudden,
Maybe killed, unknown to her mate,
One forenoon the she-bird crouched not on the nest,
Nor returned that afternoon, nor the next,
Nor ever appeared again.
And thenceforward all summer in the sound of the sea,
And at night under the full of the moon in calmer weather,
Over the hoarse surging of the sea,
Or flitting from brier to brier by day,
I saw, I heard at intervals the remaining one, the he-bird,
The solitary guest from Alabama.

Blow! blow! blow!
Blow up sea-winds along Paumanok's shore;
I wait and I wait till you blow my mate to me.

Yes, when the stars glistened,
All night long on the prong of a moss-scalloped stake,
Down almost amid the slapping waves,
Sat the lone singer wonderful causing tears.

He called on his mate,
He poured forth the meanings which I of all men know.
Yes, my brother, I know,—
The rest might not, but I have treasured every note,
For more than once dimly down to the beach gliding,
Silent, avoiding the moonbeams, blending myself with the shadows,
Recalling now the obscure shapes, the echoes, the sounds and sights after
    their sorts,
The white arms out in the breakers tirelessly tossing,
I, with bare feet, a child, the wind wafting my hair,
Listened long and long.
Listened to keep, to sing, now translating the notes,
Following you, my brother.

Soothe! soothe! soothe!
Close on its wave soothes the wave behind,
And again another behind embracing and lapping, every one close,
But my love soothes not me, not me.

Low hangs the moon, it rose late,
It is lagging—O I think it is heavy with love, with love.

O madly the sea pushes upon the land,
With love, with love.

O night! do I not see my love fluttering out among the breakers?
What is that little black thing I see there in the white?

Loud! loud! loud!
Loud I call to you, my love!

High and clear I shoot my voice over the waves,
Surely you must know who is here, is here,
You must know who I am, my love.

Low-hanging moon!
What is that dusky spot in your brown yellow?
O it is the shape, the shape of my mate!
O moon, do not keep her from me any longer.

Land! land! O land!
Whichever way I turn, O I think you could give me my mate back again if
   you only would,
For I am almost sure I see her dimly whichever way I look.
O rising stars!
Perhaps the one I want so much will rise, will rise with some of you.
O throat! O trembling throat!
Sound clearer through the atmosphere!
Pierce the woods, the earth,
Somewhere listening to catch you must be the one I want.

Shake out carols!
Solitary here, the night's carols!
Carols of lonesome love! death's carols!
Carols under that lagging, yellow, waning moon!
O under that moon where she droops almost down into the sea!
O reckless despairing carols!

But soft! sink low!
Soft! let me just murmur,
And do you wait a moment, you husky-noised sea,
For somewhere I believe I heard my mate responding to me,
So faint, I must be still, be still to listen,
But not altogether still, for then she might not come immediately to me.

Hither, my love!
Here I am! here!
With this just-sustained note I announce myself to you,
This gentle call is for you my love, for you.

Do not be decoyed elsewhere:
That is the whistle of the wind, it is not my voice,
That is the fluttering, the fluttering of the spray,
Those are the shadows of leaves.

O darkness! O in vain!

O I am very sick and sorrowful.
O brown halo in the sky near the moon, drooping upon the sea!
O troubled reflection in the sea!
O throat! O throbbing heart!
And I singing uselessly, uselessly all the night.

O past! O happy life! O songs of joy!
In the air, in the woods, over fields,
Loved! loved! loved! loved! loved!
But my mate no more, no more with me!
We two together no more.

The aria sinking.
All else continuing, the stars shining,
The winds blowing, the notes of the bird continuous echoing,
With angry moans the fierce old mother incessantly moaning,
On the sands of Paumanok's shore gray and rustling,
The yellow half-moon enlarged, sagging down, drooping, the face of the sea
    almost touching,
The boy ecstatic, with his bare feet the waves, with his hair the atmosphere
    dallying,
The love in the heart long pent, now loose, now at last tumultuously
    bursting,
The aria's meaning, the ears, the soul, swiftly depositing,
The strange tears down the cheeks coursing,
The colloquy there, the trio, each uttering,
The undertone, the savage old mother incessantly crying,
To the boy's soul's questions sullenly timing, some drowned secret hissing,
To the outsetting bard.

Demon or bird (said the boy's soul)
Is it indeed toward your mate you sing? or is it really to me?
For I, that was a child, my tongue's use sleeping, now I have heard you,
Now in a moment I know what I am for, I awake,
And already a thousand singers, a thousand songs, clearer, louder and more
    sorrowful than yours,
A thousand warbling echoes have started to life within me, never to die.

O you singer solitary, singing by yourself, projecting me,
O solitary me listening, never more shall I cease perpetuating you,
Never more shall I escape, never more the reverberations,

Never more the cries of unsatisfied love be absent from me.
Never again leave me to be the peaceful child I was before what there in the
    night,
By the sea under the yellow and sagging moon,
The messenger there aroused, the fire, the sweet hell within,
The unknown want, the destiny of me.
O give me the clew! (It lurks in the night here somewhere)
O if I am to have so much, let me have more!
A word then, (for I will conquer it)
The word final, superior to all,
Subtle, sent up—what is it?—I listen;
Are you whispering it, and have been all the time, you seawaves?
Is that it from your liquid rims and wet sands?

Whereto answering, the sea,
Delaying not, hurrying not,
Whispered me through the night, and very plainly before daybreak,
Lisped to me the low and delicious word death,
And again death, death, death, death,
Hissing melodious, neither like the bird nor like my aroused child's heart,
But edging near as privately for me, rustling at my feet,
Creeping thence steadily up to my ears and laving me softly all over,
Death, death, death, death, death.

Which I do not forget,
But fuse the song of my dusky demon and brother,
That he sang to me in the moonlight on Paumanok's gray beach,
With the thousand responsive songs at random,
My own songs awaked from that hour,
And with them the key, the word up from the waves,
The word of the sweetest song and all songs,
That strong and delicious word which, creeping to my feet,
(Or like some old crone rocking the cradle, swathed in sweet garments,
    bending aside)
The sea whispered me.

I Saw in Louisiana a Live-Oak Growing

I saw in Louisiana a live-oak growing,
All alone stood it, and the moss hung down from the branches;
Without any companion it grew there, uttering joyous leaves of dark green,
And its look, rude, unbending, lusty, made me think of myself;

But I wonder'd how it could utter joyous leaves, standing alone there,
    without its friend, its lover near—for I knew I could not;
And I broke off a twig with a certain number of leaves upon it, and twined
    around it a little moss,
And brought it away—and I have placed it in sight in my room;
It is not needed to remind me as of my own dear friends,
(For I believe lately I think of little else than of them:)
Yet it remains to me a curious token—it makes me think of manly love;
For all that, and though the live-oak glistens there in Louisiana, solitary, in
    a wide flat space,
Uttering joyous leaves all its life, without a friend, a lover, near,
I know very well I could not.

Grass

A child said *What is the grass?* fetching it to me with full hands;
How could I answer the child? I do not know what it is any more than he.

I guess it must be the flag of my disposition, out of hopeful green stuff
    woven.
Or I guess it is the handkerchief of the Lord,
A scented gift and remembrancer designedly dropt,
Bearing the owner's name some way in the corners, that we may see and
    remark, and say *Whose?*
Or I guess the grass is itself a child, the produced babe of the vegetation.
Or I guess it is a uniform hieroglyphic,
And it means, Sprouting alike in broad zones and narrow zones,
Growing among black folks as among white,
Kanuck, Tuckahoe, Congressman, Cuff, I give them the same, I receive
    them the same.
And now it seems to me the beautiful uncut hair of graves.

Tenderly will I use you curling grass,
It may be you transpire from the breasts of young men,
It may be if I had known them I would have loved them,
It may be you are from old people, or from offspring taken soon out of their
    mothers' laps,
And here you are the mothers' laps.

This grass is very dark to be from the white heads of old mothers,
Darker than the colorless beards of old men,
Dark to come from under the faint red roofs of mouths.

O I perceive after all so many uttering tongues,
And I perceive they do not come from the roofs of mouths for nothing.
I wish I could translate the hints about the dead young men and women,
And the hints about old men and mothers, and the off-spring taken soon
    out of their laps.

What do you think has become of the young and old men?
And what do you think has become of the women and children?

They are alive and well somewhere,
The smallest sprout shows there is really no death,
And if ever there was it led forward life, and does not wait at the end to
    arrest it,
And ceas'd the moment life appear'd.
All goes onward and outward, nothing collapses,
And to die is different from what any one supposed, and luckier.

                  From *Song of Myself*

Animals

I think I could turn and live with animals, they are so placid and
    self-contained;
I stand and look at them long and long.
They do not sweat and whine about their condition;
They do not lie awake in the dark and weep for their sins;
They do not make me sick discussing their duty to God;
Not one is dissatisfied—not one is demented with the mania of owning
    things;
Not one kneels to another, nor to his kind that lived thousands of years ago;
Not one is respectable or industrious over the whole earth.

                  From *Song of Myself*

To Think of Time

1

To think of time—of all that retrospection,
To think of to-day, and the ages continued henceforward.

Have you guess'd you yourself would not continue?
Have you dreaded these earth-beetles?
Have you fear'd the future would be nothing to you?

Is to-day nothing? is the beginningless past nothing?
If the future is nothing they are just as surely nothing.

To think that the sun rose in the east—that men and women were flexible,
   real, alive—that every thing was alive,
To think that you and I did not see, feel, think, nor bear our part,
To think that we are now here and bear our part.

2

Not a day passes, not a minute or second without an accouchement,
Not a day passes, not a minute or second without a corpse.

The dull nights go over and the dull days also,
The soreness of lying so much in bed goes over,
The physician after long putting off gives the silent and terrible look for an
   answer,
The children come hurried and weeping, and the brothers and sisters are
   sent for,
Medicines stand unused on the shelf, (the camphor-smell has long
   pervaded the rooms,)
The faithful hand of the living does not desert the hand of the dying,
The twitching lips press lightly on the forehead of the dying,
The breath ceases and the pulse of the heart ceases,
The corpse stretches on the bed and the living look upon it,
It is palpable as the living are palpable.
The living look upon the corpse with their eyesight,
But without eyesight lingers a different living and looks curiously on the
   corpse.

3

To think the thought of death merged in the thought of materials,
To think of all these wonders of city and country, and others taking great
   interest in them, and we taking no interest in them.
To think how eager we are in building our houses,
To think others shall be just as eager, and we quite indifferent.
(I see one building the house that serves him a few years, or seventy or
   eighty years at most,
I see one building the house that serves him longer than that.)
Slow-moving and black lines creep over the whole earth—they never
   cease—they are the burial lines,
He that was President was buried, and he that is now President shall surely
   be buried.

4

A reminiscence of the vulgar fate,
A frequent sample of the life and death of workmen,
Each after his kind.
Cold dash of waves at the ferry-wharf, posh and ice in the river, half-frozen
    mud in the streets,
A gray discouraged sky overhead, the short last daylight of December,
A hearse and stages, the funeral of an old Broadway stage-driver, the
    cortege mostly drivers.
Steady the trot to the cemetery, duly rattles the death-bell,
The gate is pass'd, the new-dug grave is halted at, the living alight, the
    hearse uncloses,
The coffin is pass'd out, lower'd and settled, the whip is laid on the coffin,
    the earth is swiftly shovel'd in,
The mound above is flatted with the spades—silence,
A minute—no one moves or speaks—it is done,
He is decently put away—is there any thing more?
He was a good fellow, free-mouth'd, quick-temper'd, not bad-looking,
Ready with life or death for a friend, fond of women, gambled, ate hearty,
    drank hearty,
Had known what it was to be flush, grew low-spirited toward the last,
    sicken'd, was help'd by a contribution,
Died, aged forty-one years—and that was his funeral.
Thumb extended, finger uplifted, apron, cape, gloves, strap, wet-weather
    clothes, whip carefully chosen,
Boss, spotter, starter, hostler, somebody loafing on you, you loafing on
    somebody, headway, man before and man behind,
Good day's work, bad day's work, pet stock, mean stock, first out, last out,
    turning-in at night,
To think that these are so much and so nigh to other drivers, and he there
    takes no interest in them.

Good-Bye, My Fancy!

Good-bye, my Fancy!
Farewell, dear mate, dear love!
I am going away, I know not where,
Or to what fortune, or whether I may ever see you again,
So Good-bye, my Fancy.
Now for my last—let me look back a moment;
The slower fainter ticking of the clock is in me,
Exit, nightfall, and soon the heart-thud stopping.

Long have we lived, joy'd, caress'd together;
Delightful—now separation—Good-bye, my Fancy.

Yet let me not be too hasty:
Long indeed have we lived, slept, filter'd, become really blended into one;
Then if we die we die together (yes, we'll remain one),
If we go anywhere we'll go together to meet what happens,
May-be we'll be better off and blither, and learn something,
May-be it is yourself now really ushering me to the true songs (who knows?),
May-be it is you the mortal knob really undoing, turning—so now finally,
Good-bye—and hail! my Fancy.

A Hub for the Universe

I have said that the soul is not more than the body,
And I have said that the body is not more than the soul,
And nothing, not God, is greater to one than one's self is,
And whoever walks a furlong without sympathy walks to his
  own funeral drest in his shroud,
And I or you pocketless of a dime may purchase the pick of the earth,
And to glance with an eye or show a bean in its pod confounds
  the learning of all times,
And there is no trade or employment but the young man following it
  may become a hero,
And there is no object so soft but it makes a hub for the wheeled universe.

From Song of Myself

CHARLES KINGSLEY
1819–1875

Young and Old

When all the world is young, lad,
  And all the trees are green;
And every goose a swan, lad,
  And every lass a queen;
Then hey for boot and horse, lad,
  And round the world away;
Young blood must have its course, lad,
  And every dog his day.

When all the world is old, lad,
    And all the trees are brown;
And all the sport is stale, lad,
    And all the wheels run down;
Creep home, and take your place there,
    The spent and maimed among:
God grant you find one face there,
    You loved when all was young.

ARTHUR HUGH CLOUGH
1819–1861

Say Not the Struggle

Say not the struggle naught availeth,
    The labour and the wounds are vain,
The enemy faints not, nor faileth,
    And as things have been they remain.

If hopes were dupes, fears may be liars;
    It may be, in yon smoke conceal'd,
Your comrades chase e'en now the fliers,
    And, but for you, possess the field.

For while the tired waves, vainly breaking,
    Seem here no painful inch to gain,
Far back, through creeks and inlets making,
    Comes silent, flooding in, the main.

And not by eastern windows only,
    When daylight comes, comes in the light;
In front the sun climbs slow, how slowly!
    But westward, look, the land is bright!

JULIA WARD HOWE
1819–1910

The Battle-Hymn of the Republic

Mine eyes have seen the glory of the coming of the Lord;
He is trampling out the vintage where the grapes of wrath are stored;
He hath loosed the fateful lightning of His terrible swift sword;
His truth is marching on.

I have seen Him in the watch-fires of a hundred circling camps;
They have builded Him an altar in the evening dews and damps;
I can read His righteous sentence by the dim and flaring lamps;
His day is marching on.

I have read a fiery gospel, writ in burnished rows of steel:
"As ye deal with my contemners, so with you my grace shall deal;
Let the Hero, born of woman, crush the serpent with his heel,
Since God is marching on."

He has sounded forth the trumpet that shall never call retreat;
He is sifting out the hearts of men before His judgment-seat:
Oh, be swift, my soul, to answer Him! be jubilant, my feet!
Our God is marching on.

In the beauty of the lilies Christ was born across the sea,
With a glory in His bosom that transfigures you and me:
As He died to make men holy, let us die to make men free,
While God is marching on.

MATTHEW ARNOLD
1822–1888

Dover Beach

The sea is calm to-night.
The tide is full, the moon lies fair
Upon the straits;—on the French coast the light
Gleams and is gone; the cliffs of England stand
Glimmering and vast, out in the tranquil bay.

Come to the window, sweet is the night-air!
Only, from the long line of spray
Where the sea meets the moon-blanch'd land,
Listen! you hear the grating roar
Of pebbles which the waves draw back, and fling,
At their return, up the high strand,
Begin, and cease, and then again begin,
With tremulous cadence slow, and bring
The eternal note of sadness in.

Sophocles long ago
Heard it on the Ægean, and it brought
Into his mind the turbid ebb and flow,
Of human misery; we
Find also in the sound a thought,
Hearing it by this distant northern sea.

The Sea of Faith
Was once, too, at the full, and round earth's shore
Lay like the folds of a bright girdle furl'd.
But now I only hear
Its melancholy, long, withdrawing roar,
Retreating, to the breath
Of the night-wind, down the vast edges drear
And naked shingles of the world.

Ah, love, let us be true
To one another! for the world, which seems
To lie before us like a land of dreams,
So various, so beautiful, so new,
Hath really neither joy, nor love, nor light,
Nor certitude, nor peace, nor help for pain;
And we are here as on a darkling plain
Swept with confused alarms of struggle and flight,
Where ignorant armies clash by night.

The Scholar-Gypsy

Go, for they call you, shepherd, from the hill;
  Go, shepherd, and untie the wattled cotes!
    No longer leave thy wistful flock unfed,
  Nor let thy bawling fellows rack their throats,

Nor the cropped herbage shoot another head.
   But when the fields are still,
And the tired men and dogs all gone to rest,
   And only the white sheep are sometimes seen
   Cross and recross the strips of moon-blanched green,
Come, shepherd, and again begin the quest!

Here, where the reaper was at work of late—
   In this high field's dark corner, where he leaves
     His coat, his basket, and his earthen cruse,
And in the sun all morning binds the sheaves,
   Then here, at noon, comes back his stores to use—
     Here will I sit and wait,
While to my ear from uplands far away
   The bleating of the folded flocks is borne,
     With distant cries of reapers in the corn—
All the live murmur of a summer's day.

Screened is this nook o'er the high, half-reaped field,
   And here till sun-down, shepherd! will I be.
   Through the thick corn the scarlet poppies peep,
   And round green roots and yellowing stalks I see
     Pale pink convolvulus in tendrils creep;
     And air-swept lindens yield
Their scent, and rustle down their perfumed showers
   Of bloom on the bent grass where I am laid,
     And bower me from the August sun with shade;
And the eye travels down to Oxford's towers.

And near me on the grass lies Glanvil's book—
   Come, let me read the oft-read tale again!
    The story of the Oxford scholar poor,
Of pregnant parts and quick inventive brain,
    Who, tired of knocking at preferment's door,
     One summer-morn forsook
His friends, and went to learn the gypsy-lore,
   And roamed the world with that wild brotherhood,
    And came, as most men deemed, to little good,
But came to Oxford and his friends no more.

But once, years after, in the country-lanes,
   Two scholars, whom at college erst he knew,

Met him, and of his way of life inquired;
Whereat he answered that the gypsy-crew,
His mates, had arts to rule as they desired
The workings of men's brains,
And they can bind them to what thoughts they will.
"And I," he said, "the secret of their art,
When fully learned, will to the world impart;
But it needs heaven-sent moments for this skill."

This said, he left them, and returned no more.—
But rumors hung about the country-side,
That the lost Scholar long was seen to stray,
Seen by rare glimpses, pensive and tongue-tied,
In hat of antique shape, and cloak of gray,
The same the gypsies wore,
Shepherds had met him on the Hurst in spring;
At some lone alehouse in the Berkshire moors,
On the warm ingle-bench, the smock-frocked boors
Had found him seated at their entering.

But, 'mid their drink and clatter, he would fly.
And I myself seem half to know thy looks,
And put the shepherds, wanderer! on thy trace;
And boys who in lone wheatfields scare the rooks
I ask if thou hast passed their quiet place;
Or in my boat I lie
Moored to the cool bank in the summer-heats,
'Mid wide grass meadows which the sunshine fills,
And watch the warm, green-muffled Cumner hills,
And wonder if thou haunt'st their shy retreats.

For most, I know, thou lov'st retired ground!
Thee at the ferry Oxford riders blithe,
Returning home on summer-nights, have met
Crossing the stripling Thames at Bab-lock-hithe,
Trailing in the cool stream thy fingers wet,
As the punt's rope chops round;
And leaning backward in a pensive dream,
And fostering in thy lap a heap of flowers
Plucked in shy fields and distant Wychwood bowers,
And thine eyes resting on the moonlit stream.

And then they land, and thou art seen no more!—
  Maidens, who from the distant hamlets come
    To dance around the Fyfield elm in May,
  Oft through the darkening fields have seen thee roam,
    Or cross a stile into the public way.
      Oft thou hast given them store
  Of flowers—the frail-leafed, white anemone,
    Dark bluebells drenched with dews of summer eves,
    And purple orchises with spotted leaves—
But none hath words she can report of thee.

And, above Godstow Bridge, when hay-time's here
  In June, and many a scythe in sunshine flames,
    Men who through those wide fields of breezy grass
  Where black-winged swallows haunt the glittering Thames,
    To bathe in the abandoned lasher pass,
      Have often passed thee near
  Sitting upon the river bank o'ergrown;
    Marked thine outlandish garb, thy figure spare,
    Thy dark vague eyes, and soft abstracted air—
But, when they came from bathing, thou wast gone!

At some lone homestead in the Cumner hills,
  Where at her open door the housewife darns,
    Thou hast been seen, or hanging on a gate
  To watch the threshers in the mossy barns.
    Children, who early range these slopes and late
      For cresses from the rills,
  Have known thee eying, all an April-day,
    The springing pastures and the feeding kine;
    And marked thee, when the stars come out and shine,
Through the long dewy grass move slow away.

In autumn, on the skirts of Bagley Wood—
  Where most the gypsies by the turf-edged way
    Pitch their smoked tents, and every bush you see
  With scarlet patches tagged and shreds of gray,
    Above the forest-ground called Thessaly—
      The blackbird, picking food,
  Sees thee, nor stops his meal, nor fears at all;
    So often has he known thee past him stray,

Rapt, twirling in thy hand a withered spray,
And waiting for the spark from heaven to fall.

And once, in winter, on the causeway chill
  Where home through flooded fields foot-travelers go,
    Have I not passed thee on the wooden bridge,
  Wrapped in thy cloak and battling with the snow,
    Thy face tow'rd Hinksey and its wintry ridge?
      And thou hast climbed the hill,
  And gained the white brow of the Cumner range;
    Turned once to watch, while thick the snowflakes fall,
    The line of festal light in Christ-Church hall—
  Then sought thy straw in some sequestered grange.

But what—I dream! Two hundred years are flown
  Since first thy story ran through Oxford halls,
    And the grave Glanvil did the tale inscribe
  That thou wert wandered from the studious walls
    To learn strange arts, and join a gypsy tribe;
      And thou from earth art gone
  Long since, and in some quiet churchyard laid—
    Some country-nook, where o'er thy unknown grave
    Tall grasses and white flowering nettles wave,
  Under a dark, red-fruited yew-tree's shade.

—No, no, thou hast not felt the lapse of hours!
  For what wears out the life of mortal men?
    'Tis that from change to change their being rolls;
    'Tis that repeated shocks, again, again,
      Exhaust the energy of strongest souls
      And numb the elastic powers,
  Till having used our nerves with bliss and teen,
    And tired upon a thousand schemes our wit,
    To the just-pausing Genius we remit
  Our worn-out life, and are—what we have been.

Thou hast not lived, why should'st thou perish, so?
  Thou hadst *one* aim, *one* business, *one* desire;
    Else wert thou long since numbered with the dead!
    Else hadst thou spent, like other men, thy fire!
      The generations of thy peers are fled,

And we ourselves shall go;
But thou possessest an immortal lot,
And we imagine thee exempt from age
And living as thou liv'st on Glanvil's page,
Because thou hadst—what we, alas! have not.

For early didst thou leave the world, with powers
Fresh, undiverted to the world without,
Firm to their mark, not spent on other things;
Free from the sick fatigue, the languid doubt,
Which much to have tried, in much been baffled, brings.
O life unlike to ours!
Who fluctuate idly without term or scope,
Of whom each strives, nor knows for what he strives,
And each half lives a hundred different lives;
Who wait like thee, but not, like thee, in hope.

Thou waitest for the spark from heaven! and we,
Light half-believers of our casual creeds,
Who never deeply felt, nor clearly willed,
Whose insight never has borne fruit in deeds,
Whose vague resolves never have been fulfilled;
For whom each year we see
Breeds new beginnings, disappointments new;
Who hesitate and falter life away,
And lose tomorrow the ground won today—
Ah! do not we, wanderer! await it too?

Yes, we await it!—but it still delays,
And then we suffer! and amongst us one,
Who most hast suffered, takes dejectedly
His seat upon the intellectual throne;
And all his store of sad experience he
Lays bare of wretched days;
Tells us his misery's birth and growth and signs,
And how the dying spark of hope was fed,
And how the breast was soothed, and how the head,
And all his hourly varied anodynes.

This for our wisest! and we others pine,
And wish the long unhappy dream would end,

And waive all claim to bliss, and try to bear;
With close-lipped patience for our only friend,
    Sad patience, too near neighbor to despair—
        But none has hope like thine!
Thou through the fields and through the woods dost stray,
    Roaming the country-side, a truant boy,
    Nursing thy project in unclouded joy,
And every doubt long blown by time away.

O born in days when wits were fresh and clear,
    And life ran gayly as the sparkling Thames;
        Before this strange disease of modern life,
With its sick hurry, its divided aims,
    Its head o'ertaxed, its palsied hearts, was rife—
        Fly hence, our contact fear!
Still fly, plunge deeper in the bowering wood!
    Averse, as Dido did with gesture stern
    From her false friend's approach in Hades turn,
Wave us away, and keep thy solitude!

Still nursing the unconquerable hope,
    Still clutching the inviolable shade,
        With a free, onward impulse brushing through,
By night, the silvered branches of the glade—
    Far on the forest-skirts, where none pursue,
        On some mild pastoral slope
Emerge, and resting on the moonlit pales
    Freshen thy flowers as in former years
    With dew, or listen with enchanted ears,
From the dark dingles, to the nightingales!

But fly our paths, our feverish contact fly!
    For strong the infection of our mental strife,
        Which, though it gives no bliss, yet spoils for rest;
And we should win thee from thy own fair life,
    Like us distracted, and like us unblest.
        Soon, soon thy cheer would die,
Thy hopes grow timorous, and unfixed thy powers,
    And thy clear aims be cross and shifting made;
    And then thy glad perennial youth would fade,
Fade, and grow old at last, and die like ours.

Then fly our greetings, fly our speech and smiles!
—As some grave Tyrian trader, from the sea,
    Descried at sunrise an emerging prow
Lifting the cool-haired creepers stealthily,
    The fringes of a southward-facing brow
        Among the Ægæan isles;
And saw the merry Grecian coaster come,
    Freighted with amber grapes, and Chian wine,
    Green, bursting figs, and tunnies steeped in brine—
And knew the intruders on his ancient home,

The young light-hearted masters of the waves—
    And snatched his rudder, and shook out more sail;
    And day and night held on indignantly
O'er the blue Midland waters with the gale,
    Betwixt the Syrtes and soft Sicily,
        To where the Atlantic raves
Outside the western straits; and unbent sails
    There, where down cloudy cliffs, through sheets of foam,
    Shy traffickers, the dark Iberians come;
And on the beach undid his corded bales.

DANTE GABRIEL ROSSETTI
1828–1882

The Blessed Damozel

The blessed damozel leaned out
    From the gold bar of Heaven;
Her eyes were deeper than the depth
    Of waters stilled at even;
She had three lilies in her hand,
    And the stars in her hair were seven.

Her robe, ungirt from clasp to hem,
    No wrought flowers did adorn,
But a white rose of Mary's gift,
    For service meetly worn;

Her hair that lay along her back
    Was yellow, like ripe corn.

Herseemed she scarce had been a day
    One of God's choristers;
The wonder was not yet quite gone
    From that still look of hers;
Albeit, to them she left, her day
    Had counted as ten years.

(To one, it is ten years of years.
    ... Yet now, and in this place,
Surely she leaned o'er me—her hair
    Fell all about my face....
Nothing: the autumn fall of leaves.
    The whole year sets apace.)

It was the rampart of God's house
    That she was standing on;
By God built over the sheer depth
    The which is Space begun;
So high, that looking downward thence
    She scarce could see the sun.

It lies in Heaven, across the flood
    Of ether, as a bridge.
Beneath, the tides of day and night
    With flame and darkness ridge
The void, as low as where this earth
    Spins like a fretful midge.

Around her, lovers, newly met
    'Mid deathless love's acclaims,
Spoke evermore among themselves
    Their heart-remembered names;
And the souls mounting up to God
    Went by her like thin flames.

And still she bowed herself and stooped
    Out of the circling charm;
Until her bosom must have made

The bar she leaned on warm,
And the lilies lay as if asleep
   Along her bended arm.

From the fixed place of Heaven she saw
   Time like a pulse shake fierce
Through all the worlds. Her gaze still strove
   Within the gulf to pierce
Its path; and now she spoke as when
   The stars sang in their spheres.

The sun was gone now; the curled moon
   Was like a little feather
Fluttering far down the gulf; and now
   She spoke through the still weather.
Her voice was like the voice the stars
   Had when they sang together.

(Ah sweet! Even now, in that bird's song,
   Strove not her accents there,
Fain to be hearkened? When those bells
   Possessed the mid-day air,
Strove not her steps to reach my side
   Down all the echoing stair?)

"I wish that he were come to me,
   For he will come," she said.
"Have I not prayed in Heaven?—on earth,
   Lord, Lord, has he not pray'd?
Are not two prayers a perfect strength?
   And shall I feel afraid?

"When round his head the aureole clings,
   And he is clothed in white,
I'll take his hand and go with him
   To the deep wells of light;
As unto a stream we will step down,
   And bathe there in God's sight.

"We two will stand beside that shrine,
   Occult, withheld, untrod,

Whose lamps are stirred continually
   With prayer sent up to God;
And see our old prayers, granted, melt
   Each like a little cloud.

"We two will lie i' the shadow of
   That living mystic tree
Within whose secret growth the Dove
   Is sometimes felt to be,
While every leaf that His plumes touch
   Saith His Name audibly.

"And I myself will teach to him,
   I myself, lying so,
The songs I sing here; which his voice
   Shall pause in, hushed and slow,
And find some knowledge at each pause,
   Or some new thing to know."

(Alas! we two, we two, thou say'st!
   Yea, one wast thou with me
That once of old. But shall God lift
   To endless unity
The soul whose likeness with thy soul
   Was but its love for thee?)

"We two," she said, "will seek the groves
   Where the lady Mary is,
With her five handmaidens, whose names
   Are five sweet symphonies,
Cecily, Gertrude, Magdalen,
   Margaret and Rosalys.

"Circlewise sit they, with bound locks
   And foreheads garlanded;
Into the fine cloth white like flame
   Weaving the golden thread,
To fashion the birth-robes for them
   Who are just born, being dead.

"He shall fear, haply, and be dumb:
   Then will I lay my cheek

To his, and tell about our love,
　　Not once abashed or weak:
And the dear Mother will approve
　　My pride, and let me speak.

"Herself shall bring us, hand in hand,
　　To Him round whom all souls
Kneel, the clear-ranged unnumbered heads
　　Bowed with their aureoles:
And angels meeting us shall sing
　　To their citherns and citoles.

"There will I ask of Christ the Lord
　　This much for him and me:—
Only to live as once on earth
　　With Love,—only to be,
As then awhile, for ever now
　　Together, I and he."

She gazed and listened and then said,
　　Less sad of speech than mild,—
"All this is when he comes." She ceased.
　　The light thrilled towards her, fill'd
With angels in strong level flight.
　　Her eyes prayed, and she smil'd.

(I saw her smile.) But soon their path
　　Was vague in distant spheres:
And then she cast her arms along
　　The golden barriers,
And laid her face between her hands,
　　And wept. (I heard her tears.)

GEORGE MEREDITH
1828–1909

Lucifer in Starlight

On a starred night Prince Lucifer uprose.
  Tired of his dark dominion swung the fiend
  Above the rolling ball in cloud part screened,
Where sinners hugged their specter of repose.
Poor prey to his hot fit of pride were those.
  And now upon his western wing he leaned,
  Now his huge bulk o'er Afric's sands careened,
Now the black planet shadowed Arctic snows.
Soaring through wider zones that pricked his scars
  With memory of the old revolt from Awe,
He reached a middle height, and at the stars,
Which are the brain of heaven, he looked, and sank.
Around the ancient track marched, rank on rank,
  The army of unalterable law.

CHRISTINA ROSSETTI
1830–1894

A Birthday

My heart is like a singing bird
  Whose nest is in a watered shoot;
My heart is like an apple-tree
  Whose boughs are bent with thick-set fruit;
My heart is like a rainbow shell
  That paddles in a halcyon sea;
My heart is gladder than all these,
  Because my love is come to me.

Raise me a dais of silk and down;
  Hang it with vair and purple dyes;
Carve it in doves and pomegranates,
  And peacocks with a hundred eyes;

Work it in gold and silver grapes,
   In leaves and silver fleurs-de-lys;
Because the birthday of my life
   Is come, my love is come to me.

EMILY DICKINSON
1830–1886

I Never Saw a Moor

I never saw a moor,
   I never saw the sea;
Yet know I how the heather looks,
   And what a wave must be.

I never spoke with God,
   Nor visited in heaven;
Yet certain am I of the spot
   As if the chart were given.

Success Is Counted Sweetest

Success is counted sweetest
By those who ne'er succeed.
To comprehend a nectar
Requires sorest need.

Not one of all the purple host
Who took the flag to-day
Can tell the definition,
So clear, of victory,

As he, defeated, dying,
On whose forbidden ear
The distant strains of triumph
Break, agonized and clear.

Because I Could Not Stop for Death

Because I could not stop for Death,
He kindly stopped for me;
The carriage held but just ourselves
And Immortality.

We slowly drove, he knew no haste,
And I had put away
My labor, and my leisure too,
For his civility.

We passed the school where children played
At wrestling in a ring;
We passed the fields of gazing grain,
We passed the setting sun.

We paused before a house that seemed
A swelling of the ground;
The roof was scarcely visible,
The cornice but a mound.

Since then 't is centuries; but each
Feels shorter than the day
I first surmised the horses' heads
Were toward eternity.

I Had Been Hungry

I had been hungry all the years;
My noon had come to dine;
I, trembling, drew the table near,
And touched the curious wine.

'Twas this on tables I had seen,
When turning, hungry, lone,
I looked in windows, for the wealth
I could not hope to own.

I did not know the ample bread;
'Twas so unlike the crumb
The birds and I had often shared
In Nature's dining-room.

The plenty hurt me, 'twas so new,—
Myself felt ill and odd,
As berry of a mountain bush
Transplanted to the road.

Nor was I hungry; so I found
That hunger was a way
Of persons outside windows,
The entering takes away.

The Soul Selects Her Own Society

The soul selects her own society
Then shuts the door;
On her divine majority
Obtrude no more.

Unmoved, she notes the chariot's pausing
At her low gate;
Unmoved, an emperor is kneeling
Upon her mat.

I've known her from an ample nation
Choose one;
Then close the valves of her attention
Like stone.

A Certain Slant of Light

There's a certain slant of light,
On winter afternoons,
That oppresses, like the weight
Of cathedral tunes.

Heavenly hurt it gives us;
We can find no scar,
But internal difference
Where the meanings are.

None may teach it anything
'Tis the seal, despair,—
An imperial affliction
Sent us of the air.

When it comes, the landscape listens,
Shadows hold their breath;
When it goes, 'tis like the distance
On the look of death.

I Died for Beauty

I died for beauty, but was scarce
Adjusted in the tomb,
When one who died for truth was lain
In an adjoining room.

He questioned softly why I failed?
"For beauty," I replied.
"And I for truth,—the two are one;
We brethren are," he said.

And so, as kinsmen met a night,
We talked between the rooms,
Until the moss had reached our lips,
And covered up our names.

I Heard a Fly Buzz When I Died

I heard a fly buzz when I died;
  The stillness round my form
Was like the stillness in the air
  Between the heaves of storm.

The eyes beside had wrung them dry,
  And breaths were gathering sure
For that last onset, when the king
  Be witnessed in his power.

I willed my keepsakes, signed away
  What portion of me I
Could make assignable,—and then
  There interposed a fly,

With blue, uncertain, stumbling buzz,
  Between the light and me;
And then the windows failed, and then
  I could not see to see.

Presentiment

Presentiment is that long shadow on the lawn
Indicative that suns go down;
The notice to the startled grass
That darkness is about to pass.

The First Day's Night Had Come

The first Day's Night had come—
And, grateful that a thing
So terrible had been endured,
I told my Soul to sing.

She said her strings were snapt,
Her bow to atoms blown;
And so, to mend her, gave me work
Until another morn.

And then a Day as huge
As Yesterday in pairs
Unrolled its horror on my face—
Until it blocked my eyes.

LEWIS CARROLL
1832–1898

Jabberwocky

'Twas brillig, and the slithy toves
   Did gyre and gimble in the wabe:
All mimsy were the borogoves,
   And the mome raths outgrabe.

"Beware the Jabberwock, my son!
   The jaws that bite, the claws that catch!
Beware the Jubjub bird, and shun
   The frumious Bandersnatch!"

He took his vorpal sword in hand;
   Long time the manxome foe he sought—

So rested he by the Tumtum tree,
   And stood awhile in thought.

And, as in uffish thought he stood,
   The Jabberwock, with eyes of flame,
Came whiffling through the tulgey wood,
   And burbled as it came!

One, two! One, two! And through and through
   The vorpal blade went snicker-snack!
He left it dead, and with its head
   He went galumphing back.

"And hast thou slain the Jabberwock?
   Come to my arms, my beamish boy!
O frabjous day! Callooh, Callay!"
   He chortled in his joy.

'Twas brillig, and the slithy toves
   Did gyre and gimble in the wabe:
All mimsy were the borogoves,
   And the mome raths outgrabe.

SIR W. S. GILBERT
1836–1911

Ko-Ko's Song

On a tree by a river a little tom-tit
   Sang "Willow, titwillow, titwillow!"
And I said to him, "Dicky-bird, why do you sit
   Singing 'Willow, titwillow, titwillow'!
Is it a weakness of intellect, birdie?" I cried,
"Or a rather tough worm in your little inside?"
With a shake of his poor little head he replied,
   "Oh, willow, titwillow, titwillow!"

He slapped at his chest, as he sat on that bough,
   Singing "Willow, titwillow, titwillow!"

And a cold perspiration bespangled his brow,
    Oh, willow, titwillow, titwillow!
He sobbed and he sighed, and a gurgle he gave,
Then he threw himself into the billowy wave,
And an echo arose from the suicide's grave—
    "Oh, willow, titwillow, titwillow!"

Now, I feel just as sure as I'm sure that my name
    Isn't Willow, titwillow, titwillow,
That 'twas blighted affection that made him exclaim
    "Oh, willow, titwillow, titwillow!"
And if you remain callous and obdurate, I
Shall perish as he did, and you will know why,
Though I probably shall not exclaim as I die,
    "Oh, willow, titwillow, titwillow!"

From *The Mikado*

ALGERNON CHARLES SWINBURNE
1837–1909

Before the Beginning of Years

Before the beginning of years
    There came to the making of man
Time, with a gift of tears;
    Grief, with a glass that ran;
Pleasure, with pain for leaven;
    Summer, with flowers that fell;
Remembrance fallen from heaven,
    And madness risen from hell;
Strength without hands to smite;
    Love that endures for a breath;
Night, the shadow of light,
    And life, the shadow of death.

And the high gods took in hand
    Fire, and the falling of tears,
And a measure of sliding sand
    From under the feet of the years;

And froth and drift of the sea;
   And dust of the labouring earth;
And bodies of things to be
   In the houses of death and of birth;
And wrought with weeping and laughter,
   And fashion'd with loathing and love,
With life before and after
   And death beneath and above,
For a day and a night and a morrow,
   That his strength might endure for a span
With travail and heavy sorrow,
   The holy spirit of man.

From the winds of the north and the south
   They gather'd as unto strife;
They breathed upon his mouth,
   They filled his body with life;
Eyesight and speech they wrought
   For the veils of the soul therein,
A time for labour and thought,
   A time to serve and to sin;
They gave him light in his ways,
   And love, and a space for delight,
And beauty and length of days,
   And night, and sleep in the night.
His speech is a burning fire;
   With his lips he travaileth;
In his heart is a blind desire,
   In his eyes foreknowledge of death;
He weaves, and is clothed with derision;
   Sows, and he shall not reap;
His life is a watch or a vision
   Between a sleep and a sleep.

THOMAS HARDY
1840–1928

The Darkling Thrush

I leant upon a coppice gate
  When Frost was spectre-gray,
And Winter's dregs made desolate
  The weakening eye of day.
The tangled vine-stems scored the sky
  Like strings of broken lyres,
And all mankind that haunted nigh
  Had sought their household fires.

The land's sharp features seemed to be
  The Century's corpse outleant,
His crypt the cloudy canopy,
  The wind his death-lament.
The ancient pulse of germ and birth
  Was shrunken hard and dry,
And every spirit upon earth
  Seemed fervorless as I.

At once a voice arose among
  The bleak twigs overhead
In a full-hearted evensong
  Of joy illimited;
An aged thrush, frail, gaunt, and small,
  In blast-beruffled plume,
Had chosen thus to fling his soul
  Upon the growing gloom.

So little cause for carolings
  Of such ecstatic sound
Was written on terrestrial things
  Afar or nigh around,
That I could think there trembled through
  His happy good-night air
Some blessed Hope, whereof he knew
  And I was unaware.

Channel Firing

That night your great guns, unawares,
Shook all our coffins as we lay,
And broke the chancel window-squares,
We thought it was the Judgment-day

And sat upright. While drearisome
Arose the howl of wakened hounds:
The mouse let fall the altar-crumb,
The worms drew back into the mounds,

The glebe cow drooled. Till God called, "No;
It's gunnery practice out at sea
Just as before you went below;
The world is as it used to be:

"All nations striving strong to make
Red war yet redder. Mad as hatters
They do no more for Christés sake
Than you who are helpless in such matters.

"That this is not the judgment-hour
For some of them's a blessed thing,
For if it were they'd have to scour
Hell's floor for so much threatening . . .

"Ha, ha. It will be warmer when
I blow the trumpet (if indeed
I ever do; for you are men,
And rest eternal sorely need)."

So down we lay again. "I wonder,
Will the world ever saner be,"
Said one, "than when He sent us under
In our indifferent century!"

And many a skeleton shook his head.
"Instead of preaching forty year,"
My neighbor Parson Thirdly said,
"I wish I had stuck to pipes and beer."

Again the guns disturbed the hour,
Roaring their readiness to avenge,
As far inland as Stourton Tower,
And Camelot, and starlit Stonehenge.

Hap

If but some vengeful god would call to me
From up the sky, and laugh: "Thou suffering thing,
Know that thy sorrow is my ecstasy,
That thy love's loss is my hate's profiting!"
Then would I bear it, clench myself, and die,
Steeled by the sense of ire unmerited;
Half-eased in that a Powerfuller than I
Had willed and meted me the tears I shed.

But not so. How arrives it joy lies slain,
And why unblooms the best hope ever sown?
—Crass Casualty obstructs the sun and rain,
And dicing Time for gladness casts a moan. . . .
These purblind Doomsters had as readily strown
Blisses about my pilgrimage as pain.

SIDNEY LANIER
1842–1881

The Marshes of Glynn

Glooms of the live-oaks, beautiful-braided and woven
With intricate shades of the vines that myriad-cloven
   Clamber the forks of the multiform boughs,—
      Emerald twilights,—
      Virginal shy lights,
Wrought of the leaves to allure to the whisper of vows,
When lovers pace timidly down through the green colonnades
Of the dim sweet woods, of the dear dark woods,
   Of the heavenly woods and glades,
That run to the radiant marginal sand-beach within
   The wide sea-marshes of Glynn;—
Beautiful glooms, soft dusks in the noon-day fire,—

Wildwood privacies, closets of lone desire,
Chamber from chamber parted with wavering arras of leaves,—
Cells for the passionate pleasure of prayer to the soul that grieves,
Pure with a sense of the passing of saints through the wood,
Cool for the dutiful weighing of ill with good;—

O braided dusks of the oak and woven shades of the vine,
While the riotous noon-day sun of the June-day long did shine
Ye held me fast in your heart and I held you fast in mine;
But now when the noon is no more, and riot is rest,
And the sun is a-wait at the ponderous gate of the West,
And the slant yellow beam down the wood-aisle doth seem
Like a lane into heaven that leads from a dream,—
Ay, now, when my soul all day hath drunken the soul of the oak,
And my heart is at ease from men, and the wearisome sound of the stroke
    Of the scythe of time and the trowel of trade is low,
        And belief overmasters doubt, and I know that I know,
        And my spirit is grown to a lordly great compass within,
That the length and the breadth and the sweep of the marshes of Glynn
Will work me no fear like the fear they have wrought me of yore
When length was fatigue, and when breadth was but bitterness sore,
And when terror and shrinking and dreary unnamable pain
Drew over me out of the merciless miles of the plain,—

Oh, now, unafraid, I am fain to face
    The vast sweet visage of space.
To the edge of the wood I am drawn, I am drawn,
Where the gray beach glimmering runs, as a belt of the dawn,
    For a mete and a mark
        To the forest-dark:—So: Affable live-oak, leaning low,—
Thus—with your favor—soft, with a reverent hand
(Not lightly touching your person, Lord of the land!),
Bending your beauty aside, with a step I stand
On the firm-packed sand,
            Free
By a world of marsh that borders a world of sea.
Sinuous southward and sinuous northward the shimmering band
Of the sand-beach fastens the fringe of the marsh to the folds of the land.
Inward and outward to northward and southward the beachlines
        linger and curl

As a silver-wrought garment that clings to and follows the firm sweet limbs
    of a girl.
Vanishing, swerving, evermore curving again into sight,
Softly the sand-beach wavers away to a dim gray looping of light.
And what if behind me to westward the wall of the woods stands high?
The world lies east: how ample, the marsh and the sea and the sky!
A league and a league of marsh-grass, waist-high, broad in the blade,
Green, and all of a height, and unflecked with a light or a shade,
Stretch leisurely off, in a pleasant plain,
To the terminal blue of the main.

Oh, what is abroad in the marsh and the terminal sea?
    Somehow my soul seems suddenly free
From the weighing of fate and the sad discussion of sin,
By the length and the breadth and the sweep of the marshes of Glynn.

Ye marshes, how candid and simple and nothing-withholding and free
Ye publish yourselves to the sky and offer yourselves to the sea!
Tolerant plains, that suffer the sea and the rains and the sun,
Ye spread and span like the catholic man who hath mightily won
God out of knowledge and good out of infinite pain
And sight out of blindness and purity out of a stain.

As the marsh-hen secretly builds on the watery sod,
Behold I will build me a nest on the greatness of God:
I will fly in the greatness of God as the marsh-hen flies
In the freedom that fills all the space 'twixt the marsh and the skies:
By so many roots as the marsh-grass sends in the sod
I will heartily lay me a-hold on the greatness of God:
Oh, like to the greatness of God is the greatness within
The range of the marshes, the liberal marshes of Glynn.

And the sea lends large, as the marsh: lo, out of his plenty the sea
Pours fast: full soon the time of the flood-tide must be:
Look how the grace of the sea doth go
About and about through the intricate channels that flow
    Here and there, everywhere,
Till his waters have flooded the uttermost creeks and the low-lying lanes,
And the marsh is meshed with a million veins,
That like as with rosy and silvery essences flow
    In the rose-and-silver evening glow.
        Farewell, my lord Sun!

The creeks overflow: a thousand rivulets run
'Twixt the roots of the sod; the blades of the marsh-grass stir;
Passeth a hurrying sound of wings that westward whir;
Passeth, and all is still; and the currents cease to run;
And the sea and the marsh are one.

How still the plains of the waters be!
The tide is in his ecstasy.
The tide is at his highest height: And it is night.

And now from the Vast of the Lord will the waters of sleep
Roll in on the souls of men,
But who will reveal to our waking ken
The forms that swim and the shapes that creep
  Under the waters of sleep?
And I would I could know what swimmeth below when the tide comes in
On the length and the breadth of the marvelous marshes of Glynn.

GERARD MANLEY HOPKINS
1844–1889

God's Grandeur

The world is charged with the grandeur of God.
It will flame out, like shining from shook foil;
It gathers to a greatness, like the ooze of oil
Crushed. Why do men then now not reck his rod?

Generations have trod, have trod, have trod;
And all is seared with trade; bleared, smeared with toil;
And wears man's smudge and shares man's smell: the soil
Is bare now, nor can foot feel, being shod.

And for all this, nature is never spent;
There lives the dearest freshness deep down things;
And though the last lights off the black West went
Oh, morning, at the brown brink eastward, springs—
Because the Holy Ghost over the bent
World broods with warm breast and with ah! bright wings.

Pied Beauty

Glory be to God for dappled things—
  For skies of couple-colour as a brinded cow;
    For rose-moles all in stipple upon trout that swim;
Fresh-firecoal chestnut-falls; finches wings;
  Landscape plotted and pieced—fold, fallow, and plough,
    And áll trádes, their gear and tackle and trim.
All things counter, original, spare, strange;
  Whatever is fickle, freckled (who knows how?)
    With swift, slow; sweet, sour; adazzle, dim;
He fathers-forth whose beauty is past change:
              Praise him.

The Candle Indoors

Some candle clear burns somewhere I come by.
I muse at how its being puts blissful back
With yellowy moisture mild night's blear-all black,
Or to-fro tender trambeams truckle at the eye.
By that window what task what fingers ply,
I plod wondering, a-wanting, just for lack
Of answer the eagerer a-wanting Jessy or Jack
There, God to aggrándize, God to glorify.—
Come you indoors, come home; your fading fire
Mend first and vital candle in close heart's vault:
You there are master, do your own desire;
What hinders? Are you beam-blind, yet to a fault
In a neighbour deft-handed? Are you that liar
And, cast by conscience out, spendsavour salt?

Spring and Fall: To a Young Child

Márgarét, are you gríeving
Over Goldengrove unleaving?
Leáves, líke the things of man, you
With your fresh thoughts care for, can you?
Ah! ás the heart grows older
It will come to such sights colder
By and by, nor spare a sigh
Though worlds of wanwood leafmeal lie;
And yet you wíll weep and know why.
Now no matter, child, the name:

Sórrow's spríngs áre the same.
Nor mouth had, no nor mind, expressed
What heart heard of, ghost guessed:
It ís the blight man was born for,
It is Margaret you mourn for.

Inversnaid

This darksome burn, horseback brown,
His rollrock highroad roaring down,
In coop and in comb the fleece of his foam
Flutes and low to the lake falls home.

A windpuff-bonnet of fawn-froth
Turns and twindles over the broth
Of a pool so pitchblack, fell-frowning,
It rounds and rounds Despair to drowning.

Degged with dew, dappled with dew
Are the groins of the braes that the brook treads through,
Wiry heathpacks, flitches of fern,
And the beadbonny ash that sits over the burn.

What would the world be, once bereft
Of wet and of wildness? Let them be left,
O let them be left, wildness and wet;
Long live the weeds and the wilderness yet.

In the Valley of the Elwy

I remember a house where all were good
To me, God knows, deserving no such thing:
Comforting smell breathed at very entering,
Fetched fresh, as I suppose, off some sweet wood.
That cordial air made those kind people a hood
All over, as a bevy of eggs the mothering wing
Will, or mild nights the new morsels of spring:

Why, it seemed of course; seemed of right it should.
Lovely the woods, waters, meadows, combes, vales,
All the air things wear that build this world of Wales;
Only the inmate does not correspond:
God, lover of souls, swaying considerate scales,

Complete thy creature dear O where it fails,
Being mighty a master, being a father and fond.

Felix Randal

Felix Randal the farrier, O he is dead then? my duty all ended,
Who have watched his mould of man, big-boned and hardy-handsome
Pining, pining, till time when reason rambled in it and some
Fatal four disorders, fleshed there, all contended?

Sickness broke him. Impatient he cursed at first, but mended
Being anointed and all; though a heavenlier heart began some
Months earlier, since I had our sweet reprieve and ransom
Tendered to him. Ah well, God rest him all road ever he offended!

This seeing the sick endears them to us, us too it endears.
My tongue had taught thee comfort, touch had quenched thy tears,
Thy tears that touched my heart, child, Felix, poor Felix Randal;

How far from then forethought of, all thy more boisterous years,
When thou at the random grim forge, powerful amidst peers,
Didst fettle for the great grey drayhorse his bright and battering sandal!

The Habit of Perfection

Elected Silence, sing to me
And beat upon my whorlèd ear,
Pipe me to pastures still and be
The music that I care to hear.

Shape nothing, lips; be lovely-dumb:
It is the shut, the curfew sent
From there where all surrenders come
Which only makes you eloquent.

Be shellèd, eyes, with double dark
And find the uncreated light:
This ruck and reel which you remark
Coils, keeps, and teases simple sight.

Palate, the hutch of tasty lust,
Desire not to be rinsed with wine:
The can must be so sweet, the crust
So fresh that come in fasts divine!

Nostrils, your careless breath that spend
Upon the stir and keep of pride,
What relish shall the censers send
Along the sanctuary side!

O feel-of-primrose hands, O feet
That want the yield of plushy sward,
But you shall walk the golden street
And you unhouse and house the Lord.

And, Poverty, be thou the bride
And now the marriage feast begun,
And lily-coloured clothes provide
Your spouse not laboured-at nor spun.

The Leaden Echo and the Golden Echo

(MAIDENS' SONG FROM ST. WINEFRED'S WELL)

THE LEADEN ECHO

How to kéep—is there any any, is there none such, nowhere known some,
    bow or brooch or braid or brace, láce, latch or catch or key to keep
Back beauty, keep it, beauty, beauty, beauty, . . . from vanishing away?
O is there no frowning of these wrinkles, rankèd wrinkles deep,
Dówn? no waving off of these most mournful messengers, still messengers,
    sad and stealing messengers of grey?
No there's none, there's none, O no there's none,
Nor can you long be, what you now are, called fair,
Do what you may do, what, do what you may,
And wisdom is early to despair:
Be beginning; since, no, nothing can be done to keep at bay
Age and age's evils, hoar hair,
Ruck and wrinkle, drooping, dying, death's worst, winding sheets, tombs
    and worms and tumbling to decay;
So be beginning, be beginning to despair.
O there's none; no no no there's none:
Be beginning to despair, to despair,
Despair, despair, despair, despair.

THE GOLDEN ECHO

Spare!
There ís one, yes I have one (Hush there!);
Only not within seeing of the sun,

Not within the singeing of the strong sun,
Tall sun's tingeing, or treacherous the tainting of the earth's air,
Somewhere elsewhere there is ah well where! one,
Óne. Yes I can tell such a key, I do know such a place,
Where whatever's prized and passes of us, everything that's
   fresh and fast flying of us, seems to us sweet of us and
   swiftly away with, done away with, undone,
Undone, done with, soon done with, and yet dearly and dangerously sweet
Of us, the wimpled-water-dimpled, not-by-morning-matchèd face,
The flower of beauty, fleece of beauty, too too apt to, ah! to fleet,
Never fleets móre, fastened with the tenderest truth
To its own best being and its loveliness of youth: it is an everlastingness of,
   O it is an all youth!
Come then, your ways and airs and looks, locks, maiden gear, gallantry and
   gaiety and grace,
Winning ways, airs innocent, maiden manners, sweet looks,
   loose locks, long locks, lovelocks, gaygear, going gallant, girlgrace—
Resign them, sign them, seal them, send them, motion them with breath,
And with sighs soaring, soaring síghs deliver
Them; beauty-in-the-ghost, deliver it, early now, long before death
Give beauty back, beauty, beauty, beauty, back to God,
   beauty's self and beauty's giver.
See; not a hair is, not an eyelash, not the least lash lost; every hair
Is, hair of the head, numbered.
Nay, what we had lighthanded left in surly the mere mould
Will have waked and have waxed and have walked with the
   wind whatwhile we slept,
This side, that side hurling a heavyheaded hundredfold
Whatwhile we, while we slumbered.
O then, weary then why should we tread? O why are we so
   haggard at the heart, so care-coiled, care-killed, so fagged,
   so fashed, so cogged, so cumbered,
When the thing we freely fórfeit is kept with fonder a care,
Fonder a care kept than we could have kept it, kept
Far with fonder a care (and we, we should have lost it) finer, fonder
A care kept.—Where kept? Do but tell us where kept, where.—
Yonder.—What high as that! We follow, now we follow.—
   —Yonder, yes yonder, yonder,
Yonder.

The Wreck of the Deutschland

To the happy memory of five Franciscan Nuns, exiles by the Falk
Laws, drowned between midnight and morning of Dec. 7th, 1875

PART THE FIRST

I   Thou mastering me
    God! giver of breath and bread;
  World's strand, sway of the sea;
    Lord of living and dead;
Thou hast bound bones and veins in me, fastened me flesh,
And after it almost unmade, what with dread,
  Thy doing: and dost thou touch me afresh?
Over again I feel thy finger and find thee.

II   I did say yes
    O at lightning and lashed rod;
  Thou heardst me truer than tongue confess
    Thy terror, O Christ, O God;
Thou knowest the walls, altar and hour and night:
The swoon of a heart that the sweep and the hurl of thee trod
  Hard down with a horror of height:
And the midriff astrain with leaning of, laced with fire of stress.

III   The frown of his face
    Before me, the hurtle of hell
  Behind, where, where was a, where was a place?
    I whirled out wings that spell
And fled with a fling of the heart to the heart of the Host.
My heart, but you were dovewinged, I can tell,
  Carrier-witted, I am bold to boast,
To flash from the flame to the flame then, tower from the grace to the grace.

IV   I am soft sift
    In an hourglass—at the wall
  Fast, but mined with a motion, a drift,
    And it crowds and it combs to the fall;
I steady as a water in a well, to a poise, to a pane,
But roped with, always, all the way down from the tall
  Fells or flanks of the voel, a vein
Of the gospel proffer, a pressure, a principle, Christ's gift.

V I kiss my hand
    To the stars, lovely-asunder
     Starlight, wafting him out of it; and
      Glow, glory in thunder;
   Kiss my hand to the dappled-with-damson west:
   Since, tho' he is under the world's splendour and wonder,
    His mystery must be instressed, stressed;
For I greet him the days I meet him, and bless when I understand.

VI Not out of his bliss
    Springs the stress felt
     Nor first from heaven (and few know this)
      Swings the stroke dealt—
   Stroke and a stress that stars and storms deliver,
   That guilt is hushed by, hearts are flushed by and melt—
    But it rides time like riding a river
(And here the faithful waver, the faithless fable and miss).

VII It dates from day
    Of his going in Galilee;
     Warm-laid grave of a womb-like grey;
      Manger, maiden's knee;
   The dense and the driven Passion, and frightful sweat;
   Thence the discharge of it, there its swelling to be,
    Though felt before, though in high flood yet—
What none would have known of it, only the heart, being hard at bay,

VIII Is out with it! Oh,
    We lash with the best or worst
     Word last! How a lush-kept plush-capped sloe
      Will, mouthed to flesh-burst,
   Gush!—flush the man, the being with it, sour or sweet,
   Brim, in a flash, full!—Hither then, last or first,
    To hero of Calvary, Christ's feet—
Never ask if meaning it, wanting it, warned of it—men go.

IX Be adored among men,
    God, three-numberèd form;
     Wring thy rebel, dogged in den,
      Man's malice, with wrecking and storm.
   Beyond saying sweet, past telling of tongue,

Thou art lightning and love, I found it, a winter and warm;
  Father and fondler of heart thou hast wrung:
Hast thy dark descending and most art merciful then.

X   With an anvil-ding
  And with fire in him forge thy will
    Or rather, rather then, stealing as Spring
      Through him, melt him but master him still:
Whether at once, as once at a crash Paul,
Or as Austin, a lingering-out sweet skill,
  Make mercy in all of us, out of us all
Mastery, but be adored, but be adored King.

PART THE SECOND

XI   "Some find me a sword; some
  The flange and the rail; flame,
    Fang, or flood" goes Death on drum,
      And storms bugle his fame.
But wé dream we are rooted in earth—Dust!
Flesh falls within sight of us, we, though our flower the same,
  Wave with the meadow, forget that there must
The sour scythe cringe, and the blear share come.

XII   On Saturday sailed from Bremen,
  American-outward-bound,
    Take settler and seamen, tell men with women,
      Two hundred souls in the round—
O Father, not under thy feathers nor ever as guessing
The goal was a shoal, of a fourth the doom to be drowned;
  Yet did the dark side of the bay of thy blessing
Not vault them, the millions of rounds of thy mercy not reeve even them in?

XIII   Into the snows she sweeps,
  Hurling the haven behind,
    The Deutschland, on Sunday; and so the sky keeps,
      For the infinite air is unkind,
And the sea flint-like, black-backed in the regular blow,
Sitting Eastnortheast, in cursed quarter, the wind;
  Wiry and white-fiery and whirlwind-swivellèd snow
Spins to the widow-making unchilding unfathering deeps.

XIV   She drove in the dark to leeward,
        She struck—not a reef or a rock
      But the combs of a smother of sand: night drew her
        Dead to the Kentish Knock;
    And she beat the bank down with her bows and the ride of her keel:
      The breakers rolled on her beam with ruinous shock;
        And canvas and compass, the whorl and the wheel
Idle for ever to waft her or wind her with, these she endured.

XV   Hope had grown grey hairs,
        Hope had mourning on,
      Trenched with tears, carved with cares,
        Hope was twelve hours gone;
    And frightful a nightfall folded rueful a day
      Nor rescue, only rocket and lightship, shone,
        And lives at last were washing away:
To the shrouds they took,—they shook in the hurling and horrible airs.

XVI   One stirred from the rigging to save
        The wild woman-kind below,
      With a rope's end round the man, handy and brave—
        He was pitched to his death at a blow,
    For all his dreadnought breast and braids of thew:
      They could tell him for hours, dandled the to and fro
        Through the cobbled form-fleece, what could he do
With the burl of the fountains of air, buck and the flood of the wave?

XVII   They fought with God's cold—
        And they could not and fell to the deck
      (Crushed them) or water (and drowned them) or rolled
        With the sea-romp over the wreck.
    Night roared, with the heart-break hearing a heart-broke rabble,
      The woman's wailing, the crying of child without check—
        Till a lioness arose breasting the babble,
A prophetess towered in the tumult, a virginal tongue told.

XVIII   Ah, touched in your bower of bone
        Are you! turned for an exquisite smart,
      Have you! make words break from me here all alone,
        Do you!—mother of being in me, heart.
    O unteachably after evil, but uttering truth,

Why, tears! is it? tears; such a melting, a madrigal start!
    Never-eldering revel and river of youth,
What can it be, this glee? the good you have there of your own?

XIX   Sister, a sister calling
    A master, her master and mine!—
    And the inboard seas run swirling and hawling;
    The rash smart sloggering brine
Blinds her; but she that weather sees one thing, one;
Has one fetch in her: she rears herself to divine
    Ears, and the call of the tall nun
To the men in the tops and the tackle rode over the storm's brawling.

XX   She was first of a five and came
    Of a coifèd sisterhood.
    (O Deutschland, double a desperate name!
    O world wide of its good!
But Gertrude, lily, and Luther, are two of a town,
Christ's lily and beast of the waste wood:
    From life's dawn it is drawn down,
Abel is Cain's brother and breasts they have sucked the same.)

XXI   Loathed for a love men knew in them,
    Banned by the land of their birth,
    Rhine refused them. Thames would ruin them;
    Surf, snow, river and earth
Gnashed: but thou art above, thou Orion of light;
Thy unchancelling poising palms were weighing the worth,
    Thou martyr-master: in thy sight
Storm flakes were scroll-leaved flowers, lily showers—sweet heaven was
                    astrew in them.

XXII   Five! the finding and sake
    And cipher of suffering Christ.
    Mark, the mark is of man's make
    And the word of it Sacrificed.
But he scores it in scarlet himself on his own bespoken,
Before-time-taken, dearest prizèd and pricèd—
    Stigma, signal, cinquefoil token
For lettering of the lamb's fleece, ruddying of the rose flake.

XXIII   Joy fall to thee, father Francis,
        Drawn to the Life that died;
        With the gnarls of the nails in thee, niche of the lance, his
            Lovescape crucified
    And seal of his seraph-arrival! and these thy daughters
    And five-livèd and leavèd favour and pride,
        Are sisterly sealed in wild waters,
To bathe in his fall-gold mercies, to breathe in his all-fire glances.

XXIV   Away in the loveable west,
        On a pastoral forehead of Wales,
    I was under a roof here, I was at rest,
        And they the prey of the gales;
    She to the black-about air, to the breaker, the thickly
    Falling flakes, to the throng that catches and quails
        Was calling "O Christ, Christ, come quickly":
The cross to her she calls Christ to her, christens her wild-worst Best.

XXV   The majesty! what did she mean?
        Breathe, arch and original Breath.
    Is it love in her of the being as her lover had been?
        Breathe, body of lovely Death.
    They were else-minded then, altogether, the men
Woke thee with a *we are perishing* in the weather of Gennesareth.
        Or is it that she cried for the crown then,
The keener to come at the comfort for feeling the combating keen?

XXVI   For how to the heart's cheering
        The down-dugged ground-hugged grey
    Hovers off, the jay-blue heavens appearing
        Of pied and peeled May!
    Blue-beating and hoary-glow height; or night, still higher,
    With belled fire and the moth-soft Milky Way,
        What by your measure is the heaven of desire,
The treasure never eyesight got, nor was ever guessed what for the hearing?

XXVII   No, but it was not these.
        The jading and jar of the cart,
    Time's tasking, it is fathers that asking for ease
        Of the sodden-with-its-sorrowing heart,
Not danger, electrical horror; then further it finds

The appealing of the Passion is tenderer in prayer apart:
    Other, I gather, in measure her mind's
Burden, in wind's burly and beat of endragonèd seas.

XXVIII   But how shall I . . . make me room there:
        Reach me a . . . Fancy, come faster—
    Strike you the sight of it? look at it loom there,
        Thing that she . . . there then! the Master,
Ipse, the only one, Christ, King, Head:
    He was to cure the extremity where he had cast her;
        Do, deal, lord it with living and dead;
Let him ride, her pride, in his triumph, despatch and have
                    done with his doom there.

XXIX   Ah! there was a heart right!
        There was single eye!
    Read the unshapeable shock night
        And knew the who and the why;
    Wording it how but by him that present and past,
    Heaven and earth are word of, worded by?—
    The Simon Peter of a soul! to the blast
Tarpeian-fast, but a blown beacon of light.

XXX   Jesu, heart's light,
        Jesu, maid's son,
    What was the feast followed the night
        Thou hadst glory of this nun?—
    Feast of the one woman without stain.
    For so conceivèd, so to conceive thee is done;
        But here was heart-throe, birth of a brain,
Word, that heard and kept thee and uttered thee outright.

XXXI   Well, she has thee for the pain, for the
        Patience; but pity of the rest of them!
    Heart, go and bleed at a bitterer vein for the
        Comfortless unconfessed of them—
No not uncomforted: lovely-felicitous Providence
Finger of a tender of, O of a feathery delicacy, the breast of the
    Maiden could obey so, be a bell to, ring of it, and
Startle the poor sheep back! is the shipwreck then a harvest,
            does tempest carry the grain for thee?

XXXII   I admire thee, master of the tides,
        Of the Yore-flood, of the year's fall;
    The recurb and the recovery of the gulf's sides,
        The girth of it and the wharf of it and the wall;
    Stanching, quenching ocean of a motionable mind;
    Ground of being, and granite of it: past all
        Grasp God, throned behind
Death with a sovereignty that heeds but hides, bodes but abides;

XXXIII   With a mercy that outrides
        The all of water, an ark
    For the listener; for the lingerer with a love glides
        Lower than death and the dark;
    A vein for the visiting of the past-prayer, pent in prison,
    The-last-breath penitent spirits—the uttermost mark
        Our passion-plungèd giant risen,
The Christ of the Father compassionate, fetched in the storm of his strides.

XXXIV   Now burn, new born to the world,
        Double-naturèd name,
    The heaven-flung, heart-fleshed, maiden-furled
        Miracle-in-Mary-of-flame,
    Mid-numbered He in three of the thunder-throne!
    Not a dooms-day dazzle in his coming nor dark as he came;
        Kind, but royally reclaiming his own;
A released shower, let flash to the shire, not a lightning of fire hard-hurled.

XXXV   Dame, at our door
        Drowned, and among our shoals,
    Remember us in the roads, the heaven-haven of the Reward:
        Our King back, oh, upon English souls!
    Let him easter in us, be a dayspring to the dimness of us, be a crimson-
        cresseted east,
    More brightening her, rare-dear Britain, as his reign rolls,
        Pride, rose, prince, hero of us, high-priest,
Our heart's charity's hearth's fire, our thoughts' chivalry's throng's Lord.

ROBERT BRIDGES
1844–1930

A Passer-By

Whither, O splendid ship, thy white sails crowding,
　Leaning across the bosom of the urgent West
That fearest nor sea rising, nor sky clouding,
　Whither away, fair rover, and what thy quest?
　Ah! soon, when Winter has all our vales opprest,
When skies are cold and misty, and hail is hurling,
　Wilt thou glide on the blue Pacific, or rest
In a summer haven asleep, thy white sails furling.

I there before thee, in the country that well thou knowest
　Already arrived am inhaling the odorous air:
I watch thee enter unerringly where thou goest,
　And anchor queen of the strange shipping there,
　Thy sails for awnings spread, thy masts bare:
Nor is aught from the foaming reef to the snow-capped, grandest
　Peak, that is over the feathery palms more fair
Than thou, so upright, so stately, and still thou standest.

And yet, O splendid ship, unhailed and nameless,
　I know not if, aiming a fancy, I rightly divine
That thou hast a purpose joyful, a courage blameless,
　Thy port assured in a happier land than mine.
　But for all I have given thee, beauty enough is thine,
As thou, aslant with trim tackle and shrouding,
　From the proud nostril curve of a prow's line
In the offing scatterest foam, thy white sails crowding.

Nightingales

Beautiful must be the mountains whence ye come,
And bright in the fruitful valleys the streams wherefrom
　Ye learn your song:
Where are those starry woods? O might I wander there,
　Among the flowers, which in that heavenly air
　　Bloom the year long!

Nay, barren are those mountains and spent the streams:
Our song is the voice of desire, that haunts our dreams,

A throe of the heart,
Whose pining visions dim, forbidden hopes profound,
　No dying cadence nor long sigh can sound,
　　For all our art.

Alone, aloud in the raptured ear of men
We pour our dark nocturnal secret; and then,
　　As night is withdrawn
From these sweet-springing meads and bursting boughs of May,
　Dream, while the innumerable choir of day
　　Welcome the dawn.

WILLIAM ERNEST HENLEY
1849–1903

Invictus

Out of the night that covers me,
　Black as the Pit from pole to pole,
I thank whatever gods may be
　For my unconquerable soul.

In the fell clutch of circumstance
　I have not winced nor cried aloud.
Under the bludgeonings of chance
　My head is bloody, but unbowed.

Beyond this place of wrath and tears
　Looms but the horror of the shade,
And yet the menace of the years
　Finds, and shall find me, unafraid.

It matters not how strait the gate,
　How charged with punishments the scroll,
I am the master of my fate:
　I am the captain of my soul.

FRANCIS THOMPSON
1859–1907

The Hound of Heaven

I fled Him, down the nights and down the days;
  I fled Him, down the arches of the years;
I fled Him, down the labyrinthine ways
  Of my own mind; and in the mist of tears
I hid from Him, and under running laughter.
        Up vistaed hopes I sped;
        And shot, precipitated,
Adown Titanic glooms of chasmèd fears,
  From those strong Feet that followed, followed after.
      But with unhurrying chase,
      And unperturbèd pace,
    Deliberate speed, majestic instancy,
        They beat—and a Voice beat
        More instant than the Feet—
    "All things betray thee, who betrayest Me."
        I pleaded, outlaw-wise,
By many a hearted casement, curtained red,
  Trellised with intertwining charities;
(For, though I knew His love Who followèd,
        Yet was I sore adread
Lest, having Him, I must have naught beside);
But, if one little casement parted wide,
  The gust of His approach would clash it to.
  Fear wist not to evade, as Love wist to pursue.
Across the margent of the world I fled,
  And troubled the gold gateways of the stars,
  Smiting for shelter on their clangèd bars;
        Fretted to dulcet jars
And silvern chatter the pale ports o' the moon.
I said to Dawn: Be sudden—to Eve: Be soon;
  With thy young skiey blossoms heap me over
      From this tremendous Lover—
Float thy vague veil about me, lest He see!
  I tempted all His servitors, but to find
My own betrayal in their constancy,
In faith to Him their fickleness to me,

Their traitorous trueness, and their loyal deceit.
To all swift things for swiftness did I sue;
  Clung to the whistling mane of every wind.
    But whether they swept, smoothly fleet,
    The long savannahs of the blue;
      Or whether, Thunder-driven,
    They clanged his chariot 'thwart a heaven
Plashy with flying lightnings round the spurn o' their feet:—
Fear wist not to evade as Love wist to pursue.
    Still with unhurrying chase,
    And unperturbèd pace,
  Deliberate speed, majestic instancy,
    Came on the following Feet,
    And a Voice above their beat—
"Naught shelters thee, who wilt not shelter Me."

I sought no more that after which I strayed
    In face of man or maid;
But still within the little children's eyes
    Seems something, something that replies,
They at least are for me, surely for me!
I turned me to them very wistfully;
But just as their young eyes grew sudden fair
    With dawning answers there,
Their angel plucked them from me by the hair.
"Come then, ye other children, Nature's—share
With me" (said I) "your delicate fellowship;
    Let me greet you lip to lip,
    Let me twine with you caresses,
      Wantoning
    With our Lady-Mother's vagrant tresses,
      Banqueting
    With her in her wind-walled palace,
    Underneath her azured daïs,
    Quaffing, as your taintless way is,
      From a chalice
Lucent-weeping out of the dayspring.
    So it was done:
I in their delicate fellowship was one—
Drew the bolt of Nature's secrecies.
    I knew all the swift importings

On the willful face of skies;
I knew how the clouds arise
Spumèd of the wild sea-snortings;
 All that's born or dies
 Rose and drooped with; made them shapers
Of mine own moods, or wailful or divine;
 With them joyed and was bereaven.
 I was heavy with the even,
 When she lit her glimmering tapers
 Round the day's dead sanctities.
 I laughed in the morning's eyes.
I triumphed and I saddened with all weather,
 Heaven and I wept together,
And its sweet tears were salt with mortal mine.
Against the red throb of its sunset-heart
 I laid my own to beat,
 And share commingling heat;
But not by that, by that, was eased my human smart.
In vain my tears were wet on Heaven's grey cheek.
For ah! we know not what each other says,
 These things and I; in sound *I* speak—
Their sound is but their stir, they speak by silences.
Nature, poor stepdame, cannot slake my drouth;
 Let her, if she would owe me,
Drop yon blue bosom-veil of sky, and show me
 The breasts o' her tenderness:
Never did any milk of hers once bless
 My thirsting mouth.
 Nigh and nigh draws the chase,
 With unperturbèd pace,
Deliberate speed, majestic instancy;
 And past those noisèd Feet
 A Voice comes yet more fleet—
"Lo! naught contents thee, who content'st not Me."

Naked I wait Thy love's uplifted stroke!
My harness piece by piece Thou hast hewn from me,
 And smitten me to my knee;
 I am defenceless utterly.
 I slept, methinks, and woke,
And, slowly gazing, find me stripped in sleep.

In the rash lustihead of my young powers,
     I shook the pillaring hours
And pulled my life upon me; grimed with smears,
I stand amid the dust o' the mounded years—
My mangled youth lies dead beneath the heap,
My days have crackled and gone up in smoke,
Have puffed and burst as sun-starts on a stream.

     Yea, faileth now even dream
The dreamer, and the lute the lutanist;
Even the linked fantasies, in whose blossomy twist
I swung the earth a trinket at my wrist,
Are yielding; cords of all too weak account
For earth with heavy griefs so overplussed.
     Ah! is Thy love indeed
A weed, albeit an amaranthine weed,
Suffering no flowers except its own to mount?
     Ah! must—
     Designer infinite!—
Ah! must Thou char the wood ere Thou canst limn with it?
My freshness spent its wavering shower i' the dust;
And now my heart is as a broken fount,
Wherein tear-drippings stagnate, spilt down ever
     From the dank thoughts that shiver
Upon the sighful branches of my mind.
     Such is; what is to be?
The pulp so bitter, how shall taste the rind?
I dimly guess what Time in mists confounds;
Yet ever and anon a trumpet sounds
From the hid battlements of Eternity;
Those shaken mists a space unsettle, then
Round the half-glimpsèd turrets slowly wash again.
     But not ere him who summoneth
     I first have seen, enwound
With glooming robes purpureal, cypress-crowned;
His name I know, and what his trumpet saith.
Whether man's heart or life it be which yields
     Thee harvest, must Thy harvest-fields
     Be dunged with rotten death?

     Now of that long pursuit
     Comes at hand the bruit;

That Voice is round me like a bursting sea:
    "And is thy earth so marred,
      Shattered in shard on shard?
    Lo, all things fly thee, for thou fliest Me!
    Strange, piteous, futile thing!
Wherefore should any set thee love apart?
Seeing none but I make much of naught" (He said),
"And human love needs human meriting:
    How hast thou merited—
Of all man's clotted clay the dingiest clot?
    Alack, thou knowest not
How little worthy of any love thou art!
Whom wilt thou find to love ignoble thee
    Save Me, save only Me?
All which I took from thee I did but take,
    Not for thy harms,
But just that thou might'st seek it in My arms.
    All which thy child's mistake
Fancies as lost, I have stored for thee at home:
    Rise, clasp My hand, and come!"

    Halts by me that footfall:
    Is my gloom, after all,
Shade of His hand, outstretched caressingly?
    "Ah, fondest, blindest, weakest,
    I am He Whom thou seekest!
Thou dravest love from thee, who dravest Me."

JOHN DAVIDSON
1859—1909

Thirty Bob a Week

I couldn't touch a step and turn a screw,
    And set the blooming world a-work for me,
Like such as cut their teeth—I hope, like you—
    On the handle of a skeleton gold key;
I cut mine on a leek, which I eat it every week:
    I'm a clerk at thirty bob as you can see.

But I don't allow it's luck and all a toss;
    There's no such thing as being starred and crossed;
It's just the power of some to be a boss,
    And the bally power of others to be bossed:
I face the music, sir; you bet I ain't a cur;
    Strike me lucky if I don't believe I'm lost!

For like a mole I journey in the dark,
    A-travelling along the underground
From my Pillar'd Halls and broad Suburban Park,
    To come the daily dull official round;
And home again at night with my pipe all alight,
    A-scheming how to count ten bob a pound.

And it's often very cold and very wet,
    And my missis stitches towels for a hunks;
And the Pillar'd Halls is half of it to let—
    Three rooms about the size of travelling trunks.
And we cough, my wife and I, to dislocate a sigh,
    When the noisy little kids are in their bunks.

But you never hear her do a growl or whine,
    For she's made of flint and roses, very odd;
And I've got to cut my meaning rather fine,
    Or I'd blubber, for I'm made of greens and sod:
So p'r'aps we are in Hell for all that I can tell,
    And lost and damn'd and served up hot to God.

I ain't blaspheming, Mr. Silver-tongue;
    I'm saying things a bit beyond your art:
Of all the rummy starts you ever sprung,
    Thirty bob a week's the rummiest start!
With your science and your books and your the'ries about spooks,
    Did you ever hear of looking in your heart?

I didn't mean your pocket, Mr., no:
    I mean that having children and a wife,
With thirty bob on which to come and go,
    Isn't dancing to the tabor and the fife:
When it doesn't make you drink, by Heaven! it makes you think,
    And notice curious items about life.

I step into my heart and there I meet
　A god-almighty devil singing small,
Who would like to shout and whistle in the street,
　And squelch the passers flat against the wall;
If the whole world was a cake he had the power to take,
　He would take it, ask for more, and eat it all.

And I meet a sort of simpleton beside,
　The kind that life is always giving beans;
With thirty bob a week to keep a bride
　He fell in love and married in his teens:
At thirty bob he stuck; but he knows it isn't luck:
　He knows the seas are deeper than tureens.

And the god-almighty devil and the fool
　That meet me in the High Street on the strike,
When I walk about my heart a-gathering wool,
　Are my good and evil angels if you like.
And both of them together in every kind of weather
　Ride me like a double-seated bike.

That's rough a bit and needs its meaning curled.
　But I have a high old hot un in my mind—
A most engrugious notion of the world,
　That leaves your lightning 'rithmetic behind:
I give it at a glance when I say "There ain't no chance,
　Nor nothing of the lucky-lottery kind."

And it's this way I make it out to be:
　No fathers, mothers, countries, climates—none;
Not Adam was responsible for me,
　Nor society, nor systems, nary one:
A little sleeping seed, I woke—I did, indeed—
　A million years before the blooming sun.

I woke because I thought the time had come;
　Beyond my will there was no other cause;
And every where I found myself at home,
　Because I chose to be the thing I was;
And in what ever shape of mollusc or of ape
　I always went according to the laws.

I was the love that chose my mother out;
  I joined two lives and from the union burst;
My weakness and my strength without a doubt
  Are mine alone for ever from the first:
It's just the very same with a difference in the name
  As "Thy will be done." You say it if you durst!

They say it daily up and down the land
  As easy as you take a drink, it's true;
But the difficultest go to understand,
  And the difficultest job a man can do,
Is to come it brave and meek with thirty bob a week,
  And feel that that's the proper thing for you.

It's a naked child against a hungry wolf;
  It's playing bowls upon a splitting wreck;
It's walking on a string across a gulf
  With millstones fore-and-aft about your neck;
But the thing is daily done by many and many a one;
  And we fall, face forward, fighting, on the deck.

A. E. HOUSMAN
1859–1936

Loveliest of Trees, the Cherry Now

Loveliest of trees, the cherry now
Is hung with bloom along the bough,
And stands about the woodland ride
Wearing white for Eastertide.

Now, of my threescore years and ten,
Twenty will not come again,
And take from seventy springs a score,
It only leaves me fifty more.

And since to look at things in bloom
Fifty springs are little room,
About the woodlands I will go
To see the cherry hung with snow.

When I Was One-and-Twenty

When I was one-and-twenty
   I heard a wise man say,
"Give crowns and pounds and guineas
   But not your heart away;
Give pearls away and rubies
   But keep your fancy free."
But I was one-and-twenty,
   No use to talk to me.

When I was one-and-twenty
   I heard him say again,
"The heart out of the bosom
   Was never given in vain;
'Tis paid with sighs a plenty
   And sold for endless rue."
And I am two-and-twenty,
   And oh, 'tis true, 'tis true.

With Rue My Heart Is Laden

With rue my heart is laden
   For golden friends I had,
For many a rose-lipt maiden
   And many a lightfoot lad.

By brooks too broad for leaping
   The lightfoot boys are laid;
The rose-lipt girls are sleeping
   In fields where roses fade.

To an Athlete Dying Young

The time you won your town the race
We chaired you through the market-place;
Man and boy stood cheering by,
And home we brought you shoulder-high.

To-day, the road all runners come,
Shoulder-high we bring you home,
And set you at your threshold down,
Townsman of a stiller town.

Smart lad, to slip betimes away
From fields where glory does not stay
And early though the laurel grows
It withers quicker than the rose.

Eyes the shady night has shut
Cannot see the record cut,
And silence sounds no worse than cheers
After earth has stopped the ears:

Now you will not swell the rout
Of lads that wore their honours out,
Runners whom renown outran
And the name died before the man.

So set, before its echoes fade,
The fleet foot on the sill of shade,
And hold to the low lintel up
The still-defended challenge-cup.

And round that early-laurelled head
Will flock to gaze the strengthless dead,
And find unwithered on its curls
The garland briefer than a girl's.

Infant Innocence

The Grizzly Bear is huge and wild;
He has devoured the infant child.
The infant child is not aware
It has been eaten by the bear.

GEORGE SANTAYANA
1863–1952

A Minuet on Reaching the Age of Fifty

Old Age, on tiptoe, lays her jewelled hand
Lightly in mine.—Come, tread a stately measure
Most gracious partner, nobly posed and bland.

Ours be no boisterous pleasure,
But smiling conversation, with quick glance
And memories dancing lightlier than we dance,

    Friends who a thousand joys
Divide and double, save one joy supreme
    Which many a pang alloys.
    Let wanton girls and boys
Cry over lovers' woes and broken toys.
Our waking life is sweeter than their dream.

Dame Nature, with unwitting hand,
Has sparsely strewn the black abyss with lights
Minute, remote, and numberless. We stand
    Measuring far depths and heights,
    Arched over by a laughing heaven,
Intangible and never to be scaled.
If we confess our sins, they are forgiven.
    We triumph, if we know we failed.

    Tears that in youth you shed,
Congealed to pearls, now deck your silvery hair;
    Sighs breathed for loves long dead
Frosted the glittering atoms of the air
        Into the veils you wear
Round your soft bosom and most queenly head;
        The shimmer of your gown
Catches all tints of autumn, and the dew
Of gardens where the damask roses blew;

The myriad tapers from these arches hung
        Play on your diamonded crown;
And stars, whose light angelical caressed
        Your virgin days,
Give back in your calm eyes their holier rays.
    The deep past living in your breast
    Heaves these half-merry sighs;
    And the soft accents of your tongue
    Breathe unrecorded charities.

        Hasten not; the feast will wait.
This is a master-night without a morrow.

No chill and haggard dawn, with after-sorrow,
    Will snuff the spluttering candle out,
Or blanch the revellers homeward straggling late.
    Before the rout
Wearies or wanes, will come a calmer trance.
Lulled by the poppied fragrance of this bower,
    We'll cheat the lapsing hour,
And close our eyes, still smiling, on the dance.

WILLIAM BUTLER YEATS
1865–1939

The Second Coming

Turning and turning in the widening gyre
The falcon cannot hear the falconer;
Things fall apart; the centre cannot hold;
Mere anarchy is loosed upon the world,
The blood-dimmed tide is loosed, and everywhere
The ceremony of innocence is drowned;
The best lack all conviction, while the worst
Are full of passionate intensity.

Surely some revelation is at hand;
Surely the Second Coming is at hand.
The Second Coming! Hardly are those words out
When a vast image out of *Spiritus Mundi*
Troubles my sight: somewhere in sands of the desert
A shape with lion body and the head of a man,
A gaze blank and pitiless as the sun,
Is moving its slow thighs, while all about it
Reel shadows of the indignant desert birds.
The darkness drops again; but now I know
That twenty centuries of stony sleep
Were vexed to nightmare by a rocking cradle,
And what rough beast, its hour come round at last,
Slouches towards Bethlehem to be born?

Sailing to Byzantium

That is no country for old men. The young
In one another's arms, birds in the trees
—Those dying generations—at their song,
The salmon-falls, the mackerel-crowded seas,
Fish, flesh, or fowl, commend all summer long
Whatever is begotten, born, and dies.
Caught in that sensual music all neglect
Monuments of unaging intellect.

An aged man is but a paltry thing,
A tattered coat upon a stick, unless
Soul clap its hands and sing, and louder sing
For every tatter in its mortal dress,
Nor is there singing school but studying
Monuments of its own magnificence;
And therefore I have sailed the seas and come
To the holy city of Byzantium.

O sages standing in God's holy fire
As in the gold mosaic of a wall,
Come from the holy fire, perne in a gyre,
And be the singing-masters of my soul.
Consume my heart away; sick with desire
And fastened to a dying animal
It knows not what it is; and gather me
Into the artifice of eternity.

Once out of nature I shall never take
My bodily form from any natural thing,
But such a form as Grecian goldsmiths make
Of hammered gold and gold enameling
To keep a drowsy Emperor awake;
Or set upon a golden bough to sing
To lords and ladies of Byzantium
Of what is past, or passing, or to come.

Leda and the Swan

A sudden blow: the great wings beating still
Above the staggering girl, her thighs caressed
By the dark webs, her nape caught in his bill,

He holds her helpless breast upon his breast.
How can those terrified vague fingers push
The feathered glory from her loosening thighs?
And how can body, laid in that white rush,
But feel the strange heart beating where it lies?
A shudder in the loins engenders there
The broken wall, the burning roof and tower
And Agamemnon dead. Being so caught up,
So mastered by the brute blood of the air,
Did she put on his knowledge with his power
Before the indifferent beak could let her drop?

For Anne Gregory

"Never shall a young man,
Thrown into despair
By those great honey-colored
Ramparts at your ear,
Love you for yourself alone
And not your yellow hair."

"But I can get a hair-dye
And set such color there,
Brown, or black, or carrot,
That young men in despair
May love me for myself alone
And not my yellow hair."

"I heard an old religious man
But yesternight declare
That he had found a text to prove
That only God, my dear,
Could love you for yourself alone
And not your yellow hair."

Two Songs from a Play

I

I saw a staring virgin stand
Where holy Dionysus died,
And tear the heart out of his side,
And lay the heart upon her hand

And bear that beating heart away;
And then did all the Muses sing
Of Magnus Annus at the spring,
As though God's death were but a play.

Another Troy must rise and set,
Another lineage feed the crow,
Another Argo's painted prow
Drive to a flashier bauble yet.
The Roman Empire stood appalled:
It dropped the reins of peace and war
When that fierce virgin and her Star
Out of the fabulous darkness called.

II

In pity for man's darkening thought
He walked that room and issued thence
In Galilean turbulence;
The Babylonian starlight brought
A fabulous, formless darkness in;
Odor of blood when Christ was slain
Made all Platonic tolerance vain
And vain all Doric discipline.

Everything that man esteems
Endures a moment or a day.
Love's pleasure drives his love away,
The painter's brush consumes his dreams;
The herald's cry, the soldier's tread
Exhaust his glory and his might:
Whatever flames upon the night
Man's own resinous heart has fed.

Among School Children

I walk through the long schoolroom questioning,
A kind old nun in a white hood replies;
The children learn to cipher and to sing,
To study reading-books and history,
To cut and sew, be neat in everything
In the best modern way—the children's eyes
In momentary wonder stare upon
A sixty year old smiling public man.

I dream of a Ledæan body, bent
Above a sinking fire, a tale that she
Told of a harsh reproof, or trivial event
That changed some childish day to tragedy—
Told, and it seemed that our two natures blent
Into a sphere from youthful sympathy,
Or else, to alter Plato's parable,
Into the yolk and white of the one shell.

And thinking of that fit of grief or rage
I look upon one child or t'other there
And wonder if she stood so at that age—
For even daughters of the swan can share
Something of every paddler's heritage—
And had that color upon cheek or hair;
And thereupon my heart is driven wild:
She stands before me as a living child.

Her present image floats into the mind—
Did quattrocento finger fashion it
Hollow of cheek as though it drank the wind
And took a mess of shadows for its meat?
And I though never of Ledæan kind
Had pretty plumage once—enough of that,
Better to smile on all that smile, and show
There is a comfortable kind of old scarecrow.

What youthful mother, a shape upon her lap
Honey of generation had betrayed,
And that must sleep, shriek, struggle to escape
As recollection or the drug decide,
Would think her son, did she but see that shape
With sixty or more winters on its head,
A compensation for the pang of his birth,
Or the uncertainty of his setting forth?

Plato thought nature but a spume that plays
Upon a ghostly paradigm of things;
Solider Aristotle played the taws
Upon the bottom of a king of kings;
World-famous golden-thighed Pythagoras

Fingered upon a fiddle stick or strings
What a star sang and careless Muses heard:
Old clothes upon old sticks to scare a bird.

Both nuns and mothers worship images,
But those the candles light are not as those
That animate a mother's reveries,
But keep a marble or a bronze repose.
And yet they too break hearts—O Presences
That passion, piety or affection knows,
And that all heavenly glory symbolize—
O self-born mockers of man's enterprise;

Labor is blossoming or dancing where
The body is not bruised to pleasure soul,
Nor beauty born out of its own despair,
Nor blear-eyed wisdom out of midnight oil.
O chestnut tree, great rooted blossomer,
Are you the leaf, the blossom or the bole?
O body swayed to music, O brightening glance,
How can we know the dancer from the dance?

RUDYARD KIPLING
1865–1936

Sestina of the Tramp-Royal

Speakin' in general, I 'ave tried 'em all—
The 'appy roads that take you o'er the world.
Speakin' in general, I 'ave found them good
For such as cannot use one bed too long,
But must get 'ence, the same as I 'ave done,
An' go observin' matters till they die.

What do it matter where or 'ow we die,
So long as we've our 'ealth to watch it all—
The different ways that different things are done,

An' men an' women lovin' in this world;
Takin' our chances as they come along,
An' when they ain't, pretendin' they are good?

In cash or credit—no, it aren't no good;
You 'ave to 'ave the 'abit or you'd die,
Unless you lived your life but one day long,
Nor didn't prophesy nor fret at all,
But drew your tucker some'ow from the world,
An' never bothered what you might ha' done.

But, Gawd, what things are they I 'aven't done!
I've turned my 'and to most, an' turned it good,
In various situations round the world—
For 'im that doth not work must surely die;
But that's no reason man should labour all
'Is life on one same shift—life's none so long.

Therefore, from job to job I've moved along.
Pay couldn't 'old me when my time was done,
For something in my 'ead upset it all,
Till I 'ad dropped whatever 't was for good,
An' out at sea, be'eld the dock-light die,
An' met my mate—the wind that tramps the world!

It's like a book, I think, this bloomin' world,
Which you can read and care for just so long,
But presently you feel that you will die
Unless you get the page you're readin' done,
An' turn another—likely not so good;
But what you're after is to turn 'em all.

Gawd bless this world! Whatever she 'ath done—
Excep' when awful long—I've found it good.
So write, before I die, " 'E liked it all!"

ERNEST DOWSON
1867–1900

Non Sum Qualis Eram Bonae sub Regno Cynarae

Last night, ah, yesternight, betwixt her lips and mine
There fell thy shadow, Cynara! thy breath was shed
Upon my soul between the kisses and the wine;
And I was desolate and sick of an old passion,
   Yea, I was desolate and bowed my head:
I have been faithful to thee, Cynara! in my fashion.

All night upon mine heart I felt her warm heart beat,
Night-long within mine arms in love and sleep she lay;
Surely the kisses of her bought red mouth were sweet;
But I was desolate and sick of an old passion,
   When I awoke and found the dawn was gray:
I have been faithful to thee, Cynara! in my fashion.

I have forgot much, Cynara! gone with the wind,
Flung roses, roses riotously with the throng,
Dancing, to put thy pale, lost lilies out of mind;
But I was desolate and sick of an old passion,
   Yea, all the time, because the dance was long:
I have been faithful to thee, Cynara! in my fashion.

I cried for madder music and for stronger wine,
But when the feast is finished and the lamps expire,
Then falls thy shadow, Cynara! the night is thine;
And I am desolate and sick of an old passion,
   Yea hungry for the lips of my desire:
I have been faithful to thee, Cynara! in my fashion.

EDGAR LEE MASTERS
1869–1950

Anne Rutledge

Out of me unworthy and unknown
The vibrations of deathless music;
"With malice toward none, with charity for all."
Out of me the forgiveness of millions toward millions,
And the beneficent face of a nation
Shining with justice and truth.

I am Anne Rutledge who sleep beneath these weeds,
Beloved in life of Abraham Lincoln,
Wedded to him, not through union,
But through separation.
Bloom forever, O Republic,
From the dust of my bosom!

EDWIN ARLINGTON ROBINSON
1869–1935

The Dark Hills

Dark hills at evening in the west,
Where sunset hovers like a sound
Of golden horns that sang to rest
Old bones of warriors under ground,
Far now from all the bannered ways
Where flash the legions of the sun,
You fade—as if the last of days
Were fading, and all wars were done.

Richard Cory

Whenever Richard Cory went down town,
We people on the pavement looked at him:
He was a gentleman from sole to crown,
Clean favored, and imperially slim.

And he was always quietly arrayed,
   And he was always human when he talked;
But still he fluttered pulses when he said,
   "Good-morning," and he glittered when he walked.

And he was rich—yes, richer than a king,
   And admirably schooled in every grace:
In fine, we thought that he was everything
   To make us wish that we were in his place.

So on we worked, and waited for the light,
   And went without the meat, and cursed the bread;
And Richard Cory, one calm summer night,
   Went home and put a bullet through his head.

Miniver Cheevy

Miniver Cheevy, child of scorn,
   Grew lean while he assailed the seasons;
He wept that he was ever born,
   And he had reasons.

Miniver loved the days of old
   When swords were bright and steeds were prancing.
The vision of a warrior bold
   Would set him dancing.

Miniver sighed for what was not,
   And dreamed, and rested from his labors;
He dreamed of Thebes and Camelot,
   And Priam's neighbors.

Miniver mourned the ripe renown
   That made so many a name so fragrant;
He mourned Romance, now on the town,
   And Art, a vagrant.

Miniver loved the Medici,
   Albeit he had never seen one;
He would have sinned incessantly
   Could he have been one.

Miniver cursed the commonplace
    And eyed a khaki suit with loathing;
He missed the mediæval grace
    Of iron clothing.

Miniver scorned the gold he sought,
    But sore annoyed was he without it;
Miniver thought, and thought, and thought,
    And thought about it.

Miniver Cheevy, born too late,
    Scratched his head and kept on thinking:
Miniver coughed, and called it fate,
    And kept on drinking.

Cassandra

    I heard one who said: "Verily,
        What word have I for children here?
    Your Dollar is your only Word,
        The wrath of it your only fear.

    "You build it altars tall enough
        To make you see, but you are blind;
    You cannot leave it long enough
        To look before you or behind.

    "When Reason beckons you to pause,
        You laugh and say that you know best;
    But what it is you know, you keep
        As dark as ingots in a chest.

    "You laugh and answer, 'We are young;
        Oh, leave us now, and let us grow:'
    Not asking how much more of this
        Will Time endure or Fate bestow.

    "Because a few complacent years
        Have made your peril of your pride,
    Think you that you are to go on
        Forever pampered and untried?

"What lost eclipse of history,
    What bivouac of the marching stars,
Has given the sign for you to see
    Millenniums and last great wars?

"What unrecorded overthrow
    Of all the world has ever known,
Or ever been, has made itself
    So plain to you, and you alone?

"Your Dollar, Dove and Eagle make
    A Trinity that even you
Rate higher than you rate yourselves;
    It pays, it flatters, and it's new.

"And though your very flesh and blood
    Be what your Eagle eats and drinks,
You'll praise him for the best of birds,
    Not knowing what the Eagle thinks.

"The power is yours, but not the sight;
    You see not upon what you tread;
You have the ages for your guide,
    But not the wisdom to be led.

"Think you to tread forever down
    The merciless old verities?
And are you never to have eyes
    To see the world for what it is?

"Are you to pay for what you have
    With all you are?"—No other word
We caught, but with a laughing crowd
    Moved on. None heeded, and few heard.

W. H. DAVIES
1870–1940

A Great Time

Sweet Chance, that led my steps abroad,
Beyond the town, where wild flowers grow—
A rainbow and a cuckoo, Lord!
  How rich and great the times are now!
    Know, all ye sheep
    And cows that keep
On staring that I stand so long
  In grass that's wet from heavy rain—
A rainbow and a cuckoo's song
  May never come together again;
    May never come
    This side the tomb.

WALTER DE LA MARE
1873–1956

The Listeners

"Is there anybody there?" said the Traveller,
  Knocking on the moonlit door;
And his horse in the silence champed the grasses
  Of the forest's ferny floor;
And a bird flew up out of the turret,
  Above the Traveller's head;
And he smote upon the door again a second time;
  "Is there anybody there?" he said.
But no one descended to the Traveller;
  No head from the leaf-fringed sill
Leaned over and looked into his grey eyes,
  Where he stood perplexed and still.
But only a host of phantom listeners
  That dwelt in the lone house then
Stood listening in the quiet of the moonlight
  To that voice from the world of men:

Stood thronging the faint moonbeams on the dark stair,
    That goes down to the empty hall,
Hearkening in an air stirred and shaken
    By the lonely Traveller's call.

And he felt in his heart their strangeness,
    Their stillness answering his cry,
While his horse moved, cropping the dark turf,
    'Neath the starred and leafy sky;
For he suddenly smote on the door, even
    Louder, and lifted his head:
"Tell them I came, and no one answered
    That I kept my word," he said.
Never the least stir made the listeners,
    Though every word he spake
Fell echoing through the shadowiness of the still house
    From the one man left awake:
Ay, they heard his foot upon the stirrup,
    And the sound of iron on stone,
And how the silence surged softly backward,
    When the plunging hoofs were gone.

An Epitaph

Here lies a most beautiful lady:
Light of step and heart was she;
I think she was the most beautiful lady
That ever was in the West Country.
But beauty vanishes; beauty passes;
However rare—rare it be;
And when I crumble, who will remember
This lady of the West Country?

ROBERT FROST
1875–1963

Stopping by Woods on a Snowy Evening

Whose woods these are I think I know.
His house is in the village though;

He will not see me stopping here
To watch his woods fill up with snow.

My little horse must think it queer
To stop without a farmhouse near
Between the woods and frozen lake
The darkest evening of the year.

He gives his harness bells a shake
To ask if there is some mistake.
The only other sound's the sweep
Of easy wind and downy flake.

The woods are lovely, dark and deep.
But I have promises to keep,
And miles to go before I sleep,
And miles to go before I sleep.

The Road Not Taken

Two roads diverged in a yellow wood,
And sorry I could not travel both
And be one traveler, long I stood
And looked down one as far as I could
To where it bent in the undergrowth;

Then took the other, as just as fair,
And having perhaps the better claim,
Because it was grassy and wanted wear;
Though as for that the passing there
Had worn them really about the same,

And both that morning equally lay
In leaves no step had trodden black.
Oh, I kept the first for another day!
Yet knowing how way leads on to way,
I doubted if I should ever come back.

I shall be telling this with a sigh
Somewhere ages and ages hence:
Two roads diverged in a wood, and I—
I took the one less traveled by,
And that has made all the difference.

Two Tramps in Mud Time

Out of the mud two strangers came
And caught me splitting wood in the yard.
And one of them put me off my aim
By hailing cheerily "Hit them hard!"
I knew pretty well why he dropped behind
And let the other go on a way.
I knew pretty well what he had in mind:
He wanted to take my job for pay.

Good blocks of beech it was I split,
As large around as the chopping block;
And every piece I squarely hit
Fell splinterless as a cloven rock.
The blows that a life of self-control
Spares to strike for the common good
That day, giving a loose to my soul,
I spent on the unimportant wood.

The sun was warm but the wind was chill.
You know how it is with an April day
When the sun is out and the wind is still,
You're one month on in the middle of May.
But if you so much as dare to speak,
A cloud comes over the sunlit arch,
A wind comes off a frozen peak,
And you're two months back in the middle of March.

A bluebird comes tenderly up to alight
And fronts the wind to unruffle a plume
His song so pitched as not to excite
A single flower as yet to bloom.
It is snowing a flake: and he half knew
Winter was only playing possum.
Except in color he isn't blue,
But he wouldn't advise a thing to blossom.

The water for which we may have to look
In summertime with a witching-wand,
In every wheelrut's now a brook,
In every print of a hoof a pond.

Be glad of water, but don't forget
The lurking frost in the earth beneath
That will steal forth after the sun is set
And show on the water its crystal teeth.

The time when most I loved my task
These two must make me love it more
By coming with what they came to ask.
You'd think I never had felt before
The weight of an ax-head poised aloft,
The grip on earth of outspread feet,
The life of muscles rocking soft
And smooth and moist in vernal heat.

Out of the woods two hulking tramps
(From sleeping God knows where last night,
But not long since in the lumber camps).
They thought all chopping was theirs of right.
Men of the woods and lumberjacks,
They judged me by their appropriate tool.
Except as a fellow handled an ax,
They had no way of knowing a fool.

Nothing on either side was said.
They knew they had but to stay their stay
And all their logic would fill my head:
As that I had no right to play
With what was another man's work for gain.
My right might be love but theirs was need.
And where the two exist in twain
Theirs was the better right—agreed.

But yield who will to their separation,
My object in living is to unite
My avocation and my vocation
As my two eyes make one in sight.
Only where love and need are one,
And the work is play for mortal stakes,
Is the deed ever really done
For Heaven and the future's sakes.

To Earthward

Love at the lips was touch
As sweet as I could bear;
And once that seemed too much;
I lived on air

That crossed me from sweet things,
The flow of—was it musk
From hidden grapevine springs
Down hill at dusk?

I had the swirl and ache
From sprays of honeysuckle
That when they're gathered shake
Dew on the knuckle.

I craved strong sweets, but those
Seemed strong when I was young;
The petal of the rose
It was that stung.

Now no joy but lacks salt
That is not dashed with pain
And weariness and fault;
I crave the stain

Of tears, the aftermark
Of almost too much love,
The sweet of bitter bark
And burning clove.

When stiff and sore and scarred
I take away my hand
From leaning on it hard
In grass and sand,

The hurt is not enough:
I long for weight and strength
To feel the earth as rough
To all my length.

The Silken Tent

She is as in a field a silken tent
At midday when a sunny summer breeze
Has dried the dew and all its ropes relent,
So that in guys it gently sways at ease,
And its supporting central cedar pole,
That is its pinnacle to heavenward
And signifies the sureness of the soul,
Seems to owe naught to any single cord,
But strictly held by none, is loosely bound
By countless silken ties of love and thought
To everything on earth the compass round,
And only by one's going slightly taut
In the capriciousness of summer air
Is of the slightest bondage made aware.

Directive

Back out of all this now too much for us,
Back in a time made simple by the loss
Of detail, burned, dissolved, and broken off
Like graveyard marble sculpture in the weather,
There is a house that is no more a house
Upon a farm that is no more a farm
And in a town that is no more a town.
The road there, if you'll let a guide direct you
Who only has at heart your getting lost,
May seem as if it should have been a quarry—
Great monolithic knees the former town
Long since gave up pretence of keeping covered.
And there's a story in a book about it:
Besides the wear of iron wagon wheels
The ledges show lines ruled southeast northwest,
The chisel work of an enormous Glacier
That braced his feet against the Arctic Pole.
You must not mind a certain coolness from him
Still said to haunt this side of Panther Mountain.
Nor need you mind the serial ordeal
Of being watched from forty cellar holes
As if by eye pairs out of forty firkins.
As for the woods' excitement over you
That sends light rustle rushes to their leaves,

Charge that to upstart inexperience.
Where were they all not twenty years ago?
They think too much of having shaded out
A few old pecker-fretted apple trees.
Make yourself up a cheering song of how
Someone's road home from work this once was,
Who may be just ahead of you on foot
Or creaking with a buggy load of grain.
The height of the adventure is the height
Of country where two village cultures faded
Into each other. Both of them are lost.
And if you're lost enough to find yourself
By now, pull in your ladder road behind you
And put a sign up CLOSED to all but me.
Then make yourself at home. The only field
Now left's no bigger than a harness gall.
First there's the children's house of make believe,
Some shattered dishes underneath a pine,
The playthings in the playhouse of the children.
Weep for what little things could make them glad.
Then for the house that is no more a house,
But only a belilaced cellar hole,
Now slowly closing like a dent in dough.
This was no playhouse but a house in earnest.
Your destination and your destiny's
A brook that was the water of the house,
Cold as a spring as yet so near its source,
Too lofty and original to rage.
(We know the valley streams that when aroused
Will leave their tatters hung on barb and thorn.)
I have kept hidden in the instep arch
Of an old cedar at the waterside
A broken drinking goblet like the Grail
Under a spell so the wrong ones can't find it,
So can't get saved, as Saint Mark says they mustn't.
(I stole the goblet from the children's playhouse.)
Here are your waters and your watering place.
Drink and be whole again beyond confusion.

JOHN MASEFIELD
1878–1967

On Growing Old

Be with me, Beauty, for the fire is dying,
My dog and I are old, too old for roving.
Man, whose young passion sets the spindrift flying,
Is soon too lame to march, too cold for loving.
I take the book and gather to the fire,
Turning old yellow leaves; minute by minute
The clock ticks to my heart; a withered wire
Moves a thin ghost of music in the spinet.
I cannot sail your seas, I cannot wander
Your cornland nor your hill-land nor your valleys
Ever again, nor share the battle yonder
Where the young knight the broken squadron rallies;
Only stay quiet, while my mind remembers
The beauty of fire from the beauty of embers.

Beauty, have pity, for the strong have power,
The rich their wealth, the beautiful their grace,
Summer of man its sunlight and its flower,
Springtime of man all April in a face.
Only, as in the jostling in the Strand,
Where the mob thrusts or loiters or is loud,
The beggar with the saucer in his hand
Asks only a penny from the passing crowd,
So, from this glittering world with all its fashion,
Its fire and play of men, its stir, its march,
Let me have wisdom, Beauty, wisdom and passion,
Bread to the soul, rain where the summers parch.
Give me but these, and though the darkness close
Even the night will blossom as the rose.

SARAH N. CLEGHORN
1876–1959

The Golf Links

The golf links lie so near the mill
That almost every day
The laboring children can look out
And see the men at play.

CARL SANDBURG
1878–1967

Evening Waterfall

What was the name you called me?—
And why did you go so soon?

The crows lift their caw on the wind,
And the wind changed and was lonely.

The warblers cry their sleepy-songs
Across the valley gloaming,
Across the cattle-horns of early stars.

Feathers and people in the crotch of a treetop
Throw an evening waterfall of sleepy-songs.

What was the name you called me?—
And why did you go so soon?

HAROLD MONRO
1879–1932

Living

Slow bleak awakening from the morning dream
Brings me in contact with the sudden day.
I am alive—this I.
I let my fingers move along my body.
Realisation warns them, and my nerves
Prepare their rapid messages and signals.
While Memory begins recording, coding,
Repeating; all the time Imagination
Mutters: You'll only die.

Here's a new day. O Pendulum move slowly!
My usual clothes are waiting on their peg.
I am alive—this I.
And in a moment Habit, like a crane,
Will bow its neck and dip its pulleyed cable,
Gathering me, my body, and our garment,
And swing me forth, oblivious of my question,
Into the daylight—why?

I think of all the others who awaken,
And wonder if they go to meet the morning
More valiantly than I;
Nor asking of this Day they will be living:
What have I done that I should be alive?
O, can I not forget that I am living?
How shall I reconcile the two conditions:
Living, and yet—to die?

Between the curtains the autumnal sunlight
With lean and yellow finger points me out;
The clock moans: Why? Why? Why?
But suddenly, as if without a reason,
Heart, Brain and Body, and Imagination
All gather in tumultuous joy together,
Running like children down the path of morning
To fields where they can play without a quarrel:

A country I'd forgotten, but remember,
And welcome with a cry.

O cool glad pasture; living tree, tall corn,
Great cliff, or languid sloping sand, cold sea,
Waves; rivers curving: you, eternal flowers,
Give me content, while I can think of you:
Give me your living breath!
Back to your rampart, Death.

VACHEL LINDSAY
1879–1931

The Leaden-Eyed

Let not young souls be smothered out before
They do quaint deeds and fully flaunt their pride.
It is the world's one crime its babes grow dull,
Its poor are ox-like, limp and leaden-eyed.
Not that they starve, but starve so dreamlessly;
Not that they sow, but that they seldom reap;
Not that they serve, but have no gods to serve;
Not that they die, but that they die like sheep.

General William Booth Enters into Heaven

(To be sung to the tune of "The Blood of the Lamb" with indicated instrument.)

(Bass drum beaten loudly.)
Booth led boldly with his big bass drum—
(Are you washed in the blood of the Lamb?)
The Saints smiled gravely and they said: "He's come."
(Are you washed in the blood of the Lamb?)
Walking lepers followed, rank on rank,
Lurching bravos from the ditches dank,
Drabs from the alleyways and drug fiends pale—
Minds still passion-ridden, soul-powers frail:—
Vermin-eaten saints with moldy breath,
Unwashed legions with the ways of Death—
(Are you washed in the blood of the Lamb?)

(Banjos.)
Every slum had sent its half-a-score
The round world over. (Booth had groaned for more.)
Every banner that the wide world flies
Bloomed with glory and transcendent dyes.
Big-voiced lasses made their banjos bang;
Tranced, fanatical they shrieked and sang:—
"Are you washed in the blood of the Lamb?"
Hallelujah! It was queer to see
Bull-necked convicts with that land make free.
Loons with trumpets blowed a blare, blare, blare
On, on upward thro' the golden air!
(Are you washed in the blood of the Lamb?)

(Bass drum slower and softer.)
Booth died blind and still by faith he trod,
Eyes still dazzled by the ways of God.
Booth led boldly, and he looked the chief,
Eagle countenance in sharp relief,
Beard a-flying, air of high command
Unabated in that holy land.

(Sweet flute music.)
Jesus came from out the court-house door,
Stretched his hands above the passing poor.
Booth saw not, but led his queer ones there
Round and round the mighty court-house square.
Then, in an instant all that blear review
Marched on spotless, clad in raiment new.
The lame were straightened, withered limbs uncurled
And blind eyes opened on a new, sweet world.

(Bass drum louder.)
Drabs and vixens in a flash made whole!
Gone was the weasel-head, the snout, the jowl!
Sages and sibyls now, and athletes clean,
Rulers of empires, and of forests green!

(Grand chorus of all instruments. Tambourines to the foreground.)
The hosts were sandalled, and their wings were fire!
(Are you washed in the blood of the Lamb?)

But their noise played havoc with the angel-choir.
(Are you washed in the blood of the Lamb?)
Oh, shout Salvation! It was good to see
Kings and Princes by the Lamb set free.
The banjos rattled and the tambourines
Jing-jing-jingled in the hands of Queens.

(Reverently sung, no instruments.)
And when Booth halted by the curb for prayer
He saw his Master thro' the flag-filled air.
Christ came gently with a robe and crown
For Booth the soldier, while the throng knelt down.
He saw King Jesus. They were face to face,
And he knelt a-weeping in that holy place.
Are you washed in the blood of the Lamb?

Factory Windows Are Always Broken

Factory windows are always broken.
Somebody's always throwing bricks,
Somebody's always heaving cinders,
Playing ugly Yahoo tricks.

Factory windows are always broken.
Other windows are let alone.
No one throws through the chapel-window
The bitter, snarling derisive stone.

Factory windows are always broken.
Something or other is going wrong.
Something is rotten—I think, in Denmark.
End of the factory-window song.

WALLACE STEVENS
1879–1955

Sunday Morning

Complacencies of the peignoir, and late
Coffee and oranges in a sunny chair,

And the green freedom of a cockatoo
Upon a rug mingle to dissipate
The holy hush of ancient sacrifice.
She dreams a little, and she feels the dark
Encroachment of that old catastrophe,
As a calm darkens among water-lights.
The pungent oranges and bright, green wings
Seem things in some procession of the dead,
Winding across wide water, without sound.
The day is like wide water, without sound,
Stilled for the passing of her dreaming feet
Over the seas, to silent Palestine,
Dominion of the blood and sepulchre.

Why should she give her bounty to the dead?
What is divinity if it can come
Only in silent shadows and in dreams?
Shall she not find in comforts of the sun,
In pungent fruit and bright, green wings, or else
In any balm or beauty of the earth,
Things to be cherished like the thought of heaven
Divinity must live within herself:
Passions of rain, or moods in falling snow;
Grievings in loneliness, or unsubdued
Elations when the forest blooms; gusty
Emotions on wet roads on autumn nights;
All pleasures and all pains, remembering
The bough of summer and the winter branch,
These are the measures destined for her soul.

Jove in the clouds had his inhuman birth.
No mother suckled him, no sweet land gave
Large-mannered motions to his mythy mind.
He moved among us, as a muttering king,
Magnificent, would move among his hinds,
Until our blood, commingling, virginal,
With heaven, brought such requital to desire
The very hinds discerned it, in a star.
Shall our blood fail? Or shall it come to be
The blood of paradise? And shall the earth
Seem all of paradise that we shall know?

The sky will be much friendlier then than now,
A part of labor and a part of pain,
And next in glory to enduring love,
Not this dividing and indifferent blue.

She says, "I am content when wakened birds,
Before they fly, test the reality
Of misty fields, by their sweet questionings;
But when the birds are gone, and their warm fields
Return no more, where, then, is paradise?"
There is not any haunt of prophecy,
Nor any old chimera of the grave,
Neither the golden underground, nor isle
Melodious, where spirits gat them home,
Nor visionary south, nor cloudy palm
Remote on heaven's hill, that has endured
As April's green endures; or will endure
Like her remembrance of awakened birds,
Or her desire for June and evening, tipped
By the consummation of the swallow's wings.

She says, "But in contentment I still feel
The need of some imperishable bliss."
Death is the mother of beauty; hence from her,
Alone, shall come fulfilment to our dreams
And our desires. Although she strews the leaves
Of sure obliteration on our paths,
The path sick sorrow took, the many paths
Where triumph rang its brassy phrase, or love
Whispered a little out of tenderness,
She makes the willow shiver in the sun
For maidens who were wont to sit and gaze
Upon the grass, relinquished to their feet.
She causes boys to pile new plums and pears
On disregarded plate. The maidens taste
And stray impassioned in the littering leaves.

Is there no change of death in paradise?
Does ripe fruit never fall? Or do the boughs
Hang always heavy in that perfect sky,
Unchanging, yet so like our perishing earth,
With rivers like our own that seek for seas

They never find, the same receding shores
That never touch with inarticulate pang?
Why set the pear upon those river-banks
Or spice the shores with odors of the plum?
Alas, that they should wear our colors there,
The silken weavings of our afternoons,
And pick the strings of our insipid lutes!
Death is the mother of beauty, mystical,
Within whose burning bosom we devise
Our earthly mothers waiting, sleeplessly.

Supple and turbulent, a ring of men
Shall chant in orgy on a summer morn
Their boisterous devotion to the sun,
Not as a god, but as a god might be,
Naked among them, like a savage source.
Their chant shall be a chant of paradise,
Out of their blood, returning to the sky;
And in their chant shall enter, voice by voice,
The windy lake wherein their lord delights,
The trees, like serafin, and echoing hills,
That choir among themselves long afterward.
They shall know well the heavenly fellowship
Of men that perish and of summer morn.
And whence they came and whither they shall go
The dew upon their feet shall manifest.

She hears, upon that water without sound,
A voice that cries, "The tomb in Palestine
Is not the porch of spirits lingering.
It is the grave of Jesus, where He lay."
We live in an old chaos of the sun,
Or old dependency of day and night,
Or island solitude, unsponsored, free,
Of that wide water, inescapable.
Deer walk upon our mountains, and the quail
Whistle about us their spontaneous cries;
Sweet berries ripen in the wilderness;
And, in the isolation of the sky,
At evening, casual flocks of pigeons make
Ambiguous undulations as they sink,
Downward to darkness, on extended wings.

The Sense of the Sleight-of-Hand Man

One's grand flights, one's Sunday baths,
One's tootings at the weddings of the soul
Occur as they occur. So bluish clouds
Occurred above the empty house and the leaves
Of the rhododendrons rattled their gold,
As if someone lived there. Such floods of white
Came bursting from the clouds. So the wind
Threw its contorted strength around the sky.

Could you have said the bluejay suddenly
Would swoop to earth? It is a wheel, the rays
Around the sun. The wheel survives the myths.
The fire eye in the clouds survives the gods.
To think of a dove with an eye of grenadine
And pines that are cornets, so it occurs,

And a little island full of geese and stars:
It may be that the ignorant man, alone,
Has any chance to mate his life with life
That is the sensual, pearly spouse, the life
That is fluent in even the wintriest bronze.

WILLIAM CARLOS WILLIAMS
1883–1963

The Yachts

contend in a sea which the land partly encloses
shielding them from the too heavy blows
of an ungoverned ocean which when it chooses

tortures the biggest hulls, the best man knows
to pit against its beating, and sinks them pitilessly.
Mothlike in mists, scintillant in the minute

brilliance of cloudless days, with broad bellying sails
they glide to the wind tossing green water
from their sharp prows while over them the crew crawls

ant-like, solicitously grooming them, releasing,
making fast as they turn, lean far over and having
caught the wind again, side by side, head for the mark.

In a well guarded arena of open water surrounded by
lesser and greater craft which, sycophant, lumbering
and flittering follow them, they appear youthful, rare

as the light of a happy eye, live with the grace
of all that in the mind is feckless, free and
naturally to be desired. Now the sea which holds them

is moody, lapping their glossy sides, as if feeling
for some slightest flaw but fails completely.
Today no race. Then the wind comes again. The yachts

move, jockeying for a start, the signal is set and they
are off. Now the waves strike at them but they are too
well made, they slip through, though they take in canvas.

Arms with hands grasping seek to clutch at the prows.
Bodies thrown recklessly in the way are cut aside.
It is a sea of faces about them in agony, in despair

until the horror of the race dawns staggering the mind,
the whole sea become an entanglement of watery bodies
lost to the world bearing what they cannot hold. Broken,

beaten, desolate, reaching from the dead to be taken up
they cry out, failing, failing! their cries rising
in waves still as the skillful yachts pass over.

ELINOR WYLIE
1885–1928

I Hereby Swear

I hereby swear that to uphold your house
I would lay my bones in quick destroying lime
Or turn my flesh to timber for all time;
Cut down my womanhood; lop off the boughs
Of that perpetual ecstasy that grows
From the heart's core; condemn it as a crime
If it be broader than a beam, or climb
Above the stature that your roof allows.
I am not the hearthstone nor the cornerstone
Within this noble fabric you have builded;
Not by my beauty was its cornice gilded;
Not on my courage were its arches thrown:
My lord, adjudge my strength, and set me where
I bear a little more than I can bear.

From *"One Person"*

D. H. LAWRENCE
1885–1930

Bavarian Gentians

Not every man has gentians in his house
in Soft September, at slow, Sad Michaelmas.

Bavarian gentians, big and dark, only dark
darkening the day-time torch-like with the smoking blueness of Pluto's
    gloom,
ribbed and torch-like, with their blaze of darkness spread blue
down flattening into points, flattened under the sweep of white day
torch-flower of the blue-smoking darkness, Pluto's dark-blue daze,
black lamps from the halls of Dis, burning dark blue,
giving off darkness, blue darkness, as Demeter's pale lamps give off light,
lead me then, lead me the way.

Reach me a gentian, give me a torch
let me guide myself with the blue, forked torch of this flower
down the darker and darker stairs, where blue is darkened on blueness,
even where Persephone goes, just now, from the frosted September
to the sightless realm where darkness was awake upon the dark
and Persephone herself is but a voice
or a darkness invisible enfolded in the deeper dark
of the arms Plutonic, and pierced with the passion of dense gloom,
among the splendour of torches of darkness, shedding darkness on the lost
　　bride and her groom.

EZRA POUND

1885–1972

An Immorality

Sing we for love and idleness,
Naught else is worth the having.

Though I have been in many a land,
There is naught else in living.

And I would rather have my sweet,
Though rose-leaves die of grieving,

Than do high deeds in Hungary
To pass all men's believing.

Sestina: Altaforte

Loquitur: En *Bertrans de Born.*
　　Dante Alighieri put this man in hell for that he was a stirrer up of strife.
　　Eccovi! Judge ye!
　　Have I dug him up again?
The scene is at his castle, Altaforte. "Papiols" is his jongleur.
"The Leopard," the device of Richard Cœur de Lion.

　　Damn it all! all this our South stinks peace.
　　You whoreson dog, Papiols, come! Let's to music!
　　I have no life save when the swords clash.
　　But ah! when I see the standards gold, vair, purple, opposing

And the broad fields beneath them turn crimson,
Then howl I my heart nigh mad with rejoicing.

In hot summer have I great rejoicing
When the tempests kill the earth's foul peace,
And the lightnings from black heav'n flash crimson,
And the fierce thunders roar me their music
And the winds shriek through the clouds mad, opposing,
And through all the riven skies God's swords clash.

Hell grant soon we hear again the swords clash!
And the shrill neighs of destriers in battle rejoicing,
Spiked breast to spiked breast opposing!
Better one hour's stour than a year's peace
With fat boards, bawds, wine and frail music!
Bah! there's no wine like the blood's crimson!

And I love to see the sun rise blood-crimson.
And I watch his spears through the dark clash
And it fills all my heart with rejoicing
And pries wide my mouth with fast music
When I see him so scorn and defy peace,
His lone might 'gainst all darkness opposing.

The man who fears war and squats opposing
My words for stour, hath no blood of crimson
But is fit only to rot in womanish peace
Far from where worth's won and the swords clash
For the death of such sluts I go rejoicing;
Yea, I fill all the air with my music.

Papiols, Papiols, to the music!
There's no sound like to swords swords opposing,
No cry like the battle's rejoicing
When our elbows and swords drip the crimson
And our charges 'gainst "The Leopard's" rush clash.
May God damn for ever all who cry "Peace!"

And let the music of the swords make them crimson!
Hell grant soon we hear again the swords clash!
Hell blot black for alway the thought "Peace"!

Ballad of the Goodly Fere

Simon Zelotes speaketh it somewhile after the Crucifixion

Ha' we lost the goodliest fere o' all
For the priests and the gallows tree?
Aye lover he was of brawny men,
O' ships and the open sea.

When they came wi' a host to take Our Man
His smile was good to see,
"First let these go!" quo' our Goodly Fere,
"Or I'll see ye damned," says he.

Aye he sent us out through the crossed high spears
And the scorn of his laugh rang free,
"Why took ye not me when I walked about
Alone in the town?" says he.

Oh we drunk his "Hale" in the good red wine
When we last made company,
No capon priest was the Goodly Fere
But a man o' men was he.

I ha' seen him drive a hundred men
Wi' a bundle o' cords swung free,
That they took the high and holy house
For their pawn and treasury.

They'll no' get him a' in a book I think
Though they write it cunningly;
No mouse of the scrolls was the Goodly Fere
But aye loved the open sea.

If they think they ha' snared our Goodly Fere
They are fools to the last degree.
"I'll go to the feast," quo' our Goodly Fere,
"Though I go to the gallows tree."

"Ye ha' seen me heal the lame and blind,
And wake the dead," says he,
"Ye shall see one thing to master all:
'Tis how a brave man dies on the tree."

A son of God was the Goodly Fere
That bade us his brothers be.
I ha' seen him cow a thousand men.
I have seen him upon the tree.

He cried no cry when they drave the nails
And the blood gushed hot and free,
The hounds of the crimson sky gave tongue
But never a cry cried he.

I ha' seen him cow a thousand men
On the hills o' Galilee,
They whined as he walked out calm between,
Wi' his eyes like the grey o' the sea,

Like the sea that brooks no voyaging
With the winds unleashed and free,
Like the sea that he cowed at Genseret
Wi' twey words spoke' suddently.

A master of men was the Goodly Fere,
A mate of the wind and sea,
If they think they ha' slain our Goodly Fere
They are fools eternally.

I ha' seen him eat o' the honey-comb
Sin' they nailed him to the tree.

Fere, *mate, companion.*

RUPERT BROOKE
1887–1915

The Great Lover

I have been so great a lover: filled my days
So proudly with the splendour of Love's praise,
The pain, the calm, and the astonishment,
Desire illimitable, and still content,

And all dear names men use, to cheat despair,
For the perplexed and viewless streams that bear
Our hearts at random down the dark of life.
Now, ere the unthinking silence on that strife
Steals down, I would cheat drowsy Death so far,
My night shall be remembered for a star
That outshone all the suns of all men's days.
Shall I not crown them with immortal praise
Whom I have loved, who have given me, dared with me
High secrets, and in darkness knelt to see
The inenarrable godhead of delight?
Love is a flame;—we have beaconed the world's night.
A city:—and we have built it, these and I.
An emperor:—we have taught the world to die.
So, for their sakes I loved, ere I go hence,
And the high cause of Love's magnificence,
And to keep loyalties young, I'll write those names
Golden for ever, eagles, crying flames,
And set them as a banner, that men may know,
To dare the generations, burn, and blow
Out on the wind of Time, shining and streaming. . . .

These I have loved:
          White plates and cups, clean-gleaming,
Ringed with blue lines; and feathery, faery dust;
Wet roofs, beneath the lamp-light; the strong crust
Of friendly bread; and many-tasting food;
Rainbows; and the blue bitter smoke of wood;
And radiant raindrops couching in cool flowers;
And flowers themselves, that sway through sunny hours,
Dreaming of moths that drink them under the moon;
Then, the cool kindliness of sheets, that soon
Smooth away trouble; and the rough male kiss
Of blankets; grainy wood; live hair that is
Shining and free; blue-massing clouds; the keen
Unpassioned beauty of a great machine;
The benison of hot water; furs to touch;
The good smell of old clothes; and other such—
The comfortable smell of friendly fingers,
Hair's fragrance, and the musty reek that lingers
About dead leaves and last year's ferns. . . .

                                      Dear names,
And thousand others throng to me! Royal flames;
Sweet water's dimpling laugh from tap or spring;
Holes in the ground; and voices that do sing:
Voices in laughter, too; and body's pain,
Soon turned to peace; and the deep-panting train;
Firm sands; the little dulling edge of foam
That browns and dwindles as the wave goes home;
And washen stones, gay for an hour; the cold
Graveness of iron; moist black earthen mould;
Sleep; and high places; footprints in the dew;
And oaks; and brown horse-chestnuts, glossy-new;
And new-peeled sticks; and shining pools on grass;—
All these have been my loves. And these shall pass.
Whatever passes not, in the great hour,
Nor all my passion, all my prayers, have power
To hold them with me through the gate of Death.
They'll play deserter, turn with traitor breath,
Break the high bond we made, and sell Love's trust
And sacramental covenant to the dust.

—Oh, never a doubt but, somewhere, I shall wake,
And give what's left of love again, and make
New friends, now strangers. . . .
                              But the best I've known
Stays here, and changes, breaks, grows old, is blown
About the winds of the world, and fades from brains
Of living men, and dies.
                         Nothing remains.

O dear my loves, O faithless, once again
This one last gift I give: that after men
Shall know, and later lovers, far-removed
Praise you, "All these were lovely"; say, "He loved."

ROBINSON JEFFERS
1887–1962

The Eye

The Atlantic is a stormy moat, and the Mediterranean,
The blue pool in the old garden,
More than five thousand years has drunk sacrifice
Of ships and blood and shines in the sun; but here the Pacific:
The ships, planes, wars are perfectly irrelevant.
Neither our present blood-feud with the brave dwarfs
Nor any future world-quarrel of westering
And eastering man, the bloody migrations, greed of power, battle-falcons,
Are a mote of dust in the great scale-pan.
Here from this mountain shore, headland beyond stormy headland
plunging like dolphins through the gray sea-smoke
Into pale sea, look west at the hill of water: it is half the
planet: this dome, this half-globe, this bulging
Eyeball of water, arched over to Asia,
Australia and white Antarctica: those are the eyelids that
never close; this is the staring unsleeping
Eye of the earth, and what it watches is not our wars.

The Bloody Sire

It is not bad. Let them play.
Let the guns bark and the bombing-plane
Speak his prodigious blasphemies.
It is not bad, it is high time,
Stark violence is still the sire of all the world's values.

What but the wolf's tooth chiseled so fine
The fleet limbs of the antelope?
What but fear winged the birds and hunger
Gemmed with such eyes the great goshawk's head?
Violence has been the sire of all the world's values.

Who would remember Helen's face
Lacking the terrible halo of spears?
Who formed Christ but Herod and Caesar,
The cruel and bloody victories of Caesar?
Violence has been the sire of all the world's values.

Never weep, let them play,
Old violence is not too old to beget new values.

EDWIN MUIR
1887–1958

The Road

There is a road that turning always
    Cuts off the country of Again.
Archers stand there on every side
    And as it runs Time's deer is slain,
    And lies where it has lain.

That busy clock shows never an hour.
    All flies and all in flight must tarry.
The hunter shoots the empty air
    Far on before the quarry,
    Which falls though nothing's there to parry.

The lion couching in the centre
    With mountain head and sunset brow
Rolls down the everlasting slope
    Bones picked an age ago,
    And the bones rise up and go.

There the beginning finds the end
    Before beginning ever can be,
And the great runner never leaves
    The starting and the finishing tree,
    The budding and the fading tree.

There the ship sailing safe in harbour
    Long since in many a sea was drowned.
The treasure burning in her hold
    So near will never be found,
    Sunk past all sound.

There a man on a summer evening
    Reclines at ease upon his tomb

And is his mortal effigy.
> And there within the womb,
> The cell of doom,

The ancestral deed is thought and done,
> And in a million Edens fall
A million Adams drowned in darkness
> For small is great and great is small,
> And a blind seed all.

MARIANNE MOORE
1887–1972

Poetry

I, too, dislike it: there are things that are important
> beyond all this fiddle.
Reading it, however, with a perfect contempt for it, one
> discovers in
it after all, a place for the genuine.
> Hands that can grasp, eyes
> that can dilate, hair that can rise
> if it must, these things are important not because a

high-sounding interpretation can be put upon them but
> because they are
useful. When they become so derivative as to become
> unintelligible,
the same thing may be said for all of us, that we
> do not admire what
> we cannot understand: the bat
> holding on upside down or in quest of something to

eat, elephants pushing, a wild horse taking a roll,
> a tire-less-wolf under
a tree, the immovable critic twitching his skin like a
> horse that feels a flea, the base-
ball fan, the statistician—
> nor is it valid
> to discriminate "against business documents and

school-books"; all these phenomena are important. One
            must make a distinction
however: when dragged into prominence by half
            poets, the result is not poetry,
nor till the poets among us can be
    "literalists of
        the imagination"—above
            insolence and triviality and can present

for inspection, imaginary gardens with real toads in
            them, shall we have
    it. In the meantime, if you demand on the one hand,
    the raw material of poetry in
        all its rawness and
        that which is on the other hand
            genuine, then you are interested in poetry.

THOMAS STEARNS ELIOT
1888–1965

The Wind Sprang up at Four O'Clock

The wind sprang up at four o'clock
The wind sprang up and broke the bells
Swinging between life and death
Here, in death's dream kingdom
The waking echo of confusing strife
Is it a dream or something else
When the surface of the blackened river
Is a face that sweats with tears?
I saw across the blackened river
The camp fire shake with alien spears.
Here, across death's other river
The Tartar horsemen shake their spears.

Gerontion

*Thou hast nor youth nor age
But as it were an after dinner sleep
Dreaming of both.*

Here I am, an old man in a dry month,
Being read to by a boy, waiting for rain.
I was neither at the hot gates
Nor fought in the warm rain
Nor knee deep in the salt marsh, heaving a cutlass,
Bitten by flies, fought.
My house is a decayed house,
And the Jew squats on the window sill, the owner,
Spawned in some estaminet of Antwerp,
Blistered in Brussels, patched and peeled in London.
The goat coughs at night in the field overhead;
Rocks, moss, stonecrop, iron, merds.
The woman keeps the kitchen, makes tea,
Sneezes at evening, poking the peevish gutter.
                              I an old man,
A dull head among windy spaces.

Signs are taken for wonders. "We would see a sign!"
The word within a word, unable to speak a word,
Swaddled with darkness. In the juvescence of the year
Came Christ the tiger
In depraved May, dogwood and chestnut, flowering judas,
To be eaten, to be divided, to be drunk
Among whispers; by Mr. Silvero
With caressing hands, at Limoges
Who walked all night in the next room;

By Hakagawa, bowing among the Titians;
By Madame de Tornquist, in the dark room
Shifting the candles; Fräulein von Kulp
Who turned in the hall, one hand on the door. Vacant shuttles
Weave the wind. I have no ghosts,
An old man in a draughty house
Under a windy knob.

After such knowledge, what forgiveness? Think now
History has many cunning passages, contrived corridors
And issues, deceives with whispering ambitions,
Guides us by vanities. Think now
She gives when our attention is distracted
And what she gives, gives with such supple confusions

That the giving famishes the craving. Gives too late
What's not believed in, or if still believed,
In memory only, reconsidered passion. Gives too soon
Into weak hands, what's thought can be dispensed with
Till the refusal propagates a fear. Think
Neither fear nor courage saves us. Unnatural vices
Are fathered by our heroism. Virtues
Are forced upon us by our impudent crimes.
These tears are shaken from the wrath-bearing tree.

The tiger springs in the new year. Us he devours. Think at last
We have not reached conclusion, when I
Stiffen in a rented house. Think at last
I have not made this show purposelessly
And it is not by any concitation
Of the backward devils.
I would meet you upon this honestly.
I that was near your heart was removed therefrom
To lose beauty in terror, terror in inquisition.
I have lost my passion: why should I need to keep it
Since what is kept must be adulterated?
I have lost my sight, smell, hearing, taste and touch:
How should I use them for your closer contact?

These with a thousand small deliberations
Protract the profit of their chilled delirium,
Excite the membrane, when the sense has cooled,
With pungent sauces, multiply variety
In a wilderness of mirrors. What will the spider do,
Suspend its operations, will the weevil
Delay? De Bailhache, Fresca, Mrs. Cammel, whirled
Beyond the circuit of the shuddering Bear
In fractured atoms. Gull against the wind, in the windy straits
Of Belle Isle, or running on the Horn,
White feathers in the snow, the Gulf claims,
And an old man driven by the Trades
To a sleepy corner.
                                        Tenants of the house,
Thoughts of a dry brain in a dry season.

Journey of the Magi

"A cold coming we had of it,
Just the worst time of the year
For a journey, and such a long journey:
The ways deep and the weather sharp,
The very dead of winter."
And the camels galled, sore-footed, refractory,
Lying down in the melting snow.
There were times we regretted
The summer palaces on slopes, the terraces,
And the silken girls bringing sherbet.
Then the camel men cursing and grumbling
And running away, and wanting their liquor and women,
And the night-fires going out, and the lack of shelters,
And the cities hostile and the towns unfriendly
And the villages dirty and charging high prices:
A hard time we had of it.
At the end we preferred to travel all night,
Sleeping in snatches,
With the voices singing in our ears, saying
That this was all folly.

Then at dawn we came down to a temperate valley,
Wet, below the snow line, smelling of vegetation;
With a running stream and a water-mill beating the darkness,
And three trees on the low sky,
And an old white horse galloped away in the meadow.
Then we came to a tavern with vine-leaves over the lintel,
Six hands at an open door dicing for pieces of silver,
And feet kicking the empty wine-skins.
But there was no information, and so we continued
And arrived at evening, not a moment too soon
Finding the place; it was (you may say) satisfactory.

All this was a long time ago, I remember,
And I would do it again, but set down
This set down
This: were we led all that way for
Birth or Death? There was a Birth, certainly,
We had evidence and no doubt. I had seen birth and death
But had thought they were different; this Birth was

Hard and bitter agony for us, like Death, our death.
We returned to our places, these Kingdoms,
But no longer at ease here, in the old dispensation,
With an alien people clutching their gods.
I should be glad of another death.

The Hippopotamus

Similiter et omnes revereantur Diaconos, ut mandatum Jesu Christi; et Episcopum, ut Jesum
Christum, existentem filium Patris; Presbyteros autem, ut concilium Dei et conjunctionem
Apostolorum. Sine his Ecclesia non vocatur; de quibus suadeo vos sic habeo.

S. IGNATII AD TRALLIANOS

And when this epistle is read among you, cause that it be read also in the church of the
Laodiceans.

The broad-backed hippopotamus
Rests on his belly in the mud;
Although he seems so firm to us
He is merely flesh and blood.

Flesh and blood is weak and frail,
Susceptible to nervous shock;
While the True Church can never fail
For it is based upon a rock.

The hippo's feeble steps may err
In compassing material ends,
While the True Church need never stir
To gather in its dividends.

The 'potamus can never reach
The mango on the mango-tree;
But fruits of pomegranate and peach
Refresh the Church from over sea.

At mating time the hippo's voice
Betrays inflexions hoarse and odd,
But every week we hear rejoice
The Church, at being one with God.

The hippopotamus's day
Is passed in sleep; at night he hunts;

God works in a mysterious way—
The Church can sleep and feed at once.

I saw the 'potamus take wing
Ascending from the damp savannas,
And quiring angels round him sing
The praise of God, in loud hosannas.

Blood of the Lamb shall wash him clean
And him shall heavenly arms enfold,
Among the saints he shall be seen
Performing on a harp of gold.

He shall be washed as white as snow,
By all the martyr'd virgins kist,
While the True Church remains below
Wrapt in the old miasmal mist.

The Hollow Men

MISTAH KURTZ—HE DEAD.
A PENNY FOR THE OLD GUY

I

We are the hollow men
We are the stuffed men
Leaning together
Headpiece filled with straw. Alas!
Our dried voices, when

We whisper together
Are quiet and meaningless
As wind in dry grass
Or rats' feet over broken glass
In our dry cellar

Shape without form, shade without colour,
Paralysed force, gesture without motion;

Those who have crossed
With direct eyes, to death's other Kingdom
Remember us—if at all—not as lost

Violent souls, but only
As the hollow men
The stuffed men.

II

Eyes I dare not meet in dreams
In death's dream kingdom
These do not appear:
There, the eyes are
Sunlight on a broken column
There, is a tree swinging
And voices are
In the wind's singing
More distant and more solemn
Than a fading star.

Let me be no nearer
In death's dream kingdom
Let me also wear
Such deliberate disguises
Rat's coat, crowskin, crossed staves
In a field
Behaving as the wind behaves
No nearer—

Not that final meeting
In the twilight kingdom

III

This is the dead land
This is cactus land
Here the stone images
Are raised, here they receive
The supplication of a dead man's hand
Under the twinkle of a fading star.

Is it like this
In death's other kingdom
Waking alone
At the hour when we are
Trembling with tenderness
Lips that would kiss
Form prayers to broken stone.

IV

The eyes are not here
There are no eyes here
In this valley of dying stars
In this hollow valley
This broken jaw of our lost kingdoms

In this last of meeting places
We grope together
And avoid speech
Gathered on this beach of the tumid river

Sightless, unless
The eyes reappear
As the perpetual star
Multifoliate rose
Of death's twilight kingdom
The hope only
Of empty men.

V

Here we go round the prickly pear
Prickly pear prickly pear
Here we go round the prickly pear
At five o'clock in the morning.

Between the idea
And the reality
Between the motion
And the act
Falls the Shadow
                              For Thine is the Kingdom

Between the conception
And the creation
Between the emotion
And the response
Falls the Shadow
                                        Life is very long

Between the desire
And the spasm

Between the potency
And the existence
Between the essence
And the descent
Falls the Shadow

For Thine is the Kingdom

For Thine is
Life is
For Thine is the

This is the way the world ends
This is the way the world ends
This is the way the world ends
Not with a bang but a whimper.

JOHN CROWE RANSOM
1888–1974

Captain Carpenter

Captain Carpenter rose up in his prime
Put on his pistols and went riding out
But had got wellnigh nowhere at that time
Till he fell in with ladies in a rout.

It was a pretty lady and all her train
That played with him so sweetly but before
An hour she'd taken a sword with all her main
And twined him of his nose for evermore.

Captain Carpenter mounted up one day
And rode straightway into a stranger rogue
That looked unchristian but be that as may
The Captain did not wait upon prologue.

But drew upon him out of his great heart
The other swung against him with a club
And cracked his two legs at the shinny part
And let him roll and stick like any tub.

Captain Carpenter rode many a time
From male and female took he sundry harms
He met the wife of Satan crying "I'm
The she-wolf bids you shall bear no more arms."

Their strokes and counters whistled in the wind
I wish he had delivered half his blows
But where she should have made off like a hind
The bitch bit off his arms at the elbows.

And Captain Carpenter parted with his ears
To a black devil that used him in this wise
O Jesus ere his threescore and ten years
Another had plucked out his sweet blue eyes.

Captain Carpenter got up on his roan
And sallied from the gate in hell's despite
I heard him asking in the grimmest tone
If any enemy yet there was to fight?

"To any adversary it is fame
If he risk to be wounded by my tongue
Or burnt in two beneath my red heart's flame
Such are the perils he is cast among.

"But if he can he has a pretty choice
From an anatomy with little to lose
Whether he cut my tongue and take my voice
Or whether it be my round red heart he choose."

It was the neatest knave that ever was seen
Stepping in perfume from his lady's bower
Who at this word put in his merry mien
And fell on Captain Carpenter like a tower.

I would not knock old fellows in the dust
But there lay Captain Carpenter on his back
His weapons were the old heart in his bust
And a blade shook between rotten teeth alack.

The rogue in scarlet and grey soon knew his mind
He wished to get his trophy and depart

With gentle apology and touch refined
He pierced him and produced the Captain's heart.

God's mercy rest on Captain Carpenter now
I thought him Sirs an honest gentleman
Citizen husband soldier and scholar enow
Let jangling kites eat of him if they can.

But God's deep curses follow after those
That shore him of his goodly nose and ears
His legs and strong arms at the two elbows
And eyes that had not watered seventy years

The curse of hell upon the sleek upstart
That got the Captain finally on his back
And took the red red vitals of his heart
And made the kites to whet their beaks clack clack.

CONRAD AIKEN
1889–1973

Music I Heard

Music I heard with you was more than music,
And bread I broke with you was more than bread;
Now that I am without you, all is desolate;
All that was once so beautiful is dead.

Your hands once touched this table and this silver,
And I have seen your fingers hold this glass.
These things do not remember you, beloved,
And yet your touch upon them will not pass.

For it was in my heart you moved among them,
And blessed them with your hands and with your eyes;
And in my heart they will remember always,—
They knew you once, O beautiful and wise.

Morning Song of Senlin

It is morning, Senlin says, and in the morning
When the light drips through the shutters like the dew,
I arise, I face the sunrise,
And do the things my fathers learned to do.
Stars in the purple dusk above the rooftops
Pale in a saffron mist and seem to die,
And I myself on a swiftly tilting planet
Stand before a glass and tie my tie.

Vine leaves tap my window,
Dew-drops sing to the garden stones,
The robin chirps in the chinaberry tree
Repeating three clear tones.

It is morning. I stand by the mirror
And tie my tie once more,
While waves far off in a pale rose twilight
Crash on a white sand shore.
I stand by a mirror and comb my hair:
How small and white my face!—
The green earth tilts through a sphere of air
And bathes in a flame of space.

There are houses hanging above the stars
And stars hung under a sea . . .
And a sun far off in a shell of silence
Dapples my walls for me . . .

It is morning, Senlin says, and in the morning
Should I not pause in the light to remember god?
Upright and firm I stand on a star unstable,
He is immense and lonely as a cloud.
I will dedicate this moment before my mirror
To him alone; for him I will comb my hair.
Accept these humble offerings, cloud of silence!
I will think of you as I descend the stair.

Vine leaves tap my window,
The snail-track shines on the stones,
Dew-drops flash from the chinaberry tree
Repeating two clear tones.

It is morning, I awake from a bed of silence,
Shining I rise from the starless waters of sleep.
The walls are about me still as in the evening,
I am the same, and the same name still I keep.

The earth revolves with me, yet makes no motion,
The stars pale silently in a coral sky.
In a whistling void I stand before my mirror,
Unconcerned, and tie my tie.

There are horses neighing on far-off hills
Tossing their long white manes,
And mountains flash in the rose-white dusk,
Their shoulders black with rains . . .
It is morning. I stand by the mirror
And surprise my soul once more;
The blue air rushes above my ceiling,
There are suns beneath my floor . . .

. . . It is morning, Senlin says, I ascend from darkness
And depart on the winds of space for I know not where,
My watch is wound, a key is in my pocket,
And the sky is darkened as I descend the stair.
There are shadows across the windows, clouds in heaven,
And a god among the stars; and I will go
Thinking of him as I might think of daybreak
And humming a tune I know . . .

Vine leaves tap at the window,
Dew-drops sing to the garden stones,
The robin chirps in the chinaberry tree
Repeating three clear tones.

EDNA ST. VINCENT MILLAY
1892–1951

Recuerdo

We were very tired, we were very merry—
We had gone back and forth all night on the ferry.
It was bare and bright, and smelled like a stable—
But we looked into a fire, we leaned across a table,
We lay on a hill-top underneath the moon;
And the whistles kept blowing, and the dawn came soon.

We were very tired, we were very merry—
We had gone back and forth all night on the ferry;
And you ate an apple, and I ate a pear,
From a dozen of each we had bought somewhere;
And the sky went wan, and the wind came cold,
And the sun rose dripping, a bucketful of gold.

We were very tired, we were very merry,
We had gone back and forth all night on the ferry.
We hailed, "Good-morrow, mother!" to a shawl-covered head,
And bought a morning paper, which neither of us read;
And she wept, "God bless you!" for the apples and pears,
And we gave her all our money but our subway fares.

JOHN PEALE BISHOP
1892–1944

The Return

Night and we heard heavy and cadenced hoofbeats
Of troops departing; the last cohorts left
By the North Gate. That night some listened late
Leaning their eyelids toward Septentrion.

Morning flared and the young tore down the trophies
And warring ornaments: arches were strong
And in the sun but stone; no longer conquest
Circled our columns; all our state was down

In fragments. In the dust, old men with tufted
Eyebrows whiter than sunbaked faces gulped
As it fell. But they no more than we remembered
The old sea-fights, the soldiers' names and sculptors'.

We did not know the end was coming: nor why
It came; only that long before the end
Were many wanted to die. Then vultures starved
And sailed more slowly in the sky.

We still had taxes. Salt was high. The soldiers
Gone. Now there was much drinking and lewd
Houses all night loud with riot. But only
For a time. Soon the taverns had no roofs.

Strangely it was the young, the almost boys,
Who first abandoned hope; the old still lived
A little, at last a little lived in eyes.
It was the young whose child did not survive.

Some slept beneath the simulacra, until
The gods' faces froze. Then was fear.
Some had response in dreams, but morning restored
Interrogation. Then O then, O ruins!

Temples of Neptune invaded by the sea
And dolphins streaked like streams sportive
As sunlight rode and over the rushing floors
The sea unfurled and what was blue raced silver.

ARCHIBALD MacLEISH
1892–1982

The End of the World

Quite unexpectedly, as Vasserot
The armless ambidextrian was lighting
A match between his great and second toe,
And Ralph the lion was engaged in biting

The neck of Madame Sossman while the drum
Pointed, and Teeny was about to cough
In waltz-time swinging Jocko by the thumb—
Quite unexpectedly the top blew off:

And there, there overhead, there, there hung over
Those thousands of white faces, those dazed eyes,
There in the starless dark the poise, the hover,
There with vast wings across the cancelled skies,
There in the sudden blackness the black pall
Of nothing, nothing, nothing—nothing at all.

WILFRED OWEN
1893–1918

Greater Love

Red lips are not so red
  As the stained stones kissed by the English dead.
Kindness of wooed and wooer
Seems shame to their love pure.
O Love, your eyes lose lure
  When I behold eyes blinded in my stead!

Your slender attitude
  Trembles not exquisite like limbs knife-skewed,
Rolling and rolling there
Where God seems not to care;
Till the fierce Love they bear
  Cramps them in death's extreme decrepitude.

Your voice sings not so soft,—
  Though even as wind murmuring through raftered loft,—
Your dear voice is not dear,
Gentle, and evening clear,
As theirs whom none now hear,
  Now earth has stopped their piteous mouths that coughed.

Heart, you were never hot,
  Nor large, nor full like hearts made great with shot;

And though your hand be pale,
Paler are all which trail
Your cross through flame and hail:
Weep, you may weep, for you may touch them not.

Arms and the Boy

Let the boy try along this bayonet-blade
How cold steel is, and keen with hunger of blood;
Blue with all malice, like a madman's flash;
And thinly drawn with famishing for flesh.

Lend him to stroke these blind, blunt bullet-heads
Which long to nuzzle in the hearts of lads,
Or give him cartridges of fine zinc teeth,
Sharp with the sharpness of grief and death.

For his teeth seem for laughing round an apple.
There lurk no claws behind his fingers supple;
And God will grow no talons at his heels,
Nor antlers through the thickness of his curls.

The Show

We have fallen in the dreams the ever-living
Breathe on the tarnished mirror of the world,
And then smooth out with ivory hands and sigh.

—*W. B. Yeats*

My soul looked down from a vague height with Death,
As unremembering how I rose or why,
And saw a sad land, weak with sweats of dearth,
Gray, cratered like the moon with hollow woe,
And pitted with great pocks and scabs of plagues.
Across its beard, that horror of harsh wire,
There moved thin caterpillars, slowly uncoiled.
It seemed they pushed themselves to be as plugs
Of ditches, where they writhed and shrivelled, killed.
By them had slimy paths been trailed and scraped
Round myriad warts that might be little hills.
From gloom's last dregs these long-strung creatures crept,
And vanished out of dawn down hidden holes.

(And smell came up from those foul openings
As out of mouths, or deep wounds deepening.)
On dithering feet upgathered, more and more,
Brown strings, towards strings of gray, with bristling spines,
All migrants from green fields, intent on mire.
Those that were gray, of more abundant spawns,
Ramped on the rest and ate them and were eaten.
I saw their bitten backs curve, loop, and straighten,
I watched those agonies curl, lift, and flatten.
Whereat, in terror what that sight might mean,
I reeled and shivered earthward like a feather.
And Death fell with me, like a deepening moan.
And He, picking a manner of worm, which half had hid
Its bruises in the earth, but crawled no further,
Showed me its feet, the feet of many men,
And the fresh-severed head of it, my head.

Anthem for Doomed Youth

What passing-bells for these who die as cattle?
Only the monstrous anger of the guns.
Only the stuttering rifles' rapid rattle
Can patter out their hasty orisons.
No mockeries for them; no prayers nor bells,
Nor any voice of mourning save the choirs,—
The shrill, demented choirs of wailing shells;
And bugles calling for them from sad shires.

What candles may be held to speed them all?
Not in the hands of boys, but in their eyes
Shall shine the holy glimmers of good-byes.
The pallor of girls' brows shall be their pall;
Their flowers the tenderness of patient minds,
And each slow dusk a drawing-down of blinds.

Strange Meeting

It seemed that out of the battle I escaped
Down some profound dull tunnel, long since scooped
Through granites which Titanic wars had groined.
Yet also there encumbered sleepers groaned,
Too fast in thought or death to be bestirred.
Then, as I probed them, one sprang up, and stared

With piteous recognition in fixed eyes,
Lifting distressful hands as if to bless.
And by his smile, I knew that sullen hall;
By his dead smile I knew we stood in Hell.
With a thousand pains that vision's face was grained;
Yet no blood reached there from the upper ground,
And no guns thumped, or down the flues made moan.
"Strange, friend," I said, "here is no cause to mourn."
"None," said the other, "save the undone years,
The hopelessness. Whatever hope is yours,
Was my life also; I went hunting wild
After the wildest beauty in the world,
Which lies not calm in eyes, or braided hair,
But mocks the steady running of the hour,
And if it grieves, grieves richlier than here.
For by my glee might many men have laughed,
And of my weeping something has been left,
Which must die now. I mean the truth untold,
The pity of war, the pity war distilled.
Now men will go content with what we spoiled,
Or, discontent, boil bloody, and be spilled.
They will be swift with swiftness of the tigress,
None will break ranks, though nations trek from progress.
Courage was mine, and I had mystery,
Wisdom was mine, and I had mastery;
To miss the march of this retreating world
Into vain citadels that are not walled.
Then when much blood had clogged their chariot-wheels
I would go up and wash them from sweet wells,
Even with truths that lie too deep for taint.
I would have poured my spirit without stint
But not through wounds; not on the cess of war.
Foreheads of men have bled where no wounds were.
I am the enemy you killed, my friend.
I knew you in this dark; for so you frowned
Yesterday through me as you jabbed and killed.
I parried; but my hands were loath and cold.
Let us sleep now. . . ."

E. E. CUMMINGS
1894–1962

What If a Much of a Which of a Wind

what if a much of a which of a wind
gives the truth to summer's lie;
bloodies with dizzying leaves the sun
and yanks immortal stars awry?
Blow king to beggar and queen to seem
(blow friend to fiend: blow space to time)
—when skies are hanged and oceans drowned,
the single secret will still be man

what if a keen of a lean wind flays
screaming hills with sleet and snow:
strangles valleys by ropes of thing
and stifles forests in white ago?
Blow hope to terror; blow seeing to blind
(blow pity to envy and soul to mind)
—whose hearts are mountains, roots are trees,
it's they shall cry hello to the spring

what if a dawn of a doom of a dream
bites this universe in two,
peels forever out of his grave
and sprinkles nowhere with me and you?
Blow soon to never and never to twice
(blow life to isn't: blow death to was)
—all nothing's only our hugest home;
the most who die, the more we live

I Sing of Olaf

i sing of Olaf glad and big
whose warmest heart recoiled at war:
a conscientious object-or

his wellbelovéd colonel (trig
westpointer most succinctly bred)
took erring Olaf soon in hand;
but—though an host of overjoyed

noncoms (first knocking on the head
him) do through icy waters roll
that helplessness which others stroke
with brushes recently employed
anent this muddy toilet bowl,
while kindred intellects evoke
allegiance per blunt instruments—
Olaf (being to all intents
a corpse and wanting any rag
upon what God unto him gave)
responds, without getting annoyed
"I will not kiss your f.ing flag"

straightway the silver bird looked grave
(departing hurriedly to shave)

but—though all kinds of officers
(a yearning nation's blueeyed pride)
their passive prey did kick and curse
until for wear their clarion
voices and boots were much the worse,
and egged the firstclassprivates on
his rectum wickedly to tease
by means of skilfully applied
bayonets roasted hot with heat—
Olaf (upon what were once knees)
does almost ceaselessly repeat
"there is some s. I will not eat"
our president, being of which
assertions duly notified
threw the yellowsonofabitch
into a dungeon, where he died

Christ (of His mercy infinite)
i pray to see; and Olaf, too

preponderatingly because
unless statistics lie he was
more brave than me: more blond than you.

ROBERT GRAVES
1895–1985

Interruption

If ever against this easy blue and silver
Hazed-over countryside of thoughtfulness
Far behind in the mind and above,
Boots from before and below approach tramping,
Watch how their premonition will display
A forward countryside, low in the distance,
A picture-postcard square of June grass,
Will warm a summer season, trim the hedges,
Cast the river about on either flank,
Start the late cuckoo emptily calling,
Invent a rambling tale of moles and voles,
Furnish a path with stiles.
Watch how the field will broaden, the feet nearing
Sprout with great dandelions and buttercups,
Widen and heighten. The blue and silver
Fogs at the border of this all-grass.
Interruption looms gigantified,
Lurches against, treads thundering through,
Blots the landscape, scatters all,
Roars and rumbles like a dark tunnel,
Is gone.
        The picture-postcard grass and trees
Swim back to central: it is a large patch,
It is a modest, failing patch of green,
The postage-stamp of its departure,
Clouded with blue and silver, closing in now
To a plain countryside of less and less,
Unpeopled and unfeathered blue and silver,
Before, behind, above.

The Legs

There was this road,
And it led up-hill,
And it led down-hill,
And round and in and out.

And the traffic was legs,
Legs from the knees down,
Coming and going,
Never pausing.

And the gutters gurgled
With the rain's overflow,
And the sticks on the pavement
Blindly tapped and tapped.

What drew the legs along
Was the never-stopping,
And the senseless, frightening
Fate of being legs.

Legs for the road,
The road for legs,
Resolutely nowhere
In both directions.

My legs at least
Were not in that rout:
On grass by the road-side
Entire I stood,

Watching the unstoppable
Legs go by
With never a stumble
Between step and step.

Though my smile was broad
The legs could not see,
Though my laugh was loud
The legs could not hear.

My head dizzied, then:
I wondered suddenly,
Might I too be a walker
From the knees down?

Gently I touched my shins.
The doubt unchained them:

They had run in twenty puddles
Before I regained them.

To Juan at the Winter Solstice

There is one story and one story only
That will prove worth your telling,
Whether as learned bard or gifted child;
To it all lines or lesser gauds belong
That startle with their shining
Such common stories as they stray into.

Is it of trees you tell, their months and virtues,
Of strange beasts that beset you,
Of birds that croak at you the Triple will?
Or of the Zodiac and how slow it turns
Below the Boreal Crown,
Prison of all true kings that ever reigned?

Water to water, ark again to ark,
From woman back to woman:
So each new victim treads unfalteringly
The never altered circuit of his fate,
Bringing twelve peers as witness
Both to his starry rise and starry fall.

Or is it of the Virgin's silver beauty,
All fish below the thighs?
She in her left hand bears a leafy quince;
When with her right she crooks a finger, smiling,
How may the King hold back?
Royally then he barters life for love.

Or of the undying snake from chaos hatched,
Whose coils contain the ocean,
Into whose chops with naked sword he springs,
Then in black water, tangled by the reeds,
Battles three days and nights,
To be spewed up beside her scalloped shore?

Much snow is falling, winds roar hollowly,
The owl hoots from the elder,

Fear in your heart cries to the loving-cup:
Sorrow to sorrow as the sparks fly upward.
The log groans and confesses
There is one story and one story only.

Dwell on her graciousness, dwell on her smiling,
Do not forget what flowers
The great boar trampled down in ivy time.
Her brow was creamy as the long ninth wave,
Her sea-blue eyes were wild.
But nothing promised that is not performed.

F. R. HIGGINS
1896–1941

Song for the Clatter-Bones

God rest that Jewy woman,
Queen Jezebel, the bitch
Who peeled the clothes from her shoulder-bones
Down to her spent teats
As she stretched out of the window
Among the geraniums, where
She chaffed and laughed like one half daft
Titivating her painted hair—

King Jehu he drove to her,
She tipped him a fancy beck;
But he from his knacky side-car spoke,
"Who'll break that dewlapped neck?"
And so she was thrown from the window;
Like Lucifer she fell
Beneath the feet of the horses and they beat
The light out of Jezebel.

That corpse wasn't planted in clover;
Ah, nothing of her was found
Save those grey bones that Hare-foot Mike
Gave me for their lovely sound;

And as once her dancing body
Made star-lit princes sweat,
So I'll just clack: though her ghost lacks a back
There's music in the old bones yet.

ALLEN TATE
1899–1979

The Mediterranean

QUEM DAS FINEM, REX MAGNE, DOLORUM?

Where we went in the boat was a long bay
A slingshot wide, walled in by towering stone—
Peaked margin of antiquity's delay,
And we went there out of time's monotone:

Where we went in the black hull no light moved
But a gull white-winged along the feckless wave,
The breeze, unseen but fierce as a body loved,
That boat drove onward like a willing slave:

Where we went in the small ship the seaweed
Parted and gave to us the murmuring shore
And we made feast and in our secret need
Devoured the very plates Aeneas bore:

Where derelict you see through the low twilight
The green coast that you, thunder-tossed, would win
Drop sail, and hastening to drink all night
Eat dish and bowl—to take that sweet land in!

Where we feasted and caroused on the sandless
Pebbles, affecting our day of piracy,
What prophecy of eaten plates could landless
Wanderers fulfil by the ancient sea?

We for that time might taste the famous age
Eternal here yet hidden from our eyes
When lust of power undid its stuffless rage;
They, in a wineskin, bore earth's paradise.

Let us lie down once more by the breathing side
Of Ocean, where our live forefathers sleep
As if the Known Sea still were a month wide—
Atlantis howls but is no longer steep!

What country shall we conquer, what fair land
Unman our conquest and locate our blood?
We've cracked the hemispheres with careless hand!
Now, from the Gates of Hercules we flood

Westward, westward till the barbarous brine
Whelms us to the tired world where tasseling corn,
Fat beans, grapes sweeter than muscadine
Rot on the vine: in that land were we born.

HART CRANE
1899–1932

To Brooklyn Bridge

How many dawns, chill from his rippling rest
The seagull's wings shall dip and pivot him,
Shedding white rings of tumult, building high
Over the chained bay waters Liberty—

Then, with inviolate curve, forsake our eyes
As apparitional as sails that cross
Some page of figures to be filed away;
—Till elevators drop us from our day . . .

I think of cinemas, panoramic sleights
With multitudes bent toward some flashing scene
Never disclosed, but hastened to again,
Foretold to other eyes on the same screen;

And Thee, across the harbor, silver-paced
As though the sun took step of thee, yet left
Some motion ever unspent in thy stride,—
Implicitly thy freedom staying thee!

Out of some subway scuttle, cell or loft
A bedlamite speeds to thy parapets,
Tilting there momently, shrill shirt ballooning,
A jest falls from the speechless caravan.

Down Wall, from girder into street noon leaks,
A rip-tooth of the sky's acetylene;
All afternoon the cloud-flown derricks turn . . .
Thy cables breathe the North Atlantic still.

And obscure as that heaven of the Jews,
Thy guerdon . . . Accolade thou dost bestow
Of anonymity time cannot raise:
Vibrant reprieve and pardon thou dost show.

O harp and altar, of the fury fused,
(How could mere toil align thy choiring strings!)
Terrific threshold of the prophet's pledge,
Prayer of pariah, and the lover's cry,—

Again the traffic lights that skim thy swift
Unfractioned idiom, immaculate sigh of stars,
Beading thy path—condense eternity:
And we have seen night lifted in thine arms.

Under thy shadow by the piers I waited;
Only in darkness is thy shadow clear.
The City's fiery parcels all undone,
Already snow submerges an iron year . . .

O Sleepless as the river under thee,
Vaulting the sea, the prairies' dreaming sod,
Unto us lowliest sometime sweep, descend
And of the curveship lend a myth to God.

Voyages (II)

And yet this great wink of eternity,
Of rimless floods, unfettered leewardings,
Samite sheeted and processioned where
Her undinal vast belly moonward bends,
Laughing the wrapt inflections of our love;

Take this Sea, whose diapason knells
On scrolls of silver snowy sentences,
The sceptred terror of whose sessions rends
As her demeanors motion well or ill,
All but the pieties of lovers' hands.

And onward, as bells off San Salvador
Salute the crocus lustres of the stars,
In these poinsettia meadows of her tides,—
Adagios of islands, O my Prodigal,
Complete the dark confessions her veins spell.

Mark how her turning shoulders wind the hours,
And hasten while her penniless rich palms
Pass superscription of bent foam and wave,—
Hasten, while they are true,—sleep, death, desire,
Close round one instant in one floating flower.

Bind us in time, O Seasons clear, and awe.
O minstrel galleons of Carib fire,
Bequeath us to no earthly shore until
Is answered in the vortex of our grave
The seal's wide spindrift gaze toward paradise.

For the Marriage of Faustus and Helen (III)

Capped arbiter of beauty in this street
That narrows darkly into motor dawn,—
You, here beside me, delicate ambassador
Of intricate slain numbers that arise
In whispers, naked of steel;

                    religious gunman!
Who faithfully, yourself, will fall too soon,
And in other ways than as the wind settles
On the sixteen thrifty bridges of the city:
Let us unbind our throats of fear and pity.

                              We even,
Who drove speediest destruction
In corymbulous formations of mechanics,—
Who hurried the hill breezes, spouting malice
Plangent over meadows, and looked down
On rifts of torn and empty houses

Like old women with teeth unjubilant
That waited faintly, briefly and in vain:

We know, eternal gunman, our flesh remembers
The tensile boughs, the nimble blue plateaus,
The mounted, yielding cities of the air!
That saddled sky that shook down vertical
Repeated play of fire—no hypogeum
Of wave or rock was good against one hour.

We did not ask for that, but have survived,
And will persist to speak again before
All stubble streets that have not curved
To memory, or known the ominous lifted arm
That lowers down the arc of Helen's brow
To saturate with blessing and dismay.

A goose, tobacco and cologne—
Three winged and gold-shod prophecies of heaven,
The lavish heart shall always have to leaven
And spread with bells and voices, and atone
The abating shadows of our conscript dust.

Anchises' navel, dripping of the sea,—
The hands Erasmus dipped in gleaming tides,
Gathered the voltage of blown blood and vine;
Delve upward for the new and scattered wine,
O brother-thief of time, that we recall.
Laugh out the meagre penance of their days
Who dare not share with us the breath released,
The substance drilled and spent beyond repair
For golden, or the shadow of gold hair.

Distinctly praise the years, whose volatile
Blamed bleeding hands extend and thresh the height
The imagination spans beyond despair,
Outpacing bargain, vocable and prayer.

Emblems of Conduct

By a peninsula the wanderer sat and sketched
The uneven valley graves. While the apostle gave
Alms to the meek the volcano burst
With sulphur and aureate rocks . . .
For joy rides in stupendous coverings
Luring the living into spiritual gates.

Orators follow the universe
And radio the complete laws to the people.
The apostle conveys thought through discipline.
Bowls and cups fill historians with adorations,—
Dull lips commemorating spiritual gates.

The wanderer later chose this spot of rest
Where marble clouds support the sea
And where was finally borne a chosen hero.
By that time summer and smoke were past.
Dolphins still played, arching the horizons,
But only to build memories of spiritual gates.

OSCAR WILLIAMS
1900–1964

The Last Supper

I

Apostles of the hidden sun
Are come unto the room of breath
Hung with the banging blinds of death,
The body twelve, the spirit one,
Far as the eye, in earth arrayed,
The night shining, the supper laid.

II

The wine shone on the table that evening of history
Like an enormous ruby in the bauble and mystery.

In the glowing walls of the flickering decanter
There moved His face as at the world's center.

The hands of Judas showed up red and hurried
And the light hit them so, like a cross carried.

The faces of the others were there and moving
In the crystal of the dome, swiftly hovering.

The saints, under a lens, shrunken to pigmies,
Gesticulated in birds or in colored enigmas.

Outside there was a storm, the sound of temblors,
The blood bubbled and sprang into the tumblers.

When the morning came like a white wall of stone,
The day lay in the glass and the blood was gone.

I Sing an Old Song

I sing an old song, bird on a charcoal bough,
Silver voice on the black black bough, singing,
Rolling heirloom eyes, burning holes in time,
Drenching the flank of nearness with drip-music:
The disturbed owner who hides everywhere
Lumbers through the miles of thick indignation:
The subconscious parts the nap-gold of afternoon.

I sing an old song, bird scything the silence,
Bundling sabres at the cornerstone of sense:
Bird, pulley on a hillheap of elves' eyelashes,
Silver piston sunk to a bud on the bough,
Sing, bird, sing, from the black black bough,
Shake the enormous atmosphere from your small fist
Of body, tear the colossal ear of the all around
Hanging loosely, like forest outside a window:
Open all the fluteholes of days until the world
Weeps music, and sweats light from every facet,
And tumbles to the smoking knees of its orbit.

I sing an old song, bead in the hair of the park,
Bird-knot in the weave of leaves, nugget in sieve

Straining gravel of Utopia to shining beginnings,
Deed, navel of matter, fleck of the future,
Knuckle knock on finality, sing, bird, sing:
Ride the groundswell of heartbreak, tap thick wrist
Of branch, lump of utterance in the cup of sunlight
Melt into the sweetness of reality, O:
Sprinkle effigies on the gauze of stillness,
Aim your gold beak from the nest, from the crook
Of the leafy black arm, toward the poised sun
Swing girders from your beak through tin pretense
Into the underground room of man, the pallid palace.

I sing an old song, bird, toe-hold of song on bough,
Bundle in the bush of radiance: birth-cry of poem!

Dwarf of Disintegration

I

WHO is it runs through the many-storied mansion of myth
With the exaggerated child's-head among pillars and palings,
Holding in his grip the balloons of innumerable windows
And chased by the flowing malevolent army of the ceilings?

It is the dwarf, the yellow dwarf, with the minted cheeks,
With the roots of the fingers, with the wafer-thin cry,
In a maze of walls, lost in the nurseries of definition—
Shadows dance on shins of trumpets in a waning sky.

Voices are wired in the walls, rats are gnawing rumors,
The throat of music is bursting with the leadpipes of lust,
And the giant's face on the dwarf's shoulders is frightened
As the battle sounds strike the panes from the near-by past.

The pillars in the palace are reclining about like pistons:
The horses of parenthesis have run away into the woods:
The king is caught on the vast flypaper of the people:
There are holes as big as hovels in the wall of platitude.

The queen is ill from planting the garden with progeny
And her eyes are crossed off by vicious marks from her face:
She telephones the dwarf who puts his head in the instrument
To find his features come out in glacial coal-bins of space.

The orgasms of distant guns attack at the lustful curtains
And soldiers are standing about in historical knots of lies
Warming frozen tag-ends of lives around the spontaneous
Combustion of bosses who are stoking hollows of hired eyes.

The swine bulge in the snake bellies of the telegraph wires
And bellow under flat clouds of ceilings in the interior;
Communication swallows the quicksilver swords of distance;
Headlines perform, in squadrons of plumes, on the warriors.

But the draughty palace of fable is full of feeble splendor:
The yellow dwarf now in possession of knowing documents
Runs after the newspapers cackling on the edge of freedom—
The golden cupboards tremble for the aging sentiments.

The music of battlefields exhilarates the hidden overhead
And injects into the air a breakdown sense of release,
And the numerals wriggle off the lock boxes of the world
Unloosing a swarm of the venomous vultures of the peace.

But the dwarf, the yellow dwarf, with sunspots for eyes
Is hunting in the archives in the moth holes in the palace,
And he tightens the torture boot around the spinal column,
The steel twilight gleaming with the sweat of his malice.

II

Now that the battle is on, keep off the palace grounds,
You can hear the dwarf rummaging in the elephant inside:
It's better to draw a curtain of birds around your eyes—
Fall into the picture book under the thumb of a landslide—

Than to come upon spiders eating the iris of the eyeball,
Glimpse the yellow dwarf digesting the members of princes,
Or see famous paintings loll, like tongues, from their frames
Into a roomful of heroes pretending to harass pretenses.

The sagging structure propped between thought and thinker,
The gilded lawns flow on under the smokescreen of the laws:
The allover attack of a decaying body infiltrates to the atom,
Even the beast in the violin hangs out with lopped-off paws.

Run! run into the first thicket of verbs, the nest of deeds!
Place a skyline between yourself and the grandiose emblem!
For the inquisition wears the hypocritical jowls of a palace,
There's nothing here to salvage, and yours is another problem.

OGDEN NASH
1902–1971

The Sea-Gull

Hark to the whimper of the sea-gull;
He weeps because he's not an ea-gull.
Suppose you were, you silly sea-gull,
Could you explain it to your she-gull?

The Turtle

The turtle lives 'twixt plated decks
Which practically conceal its sex.
I think it clever of the turtle
In such a fix to be so fertile.

Portrait of the Artist as a Prematurely Old Man

It is common knowledge to every schoolboy and even every Bachelor
    of Arts,
That all sin is divided into two parts.
One kind of sin is called a sin of commission, and that is very important,
And it is what you are doing when you are doing something you ortant,
And the other kind of sin is just the opposite and is called a sin of omission
    and is equally bad in the eyes of all right-thinking people, from Billy
    Sunday to Buddha,
And it consists of not having done something you shudda.
I might as well give you my opinion of these two kinds of sin as long as, in a
    way, against each other we are pitting them,
And that is, don't bother your head about sins of commission because
    however sinful, they must at least be fun or else you wouldn't be
    committing them.
It is the sin of omission, the second kind of sin,
That lays eggs under your skin.
The way you get really painfully bitten

Is by the insurance you haven't taken out and the checks you haven't added
   up the stubs of and the appointments you haven't kept and the bills you
   haven't paid and the letters you haven't written.
Also, about sins of omission there is one particularly painful lack of beauty,
Namely, it isn't as though it had been a riotous red letter day or night every
   time you neglected to do your duty;
You didn't get a wicked forbidden thrill
Every time you let a policy lapse or forgot to pay a bill;
You didn't slap the lads in the tavern on the back and loudly cry Whee,
Let's all fail to write just one more letter before we go home, and this round
   of unwritten letters is on me.
No, you never get any fun
Out of the things you haven't done,
But they are the things that I do not like to be amid,
Because the suitable things you didn't do give you a lot more trouble than
   the unsuitable things you did.
The moral is that it is probably better not to sin at all, but if some kind of
   sin you must be pursuing,
Well, remember to do it by doing rather than by not doing.

Reflections on Ice-Breaking

    Candy   But liquor
    Is dandy   Is quicker.

C. DAY LEWIS
1904–1972

Consider These, for We Have Condemned Them

Consider these, for we have condemned them;
Leaders to no sure land, guides their bearings lost
Or in league with robbers have reversed the signposts,
Disrespectful to ancestors, irresponsible to heirs.
Born barren, a freak growth, root in rubble,
Fruitlessly blossoming, whose foliage suffocates,
Their sap is sluggish, they reject the sun.

The man with his tongue in his cheek, the woman
With her heart in the wrong place, unhandsome, unwholesome;

Have exposed the new-born to worse than weather,
Exiled the honest and sacked the seer.
These drowned the farms to form a pleasure-lake,
In time of drought they drain the reservoir
Through private pipes for baths and sprinklers.

Getters not begetters; gainers not beginners;
Whiners, no winners; no triers, betrayers;
Who steer by no star, whose moon means nothing.
Daily denying, unable to dig:
At bay in villas from blood relations,
Counters of spoons and content with cushions
They pray for peace, they hand down disaster.

They that take the bribe shall perish by the bribe,
Dying of dry rot, ending in asylums,
A curse to children, a charge on the state.
But still their fears and frenzies infect us;
Drug nor isolation will cure this cancer:
It is now or never, the hour of the knife,
The break with the past, the major operation.

RICHARD EBERHART
1904–2005

The Groundhog

In June, amid the golden fields,
I saw a groundhog lying dead.
Dead lay he; my senses shook,
And mind outshot our naked frailty.
There lowly in the vigorous summer
His form began its senseless change,
And made my senses waver dim
Seeing nature ferocious in him.
Inspecting close his maggots' might
And seething cauldron of his being,
Half with loathing, half with a strange love,
I poked him with an angry stick.

The fever arose, became a flame
And Vigour circumscribed the skies,
Immense energy in the sun,
And through my frame a sunless trembling.
My stick had done nor good nor harm.
Then stood I silent in the day
Watching the object, as before;
And kept my reverence for knowledge
Trying for control, to be still,
To quell the passion of the blood;
Until I had bent down on my knees
Praying for joy in the sight of decay.
And so I left; and I returned
In Autumn strict of eye, to see
The sap gone out of the groundhog,
But the bony sodden hulk remained.
But the year had lost its meaning,
And in intellectual chains
I lost both love and loathing,
Mured up in the wall of wisdom.
Another summer took the fields again
Massive and burning, full of life,
But when I chanced upon the spot
There was only a little hair left,
And bones bleaching in the sunlight
Beautiful as architecture;
I watched them like a geometer,
And cut a walking stick from a birch.
It has been three years, now.
There is no sign of the groundhog.
I stood there in the whirling summer,
My hand capped a withered heart,
And thought of China and of Greece,
Of Alexander in his tent;
Of Montaigne in his tower,
Of Saint Theresa in her wild lament.

PETER QUENNELL
1905–1993

The Flight Into Egypt

Within Heaven's circle I had not guessed at this,
I had not guessed at pleasure such as this,
So sharp a pleasure,
That, like a lamp burning in foggy night,
Makes its own orb and sphere of flowing gold
And tents itself in light.

Going before you, now how many days,
Thoughts, all turned back like birds against the wind,
Wheeled sullenly towards my Father's house,
Considered his blind presence and the gathered, bustling pæan,
The affluence of his sweetness, his grace and unageing might.

My flesh glowed then in the shadow of a loose cloak
And my brightness troubled the ground with every pulse of the blood,
My wings lax on the air, my eyes open and grave,
With the vacant pride of hardly less than a god.

We passed thickets that quaked with hidden deer,
And wide shallows dividing before my feet,
Empty plains threaded, and between stiff aloes
I took the ass's bridle to climb into mountain pathways.

When cold bit you, through your peasant's mantle,
And my Father filled the air with meaningless stars,
I brought dung and dead white grass for fuel,
Blowing a fire with the breath of the holy word.

Your drudge, Joseph, slept; you would sit unmoving,
In marble quiet, or by the unbroken voice of a river,
Would sometimes bare your maiden breast to his mouth,
The suckling, to the conscious God balanced upon your knees.

Apart I considered the melodious names of my brothers,
As again in my Father's house, and the even spheres
Slowly, nightlong recalled the splendour of numbers;
I heard again the voluptuous measure of praise.

Sometimes pacing beneath clarity immeasurable
I saw my mind lie open and desert,
The wavering streams frozen up and each coppice quieted,
A whole valley in starlight with leaves and waters.

Coming at last to these farthest Syrian hills,
Attis or Adon, some ambushed lust looked out;
My skin grows pale and smooth, shrunken as silk,
Without the rough effulgence of a God.

And here no voice has spoken;
There is no shrine of any godhead here
No grove or hallowed fires,
And godhead seems asleep.

Only the vine has woven
Strange houses and blind rooms and palaces,
Into each hollow and crevice continually
Dropped yearlong irrecoverable flowers.

The sprawling vine has built us a close room
Obedient Hymen fills the air with mist;
And to make dumb our theft
The white and moving sand that will not bear a print.

ESTHER MATHEWS
1902–1991

Song

I can't be talkin' of love, dear,
I can't be talkin' of love.
If there be one thing I can't talk of
That one thing do be love.

But that's not sayin' that I'm not lovin'—
Still water, you know, runs deep,
An' I do be lovin' so deep, dear,
I be lovin' you in my sleep.

But I can't be talkin' of love, dear,
I can't be talkin' of love,
If there be one thing I can't talk of
That one thing do be love.

WILLIAM EMPSON
1906–1984

Legal Fiction

Law makes long spokes of the short stakes of men.
Your well fenced out real estate of mind
No high flat of the nomad citizen
Looks over, or train leaves behind.

Your rights extend under and above your claim
Without bound; you own land in Heaven and Hell;
Your part of earth's surface and mass the same,
Of all cosmos' volume, and all stars as well.

Your rights reach down where all owners meet, in Hell's
Pointed exclusive conclave, at earth's centre
(Your spun farm's root still on that axis dwells);
And up, through galaxies, a growing sector.

You are nomad yet; the lighthouse beam you own
Flashes, like Lucifer, through the firmament.
Earth's axis varies; your dark central cone
Wavers, a candle's shadow, at the end.

VERNON WATKINS
1906–1967

Discoveries

The poles are flying where the two eyes set:
America has not found Columbus yet.

Ptolemy's planets, playing fast and loose,
Foretell the wisdom of Copernicus.

Dante calls Primum Mobile, the First Cause:
Love that moves the world and the other stars.

Great Galileo, twisted by the rack,
Groans the bright sun from heaven, then breathes it back.

Blake, on the world alighting, holds the skies,
And all the stars shine down through human eyes.

Donne sees those stars, yet will not let them lie:
"We're tapers, too, and at our own cost die."

The shroud-lamp catches. Lips are smiling there.
"Les flammes—déjà?"—The world dies, or Voltaire.

Swift, a cold mourner at his burial-rite,
Burns to the world's heart like a meteorite.

Beethoven deaf, in deafness hearing all,
Unwinds all music from sound's funeral.

Three prophets fall, the litter of one night,
Blind Milton gazes in fixed deeps of light.

Beggar of those Minute Particulars,
Yeats lights again the turmoil of the stars.

Motionless motion! Come, Tiresias,
The eternal flies, what's passing cannot pass.

"Solace in flight," old Heraclitus cries;
Light changing to Von Hügel's butterflies.

Rilke bears all, thinks like a tree, believes,
Sinks in the hand that bears the falling leaves.

The stars! The signs! Great Angelo hurls them back.
His whirling ceiling draws the zodiac.

The pulse of Keats testing the axiom;
The second music when the sound is dumb.

The Christian Paradox, bringing its great reward
By loss; the moment known to Kierkegaard.

W. H. AUDEN
1907–1973

Musée des Beaux Arts

About suffering they were never wrong,
The Old Masters: how well they understood
Its human position; how it takes place
While someone else is eating or opening a window or just walking
    dully along;
How, when the aged are reverently, passionately waiting
For the miraculous birth, there always must be
Children who did not specially want it to happen, skating
On a pond at the edge of the wood:
They never forgot
That even the dreadful martyrdom must run its course
Anyhow in a corner, some untidy spot
Where the dogs go on with their doggy life and the torturer's horse
Scratches its innocent behind on a tree.

In Brueghel's *Icarus*, for instance: how everything turns away
Quite leisurely from the disaster; the ploughman may
Have heard the splash, the forsaken cry,
But for him it was not an important failure; the sun shone
As it had to on the white legs disappearing into the green
Water; and the expensive delicate ship that must have seen
Something amazing, a boy falling out of the sky,
Had somewhere to get to and sailed calmly on.

In Memory of W. B. Yeats
d. Jan. 1939

I

He disappeared in the dead of winter:
The brooks were frozen, the air-ports almost deserted,
And snow disfigured the public statues;
The mercury sank in the mouth of the dying day.
O all the instruments agree
The day of his death was a dark cold day.

Far from his illness
The wolves ran on through the evergreen forests,
The peasant river was untempted by the fashionable quays;
By mourning tongues
The death of the poet was kept from his poems.

But for him it was his last afternoon as himself,
An afternoon of nurses and rumours;
The provinces of his body revolted,
The squares of his mind were empty,
Silence invaded the suburbs,
The current of his feeling failed: he became his admirers.

Now he is scattered among a hundred cities
And wholly given over to unfamiliar affections;
To find his happiness in another kind of wood
And be punished under a foreign code of conscience.
The words of a dead man
Are modified in the guts of the living.

But in the importance and noise of to-morrow
When the brokers are roaring like beasts on the floor of the Bourse,
And the poor have the sufferings to which they are fairly accustomed,
And each in the cell of himself is almost convinced of his freedom;
A few thousand will think of this day
As one thinks of a day when one did something slightly unusual.

O all the instruments agree
The day of his death was a dark cold day.

II

You were silly like us: your gift survived it all;
The parish of rich women, physical decay,
Yourself; mad Ireland hurt you into poetry.
Now Ireland has her madness and her weather still,
For poetry makes nothing happen: it survives
In the valley of its saying where executives
Would never want to tamper; it flows south
From ranches of isolation and the busy griefs,
Raw towns that we believe and die in; it survives,
A way of happening, a mouth.

III

Earth, receive an honoured guest;
William Yeats is laid to rest:
Let the Irish vessel lie
Emptied of its poetry.

Time that is intolerant
Of the brave and innocent,
And indifferent in a week
To a beautiful physique,

Worships language and forgives
Everyone by whom it lives;
Pardons cowardice, conceit,
Lays its honours at their feet.

Time that with this strange excuse
Pardoned Kipling and his views,
And will pardon Paul Claudel,
Pardons him for writing well.

In the nightmare of the dark
All the dogs of Europe bark,
And the living nations wait,
Each sequestered in its hate;

Intellectual disgrace
Stares from every human face,
And the seas of pity lie
Locked and frozen in each eye.

Follow, poet, follow right
To the bottom of the night,
With your unconstraining voice
Still persuade us to rejoice;

With the farming of a verse
Make a vineyard of the curse,
Sing of human unsuccess
In a rapture of distress;

In the deserts of the heart
Let the healing fountain start,
In the prison of his days
Teach the free man how to praise.

September 1, 1939

I sit in one of the dives
On Fifty-second Street
Uncertain and afraid
As the clever hopes expire
Of a low dishonest decade:
Waves of anger and fear
Circulate over the bright
And darkened lands of the earth,
Obsessing our private lives;
The unmentionable odour of death
Offends the September night.

Accurate scholarship can
Unearth the whole offence
From Luther until now
That has driven a culture mad,
Find what occurred at Linz,
What huge imago made
A psychopathic god:
I and the public know
What all schoolchildren learn,
Those to whom evil is done
Do evil in return.

Exiled Thucydides knew
All that a speech can say

About Democracy,
And what dictators do,
The elderly rubbish they talk
To an apathetic grave;
Analysed all in his book,
The enlightenment driven away,
The habit-forming pain,
Mismanagement and grief:
We must suffer them all again.

Into this neutral air
Where blind skyscrapers use
Their full height to proclaim
The strength of Collective Man,
Each language pours its vain
Competitive excuse:
But who can live for long
In an euphoric dream;
Out of the mirror they stare,
Imperialism's face
And the international wrong.

Faces along the bar
Cling to their average day:
The lights must never go out,
The music must always play,
All the conventions conspire
To make this fort assume
The furniture of home;
Lest we should see where we are,
Lost in a haunted wood,
Children afraid of the night
Who have never been happy or good.

The windiest militant trash
Important Persons shout
Is not so crude as our wish:
What mad Nijinsky wrote
About Diaghilev
Is true of the normal heart;
For the error bred in the bone

Of each woman and each man
Craves what it cannot have,
Not universal love
But to be loved alone.

From the conservative dark
Into the ethical life
The dense commuters come,
Repeating their morning vow;
"I *will* be true to the wife,
I'll concentrate more on my work,"
And helpless governors wake
To resume their compulsory game:
Who can release them now,
Who can reach the deaf,
Who can speak for the dumb?

All I have is a voice
To undo the folded lie,
The romantic lie in the brain
Of the sensual man-in-the-street
And the lie of Authority
Whose buildings grope the sky:
There is no such thing as the State
And no one exists alone;
Hunger allows no choice
To the citizen or the police;
We must love one another or die.

Defenceless under the night
Our world in stupour lies;
Yet, dotted everywhere,
Ironic points of light
Flash out wherever the Just
Exchange their messages:
May I, composed like them
Of Eros and of dust,
Beleaguered by the same
Negation and despair,
Show an affirming flame.

LOUIS MacNEICE
1907–1963

Bagpipe Music

It's no go the merrygoround, it's no go the rickshaw,
All we want is a limousine and a ticket for the peepshow.
Their knickers are made of crepe-de-chine, their shoes are made of python,
Their halls are lined with tiger rugs and their walls with heads of bison.

John MacDonald found a corpse, put it under the sofa,
Waited till it came to life and hit it with a poker,
Sold its eyes for souvenirs, sold its blood for whiskey,
Kept its bones for dumb-bells to use when he was fifty.

It's no go the Yogi-Man, it's no go Blavatsky,
All we want is a bank balance and a bit of skirt in a taxi.

Annie MacDougall went to milk, caught her foot in the heather,
Woke to hear a dance record playing of Old Vienna.
It's no go your maidenheads, it's no go your culture,
All we want is a Dunlop tyre and the devil mend the puncture.

The Laird o' Phelps spent Hogmanay declaring he was sober,
Counted his feet to prove the fact and found he had one foot over.
Mrs. Carmichael had her fifth, looked at the job with repulsion,
Said to the midwife "Take it away; I'm through with over-production."

It's no go the gossip column, it's no go the Ceilidh,
All we want is a mother's help and a sugar-stick for the baby.

Willie Murray cut his thumb, couldn't count the damage,
Took the hide of an Ayrshire cow and used it for a bandage.
His brother caught three hundred cran when the seas were lavish,
Threw the bleeders back in the sea and went upon the parish.

It's no go the Herring Board, it's no go the Bible,
All we want is a packet of fags when our hands are idle.

It's no go the picture palace, it's no go the stadium,
It's no go the country cot with a pot of pink geraniums.
It's no go the Government grants, it's no go the elections,

Sit on your arse for fifty years and hang your hat on a pension.
It's no go my honey love, it's no go my poppet;
Work your hands from day to day, the winds will blow the profit.
The glass is falling hour by hour, the glass will fall for ever,
But if you break the bloody glass you won't hold up the weather.

Among These Turf-Stacks

Among these turf-stacks graze no iron horses
Such as stalk such as champ in towns and the soul of crowds,
Here is no mass-production of neat thoughts
No canvas shrouds for the mind nor any black hearses:
The peasant shambles on his boots like hooves
Without thinking at all or wanting to run in grooves.

But those who lack the peasant's conspirators
The tawny mountain, the unregarded buttress,
Will feel the need of a fortress against ideas and against the
Shuddering insidious shock of the theory-vendors
The little sardine men crammed in a monster toy
Who tilt their aggregate beast against our crumbling Troy.

For we are obsolete who like the lesser things,
Who play in corners with looking-glasses and beads;
It is better we should go quickly, go into Asia
Or any other tunnel where the world recedes,
Or turn blind wantons like the gulls who scream
And rip the edge off any ideal or dream.

STEPHEN SPENDER
1909–1995

Ultima Ratio Regum

The guns spell money's ultimate reason
In letters of lead on the spring hillside.
But the boy lying dead under the olive trees
Was too young and too silly
To have been notable to their important eye.
He was a better target for a kiss.

When he lived, tall factory hooters never summoned him.
Nor did restaurant plate-glass doors revolve to wave him in.
His name never appeared in the papers.
The world maintained its traditional wall
Round the dead with their gold sunk deep as a well,
Whilst his life, intangible as a Stock Exchange rumour, drifted outside.

O too lightly he threw down his cap
One day when the breeze threw petals from the trees.
The unflowering wall sprouted with guns,
Machine-gun anger quickly scythed the grasses;
Flags and leaves fell from hands and branches;
The tweed cap rotted in the nettles.

Consider his life which was valueless
In terms of employment, hotel ledgers, news files.
Consider. One bullet in ten thousand kills a man.
Ask. Was so much expenditure justified
On the death of one so young and so silly
Lying under the olive tree, O world, O death?

I Think Continually of Those Who Were Truly Great

I think continually of those who were truly great.
Who, from the womb, remembered the soul's history
Through corridors of light where the hours are suns,
Endless and singing. Whose lovely ambition
Was that their lips, still touched with fire,
Should tell of the spirit clothed from head to foot in song.
And who hoarded from the spring branches
The desires falling across their bodies like blossoms.

What is precious is never to forget
The delight of the blood drawn from ageless springs
Breaking through rocks in worlds before our earth;
Never to deny its pleasure in the simple morning light,
Nor its grave evening demand for love;
Never to allow gradually the traffic to smother
With noise and fog the flowering of the spirit.

Near the snow, near the sun, in the highest fields
See how those names are fêted by the waving grass,

And by the streamers of white cloud,
And whispers of wind in the listening sky;
The names of those who in their lives fought for life,
Who wore at their hearts the fire's centre.
Born of the sun they traveled a short while towards the sun,
And left the vivid air signed with their honour.

ALFRED HAYES
1911–1985

The Slaughter-House

Under the big 500-watted lamps, in the huge sawdusted government
    inspected slaughter-house,
head down from hooks and clamps, run on trolleys over troughs,
    the animals die.
Whatever terror their dull intelligences feel
    or what agony distorts their most protruding eyes
the incommunicable narrow skulls conceal.
    Across the sawdusted floor,
ignorant as children, they see the butcher's slow methodical approach
in the bloodied apron, leather cap above, thick square shoes below,
struggling to comprehend this unique vision upside down,
and then approximate a human scream as from the throat slit like a letter
the blood empties, and the windpipe, like a blown valve, spurts steam.
But I, sickened equally with the ox and lamb, misread my fate,
mistake the butcher's love who kills me for the meat I am
to feed a hungry multitude beyond the sliding doors. I, too, misjudge the real
purpose of this huge shed I'm herded in: not for my love or lovely wool am
    I here,
but to make some world a meal.
See, how on the unsubstantial air
I kick, bleating my private woe,
    as upside down my rolling sight
somersaults, and frantically I try to set my world upright; too late learning
    why I'm hung here,
whose nostrils bleed, whose life runs out from eye and ear.

W. R. RODGERS
1911–1969

Neither Here nor There

In that land all Is and nothing's Ought;
No owners or notices, only birds;
No walls anywhere, only lean wire of words
Worming brokenly out from eaten thought;
No oats growing, only ankle-lace grass
Easing and not resenting the feet that pass;
No enormous beasts, only names of them;
No bones made, bans laid, or boons expected,
No contracts, entails, hereditaments,
Anything at all that might tie or hem.

In that land all's lackadaisical;
No lakes of coddled spawn, and no locked ponds
Of settled purpose, no netted fishes;
But only inkling streams and running fronds,
Fritillaried with dreams, weedy with wishes;
Nor arrogant talk is heard, haggling phrase,
But undertones, and hesitance, and haze;
On clear days mountains of meaning are seen
Humped high on the horizon; no one goes
To con their meaning, no one cares or knows.

In that land all's flat, indifferent; there
Is neither springing house nor hanging tent,
No aims are entertained, and nothing is meant,
For there are no ends and no trends, no roads,
Only follow your nose to anywhere.
No one is born there, no one stays or dies,
For it is a timeless land, it lies
Between the act and the attrition, it
Marks off bound from rebound, make from break, tit
From tat, also to-day from to-morrow.
No Cause there comes to term, but each departs
Elsewhere to whelp its deeds, expel its darts;
There are no homecomings, of course, no good-byes
In that land, neither yearning nor scorning,
Though at night there is the smell of morning.

ELIZABETH BISHOP
1911–1979

The Imaginary Iceberg

We'd rather have the iceberg than the ship
Although it meant the end of travel.
Although it stood stock still like cloudy rock
And all the sea were moving marble.
We'd rather have the iceberg than the ship;
We'd rather own this breathing plain of snow
Though the ship's sails were laid upon the sea
As the snow lies undissolved upon the water.
O solemn, floating field,
Are you aware an iceberg takes repose
With you, and when it wakes may pasture on your snows?

This is a scene a sailor'd give his eyes for.
The ship's ignored. The iceberg rises
And sinks again; its glassy pinnacles
Correct elliptics in the sky.
This is a scene where he who treads the boards
Is artlessly rhetorical. The curtain
Is light enough to rise on finest ropes
That airy twists of snow provide.
The wits of these white peaks
Spar with the sun. Its weight the iceberg dares
Upon a shifting stage and stands and stares.

This iceberg cuts its facets from within.
Like jewelry from a grave
It saves itself perpetually and adorns
Only itself, perhaps the snows
Which so surprise us lying on the sea.
Goodbye, we say, goodbye, the ship steers off
Where waves give in to one another's waves
And clouds run in a warmer sky.
Icebergs behoove the soul
(Both being self-made from elements least visible)
To see them so: fleshed, fair, erected indivisible.

LAWRENCE DURRELL
1912–1990

A Ballad of the Good Lord Nelson

The Good Lord Nelson had a swollen gland,
Little of the scripture did he understand
Till a woman led him to the promised land
    Aboard the Victory, Victory O.

Adam and Evil and a bushel of figs
Meant nothing to Nelson who was keeping pigs,
Till a woman showed him the various rigs
    Aboard the Victory, Victory O.

His heart was softer than a new laid egg,
Too poor for loving and ashamed to beg,
Till Nelson was taken by the Dancing Leg
    Aboard the Victory, Victory O.

Now he up and did up his little tin trunk
And he took to the ocean on his English junk,
Turning like the hour-glass in his lonely bunk
    Aboard the Victory, Victory O.

The Frenchman saw him a-coming there
With the one-piece eye and the valentine hair,
With the safety-pin sleeve and occupied air
    Aboard the Victory, Victory O.

Now you all remember the message he sent
As an answer to Hamilton's discontent—
There were questions asked about it in the Parliament
    Aboard the Victory, Victory O.

Now the blacker the berry, the thicker comes the juice.
Think of Good Lord Nelson and avoid self-abuse,
For the empty sleeve was no mere excuse
    Aboard the Victory, Victory O.

"England Expects" was the motto he gave
When he thought of little Emma out on Biscay's wave,

And remembered working on her like a galley-slave
    Aboard the Victory, Victory O.

The first Great Lord in our English land
To honour the Freudian command,
For a cast in the bush is worth two in the hand
    Aboard the Victory, Victory O.

Now the Frenchman shot him there as he stood
In the rage of battle in a silk-lined hood
And he heard the whistle of his own hot blood
    Aboard the Victory, Victory O.

Now stiff on a pillar with a phallic air
Nelson stylites in Trafalgar Square
Reminds the British what once they were
    Aboard the Victory, Victory O.

If they'd treat their women in the Nelson way
There'd be fewer frigid husbands every day
And many more heroes on the Bay of Biscay
    Aboard the Victory, Victory O.

F. T. PRINCE
1912–2003

Soldiers Bathing

The sea at evening moves across the sand.
Under a reddening sky I watch the freedom of a band
Of soldiers who belong to me. Stripped bare
For bathing in the sea, they shout and run in the warm air;
Their flesh, worn by the trade of war, revives
And my mind towards the meaning of it strives.
All's pathos now. The body that was gross,
Rank, ravening, disgusting in the act or in repose,
All fever, filth and sweat, its bestial strength
And bestial decay, by pain and labor grows at length
Fragile and luminous. Poor bare forked animal,

Conscious of his desires and needs and flesh that rise and fall,
Stands in the soft air, tasting after toil
The sweetness of his nakedness: letting the sea-waves coil
Their frothy tongues about his feet, forgets
His hatred of the war, its terrible pressure that begets
That machinery of death and slavery,
Each being a slave and making slaves of others; finds that he
Remembers his proud freedom in a game,
Mocking himself; and comically mimics fear and shame.

He plays with death and animality.
And, reading in the shadows of his pallid flesh, I see
The idea of Michelangelo's cartoon
Of soldiers bathing, breaking off before they were half done
At some sortie of the enemy, an episode
Of the Pisan wars with Florence. I remember how he showed
Their muscular limbs that clamber from the water
And heads that turn across the shoulder, eager for the slaughter,
Forgetful of their bodies that are bare
And hot to buckle on and use the weapons lying there.
—And I think too of the theme another found
When, shadowing men's bodies on a sinister red ground—
Was it Ucello or Pollaiuolo?—
Painted a naked battle: warriors, straddled, hacked the foe,
Dug their bare toes into the soil and slew
The brother-naked man who lay between their feet and drew
His lips back from his teeth in a grimace.

They were Italians who knew war's sorrow and disgrace
And showed the thing suspended, stripped. A theme
Born out of the experience of that horrible extreme
Of war beneath a sky where the air flows
With *Lachrimae Christi*. For that rage, that bitterness, those blows
That hatred of the slain, what could it be
But indirectly or directly a commentary
On the Crucifixion? and the picture burns
With indignation and pity and despair by turns
Because it is the obverse of the scene
Where Christ hangs murdered, stripped, upon the Cross. I mean,
That is the explanation of its rage.

And we too have our bitterness and pity that engage
Blood, spirit in this war. But night begins,
Night of the mind: who nowadays is conscious of our sins?
Though every human deed concerns our blood,
And even we must know what nobody has understood,
That some great love is over all we do
And that is what has driven us to fury, for so few
Can suffer all the terror of that love:
The terror of that love has set us spinning in this groove
Greasy with our blood.
                    These dry themselves and dress,
Resume their shirts, forget the fright and shame of nakedness.
Because to love is terrible we prefer
The freedom of our crimes; yet, as I drink the dusky air,
I feel a strange delight that fills me full,
Strange gratitude, as if evil itself were beautiful,
And kiss the wound in thought, while in the west
I watch a streak of red that might have issued from Christ's breast.

DELMORE SCHWARTZ
1913–1966

The Heavy Bear

"the withness of the body"—WHITEHEAD

The heavy bear who goes with me,
A manifold honey to smear his face,
Clumsy and lumbering here and there,
The central ton of every place,
The hungry beating brutish one
In love with candy, anger, and sleep,
Crazy factotum, dishevelling all,
Climbs the building, kicks the football,
Boxes his brother in the hate-ridden city.

Breathing at my side, that heavy animal,
That heavy bear who sleeps with me,
Howls in his sleep for a world of sugar,

A sweetness intimate as the water's clasp,
Howls in his sleep because the tight-rope
Trembles and shows the darkness beneath.
—The strutting show-off is terrified,
Dressed in his dress-suit, bulging his pants,
Trembles to think that his quivering meat
Must finally wince to nothing at all.

That inescapable animal walks with me,
Has followed me since the black womb held,
Moves where I move, distorting my gesture,
A caricature, a swollen shadow,
A stupid clown of the spirit's motive,
Perplexes and affronts with his own darkness,
The secret life of belly and bone,
Opaque, too near, my private, yet unknown,
Stretches to embrace the very dear

With whom I would walk without him near,
Touches her grossly, although a word
Would bare my heart and make me clear,
Stumbles, flounders, and strives to be fed
Dragging me with him in his mouthing care,
Amid the hundred million of his kind,
The scrimmage of appetite everywhere.

KARL SHAPIRO
1913–2000

Scyros

Snuffle and sniff and handkerchief
The doctor punched my vein
The captain called me Cain
Upon my belly sat the sow of fear
With coins on either eye
The President came by
And whispered to the braids what none could hear

High over where the storm
Stood steadfast cruciform
The golden eagle sank in wounded wheels
White negroes laughing still
Crept fiercely on Brazil
Turning the navies upward on their keels

Now one by one the trees
Stripped to their naked knees
To dance upon the heaps of shrunken dead
The roof of England fell
Great Paris tolled her bell
And China staunched her milk and wept for bread

No island singly lay
But lost its name that day
The Ainu dived across the plunging sands
From dawn to dawn to dawn
King George's birds came on
Strafing the tulips from his children's hands

Thus in the classic sea
Southeast from Thessaly
The dynamited mermen washed ashore
And tritons dressed in steel
Trolled heads with rod and reel
And dredged potatoes from the Aegean floor

Hot is the sky and green
Where Germans have been seen
The moon leaks metal on the Atlantic fields
Pink boys in birthday shrouds
Loop lightly through the clouds
Or coast the peaks of Finland on their shields

That prophet year by year
Lay still but could not hear
Where scholars tapped to find his new remains
Gog and Magog ate pork
In vertical New York
And war began next Monday on the Danes.

GEORGE BARKER

1913–1991

Sonnet to My Mother

Most near, most dear, most loved and most far,
Under the window where I often found her
Sitting as huge as Asia, seismic with laughter,
Gin and chicken helpless in her Irish hand,
Irresistible as Rabelais but most tender for
The lame dogs and hurt birds that surround her,—
She is a procession no one can follow after
But be like a little dog following a brass band.

She will not glance up at the bomber or condescend
To drop her gin and scuttle to a cellar,
But lean on the mahogany table like a mountain
Whom only faith can move, and so I send
O all my faith and all my love to tell her
That she will move from mourning into morning.

Memorial for Two Young Seamen

(Lost overboard in a storm in Mid-Pacific, January 1940)

I The seagull, spreadeagled, splayed on the wind,
Span backwards shrieking, belly facing upward,
Fled backwards with a gimlet in its heart
To see the two youths swimming hand in hand
Through green eternity. O swept overboard
Not could the thirty-foot jaws them part,
Or the flouncing skirts that swept them over
Separate what death pronounced was love.

I saw them, the hand flapping like a flag,
And another like a dolphin with a child
Supporting him. Was I the shape of Jesus
When to me hopeward their eyeballs swivelled,
Saw I was standing in the posture of vague
Horror, oh paralyzed with mere pity's peace?

II From thorax of storms the voices of verbs
Shall call to me without sound, like the vowel

Round which cyclones rage, to nurse my nerve,
My shaken, my broken, my oh I shall grovel
Heart. I taste sea swilling in my bowels,
As now I sit shivering in the swing of waves
Like a face in a bubble. As the hull heaves
I and my mind go walking over hell.

The greedy bitch with sailors in her guts,
Green as a dream and formidable as God,
Spitting at stars, gnawing at shores, mad, randy,
Riots with us on her abdomen and puts
Eternity in our cabins, pitches our pod
To the mouth of the death for which no one is ready.

III At midday they looked up and saw their death
Standing up overhead as loud as thunder
As white as angels and formidable as God:
Then, then the shock, the last gasp of breath,
As grazing the bulwarks they swept over and under,
All the green arms around them that load
Their eyes, their ears, their stomachs with eternals,
Whirled away in a white pool to the stern.

But the most possible of all miracles
Is that the useful tear that did not fall
From the corner of their eyes, was the prize,
The flowers, the gifts, the crystal sepulcher,
The funeral contribution and memorial,
The perfect and non-existent obsequies.

Dog, Dog in My Manger

Dog, dog in my manger, drag at my heathen
Heart where the swearing smoke of Love
Goes up as I give everything to the blaze.
Drag at my fires, dog, drag at my altars
Where Aztec I over my tabernacle raise
The Absalom assassination I my murder.

Dog, drag off the gifts too much I load
My life as wishing tree too heavy with:
And, dog, guide you my stray down quiet roads

Where peace is—be my engine of myth
That, dog, so drags me down my time
Sooner I shall rest from my overload.

Dog, is my shake when I come from water,
The cataract of my days, as red as danger?
O my joy has jaws that seize in fangs
The gift and hand of love always I sought for.
They come to me with kingdoms for my paucity—
Dog, why is my tooth red with their charity?

Mourn, dog, mourn over me where I lie
Not dead but spinning on the pinpoint hazard,
The fiftieth angel. Bay, bay in the blizzard
That brings a tear to my snowman's eye
And buries us all in what we most treasured.
Dog, why do we die so often before we die?

Dog, good dog, trick do and make me take
Calmly the consciousness of the crime
Born in the blood simply because we are here.
Your father burns for his father's sake,
So will a son burn in a further time
Under the bush of joy you planted here.

Dog, dog, your bone I am, who tear my life
Tatterdemalion from me. From you I have no peace,
No life at all unless you break my bone,
No bed unless I sleep upon my grief
That without you we are too much alone,
No peace until no peace is a happy home:
O dog my god, how can I cease to praise!

HENRY REED
1914–1986

Naming of Parts

To-day we have naming of parts. Yesterday,
We had daily cleaning. And to-morrow morning,
We shall have what to do after firing. But to-day,
To-day we have naming of parts. Japonica
Glistens like coral in all of the neighbouring gardens,
    And to-day we have naming of parts.

This is the lower sling swivel. And this
Is the upper sling swivel, whose use you will see,
When you are given your slings. And this is the piling swivel,
Which in your case you have not got. The branches
Hold in the gardens their silent, eloquent gestures,
    Which in our case we have not got.

This is the safety-catch, which is always released
With an easy flick of the thumb. And please do not let me
See anyone using his finger. You can do it quite easy
If you have any strength in your thumb. The blossoms
Are fragile and motionless, never letting anyone see
    Any of them using their finger.

And this you can see is the bolt. The purpose of this
Is to open the breech, as you see. We can slide it
Rapidly backwards and forwards: we call this
Easing the spring. And rapidly backwards and forwards
The early bees are assaulting and fumbling the flowers:
    They call it easing the Spring.

They call it easing the Spring: it is perfectly easy
If you have any strength in your thumb: like the bolt,
And the breech, and the cocking-piece, and the point of balance,
Which in our case we have not got; and the almond-blossom
Silent in all of the gardens and the bees going backwards and forwards,
    For to-day we have naming of parts.

JOHN MANIFOLD
1915–1985

Fife Tune
(6/8) for Sixth Platoon, 308th I.T.C.

One morning in spring
We marched from Devizes
All shapes and all sizes
Like beads on a string,
But yet with a swing
We trod the bluemetal
And full of high fettle
We started to sing.

She ran down the stair
A twelve-year-old darling
And laughing and calling
She tossed her bright hair;
Then silent to stare
At the men flowing past her—
There were all she could master
Adoring her there.

It's seldom I'll see
A sweeter or prettier;
I doubt we'll forget her
In two years or three.
And lucky he'll be
She takes for a lover
While we are far over
The treacherous sea.

ROBERT LOWELL
1917–1977

The Drunken Fisherman

Wallowing in this bloody sty,
I cast for fish that pleased my eye
(Truly Jehovah's bow suspends
No pots of gold to weight its ends);
Only the blood-mouthed rainbow trout
Rose to my bait. They flopped about
My canvas creel until the moth
Corrupted its unstable cloth.

A calendar to tell the day;
A handkerchief to wave away
The gnats; a couch unstuffed with storm
Pouching a bottle in one arm;
A whiskey bottle full of worms;
And bedroom slacks: are these fit terms
To mete the worm whose molten rage
Boils in the belly of old age?

Once fishing was a rabbit's foot—
O wind blow cold, O wind blow hot,
Let suns stay in or suns step out:
Life danced a jig on the sperm-whale's spout—
The fisher's fluent and obscene
Catches kept his conscience clean.
Children, the raging memory drools
Over the glory of past pools.

Now the hot river, ebbing, hauls
Its bloody waters into holes;
A grain of sand inside my shoe
Mimics the moon that might undo
Man and Creation too; remorse
Stinking, has puddled up its source;
Here tantrums thrash to a whale's rage.
This is the pot-hole of old age.

Is there no way to cast my hook
Out of this dynamited brook?
The Fisher's sons must cast about
When shallow waters peter out.
I will catch Christ with a greased worm,
And when the Prince of Darkness stalks
My bloodstream to its Stygian term . . .
On water the Man-Fisher walks.

GENE DERWOOD

1909–1954

Elegy

On Gordon Barber, Lamentably Drowned in his Eighteenth Year

When in the mirror of a permanent tear
Over the iris of your mother's eye
I beheld the dark tremor of your face, austere
With space of death, spun too benign for youth,
Icicle of the past to pierce her living sigh—
I saw you wish the last kiss of mother's mouth,
Who took the salted waters rather in the suck
Of seas, sighing yourself to fill and drench
With water the plum-rich glory of your breast
Where beat the heart escaping from war's luck.

Gordon, I mourn your wrist, your running foot,
Your curious brows, your thigh, your unborn daughters,
Yet mourn more deep the drought-caught war dry boy
Who goes, a killer, to join you in your sleep
And envy you what made you blench
Taking your purple back to drought-less waters.
What choke of terror filled you in the wet
What fierce surprise caught you when play turned fate
And all the rains you loved became your net,
Formlessly yielding, yet stronger than your breath?
Then did you dream of mother or hopes hatched
When the cold cramp held you from nape to foot
And time dissolved, promise dissolved, in Death?

Did you cry "cruel" to all the hands that stretched
Not near, but played afar, when you sank down
Your sponge of lungs hurt to the quick
Till you had left the quick to join the dead,
Whom, now, your mother mourns grief-sick.
You were too young to drown.

Never will you take bride to happy bed,
Who lay awash in water yet no laving
Needed, so pure so young for sudden leaving.

Gone, gone is Gordon, tall and brilliant lad
Whose mind was science. Now hollow his skull
A noble sculpture, is but sunken bone,
His cells from water come by water laid
Grave-deep, to water gone.
Lost, lost the hope he had
Washed to a cipher his splendour and his skill.

But Gordon's gone, it's other boys who live afraid.

Two years, and lads have grown to hold a gun.
In dust must splendid lads go down and choke,
Red dry their hands and dry their one day's sun
From which they earthward fall to fiery tomb
Bomb-weighted, from bloodying children's hair.

Never a boy but takes as cross Cain's crime
And goes to death by making death, to pass
Death's gate distorted with the dried brown grime—
Better the watery death than death by air
Or death by sand
Where fall hard fish of fear
Loud in unwetted dust.

Spun on a lucky wave, O early boy!
Now ocean's fish you are
As heretofore.
Perhaps you had sweet mercy's tenderness
To win so soon largesse of choice
That you, by grace, went gayly to the wave
And all our mourning should be to rejoice.

With God Conversing

Red paths that wander through the gray, and cells
Of strangeness, rutted mouldings in the brain,
Untempered fevers heated by old kills,
By the pampered word, by the pat printed rune,
Unbalanced coil under glaucous blooms of thought,
A turning mind, unmitigated thinking that
Feeds human hunger and eats us alive
While cringing to the death, expecting love,—
Such make the self we are. And do you make it?
And practice on us? For we cannot take it.

Listen. Grow mild before the flicking lash
Seems welded to your hand, self-wounder.
What are we, cry we, while our pain leaps lush,
Too jungle thick: the jungle where we wander,
No seeded faith before, nor after, miracle,
Of bidden faith in things unseen, no particle.
For we think only through our troubled selves,
We note the worm that in the apple delves,
See gibbous moons and spots upon the sun,
Speak gibberish, and keep the poor in sin.

Plus birth and death must war-lash winnow
While every pod-burst leaf of May sucks life?
Because we think shall we be less than minnow,
Cat, carrot, rat, bat and such from sense aloof?
What doorless maze is this we wander through
With fuming souls parched of our morning dew?
Reason confounds as it presents to NAUGHT:
Earth worn, man moving into self-made night.
Reason-begotten science sets war's pace
And, civil-mouthed, makes civilization pass.

Created in your image, made up of words,
Till words reduce you to a zero—O,
We, then, reflecting you, are less than birds,
Bugs, or empty dugs, still less than minus no.
There must be something wrong with being wise—
Talking we go, wondering and wandering with woes,
Big thoughts have got us, hence we organize,

Govern our heroes with unmeant yeas and nays,
And breathe in dungeons of our nervous mesh
An air too blank to snare meandering flesh.

Night melting dawn shall turn the renewed sky,
Aurora Borealis and Australis
Fanfaring leap the poles, the moon fall by;
But if our science does not quickly fail us
How long for us will space blue light the dun
Of populaces, while wonderers eye the sun?
The gloomy silhouettes of wings we forged
With reason reasonless, are now enlarged,
The falsified subconscious, beast-a-woken?
We-you? Post-suicides, shall we awaken?

After Reading St. John the Divine

Moon's glow by seven fold multiplied, turned red,
Burned fierce by the coronal limbs at last
Out-leaping insulating space, a-blast
The searing heat sheeting round earth ahead
Of the scorched geoid's course; and I a-bed
Watching that increased flame and holding fast
To pulse and pillow. Worse! No shadow cast
By chair or cat. All people waking dead . . .

Earth lurches spacial waste; my room is hot;
That moon waxes her monstrous, brimstone disk;
Thick fear stretches before the febrile light;
Green fires pierce at my clenching eye's blind spot . . .
My buried soul, rising to face the risk,
With one pure deed restores the natural night.

DYLAN THOMAS
1914–1953

A Refusal to Mourn the Death, by Fire, of a Child in London

Never until the mankind making
Bird beast and flower
Fathering and all humbling darkness
Tells with silence the last light breaking
And the still hour
Is come of the sea tumbling in harness

And I must enter again the round
Zion of the water bead
And the synagogue of the ear of corn
Shall I let pray the shadow of a sound
Or sow my salt seed
In the least valley of sackcloth to mourn

The majesty and burning of the child's death.
I shall not murder
The mankind of her going with a grave truth
Nor blaspheme down the stations of the breath
With any further
Elegy of innocence and youth

Deep with the first dead lies London's daughter,
Robed in the long friends,
The grains beyond age, the dark veins of her mother
Secret by the unmourning water
Of the riding Thames.
After the first death, there is no other.

Light Breaks Where No Sun Shines

Light breaks where no sun shines;
Where no sea runs, the waters of the heart
Push in their tides;
And, broken ghosts with glowworms in their heads,
The things of lights
File through the flesh where no flesh decks the bones.

A candle in the thighs
Warms youth and seed and burns the seeds of age;
Where no seed stirs,
The fruit of man unwrinkles in the stars,
Bright as a fig;
Where no wax is, the candle shows its hairs.

Dawn breaks behind the eyes;
From poles of skull and toe the windy blood
Slides like a sea;
Nor fenced, nor staked, the gushers of the sky
Spout to the rod
Divining in a smile the oil of tears.

Night in the sockets rounds,
Like some pitch moon, the limit of the globes;
Day lights the bone;
Where no cold is, the skinning gales unpin
The winter's robes;
The film of spring is hanging from the lids.

Light breaks on secret lots,
On tips of thought where thoughts smell in the rain;
When logics die,
The secret of the soil grows through the eye,
And blood jumps in the sun;
Above the waste allotments the dawn halts.

After the Funeral
(In Memory of Ann Jones)

After the funeral, mule praises, brays,
Windshake of sailshaped ears, muffle-toed tap
Tap happily of one peg in the thick
Grave's foot, blinds down the lids, the teeth in black,
The spittled eyes, the salt ponds in the sleeves,
Morning smack of the spade that wakes up sleep,
Shakes a desolate boy who slits his throat
In the dark of the coffin and sheds dry leaves
That breaks one bone to light with a judgment clout,
After the feast of tear-stuffed time and thistles
In a room with a stuffed fox and a stale fern,
I stand, for this memorial's sake, alone

In the snivelling hours with dead, humped Ann
Whose hooded, fountain heart once fell in puddles
Round the parched worlds of Wales and drowned each sun
(Though this for her is a monstrous image blindly
Magnified out of praise; her death was a still drop;
She would not have me sinking in the holy
Flood of her heart's fame; she would lie dumb and deep
And need no druid of her broken body).
But I, Ann's bard on a raised hearth, call all
The seas to service that her wood-tongued virtue
Babble like a bellbuoy over the hymning heads,
Bow down the walls of the ferned and foxy woods
That her love sing and swing through a brown chapel,
Bless her bent spirit with four, crossing birds.
Her flesh was meek as milk, but this skyward statue
With the wild breast and blessed and giant skull
Is carved from her in a room with a wet window
In a fiercely mourning house in a crooked year.
I know her scrubbed and sour humble hands
Lie with religion in their cramp, her threadbare
Whisper in a damp word, her wits drilled hollow,
Her fist of a face died clenched on a round pain;
And sculptured Ann is seventy years of stone.
These cloud-sopped, marble hands, this monumental
Argument of the hewn voice, gesture and psalm
Storm me forever over her grave until
The stuffed lung of the fox twitch and cry Love
And the strutting fern lay seeds on the black sill.

Fern Hill

Now as I was young and easy under the apple boughs
About the lilting house and happy as the grass was green,
   The night above the dingle starry,
    Time let me hail and climb
   Golden in the heydays of his eyes,
And honoured among wagons I was prince of the apple towns
And once below a time I lordly had the trees and leaves
    Trail with daisies and barley
   Down the rivers of the windfall light.

And as I was green and carefree, famous among the barns
About the happy yard and singing as the farm was home,

In the sun that is young once only,
          Time let me play and be
     Golden in the mercy of his means,
And green and golden I was huntsman and herdsman, the calves
Sang to my horn, the foxes on the hills barked clear and cold,
          And the sabbath rang slowly
          In the pebbles of the holy streams.

All the sun long it was running, it was lovely, the hay-
Fields high as the house, the tunes from the chimneys, it was air
          And playing, lovely and watery
          And fire green as grass.
          And nightly under the simple stars
As I rode to sleep the owls were bearing the farm away,
All the moon long I heard, blessed among stables, the nightjars
          Flying with the ricks, and the horses
          Flashing into the dark.

And then to awake, and the farm, like a wanderer white
With the dew, come back, the cock on his shoulder: it was all
          Shining, it was Adam and maiden,
          The sky gathered again
          And the sun grew round that very day.
So it must have been after the birth of the simple light
In the first, spinning place, the spellbound horses walking warm
          Out of the whinnying green stable
          On to the fields of praise.

And honoured among foxes and pheasants by the gay house
Under the new made clouds and happy as the heart was long,
          In the sun born over and over,
          I ran my heedless ways,
          My wishes raced through the house-high hay
And nothing I cared, at my sky blue trades, that time allows
In all his tuneful turning so few and such morning songs
          Before the children green and golden
          Follow him out of grace,

Nothing I cared, in the lamb white days, that time would take me
Up to the swallow thronged loft by the shadow of my hand,
          In the moon that is always rising,
          Nor that riding to sleep

I should hear him fly with the high fields
And wake to the farm forever fled from the childless land.
Oh as I was young and easy in the mercy of his means,
    Time held me green and dying
       Though I sang in my chains like the sea.

Poem in October

  It was my thirtieth year to heaven
Woke to my hearing from harbour and neighbour wood
    And the mussel pooled and the heron
        Priested shore
      The morning beckon
With water praying and call of seagull and rook
And the knock of sailing boats on the net-webbed wall
      Myself to set foot
       That second
In the still sleeping town and set forth.

  My birthday began with the water—
Birds and the birds of the winged trees flying my name
    Above the farms and the white horses
       And I rose
      In rainy autumn
And walked abroad in a shower of all my days.
High tide and the heron dived when I took the road
      Over the border
       And the gates
Of the town closed as the town awoke.

    A springful of larks in a rolling
Cloud and the roadside bushes brimming with whistling
    Blackbirds and the sun of October
        Summery
      On the hill's shoulder,
Here were fond climates and sweet singers suddenly
Come in the morning where I wandered and listened
      To the rain wringing
       Wind blow cold
In the wood faraway under me.

    Pale rain over the dwindling harbour
And over the sea-wet church the size of a snail

With its horns through mist and the castle
        Brown as owls,
            But all the gardens
Of spring and summer were blooming in the tall tales
Beyond the border and under the lark-full cloud.
            There could I marvel
                My birthday
Away but the weather turned around.

    It turned away from the blithe country,
And down the other air and the blue altered sky
    Streamed again a wonder of summer
                With apples
            Pears and red currants,
And I saw in the turning so clearly a child's
Forgotten mornings when he walked with his mother
            Through the parables
                Of sunlight
    And the legends of the green chapels

    And the twice told fields of infancy
That his tears burned my cheeks and his heart moved in mine.
        These were the woods the river and sea
                Where a boy
                In the listening
Summertime of the dead whispered the truth of his joy
To the trees and the stones and the fish in the tide.
            And the mystery
                Sang alive
    Still in the water and singing birds.

    And there could I marvel my birthday
Away but the weather turned around. And the true
        Joy of the long-dead child sang burning
                In the sun.
            It was my thirtieth
Year to heaven stood there then in the summer noon
Though the town below lay leaved with October blood.
            O may my heart's truth
                Still be sung
    On this high hill in a year's turning.

INDEX OF FIRST LINES

INDEX OF AUTHORS AND TITLES

ABOUT THE EDITOR

Oscar Williams (1900–1964), editor of this book, was himself a distinguished poet. The author of five books of poetry, including *That's All That Matters* and *Selected Poems*, he has been called "clever, disconcerting, rash" (Lionel Abel) and "a very real and important poet . . . (whose) powerful imagery and unique personal idiom will add a permanent page to American poetry" (Dylan Thomas).

Mr. Williams achieved literary distinction not only as a highly original and vigorous American poet but also as one of the great poetry anthologists of his time. His most outstanding anthologies are *The Little Treasury Series*, *The War Poets*, *Immortal Poems of the English Language*, *The Pocket Book of Modern Verse* and *The New Pocket Anthology of American Verse*, the latter three published by Pocket Books. These are accepted as present-day classics in their fields and are in wide use in colleges and universities. Other anthologies include a revised edition of Palgrave's *The Golden Treasury*, *The Major British Poets*, *The Major American Poets*, and *The Silver Treasury of Light Verse*.

Mr. Williams's last and most ambitious anthology was *Master Poems of the English Language*, now also published by Pocket Books. A huge work of over 1,100 pages, illustrated with portraits of the poets and combining a comprehensive anthology with a broad sampling of critical writing, it is a superb contribution by the man Robert Lowell called "probably the best anthologist in America."